Study Guide

to accompany

INTRODUCTION to FINANCE

LAWRENCE J. GITMAN
San Diego State University

JEFF MADURA
Florida Atlantic University

KURT R. JESSWEIN
Murray State University

Boston San Francisco New York
London Toronto Sydney Tokyo Singapore Madrid
Mexico City Munich Paris Cape Town Hong Kong Montreal

Study Guide to accompany Gitman/Madura, *Introduction to Finance*

ISBN: 0-201-70094-8

3 4 5 6 7 8 9 10-VG-40302

Contents

Preface

To the student:

This study guide is intended to supplement the accompanying textbook, *Introduction to Finance*. As a supplement, it will review concepts presented in the text and reinforce the application of these concepts through practice problems and sample exams. The best way to be successful in learning finance is to try working through many different problems that will test your ability to use the concepts you have learned. The field of finance, similar to accounting, is one that requires practice, practice, and more practice!

This study guide is organized as follows:

Chapter Summary organized around the learning goals for each chapter

Chapter Outline with the specific learning goal noted in each section. The learning goals are highlighted on the left side of the page.

Sample Problem Solutions

Study Tips

Sample Exam, usually including 10-15 True/False questions, 15-20 Multiple Choice questions, and 2 Essay questions or Problems

Answer Key for the exam

After reading the chapter notes, see if you can work through the sample problems without looking at the solutions. Once you have attempted a problem, check your answer with the given solution.

Additionally, the sample exam is presented to test your knowledge and the application of the presented material. Try taking the exam and then check your answers on the answer sheet. If you are unsure of any of the answers presented, review the study guide and/or the textbook.

Chapter 1

THE FINANCIAL ENVIRONMENT

Chapter Summary

The *Introduction to Finance* text used in your finance course is organized around learning goals. Each chapter in this Study Guide will begin by listing these learning goals along with a brief summary of the critical points associated with each learning goal. After reading the chapter outline that follows, you should check to see if you can answer the questions raised by the learning goals.

Define the term finance and explain why finance is relevant to students. Finance is the process by which money is transferred among businesses, individuals, and governments. Virtually all individuals and organizations earn or raise money and spend or invest money.

An understanding of finance can prepare students for careers in managerial finance, or in other areas of business, including work in financial institutions or in financial markets. It can also equip students to decide what types of investments to make, which securities to invest in, and how much to invest.

LG 2

Identify the components of the financial environment. The components are (1) financial managers, who are responsible for investment decisions and financing decisions, (2) investors, who supply the funds to firms that need funding, and (3) financial markets, which facilitate the flow of funds from investors to financial managers.

LG 3

Explain how investors monitor managers to ensure that managerial decisions are in the best interests of the owners. Investors buy and sell the firm's stock, an activity that determines the equilibrium price of the stock. If the managers make poor decisions inconsistent with maximizing the value of the stock, the investors will sell the stock, placing downward pressure on its price. To the extent that managers' compensation levels are tied to the price of the stock, they are penalized when they do not focus on satisfying owners. In addition, investors can initiate various forms of shareholder activism. Some investors may even consider acquiring enough shares to take control of the firm.

LG 4 ***Describe how the financial environment has become internationalized.*** The international financial environment provides additional investment opportunities for firms and investors, which may allow them to improve their stream of cash flows. However, the international environment can also cause future cash flows to be subject to more uncertainty because of currency exchange rate risk and other factors specific to foreign countries.

Chapter Outline

Definition of Finance and its Relevancy

LG 1 Finance represents the processes that transfer money among businesses, individuals, and governments.

An understanding of finance prepares students for careers in business and government. It also prepares them for making decisions as investors.

Components of the Financial Environment

LG 2 There are three key components making up the financial environment: financial managers, investors, and financial markets.

Financial managers are responsible for deciding how to invest a company's funds to expand its business and how to obtain funds (financing). They are expected to make financial decisions that will maximize the firm's value, and therefore maximize the value of the firm's stock price.

Financial managers rely on efficient accounting and information systems to help them fund the marketing and production activities of a firm.

Investment decisions made by financial managers assure the continued profitability and success of a firm. Such decisions determine the composition of assets found on the left-hand side of the balance sheet. Investment decisions are intended to generate returns proportionate to the risk taken with the investment.

Financing decisions assure access to or supply of funding resources at the lowest cost possible. Such decisions determine the composition of the liabilities and equity positions found on the right-hand side of the balance sheet. The two types of financing are debt financing (using funds borrowed from investors) and equity financing (using funds invested by the owners).

Investors represent individuals or financial institutions that provide funds to firms, government agencies, or individuals who need funds. Individual investors provide funds to firms by purchasing their securities (stocks and bonds) and financial institutions provide funds either by providing loans or by purchasing securities.

The firm can obtain debt financing in the form of loans or debt securities with the lenders or security purchasers receiving periodic interest payments as compensation for the use of their funds as well as the return of the principal (amount loaned or invested) at the end of the financing period.

The firm can obtain equity financing by selling ownership shares to investors. Investors are compensated by the return on the stock from periodic dividend payments and from the increase in the value (price) of the stock over time. There is no maturity on stock, but investors can sell stock they own to other investors.

All investments are subject to some form(s) of risk, because of the uncertainty surrounding the returns generated by the investment. Investors expect a return for the risk they accept, though the actual returns earned may differ from those originally expected.

Financial markets represent forums that facilitate the flow of funds between investors, firms, and government units and agencies. Each financial market is served by financial institutions that act as intermediaries. Each component of the market is interrelated with others; the financing decision of one is the investment decision of the other.

Investor Monitoring of Firms

Investors attempt to make decisions that will enhance their own stream of expected cash flows. They purchase and sell securities based on their expectations of the future performance of the firms in which they invest. Favorable information about a firm's future performance tends to increase the demand for the firm's stock and therefore the price of the stock. Unfavorable information has the opposite effect.

Investors influence the value of a firm by buying or selling the firm's stock based on their assessment of the investment decisions made by the firm's management. They (particularly the institutional investors) also may influence the firm through shareholder activism in which they exercise their voting (ownership) power to influence decisions made by a firm's management or board of directors. They may also influence the firm by threatening to acquire enough stock to gain control over it.

To monitor the firms, investors rely on the published financial statements provided by the firms as well as other third party information. Such monitoring is made more difficult due to asymmetric information, or the fact that the firm's managers may have access to information that is unavailable to the investors.

International Finance Environment

In response to a reduction in various international barriers, financial managers and investors commonly pursue investment opportunities in foreign countries. Firms may engage in international trade transactions (importing and exporting) or in direct foreign investment to acquire foreign assets such as production facilities.

International opportunities can expose firms to different risks than domestic opportunities.

Exchange rate risk represents the risk that expected cash flows can be adversely affected by movements in the price of one currency in relation to another (the exchange rate). The depreciation (weakening) of a foreign currency against the U.S. dollar reduces the dollar cash inflows from the specified business activity. The appreciation (strengthening) of a foreign currency against the U.S. dollar increases the dollar cash outflows.

Investors can invest in securities of foreign firms. Foreign investments often offer higher returns than U.S. investments but subject the investors to exchange rate risk.

Sample Problem Solutions

In this section of the Study Guide, you will find solutions to the types of problems presented in your textbook. You will be warned about typical mistakes made in solving the problems, as well as explanations of why a particular method is used. You should review these problems carefully before working on homework assignments or the sample exam.

This first chapter does not contain any mathematical models, so no problem solutions are provided. The remaining chapters will typically include a variety of problems for you to solve.

Study Tips

This is the place in your Study Guide where you will find notes, tips, and warnings about the chapter to help you complete assignments and prepare for examinations. Think of these as useful explanations of particularly confusing points in the chapter or as reminders of items particularly critical to your success in the course.

1. Remember that the financial environment is made up of three main components: financial managers, investors and financial markets.
   a. Financial managers help firms decide how to invest funds in activities that increase the value of the firm and how to best raise those funds.
   b. Investors decide in which firms to invest their funds.
   c. Financial markets facilitate the transfer of funds from the investors to the users of funds.

2. Wealth maximization is the key assumption made in the study of finance.
   a. The goal of financial managers is to maximize the wealth of the shareholders of a firm.
   b. The goal of investors is to maximize the expected cash flows from their own investors (i.e., maximize their own personal wealth).

3. The reduction of international barriers has expanded the financing and investment opportunities for financial managers and investors alike. Understanding the international financial markets is critical to having a full understanding of finance.

Sample Exam

True/False

T F 1. The primary role of a financial manager is to plan for the acquisition and use of funds to maximize the value of the firm.

T F 2. Financial managers must execute their duties independent of the other activities of the firm in order to properly maximize the value of the firm.

T F 3. Maximizing a firm's expected profit is the same as maximizing the wealth of the individual shareholders (owners) of the firm.

T F 4. If a firm's stock price falls during the year, this indicates that the firm's managers are not acting in the shareholders' best interest.

T F 5. The finance function is relatively independent of most other corporate functions. Marketing decisions, for example, may affect the firm's need for funds but are not affected by conditions in financial markets or other financing issues.

T F 6. Good investment opportunities are rare for firms so they have few difficulties in raising sufficient capital to fund new growth opportunities.

T F 7. Managers who depart from the principle of shareholder wealth maximization face threats of being taken over by groups who are more aligned with stockholder interests.

T F 8. Finance is concerned with the processes, institutions, markets, and instruments involved in the transfer of money among and between individuals, businesses and government.

T F 9. Return and risk are the key determinants of share price, which represents the wealth of the owners in the firm.

T F 10. Higher risk tends to result in a higher share price since the stockholder must be compensated for the greater risk.

T F 11. New information about a company, either positive or negative, will likely have little or no effect on the value of the company's stock.

T F 12. Hostile takeovers typically occur when the acquirer feels that the target firm is being poorly managed and, as a result, is undervalued in the marketplace.

T F 13. Financial intermediaries channel the savings of individuals, businesses, and governments into loans or investments.

T F 14. If a foreign currency is worth less today than yesterday when compared to the U.S. dollar, the currency is said to have appreciated with respect to the dollar.

T F 15. Exchange rate risk is the potential for positive cash flows from a foreign business activity to decline in value when denominated in the parent company's home currency.

Multiple Choice

1. The true owners of the corporation is/are the
   a. board of directors.
   b. chief executive officer.
   c. stockholders.
   d. creditors.

2. The financial manager's investment decisions determine
   a. both the mix and the type of assets found on the firm's balance sheet.
   b. both the mix and the type of liabilities found on the firm's balance sheet.
   c. both the mix and the type of assets and liabilities found on the firm's balance sheet.
   d. both the mix and the type of the firm's short-term and long-term financing.

3. The financial manager's financing decisions determine
   a. both the mix and the type of assets found on the firm's balance sheet.
   b. the most appropriate mix of short-term and long-term financing.
   c. both the mix and the type of assets and liabilities found on the firm's balance sheet.
   d. the proportion of the firm's earnings to be paid as dividend.

4. The primary goal of the financial manager is
   a. minimizing risk.
   b. maximizing profit.
   c. maximizing wealth.
   d. minimizing return.

5. Corporate owners receive realizable return through
   a. earnings per share and cash dividends.
   b. increase in share price and cash dividends.
   c. increase in share price and earnings per share.
   d. profit and earnings per share.

6. The wealth of the owners of a corporation is represented by
   a. profits.
   b. earnings per share.
   c. share price.
   d. cash flow.

7. Return and risk are the key determinants in share price. Increased return results in _________, other things remaining the same.
   a. a lower share price
   b. a higher share price
   c. an unchanged share price
   d. an undetermined share price

8. Return and risk are the key determinants in share price. Increased risk, other things remaining the same, results in
   a. a lower share price.
   b. a higher share price.
   c. an unchanged share price.
   d. an undetermined share price.

9. Financial managers evaluating decision alternatives or potential actions must consider
   a. only risk.
   b. only return.
   c. both risk and return.
   d. risk, return, and the impact on share price.

10. As the risk of a stock investment increases,
    a. return will increase.
    b. return will decrease.
    c. required rate of return will decrease.
    d. required rate of return will increase.

11. One way often used to ensure that management decisions are in the best interest of the stockholders is to
    a. threaten to fire managers who are seen as not performing adequately.
    b. remove management's perquisites.
    c. tie management compensation to the performance of the company's common stock price.
    d. tie management compensation to the level of earnings per share.

12. When fewer units of a foreign currency are required to buy one dollar, the currency is said to have _______ with respect to the dollar.
    a. appreciated
    b. depreciated
    c. consolidated
    d. remained fixed

13. ________ is the chance of loss or the variability of returns associated with a given investment.
    a. Return
    b. Value
    c. Risk
    d. Information asymmetry

14. Holders of equity capital (common stock)
    a. own the firm.
    b. receive interest payments.
    c. receive guaranteed income.
    d. have loaned money to the firm.

15. As a form of financing, equity capital (common stock)
    a. has a maturity date.
    b. is only liquidated in bankruptcy.
    c. is temporary.
    d. has priority over bonds.

16. Investors who wish to avoid risk are known as
    a. risk-averse.
    b. risk-tolerant.
    c. market makers.
    d. paranoid.

17. Investors typically monitor the activities of a firm through each of the following except
    a. reading the firm's financial statements.
    b. calling the firm's 800 number.
    c. reading the *Wall Street Journal.*
    d. reading reports from Moody's and Standard & Poor's.

18. Which of the following would not be an example of shareholder activism?
    a. Suing the firm's board of directors.
    b. Changing the membership of a firm's board of directors.
    c. Selling 50% of one's investment in the firm.
    d. Influencing the hiring of a new chief executive officer of the firm.

19. If a U.S. investor owns stock in a Japanese firm, an increase in the value of the Japanese currency will
    a. hurt the U.S. investor.
    b. benefit the U.S. investor.
    c. have no effect on the wealth of the U.S. investor.
    d. benefit the U.S. investor only if he lives in a state that does not have an income tax.

20. Investor monitoring of firms is made more difficult due to ________, or the fact that the firm's managers may have access to information that is unavailable to the investors.
    a. asymmetric information
    b. internationalization of business activities
    c. shareholder activism
    d. wealth maximization

Essay

1. Why is asymmetric information a concern for investors?

2. Explain why the value of a stock may go down.

Chapter 1 Answer Key

True/False

1. T
2. F
3. F
4. F
5. F
6. F
7. T
8. T
9. T
10. F
11. F
12. T
13. T
14. F
15. T

Multiple Choice

1. C
2. A
3. B
4. C
5. B
6. C
7. B
8. A
9. D
10. D
11. C
12. A
13. C
14. A
15. B
16. A
17. B
18. C
19. B
20. A

Essay

1. Asymmetric information refers to the condition where the managers of a firm have more information about the firm than the investors. Investors prefer that any such asymmetric information be eliminated or reduced. Individual investors often allow specific institutional investors (e.g., full-service brokers) to make and monitor their investment decisions for them due to the belief that these institutional investors have information advantages that individual investors do not.

2. Stock prices reflect investor expectations about a firm based upon the information available on the firm. Any new negative information on the future performance of the firm, whether specifically about the firm or about economic conditions in general, can have a negative impact on the value of the stock as more investors will attempt to sell the stock than to buy it.

FINANCIAL INSTITUTIONS AND MARKETS

Chapter Summary

Chapter 2 provides an overview of the various financial institutions and markets that serve managers of firms and investors who invest in firms, and how these different institutions and markets facilitate the flow of funds. The roles of managers, financial markets, and investors in channeling financial flows are discussed.

LG 1 ***Explain how financial institutions serve as intermediaries between investors and firms.*** Financial institutions channel the flow of funds between investors and firms. Individuals deposit funds at commercial banks, purchase shares of mutual funds, purchase insurance protection with insurance premiums, and contribute to pension plans. All of these financial institutions provide credit to firms by purchasing debt securities or providing loans or other credit products. In addition, all of these financial institutions except commercial banks purchase stocks issued by firms.

LG 2 ***Provide an overview of financial markets.*** Financial market transactions can be distinguished by whether they involve new or existing securities, whether the transaction of new securities reflects a public offering or a private placement, and whether the securities have short-term or long-term maturities. New securities are issued by firms in the primary market and purchased by investors. If investors desire to sell the securities they have previously purchased, they use the secondary market. The sale of new securities to the general public is referred to as a public offering; the sale of new securities to one investor or a group of investors is referred to as a private placement. Securities with short-term maturities are called money market securities, and securities with long-term maturities are called capital market securities.

LG 3 ***Explain how firms and investors trade money market and capital market securities in the financial markets in order to satisfy their needs.*** Firms obtain short-term funds by issuing commercial paper. Individual and institutional investors that wish to invest funds for a short-term period commonly purchase Treasury bills, commercial paper, and negotiable CDs. Firms that need long-term funds may issue bonds or stock. Institutional and individual investors invest funds for a long-term period by purchasing bonds or stock.

Describe the major securities exchanges. The major securities exchanges are the New York Stock Exchange and the NASDAQ-AMEX exchange. The stocks of the largest U.S. publicly traded firms are typically traded on the New York Stock Exchange, whereas stocks of smaller firms are traded on the NASDAQ-AMEX exchange.

LG 5

Describe derivative securities and explain why they are used by firms and investors. Derivative securities are financial contracts whose values are derived from the values of underlying financial assets. They are commonly used by firms to reduce their exposure to a particular type of risk. Investors may use derivative securities to enhance their returns or reduce their exposure to some types of risk.

LG 6

Describe the foreign exchange market. The foreign exchange market is composed of the spot market and the forward market. The spot market makes possible the immediate exchange of one currency for another at the prevailing exchange rate (spot rate). The forward market allows for the negotiation of contracts (forward contracts) that specify the exchange of an amount of one currency for at a particular future date and at a particular exchange rate (the forward rate).

Chapter Outline

Financial Institutions

Financial institutions serve as intermediaries by channeling the savings of individuals, business, and governments into loans and investments. The primary suppliers of funds to financial institutions are individuals; the primary demanders of funds are firms and governments.

The major financial institutions in the United States are the commercial banks and other savings institutions, mutual funds, securities firms, insurance companies, and pension funds.

1. Individuals deposit funds at commercial banks, which use the deposited funds to provide commercial loans to firms and personal loans to individuals, and purchase debt securities issued by firms or government agencies. Commercial banks act as intermediaries by consolidating small deposits of individuals into large loans for firms, and by assessing the creditworthiness of the firms wishing to borrow funds and diversifying the loans across several borrowers on behalf of the depositors. Because of their unique position in the economy, banks are regulated (by the Federal Deposit Insurance Corporation, the Federal Reserve Board, and others) to help promote

competition among banking institutions and to limit the risks banks take on. The goal of regulation is for bank customers to be charged reasonable prices for the services they obtain, while maintaining the stability of the financial system.

2. Individuals purchase shares of mutual funds, which use the proceeds to invest in securities. Mutual funds are owned by investment companies and enable small investors to enjoy the benefits of investing in a diversified portfolio of securities purchased on their behalf by professional investment managers.

3. Individuals may also use the services of securities firms, a category of firms that includes investment banks, investment companies, and brokerage firms. Securities firms serve as intermediaries by (a) helping firms and government agencies place (sell) securities with investors and (b) helping investors buy or sell securities.

4. Individuals purchase insurance (life, property and casualty, and health) protection with insurance premiums. The insurance companies pool these payments and invest the proceeds in various securities until the funds are needed to pay off claims by policyholders. Because they often own large blocks of a firm's stocks or bonds, they frequently attempt to influence the management of the firm to improve the firm's performance, and ultimately, the performance of the securities they own.

5. Individuals make contributions to pension plans, either directly or through their employer, which then invest the proceeds on behalf of the employees. Pension plans also often own large blocks of a firm's stocks or bonds and, like insurance companies, are likely to be active shareholders

Two major changes taking place in the financial markets and institutions areas are consolidation and globalization. The consolidation of financial institutions is leading to large financial conglomerates offering a wide range of financial services. Globalization has occurred as barriers to various forms of international commerce are making it easier and more profitable to engage in international financial activities.

Financial Markets

Financial market transactions can be distinguished by whether they involve new or existing securities, whether the transaction of new securities reflects a public offering or a private placement, and whether the securities have short-term or long-term maturities.

New securities are issued by firms in the primary market, and purchased by investors. If investors desire to sell the securities that they previously purchased, they use the secondary market. The sale of new securities to the general public is referred to as a public offering and the first offering of stock is called an initial public offering. The sale of new securities to one investor or a group of investors (institutional investors) is referred to as a private placement.

Securities with short-term maturities (1 year or less) are called money market securities, while securities with longer-term maturities are called capital market securities.

There are also important debt and equity markets outside of the United States. The Eurobond market allows large corporations or governments to issue bonds denominated in dollars but sold to investors located outside of the United States. Alternatives to Eurobonds are foreign bonds, which are bonds sold in foreign countries but denominated in the country's home currency. The international equity markets have also grown in importance, making it easier for large firms to raise equity capital in more than one country and for governments to sell their state-owned companies to private investors.

Money Market Securities

Treasury bills are short-term debt securities issued in maturities of 13 weeks, 26 weeks, and one-year by the U.S. Treasury. Their par value (principal to be paid at maturity) is a minimum of $10,000 and they are sold at a discount from the par value.

Commercial paper is a short-term debt security issued by well-known, creditworthy firms that serves as an alternative to a short-term loan from a bank. Like Treasury bills, it is sold at a discount from par; unlike Treasury bills, investors are subject to default risk on their investment so the required return on commercial paper is slightly higher than on Treasury bills.

Negotiable certificates of deposits (NCDs) are short-term debt securities issued by financial institutions. Like commercial paper, the required returns on NCDs are slightly above the return on Treasury bills. Unlike Treasury bills and commercial paper, NCDs provide interest payments and are not sold at a discount.

Firms and investors can also use foreign money markets to borrow or invest funds for short-term periods, perhaps enjoying lower financing costs or higher investment returns than comparable U.S. investments.

Capital Market Securities

Bonds are long-term debt securities issued by firms and governments to raise large amounts of long-term funds.

1. Treasury bonds are issued with typical maturities of 10 to 30 years by the U.S. Treasury and generally pay interest every six months. They are often referred to as risk-free investments since they are backed by the federal government. There is a very active primary and secondary market in the trading of Treasury bonds.

2. Municipal bonds are issued by municipalities to support their expenditures and can be either general obligation bonds (backed by the municipality's ability to tax) or revenue bonds (with repayment made from the funds generated by the project financed). The interest paid on municipal bonds is exempt from federal income taxes

so the cost of funds to the municipalities and the pre-tax return to investors are lower than other bonds. Interest is paid on a semiannual basis.

3. Corporate bonds are issued by corporations to finance their investment in long-term assets, such as building or machinery. Typical maturities are from 10 to 30 years, and interest is paid semiannually.

Common stock represents units of ownership interest, or equity, in a corporation. Common stockholders expect to earn a return by receiving dividends, by realizing gains through the increases in share prices, or both.

Preferred stock is a special form of ownership. Preferred stockholders are paid a fixed periodic dividend before any dividends can be paid to common stockholders. Preferred stock thus has a "preference" over common stock, much like bonds.

Major Securities Exchanges

Securities exchanges provide the marketplace in which firms raise funds through the sale of new securities and in which purchasers of securities can maintain liquidity by being able to resell them easily when necessary.

Organized security exchanges, most notably the New York Stock Exchange, are tangible organizations that act as secondary (auction) markets in which securities are bought and sold. The stocks of most large U.S. publicly traded firms are traded on the New York Stock Exchange.

The over-the-counter exchange (OTC), linked through the National Association of Securities Dealers Automated Quote (NASDAQ) System, is an intangible market for the purchase and sale of securities not listed on the organized exchanges and the primary market for selling all new public issues.

Derivative Securities Markets

Derivative securities (also called derivatives) are financial contracts whose values are derived for the values of underlying financial assets. Examples of derivative securities are stock options and financial futures.

Derivative securities are used by firms to reduce their exposure to a particular type of risk. Investors may use them to enhance their returns (by speculating on future changes in the prices of the underlying assets) or to reduce their exposure to different types of risk.

The Foreign Exchange Market

The foreign exchange market consists of large international banks around the world buying and selling currencies to facilitate the international purchases of products, services, and securities. It is composed of the spot market and the forward market.

The spot market enables immediate exchange of one currency for another at the prevailing exchange rate (spot rate). The forward market allows for the negotiation of contracts (forward contracts) that specify the exchange of an amount of one currency for another at a particular future date and at a particular exchange rate (the forward rate).

Sample Problem Solutions

Sample Problem 1: Treasury Bill Returns

You are purchasing a 1-year Treasury bill with a par value of $10,000 and a price of $9,550. If you hold the Treasury bill until maturity, how much will your return be?

Solution to Sample Problem 1

($10,000 - $9,550) / $9,550 = 4.71%.

Sample Problem 2: Foreign Exchange Calculations

Jones International must pay 200,000 Swiss francs for purchasing inventory from a Swiss firm. Payment is due in one month. The one-month forward rate of the Swiss franc is $0.61, and Jones expects the spot rate for the Swiss franc to be $0.62 one month from now. Should Jones use a forward contract to buy the Swiss francs they need now or wait until next month to make their payment of Swiss francs?

Solution to Sample Problem 2

If they wait and the spot rate for Swiss francs next month is as expected ($0.62), they will need to make a total payment of $124,000 (200,000 x $0.62).
If they enter a contract to buy the Swiss francs in one month at today's forward rate ($0.61), they will need to make a total payment of $122,000 (200,000 x $0.61).

By hedging with a forward contract, Jones expects to save $2,000.

Study Tips

1. Be sure to understand the differences between securities. Money market securities are used to borrow funds (or invest) for a short amount of time and capital market securities are generally used to borrow (or invest) for longer periods of time.

2. The international financial markets are becoming increasingly important alternatives for both borrowers and investors and need to be understood as well as their domestic counterparts.

Sample Exam

True/False

T F 1. Primary and secondary markets are markets for short-term and long-term securities, respectively.

T F 2. Financial markets are intermediaries that channel the savings of individuals, businesses, and government into loans or investments.

T F 3. The money market involves trading of securities with maturities of one year or less while the capital market involves the buying and selling of securities with maturities of more than one year.

T F 4. A bond issued by a U.S. firm that is denominated in Swiss Francs and sold in Switzerland would be an example of a foreign bond.

T F 5. Holders of equity have claims on both income and assets that are secondary to the claims of creditors.

T F 6. Preferred stock is a special form of stock having a fixed periodic dividend that must be paid prior to payment of any interest to outstanding bonds.

T F 7. Unlike the organized exchanges, the OTC handles both outstanding securities and new public issues, making it both a secondary and a primary market.

T F 8. Commercial banks obtain most of their funds from borrowing in the capital markets.

T F 9. Credit unions are the largest type of financial intermediary handling individual savings.

T F 10. A mutual fund is a type of financial intermediary that obtains funds through the sale of shares and uses the proceeds to acquire bonds and stocks issued by various business and governmental units.

T F 11. IPO stands for Interest and Principal Obligation.

T F 12. The two primary types of municipal bonds are general obligation and revenue bonds.

T F 13. The forward exchange rate is the rate of exchange between two currencies at some specified future date.

T F 14. The spot exchange rate is the prevailing rate of exchange between two currencies.

T F 15. Derivative securities derive their values from underlying assets.

Multiple Choice

1. A ______ is the largest financial intermediary handling individual savings. It receives premium payments that are placed in loans or investments to accumulate funds to cover future benefits.
   a. life insurance company
   b. commercial bank
   c. savings bank
   d. credit union

2. The key participants in financial transactions are individuals, businesses, and governments. Individuals are net ______ of funds, and businesses are net ______ of funds.
   a. suppliers; demanders
   b. purchasers; sellers
   c. demanders; suppliers
   d. users; providers

3. Which of the following is not a financial institution?
   a. A pension fund
   b. A newspaper publisher
   c. A commercial bank
   d. An insurance company

4. A ______ is set up so that employees of corporations or governments can receive income after retirement.
   a. life insurance company
   b. pension fund
   c. savings bank
   d. credit union

5. A ______ is a type of financial intermediary that pools savings of individuals and makes them available to business and government demanders. Funds are obtained through the sale of shares.
   a. mutual fund
   b. savings and loans
   c. savings bank
   d. credit union

6. Most businesses raise money by selling their securities in
   a. a direct placement.
   b. a stock exchange.
   c. a public offering.
   d. a private placement.

7. Which of the following is not a service provided by financial institutions?
   a. Buying the businesses of customers
   b. Investing customers' savings in stocks and bonds
   c. Paying savers' interest on deposited funds
   d. Lending money to customers

8. Government usually
   a. borrows funds directly from financial institutions.
   b. maintains permanent deposits with financial institutions.
   c. is a net supplier of funds.
   d. is a net demander of funds.

9. By definition, the money market involves the buying and selling of
   a. funds that mature in more than one year.
   b. flows of funds.
   c. stocks and bonds.
   d. short-term funds.

10. The ______ is created by a financial relationship between suppliers and demanders of short-term funds.
   a. financial market
   b. money market
   c. stock market
   d. capital market

11. Firms that require funds from external sources can obtain them from
    a. financial markets.
    b. private placement.
    c. financial institutions.
    d. All of the above.

12. The two key financial markets are
    a. money market and capital market.
    b. capital market and secondary market.
    c. primary market and secondary market.
    d. primary market and money market.

13. Long-term debt of a business or corporation typically has maturities of between
    a. 6 months and 1 year.
    b. 1 and 5 years.
    c. 5 and 20 years.
    d. 10 and 30 years.

14. If a bond pays $1,000 plus interest at maturity, $1,000 is called the
    a. par value.
    b. long-term value.
    c. stated value.
    d. market value.

15. ______ is hired by a firm to find prospective buyers for its new stock or bond issue.
    a. A commercial loan officer
    b. An investment banker
    c. A securities analyst
    d. A trust officer

16. The major securities traded in the capital markets are
    a. stocks and bonds.
    b. bonds and commercial paper.
    c. commercial paper and Treasury bills.
    d. Treasury bills and certificates of deposit.

17. International Advisors, Inc. (IAI) is receiving a payment of 100,000 Euros in three months. The spot rate for the Euro is currently $0.92 per Euro, but IAI has entered into a three-month forward contract with their bank at $0.94 per Euro. How much will IAI receive in three months?
    a. $92,000
    b. $94,000
    c. $106,383
    d. $108,696

18. Long-term debt instruments used by both government and business are known as
    a. bonds.
    b. equities.
    c. stocks.
    d. bills.

19. The ______ stock exchange is a primary market where new public issues are sold.
    a. regional
    b. American
    c. New York
    d. over-the-counter

20. You are purchasing a 1-year Treasury bill with a par value of $10,000 and a price of $9,600. If you hold the Treasury bill until maturity, how much will your return be?
    a. 4.00%
    b. 4.17%
    c. 5.25%
    d. 9.60%

Essay

1. Describe the primary differences between the money markets and the capital markets.

2. Discuss the roles of the key financial institutions serving as intermediaries between investors and firms.

Chapter 2 Answer Key

True/False

1. F
2. F
3. T
4. T
5. T
6. F
7. T
8. F
9. F
10. T
11. F
12. T
13. T
14. T
15. T

Multiple Choice

1. A
2. A
3. B
4. B
5. A
6. C
7. A
8. D
9. D
10. B
11. D
12. A
13. D
14. A
15. B
16. A
17. B
18. A
19. D
20. B

Essay

1. Money markets deal with short-term debt securities maturing within one year. Examples of money market instruments include Treasury bills and commercial paper. Capital markets deal with longer-term debt and equity securities. Examples of capital market securities include Treasury bonds, corporate bonds, preferred stock, and common stock equity.

2. The major financial institutions in the United States include 1) commercial banks and other savings institutions, which use deposited funds to provide commercial loans to firms and personal loans to individuals; 2) mutual funds, which use the proceeds from selling shares to investors to invest in securities; 3) securities firms, which help borrowers place (sell) securities and help investors buy or sell securities; 4) insurance companies, which pool insurance premiums and invest the proceeds in securities, and 5) pension plans, which invest retirement funds on behalf of the employees.

CORPORATE SECURITIES: BONDS AND STOCKS

Chapter Summary

Chapter 3 discusses the key aspects of the two basic corporate securities, bonds and stocks. By issuing these securities, firms are able to raise long-term funds with which to expand the business. The roles of financial managers, financial markets, and investors in issuing corporate securities and making transactions in them are highlighted.

LG 1 ***Describe the legal aspects of bond financing and bond cost.*** Corporate bonds are debt instruments indicating that a corporation has borrowed a certain amount that it promises to repay in the future. Most bonds are issued with maturities of 10 to 30 years and a par value of $1,000. The bond indenture, enforced by a trustee, states all conditions of the bond issue. It contains both standard debt provisions and restrictive covenants, which may include a sinking-fund requirement. The interest rate on a bond depends on its maturity, the offering size, the issuer risk, and the basic cost of money.

LG 2 ***Discuss the general features, ratings, popular types, and international issues of corporate bonds.*** A bond issue may include a conversion feature, a call feature, or stock purchase warrants. Bond ratings by independent agencies indicate the risk of a bond issue. A variety of traditional and contemporary types of bonds, some unsecured and others secured, are available. Eurobonds and foreign bonds enable established, creditworthy companies and governments to borrow large amounts internationally.

LG 3 ***Differentiate between debt and equity capital.*** Holders of equity capital (common and preferred stock) are owners of the firm. Typically, only common stockholders have a voice in management through their voting rights. Equity holders have claims on income and assets that are secondary to the claims of creditors, there is no maturity date, and the firm does not benefit from tax deductibility of dividends, paid to stockholders, as is the case for interest paid to debtholders.

LG 4 ***Review the rights and features of common stock.*** A common stockholder is a residual owner who receives what is left after all other claims have been satisfied. The common stock of a firm can be privately owned, closely owned, or publicly owned. It can be sold with or without a par value. Preemptive rights allow common stockholders to avoid dilution of ownership when new shares are issued. Not all shares authorized in the corporate charter are outstanding. If a firm has treasury stock, it will have issued more shares than are outstanding. Some firms have two or more classes of common stock that differ mainly in having unequal voting rights. Proxies transfer voting rights from one party to another. Dividend distributions to common stockholders are made at the discretion of the firm's board of directors. Firms can issue stock in foreign markets. The stock of many foreign corporations is traded in the form of American Depository Receipts (ADRs) in U.S. markets.

Discuss the rights and features of preferred stock. Preferred stockholders have preference over common stockholders with respect to the distribution of earnings and assets and so are normally not given voting privileges. Preferred stock issues may have certain restrictive covenants, cumulative dividends, a call feature, and a conversion feature.

LG 6

Understand the role of the investment banker in securities offerings. Corporations can raise long-term funds through a public offering, the sale of either bonds or stock to the general public. Investment bankers purchase securities from corporate and government issuers and resell them to the general public. Their primary function is underwriting, which guarantees the issuer a specified amount from the issue. Some public offerings are instead sold on a best-efforts basis. The investment bank, which may syndicate the underwriting, forms a selling group, fulfills legal requirements, and prices and distributes the issue. An alternative to public offerings is private placement of securities.

Chapter Outline

Legal Aspect of Bond Financing

Corporate bonds are debt instruments indicating that a corporation has borrowed a certain amount that it promises to repay in the future The bond indenture is the legal agreement between the issuer and the investors and states all conditions of the bond issue. The indenture is enforced by a third-party trustee, and usually contains:

1. Standard debt provisions, such as maintaining satisfactory accounting records and periodically providing audited financial statements, and

2. Restrictive covenants, which are operating and financial constraints that ensure the repayment of debt at maturity, as limiting the sales of corporate assets and requiring a sinking-fund that systematically retires bonds prior to maturity.

Cost of Bonds to Issuer

The interest rate on a bond depends on:

1. the bond's maturity (longer-term debt typically has a higher interest rate than shorter-term debt);

2. the offering size (relatively fixed administrative costs of issuing bonds favors larger issues, but larger issues also pose higher risk of default);

3. the issuer's risk (the higher the potential a firm will default, the higher return expected by the investor); and

4. the basic cost of money (which forms the foundation for the interest rate paid on all debt).

General Features of Corporate Bonds

Most bonds are issued with maturities of 10 to 30 years and a par value of $1,000. They usually make semiannual interest payments. A bond issue may include any of the following:

1. a conversion feature that allows the bondholders to exchange their bonds for a stated number of shares of common stock;

2. a call feature that allows the issuer the opportunity to repurchase bonds at a stated call price (at a premium above its par value) prior to maturity;

3. stock purchase warrants that allow the bondholders to purchase a stated number of shares of common stock at a specified price over a certain period of time.

The riskiness of corporate bonds is often assessed by independent agencies such as Moody's and Standard & Poor's.

A variety of different bond types is available. These can be classified as:

1. traditional (the basic types that have been around for years such as debentures and subordinated debentures) and contemporary (newer, more innovative types such as zero-coupon and floating rate bonds); or

2. unsecured (backed only by the reputation of the issuer) and secured (backed by collateral of the issuer).

Established, creditworthy companies and governments can often borrow large amounts internationally by issuing Eurobonds or foreign bonds.

1. Eurobonds are issued by an international borrower and sold to investors in countries with currencies other than the currency in which the bond is denominated.

2. Foreign bonds are issued in a host country's financial market, in the host country's currency, by a foreign borrower.

Differences between Debt and Equity

There are four key differences between debt and equity capital.

1. Holders of equity capital (common and preferred stock) are owners of the firm but typically only common stockholders have a voice in management through their voting rights.

2. Equity holders have claims on income and assets that are secondary, or subordinate, to the claims of creditors (debt holders).

3. Equity has no specified maturity date; debt usually has a stated maturity date.

4. Dividends paid to stockholders are not tax deductible; interest paid to debt holders is deductible.

Common Stock

A common stockholder is a residual owner who receives what is left after all other claims have been satisfied. The common stock of a firm can be privately owned, closely owned, or publicly owned.

Common stock can be sold with or without a par value, a relatively useless value for a stock, established for legal reasons.

Preemptive rights allow common stockholders to maintain their proportionate share of ownership (in voting rights and of the firm's earnings) when new shares are issued.

A corporate charter authorizes a firm to issue a specified amount of shares. Firms usually issue less than the total authorized. In addition, if a firm repurchases any of the outstanding stock, the shares become treasury stock.

Some firms have two or more classes of common stock that differ mainly in having unequal voting rights. Since most small shareholders do not attend annual meetings to vote, proxy statements are used to transfer their voting rights to another party.

The payment of dividends to common stockholders is at the discretion of the firm's board of directors and is usually paid quarterly, either in cash or in stock.

To broaden its ownership base, firms can also issue stock in foreign markets. The shares of most foreign firms entering the U.S. market trade in the form of American Depository Receipts (ADRs).

Preferred Stock

Preferred stockholders have preference over common stockholders (but not creditors) with respect to the distribution of earnings and assets of the firm. Preferred stock normally does not include voting privileges. Key features of preferred stock may include:

1. Restrictive covenants, call features, and conversion features similar to those of debt; and

2. Cumulative dividends in which all preferred stock dividends, including those in arrears (that is, not paid in previous periods), must be paid prior to the payment of any common stock dividends

The Role of the Investment Banker

Corporations can raise long-term funds through a public offering, the sale of either bonds or stock to the general public. Investment bankers help corporations raise funds by purchasing their securities and reselling them to the general public. Their primary function is underwriting, which guarantees the issuer a specified amount from the issue, although some public offerings are instead sold on a best-efforts basis.

The investment bank often syndicates the underwriting, bringing in other investment banks to help underwrite the offering. The syndicate is then responsible for:

1. forming a selling group;
2. fulfilling the legal requirements established by the Securities and Exchange Commission; and
3. pricing and distributing the issue.

An alternative to public offerings is the private placement (direct sale) of securities to one or more institutional investors.

Sample Problem Solutions

Sample Problem 1: Issuing Common Stock

Examine the section of the balance sheet below to determine how many shares of common stock the firm could issue without obtaining shareholder approval.

Stockholders' Equity	
Common stock ($1.00 per share, 500,000 shares authorized, 300,000 shares issued)	$300,000
Paid in Capital in excess of par	700,000
Retained earnings	2,000,000
Less: Cost of treasury stock (20,000 shares)	(200,000)
Total Stockholders' Equity	$2,800,000

Solution to Sample Problem 1

500,000 shares have been authorized; if any more than this number is issued, stockholder approval will be needed. Of this 500,000, only 300,000 shares have been issued of which 20,000 shares are being held as treasury stock. The firm can issue the remaining 200,000 shares plus resell the treasury stock (20,000). In total, 220,000 shares can be sold without shareholder approval.

Sample Problem 2: Preferred stock

Joe's Garage, Inc. has an outstanding issue of 8 percent, $150 preferred stock.

a. How much is the annual preferred stock dividend?

b. If the preferred stock is *noncumulative* and the dividends have not been paid for the past three years, how much would have to be paid on each share of preferred stock prior to paying any common stock dividends?

c. If the preferred stock is *cumulative* and the dividends have not been paid for the past three years, how much would have to be paid on each share of preferred stock prior to paying any common stock dividends?

Solution to Sample Problem 2

a. The annual preferred stock dividend is found by multiplying the dividend percentage (8%) by the stated value of the stock ($150). This results in an annual preferred stock dividend of $12 ($150 x 0.08).

b. If the preferred stock is *noncumulative*, only the current dividend of $12 per share is paid prior to the payment of any common stock dividends.

c. If the preferred stock is *cumulative*, all dividends in arrears ($12 per share for three years) plus the current dividend of $12 per share, or a total of $48 per share, must be paid prior to the payment of any common stock dividends.

Study Tips

1. Be sure to understand the key legal and operational differences between bonds, preferred stock, and common stock. The relative cost of each from the perspective of the issuer and the relative return and risk tradeoffs of each from the perspective of the investor are determined in large part by these differences.

Sample Exam

True/False

T F 1. Restrictive covenants are contractual clauses in long-term debt agreements that place certain operating and financial constraints on the borrower.

T F 2. Debentures are unsecured bonds that any corporation can issue.

T F 3. The call premium is the amount by which the market price exceeds the call price of the bond.

T F 4. A Eurobond is a bond issued by an international borrower and sold to investors in countries with currencies other than the country in which the bond is denominated.

T F 5. There is an inverse relationship between the quality or rating of a bond and the rate of return it must provide bondholders.

T F 6. The conversion feature of a bond is a feature that is included in almost all corporate bond issues that gives the issuer the opportunity to repurchase bonds at a stated price prior to maturity.

T F 7. The claims of the equity holders on the firm's assets have priority over the claims of creditors because the equity holders are the owners of the firm.

T F 8. Stock rights allow stockholders to purchase additional shares of stock in direct proportion to the number of shares they own.

T F 9. Preferred stock is often considered a quasi-debt since it yields a fixed periodic payment.

T F 10. Cumulative preferred stocks are preferred stocks for which all passed (unpaid) dividends in arrears must be paid along with the current dividend prior to the payment of dividends to common stockholders.

T F 11. A common stockholder has no guarantee of receiving any cash inflows, but receives what is left after all other claims on the firm's income and assets have been satisfied.

T F 12. American Depositary Receipts are claims issued by U.S. banks representing ownership of shares of a foreign company's stock held on deposit by the U.S. bank in the foreign market and issued in dollars to U.S. investors.

T F 13. Dilution of ownership occurs when a new stock issue results in each present stockholder having a larger number of shares and, thus, a claim to a larger part of the firm's earnings than previously.

T F 14. A public offering is the sale of a new security issue, typically debt or preferred stock, directly to an investor or group of investors.

T F 15. Investment bankers make investments for corporations.

Multiple Choice

1. The legal contract setting forth the terms and provisions of a corporate bond is
   a. a loan document.
   b. a promissory note.
   c. an indenture.
   d. a debenture.

2. A ______ is a restrictive provision on a bond that provides for the systematic retirement of the bonds prior to their maturity.
   a. redemption clause
   b. sinking-fund requirement
   c. conversion feature
   d. subordination clause

3. A ______ is a complex and lengthy legal document stating the conditions under which a bond has been issued.
   a. sinking fund
   b. bond indenture
   c. bond debenture
   d. warrant

4. ______ is a paid individual, corporation, or commercial bank trust department that acts as a third party to a bond indenture to ensure that the issuer does not default on its contractual responsibilities to the bondholders.
   a. A bond issuer
   b. A bond rating agency
   c. A trustee
   d. An investment banker

5. The ______ feature permits the issuer to repurchase bonds at a stated price prior to maturity.
   a. put
   b. capitalization
   c. call
   d. conversion

6. The ______ feature allows the bondholder to change each bond into a stated number of shares of stock.
   a. put
   b. capitalization
   c. call
   d. conversion

7. The riskiness of publicly traded bond issues is rated by independent agencies. According to Moody's rating system, an Aaa bond and a Caa bond are ______ and ______, respectively.
   a. speculative; investment grade
   b. prime quality; medium grade
   c. prime quality; speculative
   d. medium grade; lowest grade

8. _____ became popular vehicles used to finance mergers and takeovers.
   a. Floating rate bonds
   b. Convertible debentures
   c. Income bonds
   d. Junk bonds

9. An example of a standard debt provision is
   a. restricting the corporation from disposing of fixed assets.
   b. imposing constraints on subsequent borrowing.
   c. limiting the corporation's annual cash dividend payments.
   d. requiring the payment of taxes and other liabilities when due.

10. The major factor(s) affecting the cost, or interest rate, on a bond is (are) its
   a. basic cost of money.
   b. maturity.
   c. issuer risk.
   d. All of the above.

11. Holders of equity capital
   a. receive guaranteed income.
   b. have loaned money to the firm.
   c. own the firm.
   d. receive interest payments.

12. The claims of the equity holders on income have priority over
   a. the claims of the preferred stockholders.
   b. the claims of the creditors.
   c. the claims of the unsecured creditors.
   d. no one.

13. A firm has issued cumulative preferred stock with a $100 par value and a 12 percent annual dividend. For the past two years, the board of directors has decided not to pay a dividend. The preferred stockholders must be paid _____ prior to paying the common stockholders.
   a. $0/share
   b. $12/share
   c. $24/share
   d. $36/share

14. ______ are promised a fixed periodic dividend that must be paid prior to paying any common stock dividends.
   a. Creditors
   b. Bondholders
   c. Preferred stockholders
   d. Common stockholders

15. Shares of stock currently owned by the firm's shareholders are called
    a. authorized.
    b. issued.
    c. outstanding.
    d. treasury shares.

16. Common stockholders expect to earn a return by receiving
    a. dividends.
    b. annual interest.
    c. semiannual interest.
    d. fixed periodic dividends.

17. An 8 percent preferred stock with a market price of $110 per share and a $100 par value pays a cash dividend of _____.
    a. $4.00
    b. $8.00
    c. $8.80
    d. $80.00

18. The _____ are sometimes referred to as the residual owners of the corporation.
    a. common stockholders
    b. preferred stockholders
    c. secured creditors
    d. unsecured creditors

19. Treasury stock results from the
    a. firm selling stock for greater than its par value.
    b. cumulative feature on preferred stock.
    c. repurchase of outstanding stock.
    d. authorization of additional shares of stock by the board of directors.

20. Which of the following is not a characteristic of preferred stock?
    a. It is often considered quasi-debt due to fixed payment obligation.
    b. It has less restrictive covenants than debt.
    c. It gives the holder voting rights, which permit selection of the firm's directors.
    d. Its holders have priority over common stockholders in the liquidation of assets.

Essay

1. Differentiate between a bond indenture and a debenture.

2. What are the key differences between corporate bonds, preferred stock, and common stock?

Chapter 3 Answer Key

True/False

1. T
2. F
3. F
4. T
5. T
6. F
7. F
8. T
9. T
10. T
11. T
12. T
13. F
14. F
15. F

Multiple Choice

1. C
2. B
3. B
4. C
5. C
6. D
7. C
8. D
9. D
10. D
11. C
12. D
13. D
14. C
15. C
16. A
17. B
18. A
19. C
20. C

Essay

1. A bond indenture is the legal agreement between the issuer and the investors and states all conditions (standard debt provisions and restrictive covenant). A debenture is a formal name for an unsecured corporate bond.

2. Among the key differences are: 1) equity capital (common and preferred stock) represents ownership of a firm with common stockholders having a voice in management through their voting rights; 2) equity holders have claims on income and assets that are secondary, or subordinate, to the claims of creditors (bond holders); 3) equity has no specified maturity date; debt usually has a stated maturity date; and 4) dividends paid to stockholders is not tax deductible; interest paid to debt holders is deductible.

INTEREST RATE FUNDAMENTALS

Chapter Summary

Chapter 4 explains why interest rates vary over time, and why interest rates vary among different debt securities at a given point in time. The variation in interest rates over time and in debt securities at a particular point in time is largely attributed to the required return applied to a firm's managers and its investors. The roles of financial managers, financial markets, and investors in affecting the required return on funds and therefore causing variation in interest rates over time and among debt securities at a given point in time are discussed. This is a very important chapter in that interest rates will play a major role throughout the remainder of the textbook.

LG 1 ***Discuss the components that influence the risk-free interest rate at a given point it time.*** The interest rate on a risk-free debt security is composed of the real rate of interest and the expected rate of inflation. Thus, the stated interest rate exceeds the expected rate of inflation by an amount that reflects the real rate of interest that investors expect to earn. The real rate of interest is the return investors expect to earn after accounting for inflation.

LG 2 ***Explain why the risk-free interest rate changes over time.*** The risk-free interest rate changes over time in response to changes in the supply of funds available and in the demand for funds. An increase in the supply of funds or a decrease in the demand for funds places downward pressure on the risk-free interest rate, and therefore on interest rates of all other debt securities. Conversely, a decrease in the supply of funds or an increase in the demand for funds places upward pressure on the risk-free interest rate, and therefore on interest rates of all other debt securities. The key factors that affect the aggregate supply of funds are shifts in savings by investors and shifts in monetary policy. The key factors that affect the aggregate demand for funds are shifts in the government demand for funds, in business demand for funds, and in household demand for funds.

LG 3 ***Explain why the risk-free rate of interest varies among possible maturities (investment horizons).*** At a given time, the risk-free rate of interest varies among maturities. This can be observed by reviewing the term structure of interest rates, which shows the annualized yields of Treasury securities for various maturities. The risk-free (Treasury) securities with different maturities offer different annualized yields at a given point in time because of differences in 1) liquidity levels of the securities for each investment horizon, 2) interest rate expectations, and 3) the demand and supply of funds for each investment horizon.

LG 4

Explain the relationship between risk and the nominal interest rate on a debt security. The nominal interest rate of a risky debt security is composed of its nominal risk-free interest rate and the risk premium. Because the risk-free component is the same for all risky debt securities at a given time, the difference in nominal interest rates among the debt securities is attributed to the risk premium. The nominal interest rates are higher for debt securities that entail more risk because investors require a higher risk premium to invest in those securities.

LG 5

Explain why the returns required on risky assets change over time. The returns required on risky assets change in response to changes in the risk-free rate or in the risk premium required by investors. As the risk-free rate changes, the required return on a security changes by the same amount and in the same direction, assuming that there is no change in the risk premium. When the risk of a security increases, there is an increase in the return that investors require to invest in the security.

Chapter Outline

Risk-Free versus Real Rate of Return

LG 1

The interest rate represents the cost of borrowing money. The risk-free rate of interest, R_F, is the required return on a risk-free asset (U.S. Treasury bills are often considered risk-free assets). This *nominal* or *stated* risk-free rate is composed of the real rate of interest and the expected rate of inflation. The real rate of interest is the return investors expect to earn after accounting for inflation.

Borrowers other than the U.S. Treasury usually pay a premium above the prevailing risk-free rate.

Changes in the Risk-Free Interest Rate

LG 2

The risk-free interest rate changes over time in response to changes in the supply of funds available and in the demand for funds. An increase in the supply of funds or a decrease in the demand for funds places downward pressure on the risk-free interest rate and therefore on interest rates of all other debt securities.

The supply of funds may increase due to:

- increased savings by domestic investors that result from increases in disposable income;
- shifts in savings by international investors into the U.S. economy; and
- monetary policy actions by the Federal Reserve (such as buying securities through open market operations or reducing the discount rate) that can increase the money supply.

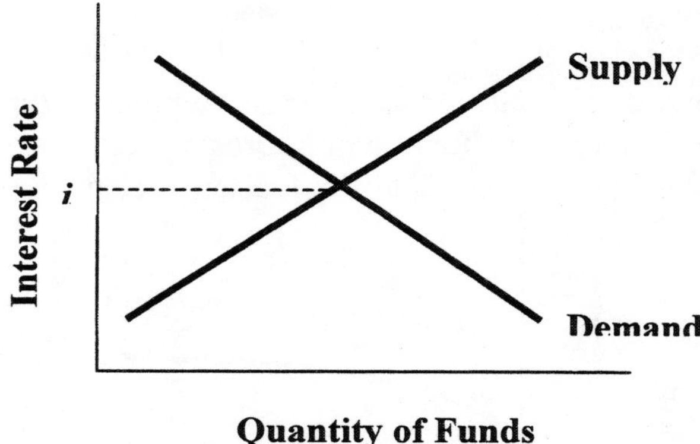

The demand for funds may decrease due to:

- reductions in the level of federal government borrowing;
- domestic businesses reducing their spending plans and decreasing their level of borrowing and foreign firms reducing their demand for dollar-denominated financing; and
- households reducing their borrowing for purchases of homes and automobiles.

A decrease in the supply of funds or an increase in the demand for funds places upward pressure on the risk-free interest rate, and therefore on interest rates of all other debt securities.

The supply of funds may decrease due to:

- decreased savings by domestic investors that result from decreases in disposable income;
- shifts in savings by international investors away from the U.S. economy; and
- monetary policy actions by the Federal Reserve (such as selling securities through open market operations or raising the discount rate) that can decrease the money supply.

The demand for funds may increase due to:

- government borrowing more than its normal amount;
- business expansion plans increasing the level of borrowing by firms, both domestically and internationally if foreign firms demand dollar-denominated financing; and
- households increasing their borrowing to purchase homes and automobiles.

Term Structure of Interest Rates

At a given time, the risk-free rate of interest varies among maturities. This can be observed by reviewing the term structure of interest rates, also known as the yield curve, which shows the annualized yields of Treasury securities for various maturities.

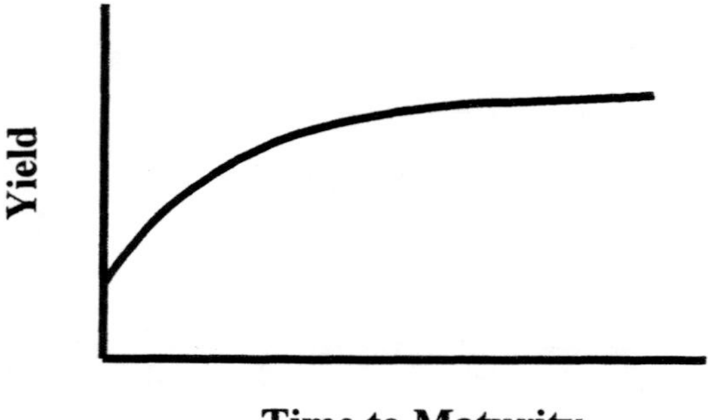

Time to Maturity

There are three general theories that help explain the shape of the yield curve for a specific time period.

The expectations theory suggests that the yield curve reflects investor expectations about future interest rates and inflation. An upward sloping yield curve would be indicative of expectations of future increases in interest rates.

The liquidity preference theory suggests that investors perceive short-term securities to be less risky than longer-term securities due to their lower level of liquidity. Investors require a premium for tying up their funds for longer periods, and borrowers are generally willing to pay the premium for securing their long-term financing.

The market segmentation theory suggests that there are different sources of supply and demand for securities at different maturities and the yield curve reflects the relationship among these individual segments.

Risk Premiums

The nominal interest rate of a risky debt security is composed of its nominal risk-free interest rate and the risk premium. Because the risk-free component is the same for all risky debt securities at a given time, the difference in nominal interest rates among the debt securities is attributed to the risk premium.

The risk premium on risky securities consists of a number of components.

1. Most important is probably the default risk of the issuer, the possibility that the issuer will default on its payments (of interest or principal) to investors at the scheduled time.

2. Other risk factors of a particular security may include:

   - maturity risk (the value of a longer-term security is more sensitive to given changes in interest rates than a short-term security);
   - liquidity risk (securities that can not be easily converted into cash are riskier than those that can be converted);
   - tax risk (the chance that unfavorable changes in the tax laws may adversely affect the return of a given security); and
   - contractual provisions that can either increase (e.g., call provisions) or decrease (e.g., convertibility) the total risk premium for the security.

Risk and Return

The nominal interest rates are higher for debt securities that entail more risk because investors require a higher risk premium to invest in those securities.

Explaining Shifts in the Required Returns on Debt Securities

LG 5

The returns required on risky assets change in response to changes in the risk-free rate or in the risk premium required by investors.

As the risk-free rate changes, the required return on a debt security changes by the same amount and in the same direction, assuming that there is no change in the risk premium. Even if the risk-free rate does not change, the risk premium (and the required return) on a debt security may change due to changes in the perceived default risk of the issuer of the security.

Changes in the risk-free rate or in the risk premiums similarly affect the required returns on equity securities.

Sample Problem Solutions

Sample Problem 1: Plotting the Yield Curve

Plot the yield curve given the following data:

Maturity	Yield
1 year	4.0%
3 year	4.5%
5 year	5.0%
10 year	6.0%
15 year	7.0%
20 year	7.5%
30 year	8.0%

Solution to Sample Problem 1

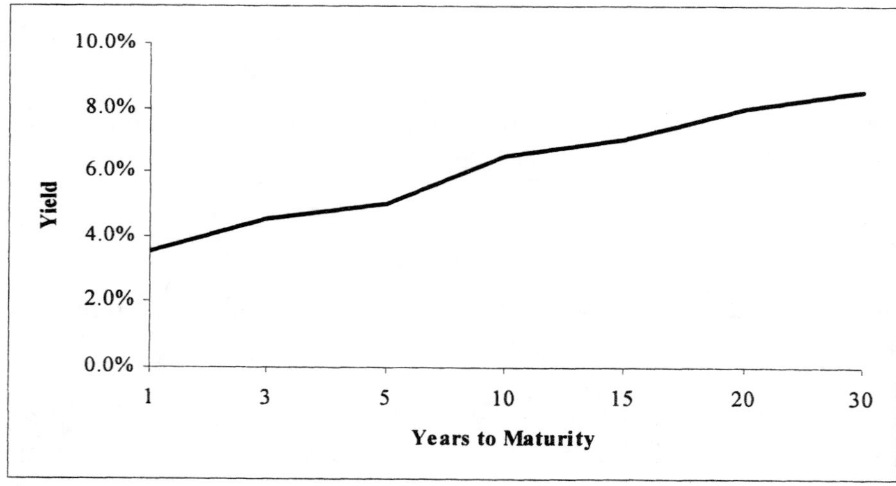

Study Tips

1. Because these terms will be used in later chapters, be sure to know the difference between the real rate, the risk-free rate, and the nominal interest rate. The real rate of interest is the return the suppliers of funds (investors) expect to earn after accounting for inflation. The risk-free rate is the real rate plus an adjustment for expected inflation. The nominal interest rate includes all of the risk premiums (inflation, default, maturity, liquidity, etc.) that apply to a particular security.

2. The yield curve is a picture of the term structure of interest rates. It shows the difference in yields of securities that differ only in their time to maturity and is usually upward sloping.

3. As risk increases, so does the required return on a security.

Sample Exam

True/False

T F 1. If the Federal Reserve tightens the money supply, other things held constant, short-term interest rates will be pushed upward, and this increase will probably be greater than the increase in rates in the long-term market.

T F 2. The term structure may be defined as the relationship between interest rates and maturities of similar securities.

T F 3. The expectations theory postulates that the term structure of interest rates is based on expectations regarding future interest rates.

T F 4. The yield curve is upward sloping, or normal, if short-term rates are higher than long-term rates.

T F 5. The real rate of interest is the actual rate of interest charged by the suppliers of funds and paid by the demanders.

T F 6. The longer the maturity of a Treasury (or any other) security, the smaller the interest rate risk.

T F 7. A downward-sloping yield curve indicates generally cheaper short-term borrowing costs than long-term borrowing costs.

T F 8. Although Treasury securities have no risk of default or illiquidity, they do suffer from "maturity risk" – the risk that interest rates will change in the future and thereby impact longer maturities more than shorter maturities.

T F 9. Liquidity preference theory suggests that for any given issuer, long-term interest rates tend to be higher than short-term rates due to the lower liquidity and higher responsiveness to general interest rate movements of longer-term securities; this causes the yield curve to be upward-sloping.

T F 10. A yield curve that reflects relatively similar borrowing costs for both short- and long-term loans is called a normal yield curve.

T F 11. Upward-sloping yield curves result from higher future inflation expectations, lender preferences for shorter maturity loans, and greater supply of short-term as opposed to long-term loans relative to their respective demand.

T F 12. Open market operations refer to the trading of stocks and bonds in relatively unregulated markets.

T F 13. Increases in government spending tend to increase interest rates.

T F 14. Increases in risk are inversely related to increases in expected return.

T F 15. Changes in interest rates directly affect bond prices, but have no effect on stock prices.

Multiple Choice

1. Your uncle would like to restrict his interest rate risk and his default risk, but he would still like to invest in corporate bonds. He would most likely invest in
   a. AAA bonds with 10 years to maturity.
   b. BBB bonds with 10 years to maturity.
   c. AAA bonds with 5 years to maturity.
   d. BBB bonds with 5 years to maturity.

2. Which of the following factors is/are likely to increase market interest rates?
   a. Corporations increase their demand for capital.
   b. Households become less willing to save.
   c. Expected inflation increases.
   d. All of the above.

3. Which of the following statements is most correct? Other things held constant,
   a. the "liquidity preference theory" would generally lead to an upward-sloping yield curve.
   b. the "expectations theory" would generally lead to an upward-sloping yield curve.
   c. the yield curve under "normal" conditions should be horizontal (i.e., flat.)
   d. a downward-sloping yield curve would suggest that investors expect interest rates to increase in the future.

4. The ______ rate of interest creates an equilibrium between the supply of savings and the demand for investment funds.
   a. nominal
   b. real
   c. risk-free
   d. inflationary

5. The ______ is the annual rate of interest earned on a security purchased on a given date and held to maturity.
   a. risk-free rate
   b. yield to maturity
   c. term structure
   d. yield curve

6. The ______ is/are a graphic depiction of the term structure of interest rates.
   a. risk-return profile
   b. aggregate demand curve
   c. yield curve
   d. supply and demand functions

7. ______ yield curve reflects higher expected future rates of interest.
   a. A downward-sloping
   b. A linear
   c. An upward-sloping
   d. A flat

8. Generally, an increase in risk will result in ______ required return or interest rate.
   a. a lower
   b. a higher
   c. an unchanged
   d. an undetermined

9. The nominal rate of interest is composed of
   a. the risk-free rate plus an inflationary expectation.
   b. the risk-free rate plus a risk premium.
   c. the real rate plus an inflationary expectation.
   d. the real rate plus a risk premium.

10. The ______ rate of interest is typically the required rate of return on a three-month U.S. Treasury bill.
    a. nominal
    b. real
    c. risk-free
    d. premium

11. A downward-sloping yield curve that indicates generally cheaper long-term borrowing costs than short-term borrowing costs is called a(n)
    a. normal yield curve.
    b. inverted yield curve.
    c. flat yield curve.
    d. None of the above.

12. The theory suggesting that for any given issuer, long-term interest rates tends to be higher than short-term rates is called the
    a. expectation hypothesis.
    b. liquidity preference theory.
    c. market segmentation theory.
    d. None of the above.

13. Which of the following theories is not one cited to explain the general shape of the yield curve?
    a. Expectations hypothesis
    b. Market segmentation theory
    c. Liquidity preference theory
    d. Security markets theory

14. The required return on a stock may change due to
    a. shifts in the risk-free rate of interest.
    b. shifts in the risk-premium on all equity securities.
    c. shifts in the perceived level of riskiness of the firm.
    d. All of the above.

15. Generally, a decrease in risk will result in _____ required rate of return.
    a. an unchanged
    b. a higher
    c. a lower
    d. an undetermined

16. Holding all else constant, reduced government spending would likely
    a. increase interest rates.
    b. decrease interest rates.
    c. not affect interest rates.
    d. increase some interest rates, decrease others.

17. The theory that explains only the tendency for the yield curve to be upward-sloping is the
    a. expectations hypothesis.
    b. liquidity preference theory.
    c. market segmentation theory.
    d. investor perception theory.

18. At any time, the slope of the yield curve is affected by
    a. liquidity preferences.
    b. the comparative equilibrium of supply and demand in the short-term and long-term market segments.
    c. inflationary expectations.
    d. All of the above.

19. Which of the following does not represent a risk premium?
    a. Default risk
    b. Inflationary risk
    c. Tax treatment risk
    d. Liquidity risk

20. The theory that states that investors and borrowers choose securities with maturities that satisfy their forecasted cash needs is the
    a. market preference theory.
    b. liquidity preference theory.
    c. expectations theory.
    d. market segmentation theory.

Essay

1. Describe the three main theories of the term structure of interest rates.

2. What factors can affect the current level of interest rates?

Chapter 4 Answer Key

True/False

1. T
2. T
3. T
4. F
5. F
6. F
7. F
8. T
9. T
10. F
11. T
12. F
13. T
14. F
15. F

Multiple Choice

1. C
2. D
3. A
4. B
5. B
6. C
7. C
8. B
9. B
10. C
11. B
12. B
13. D
14. D
15. C
16. B
17. B
18. D
19. C
20. D

Essay

1. The three main theories of the term structure of interest rates are: 1) the expectations theory that suggests that the yield curve reflects investor expectations about future interest rates and inflation where a positive slope implies expectations of higher interest rates; 2) the liquidity preference theory that suggests that due to liquidity concerns, investors require a premium for tying up their funds for longer periods, and borrowers are willing to pay the premium for securing their long-term financing; and 3) the market segmentation theory that suggests that there are different sources of supply and demand for securities at different maturities and the yield curve reflects the relationship among these individual segments.

2. Anything that affects the demand for or supply of funds in the economy can affect the current level of interest rates. Changing demand factors include changes in the level of government, business, or household borrowing. Changing supply factors include changes in the savings rate by households, business, or government or the impact of monetary policy actions by the Fed.

TIME VALUE OF MONEY

Chapter Summary

Chapter 5 presents both the key conceptual and computational aspects of the time value of money. It differentiates between future value and present value and demonstrates computations of the key techniques: future value and present value of a single amount, future value and present value of annuities, present value of perpetuities, and present values of a mixed stream cash flows goals. It discusses procedures for finding nominal and effective annual rates of return at various compounding frequencies, and demonstrates various applications of time value techniques. This is the critical chapter in the textbook, in that the techniques learned here will be used throughout the remaining chapters.

LG 1

Discuss the role of time value in finance and the use of computational aids to simplify its application. Financial managers and investors use time value of money techniques when assessing the value of the expected cash flow streams associated with investment alternatives. Alternatives can be assessed by either compounding to find future value or discounting to find present value. Because they are at time zero when making decisions, financial mangers and investors rely primarily on present value techniques. Both financial tables and financial calculators can streamline the application of time value techniques.

Understand the concept of future value and its calculation for a single amount. Future value relies on compound interest to measure future amounts: the initial principal or deposit in one period, along with the interest earned on it, becomes the beginning principal of the following period.

LG 3

Understand the concept of present value, its calculation for a single amount, and the relationship of present value to future value. Present value is the inverse of future value. The present value of a future amount is the amount of money today that is equivalent to the given future amount, considering the return that can be earned on the current money.

Find the future value and present value of an ordinary annuity, the future value of an annuity due, and the present value of a perpetuity. An annuity is a pattern of equal periodic cash flows. For an ordinary annuity, the cash flows occur at the end of the period. For an annuity due, cash flows occur at the beginning of the period. The future value of an ordinary annuity can be found by using the future value interest factor of an annuity; the present value of an ordinary annuity can be found by using the present value interest factor of an annuity. A simple conversion can be applied to use the future value interest factors for an ordinary annuity to find the future value of an annuity due. The present value of a perpetuity–an infinite-lived annuity–is found using 1 divided by the discount rate to represent the present value interest factor.

Calculate the present value of a mixed stream of cash flows. A mixed stream of cash flows is a stream of unequal periodic cash flows that reflects no particular pattern. The present value of a mixed stream of cash flows is the sum of the present values of each individual cash flow.

LG 6

Understand the effects that compounding more frequently than annually has on future value and the true rate of interest of. Interest can be compounded at intervals ranging from annually to daily, and even continuously. The more frequently interest is compounded, the larger the future amount that will be accumulated and the higher the true or effective annual rate (EAR). The annual percentage rate (APR)–a nominal annual rate–is quoted on credit cards and loans. The annual percentage yield (APY)–an effective annual rate–is quoted on savings products.

LG 7

Describe the procedures involved in determining deposits to accumulate a future sum, loan amortization, and finding interest or growth rates. The periodic deposit to accumulate a given future sum can be found by solving the equation for the future value of an annuity for the annual payment. A loan can be amortized into equal periodic payments by solving the equation for the present value of an annuity for the periodic payment. Interest or growth rates can be estimated by finding the unknown interest rate in the equation for the present value of a single amount, an annuity, or a mixed stream.

Chapter Outline

Time Value of Money

Financial managers and investors use time value of money techniques when assessing the value of the expected cash flow streams associated with various investment alternatives. Alternatives can be assessed by either compounding to find future value or discounting to find present value.

Future value techniques typically measure cash flows at the end of a project's life. The future value techniques use compounding to find the future value of each cash flow at the end of the investment's life and then sum those values to find the investment's future value.

The present value technique uses discounting to find the present value of each cash flow at time zero (the present time) and then sums these values to find the investment's value today. Because they are at time zero when making decisions, financial mangers and investors rely primarily on present value techniques.

Computational Aids

The calculation of future and present value is aided by the use of financial tables and financial calculators. The financial tables are found on the Financial Tables card in your textbook and contain factors that simplify the arithmetic involved in the calculations.

Financial calculators are an alternative to financial tables. There are a variety of inexpensive yet very powerful calculators available and they are highly recommended. While they do streamline and simplify the calculations, you will still need to understand the basic underlying financial concepts to use the calculator efficiently and correctly. The web site for your textbook contains a financial calculator guide that provides some tips on the use of the more popular models.

Future Value of A Single Amount

The future value of a present amount (typically called the principal) is found by applying compound interest over a specified period of time.

Example: If you would place $1,000 into a savings account earning 8% interest, at the end of one year you would have $1,000 in principal plus $80 in interest for a total of $1,080.

FV at end of Year 1 = $1,000 x (1 + .08) = $1,080

If you would leave the $1,080 in the account for another year, the principal and the interest earned in Year 1 will be compounded for an additional year. The new amount at the end of Year 2 would be $1,166.40.

FV at end of Year 2 = $1,080 x (1 + .08) = $1,166.40

The calculation of future values can be simplified in several ways.

1. To avoid compounding interest at each year's end, the following equation can be used to find the future value of a single amount of money, over any number of periods.

$$FV_n = PV \times (1+i)^n$$

Where:

FV_n	= The future value at the end of the period
PV	= Initial principal, or present value
i	= The annual rate of interest paid
n	= The number of periods, typically years

Using the previous example, the future value of $1,000 compounded annually at 8% for two years can be found by:

$$FV_n = \$1{,}000 \times (1+.08)^2$$
$$FV_n = \$1{,}166.40$$

2. Future value interest tables provide a pre-calculated future value interest factor (FVIF). The FVIF is simply the $(1+i)^n$ portion of the future value formula.

$$FVIF_{i,n} = (1+i)^n$$

Returning to the previous example, the future value of $1,000 compounded annually at 8% for two years can be found by using the FVIF table:

$$FV_n = PV \times FVIF_{8\%,2}$$
$$FV_n = \$1{,}000 \times (1.1664) = \$1{,}166.40$$

3. Financial calculators can also be used to simplify the calculation of future values. First, punch in $1,000 and depress PV; next, punch in 2 and enter N; then punch in 8 and depress I (which is equivalent to *i* in your textbook's notation); finally, to calculate the future value, depress CPT and then FV. The future value of $1,166.40 should appear on the calculator display. Note: Many calculators will display a minus sign (i.e., -1166.40), which should be ignored at this point. See the financial calculator guide at the book's web site for an explanation of why this occurs.

Present Value of A Single Amount

The process of finding present values is referred to as discounting cash flows and is the inverse of finding future values. It is the current dollar value of a future amount, or the amount of money that would have to be invested today at a given interest rate over a specified period to equal the future amount.

The calculation of present values is similar to that for future values. The basic formula to calculate a present value can be written as:

$$PV_n = \frac{FV_n}{(1+i)^n}$$

Example: Assume you wish to find the present value of $800 that will be received four years from now. You are earning 12% on your money. What is the most you would be willing to pay today to receive the $800 four years from now?

1. Using the basic formula, the present value of $800 discounted annually at 12% for four years can be found as follows:

$$PV_n = \frac{\$800}{(1+.12)^4}$$
$$PV_n = \$508.41$$

2. Alternatively, you could use the pre-calculated Present Value Interest Factors (PVIF), found in present value interest tables. The PVIF is simply the $1/(1+i)^n$ portion of the present value formula.

$$PVIF_{i,n} = \frac{1}{(1+i)^n}$$

Returning to the previous example, the present value of $800 discounted annually for four years at 12% can be found by using the PVIF table:

$$PV_n = FV \times PVIF_{12\%,4}$$
$$PV_n = \$800 \times (0.6355) = \$508.41$$

3. A financial calculator can also be used. Simply enter FV = 800, N = 4, I = 12, and CPT the PV, which should equal $508.41.

Annuities

An annuity is a pattern of equal periodic cash flows. For an ordinary annuity, the cash flows occur at the end of the period. For an annuity due, cash flows occur at the beginning of the period.

Future Value of an Annuity

The future value of an ordinary annuity can be found by using the future value interest factor of an annuity (FVIFA) or by using a financial calculator.

Example: You wish to invest $2,000 at the end of each year for 20 years into an account paying 10% annually. How much will be in this account after 20 years?

1. Using the FVIFA table, the formula to calculate the future value of an ordinary annuity is:

$$FVA_{(ordinary\ annuity)} = PMT \times FVIFA_{i,n}$$

   Given the example here, the future value of the annuity would be:

$$FVA_{(ordinary\ annuity)} = \$2{,}000 \times FVIFA_{10\%,20}$$
$$FVA_{(ordinary\ annuity)} = \$2{,}000 \times 57.27 = \$114{,}540$$

2. Using a financial calculator and entering 2000 = PMT, 20 = N, 10 = I, and CPT the FV, your result should be equal to $114,540.

Future Value of an Annuity Due

The future value of an annuity due can also be found by using the future value interest factor of an annuity (FVIFA) or by using a financial calculator. Note that since the annuity payments are received at the beginning of each period, rather than the end, the FVIFA formula must be converted to the following:

$$FVA_{(annuity\ due)} = PMT \times FVIFA_{i,n} \times (1+i)$$

Example: You wish to invest $2,000 at the *beginning* of each year for 20 years into an account paying 10% annually. How much will be in this account after 20 years?

1. Using the FVIFA table, the formula to calculate the future value of an ordinary annuity is:

$$FVA_{(annuity\ due)} = \$2{,}000 \times FVIFA_{10\%,20} \times (1+.10)$$
$$FVA_{(annuity\ due)} = \$2{,}000 \times 57.27 \times 1.10 = \$125{,}994$$

2. Using a financial calculator and entering 2000 = PMT, 20 = N, 10 = I, and CPT the FV, your result should be equal to $114,540. Multiplying the result by (1+.10) gives a final result of $125,994. An alternative method using a financial calculator is found in the financial calculator guide of the book's web site.

Present Value of an Ordinary Annuity

The present value of an ordinary annuity can be found by using the present value interest factor of an annuity.

Example: Having recently won a sweepstakes, you expect to receive $5,000 at the end of each year for 30 years. You are currently earning 9% on your investments. How much is this stream of payment worth to you today?

1. Using the PVIFA table, the formula to calculate the present value of an ordinary annuity is as follows:

$$PVA_{(ordinary\ annuity)} = PMT \times PVIFA_{i,n}$$

Given the example here, the future value of the annuity would be:

$$PVA_{(ordinary\ annuity)} = \$5{,}000 \times PVIFA_{9\%,30}$$
$$PVA_{(ordinary\ annuity)} = \$5{,}000 \times 10.274 = \$51{,}370$$

2. Using a financial calculator and entering 5000 = PMT, 30 = N, 9 = I, and CPT the PV, your result should be equal to $51,368.27 (the difference is due to rounding).

Present Value of an Annuity Due

The present value of an annuity due can also be found by using the present value interest factor of an annuity (PVIFA) or by using a financial calculator. As with the future value formula, the PVIFA formula must be converted for an annuity due to the following:

$$PVA_{(annuity\ due)} = PMT \times PVIFA_{i,n} \times (1+i)$$

Example: You expect to receive $5,000 at the *beginning* of each year for 30 years. How much is this stream of payments worth today if you normally earn 9% on your investments?

1. Using the FVIFA table, the formula to calculate the future value of an ordinary annuity is:

$$PVA_{(annuity\ due)} = \$5{,}000 \times PVIFA_{9\%,30} \times (1+.09)$$
$$PVA_{(annuity\ due)} = \$5{,}000 \times 10.274 \times 1.09 = \$55{,}993.30$$

2. Using a financial calculator and entering 5000 = PMT, 30 = N, 9 = I, and CPT the PV, your result should be equal to $51,368.27. Multiplying the result by (1+.09) gives a final result of $55,991.41.

Present Value of a Perpetuity

The present value of a perpetuity–an infinite-lived annuity–is found by using 1 divided by the discount rate to represent the present value interest factor.

Example: What is the present value of a stream of payments of $100 that will go on forever, assuming a 10% interest rate?

The present value interest factor for a perpetuity is 1/.10, which equals 10. The present value for the perpetuity of $100 is therefore $1,000 ($100 x 10).

Present Value of Mixed Stream of Cash Flows

The present value of a mixed stream of cash flows is the sum of the present values of each individual cash flow.

Example: Assume you wish to find the present value of the following series of cash flows: $500 in Year 1, $600 in Years 2 and 3, and $700 in Year 4 and the annual interest rate is 10%.

1. Using either the basic present value formula or the present value interest factors, you could find the present value of the cash flows to be:

$$\begin{aligned} \mathbf{PV_1} &= \mathbf{\$500 \times (PVIF_{10\%,1})} = && \mathbf{\$454.55} \\ \mathbf{PV_2} &= \mathbf{\$600 \times (PVIF_{10\%,2})} = && \mathbf{495.87} \\ \mathbf{PV_3} &= \mathbf{\$600 \times (PVIF_{10\%,3})} = && \mathbf{450.79} \\ \mathbf{PV_4} &= \mathbf{\$700 \times (PVIF_{10\%,4})} = && \underline{\mathbf{478.11}} \\ & && \mathbf{\$1,879.32} \end{aligned}$$

2. A financial calculator could also be used, either as an alternative to using the present value interest factors or, preferably, using the cash flow functions found in most financial calculators that makes a calculation of the present value of the entire cash flow stream. This alternative method is demonstrated in the financial calculator guide of the book's web site and produces similar results as above.

Compounding More Frequently Than Annually

Interest is often compounded at intervals more frequently than once a year. Besides annual compounding, financial institutions often use semiannual, quarterly, monthly, daily, and even continuous compounding.

Future Value with Compounding More Frequently Than Annually

The basic equation for finding the future value of a single amount of money, over any number of periods, can be modified as follows:

$$FVIF_{i,n} = \left(1 + \frac{i}{m}\right)^{m \times n}$$

Where ***m*** represents the number of times per year interest is compounded.

Example: Returning to our first example, we found that the future value of $1,000 compounded annually at 8% for two years was equal to $1,166.40.

$$FV_n = \$1{,}000 \times (1 + .08)^2$$
$$FV_n = \$1{,}166.40$$

With quarterly compounding, the future value would instead become:

$$FV_n = \$1{,}000 \times (1 + .08/4)^{2 \times 4}$$
$$FV_n = \$1{,}000 \times (1.02)^8$$
$$FV_n = \$1{,}171.66$$

The more frequently interest is compounded, the larger the future amount that will be accumulated.

In extreme cases, interest can be compounded on a continuous basis. In this case, the FVIF is calculated as:

$$FVIF_{i,n} = e^{i \times n}$$

Where ***e*** is the exponential function that has an approximate value of 2.7183.

Example: $1,000 invested at 8% interest compounded continuously is equal to:

$$FV_n = \$1{,}000 \times e^{.08 \times 2}$$
$$FV_n = \$1{,}173.51$$

Nominal and Effective Interest Rates

To compare loan costs or investment returns over different compounding periods, nominal and effective interest rates must be distinguished.

1. The nominal, or stated, annual rate is the contractual annual rate charged by the lender or promised by the borrower.

2. The true, effective annual rate (EAR) is the annual rate of interest actually paid or earned and reflects the impact of compounding frequency. The EAR is calculated as follows:

$$EAR = \left(1 + \frac{i}{m}\right)^m - 1$$

Example: Although the stated interest rate in our example above is 8%, the effective annual rate based on quarterly or monthly compounding would be:

$$EAR = \left(1 + \frac{.08}{4}\right)^4 - 1 = 8.24\%$$

$$EAR = \left(1 + \frac{.08}{12}\right)^{12} - 1 = 8.30\%$$

The annual percentage rate (APR)–a nominal annual rate–is the interest rate quoted on credit cards and loans.

The annual percentage yield (APY)–an effective annual rate–is the interest rate quoted on savings products.

Special Applications of Time Value

Future value and present value techniques have a number of important applications in finance. Three of the most often used are (1) deposits needed to accumulate a future sum, (2) amortization of loans, and (3) interest or growth rates.

1. **Deposits needed to accumulate a future sum**

   Often it is necessary to calculate the annual deposits needed to accumulate a certain amount of money *n* periods from now. The equation that makes it possible to find the necessary deposits is a variation of the equation used to find the future value of an annuity.

$$FVA_{(ordinary annuity)} = PMT \times FVIFA_{i,n}$$

   To find the necessary deposits simply solve the equation to determine payments.

$$PMT = \frac{FVA_{(ordinary\ annuity)}}{FVIFA_{i,n}}$$

Example: You want to save the down payment on a house. If you need to accumulate \$15,000 over the next four years, how much must you save each year if your account pays 8% interest per year?

$$PMT = \frac{\$15{,}000}{FVIFA_{8\%,4}} = \frac{\$15{,}000}{4.5061} = \$3{,}328.81$$

Alternatively, a financial calculator could be used, entering FV = \$15,000, N = 4, I = 8%, and computing (CPT) for the PMT.

2. **Loan Amortization**

Loan amortization refers to the determination of the equal annual loan payments necessary to provide the lender with a specified interest return and repay the loan principal over a specified period. To find loan payments use the formula for the present value of an annuity and rearrange the terms.

$$PVA_{(ordinary\ annuity)} = PMT \times PVIFA_{i,n}$$

$$PMT = \frac{PVA_{(ordinary\ annuity)}}{PVIFA_{i,n}}$$

Example: What is the annual payment due on a \$20,000, 9% loan repayable with equal installments over 8 years?

$$PMT = \frac{\$20{,}000}{PVIFA_{9\%,8}} = \frac{\$20{,}000}{5.5348} = \$3{,}613.49$$

Alternatively, a financial calculator could be used, entering PV = \$20,000, N = 8, I = 9%, and computing (CPT) for the PMT.

3. **Interest Growth Rates**

It is often necessary to calculate the annual rate of growth exhibited by a stream of cash flows. For example, you may want to know the annual compounded rate of growth in the dividends paid by a firm. To do this, use only the first and last cash flows in the series, ignoring all cash flows in between. Determine how many periods there were in the growth period, then use the present value equation to solve for the interest rate that will equate the present value (first cash flow) and the future value (last cash flow).

Example: Assume that the dividend from High-Flying, Inc. was $2.00 in 1994, $2.25 in 1995, $2.35 in 1996, $1.90 in 1997, $2.00 in 1998, and $2.50 in 1999. What is the annual compounded growth rate in the dividends?

Remember to ignore all but the first and last cash flow. Thus, the PV will be $2.00 and the FV will be $2.50. There are five growth periods (1994-95, 1995-96, 1996-97, 1997-98, 1998-99). Given this information, we need to find the PVIF that equates the future value of $2.50 five years from now with a present value of $2.00.

$$PV = FV \times PVIF_{i\%,5}$$
$$\$2.00 = \$2.50 \times PVIF_{i\%,5}$$
$$0.80 = PVIF_{i\%,5}$$

Looking at the PVIF table we need to find the factor closest to 0.80 on the row across from 5 periods. This value falls between 4 and 5% so estimate the growth rate as approximately 4.5%.

Alternatively, and in this case preferably if precision is needed, a financial calculator could be used. By entering PV = -2, FV = 2.50, and N = 5, the calculator can compute (CPT) the interest rate, which in this case would be 4.56%.

Sample Problem Solutions

Sample Problems: Future Value (Compounding)

$$FV_n = PV \times (1 + i)^n$$

Sample Problem 1:

You deposit $200 in the bank and leave it for 3 years at an annual rate of 7%. Interest is paid annually. How much will be in your account at the end of the third year?

Solution to Sample Problem 1:

Using the equation above, $\$200(1.07)^3 = \$245.01$.

Sample Problem 2:

Now assume that instead of annual compounding, the bank pays interest to you on a semiannual basis. How much will your $200 deposit be worth in three years at an annual rate of 7%, compounded monthly?

Solution to Sample Problem 2:

We first must adjust the future value equation to take into account compounding (i.e., $FV = PV \times (1+i/m)^{m \times n}$ where m = the number of compounding periods per year). In this case, the deposit will be worth $\$200(1+.07/2)^{2x3} = \$200(1.035)^6 = \$245.85$.

Sample Problem 3:

Now assume the bank pays interest to you on a monthly basis. How much will your $200 deposit be worth in three years at an annual rate of 7%, compounded monthly?

Solution to Sample Problem 3:

Adjusting the future value equation to take into account compounding, the deposit will be worth $\$200(1+.07/12)^{3x12} = \$200(1.005833)^{36} = \$246.59$.

Sample Problem 4:

Your aunt left you a trust fund worth $20,000 when you were 2 years old that has been earning 11% for 18 years. How much is in the fund now? Assume annual compounding.

Solution to Sample Problem 4:

Using the equation above, $\$20{,}000(1.11)^{18} = \$130{,}871$.

Sample Problems: Present Value (Discounting)

$$PV_n = \frac{FV}{(1+i)^n}$$

Sample Problem 5:

Compute the present value of $5,000 to be received in 1 year if interest rates are 8%.

Solution to Sample Problem 5:

Using the equation above, $\$5,000/(1.08)^1 = \$4,629.63$.

Sample Problem 6:

Compute the present value of $10,000 to be received in 3 years if interest rates are 10%.

Solution to Sample Problem 6:

Using the equation above, $\$10,000/(1.10)^3 = \$7,513.15$.

Sample Problem 7:

You have just had your income taxes completed by EZ-File and found out you are due a refund of $500, which you would expect to receive in two months. If you normally can earn 9% on your money, how much must EZ-File offer you now for your future cash refund of $500?

Solution to Sample Problem 7:

Since the payment is expected in two months, a monthly interest rate should be used. Because of this, the equation for calculating the present value of $500 becomes $\$500/(1+.09/12)^{2x1} = \$500/(1.0075)^2$, which equals $492.58. You would thus be satisfied to assign your $500 refund to EZ-File in exchange for receiving $492.58 today.

Sample Problem 8:

Your have recently inherited a trust fund of $50,000 that you are not legally able to access for 10 years. An attorney offers you $20,000 to assign the trust proceeds to her. If your required rate of return is 10%, should you agree to the deal?

Solution to Sample Problem 8:

$PV = \$50,000/(1.10)^{10} = \$19,277.16$
$PV = \$50,000(PVIF_{10\%,10}) = \$50,000(0.3855) = \$19,275.00$

If you invest $19,277.16 today at 10% per year, it will grow to $50,000 after 10 years. If you had the $20,000 from the attorney and invested it, you would have more than $50,000 at the end of 10 years. You should accept the offer.

Sample Problem 9:

Your have just been awarded a scholarship that will pay you $1,000 at the end of the first year, $2,000 at the end of the second year, and $3,000 at the end of the third year. If your required rate of return is 8%, what is the present value of the scholarship?

Solution to Sample Problem 9:

Because we have a stream of uneven cash flows, we need to find the present value of each cash flow individually and sum up the total.

$PV_{\$1,000} = \$1,000 \div (1.08) = \$925.93$
$PV_{\$2,000} = \$2,000 \div (1.08)^2 = \$1,714.68$
$PV_{\$3,000} = \$3,000 \div (1.08)^3 = \$2,381.50$
$PV_{all} = \$925.93 + \$1,714.68 + \$2,381.50 = \$5,022.11$

Sample Problems: Future Value of an Annuity

$$FVA_{(ordinary\ annuity)} = PMT \times FVIFA_{i,n}$$

Sample Problem 10:

Compute the future value of $2,000 put into a retirement account each year for 20 years that earns 12% per year.

Solution to Sample Problem 10:

Using the equation above and the FVIFA table, $\$2,000(FVIFA_{12\%,20}) = \$2,000 \times 72.0524 = \$144,104.80$.

Sample Problem 11:

You deposit $100 per month into a bank account for two years. If your account pays an average of 12% per year, how much will your account be worth in two years? Assume monthly compounding.

Solution to Sample Problem 11:

$\$100(FVIFA_{12\%/12,2x12}) = \$100(FVIFA_{1\%,24}) = \$100(26.9375) = \$2,693.75$.

Sample Problem 12:

Assume the same situation as before but now you deposit your $100 into your bank account at the beginning of each year. If your account pays an average of 12% per year, how much will your account be worth in two years? Assume monthly compounding.

Solution to Sample Problem 12:

Having the cash flows (deposits) occur at the beginning of each period turns this into an annuity due problem. This requires a slight adjustment to the ordinary annuity formula so that the FVIF for an annuity due is simply the $FVIF_{ordinary\ annuity}$ times (1 plus the interest rate). Thus, the annuity due becomes $100($FVIFA_{1\%,24}$)(1 + i) = $100(26.9375)(1+.01) = $2,720.69.

Sample Problems: Present Value of an Annuity

$$PVA_{(ordinary\ annuity)} = PMT \times PVIFA_{i,n}$$

Sample Problem 13:

Compute the present value of retirement benefits that pays $3,000 per year for 15 years if your required return is 10%.

Solution to Sample Problem 13:

Using the equation above, $3,000($PFIVA_{10\%,15}$) = $3,000(7.6061) = $22,818.30.

Sample Problem 14:

What would be the present value of retirement benefits if the first payment did not occur until five years from now?

Solution to Sample Problem 14:

This is a slightly more difficult problem in that it combines both present value of an annuity and present value of a single amount concepts. The problem is solved in two steps. First, the 15-year annuity is valued as it was in the previous problem so that its present value would be $22,818.30. Second, because the annuity will not begin until five years, we need to find the present value of this amount by discounting it for five years. Thus, the end result is as follows:

$3,000($PFIVA_{10\%,15}$) = $3,000(7.6061) = $22,818.30
$22,818.30($PVIF_{10\%,5}$) = $22,818.30(0.6209) = $14,167.88.

Sample Problem 15:

What would be the present value of the retirement benefits if you received the payments at the beginning of each year?

Solution to Sample Problem 15:

Having the cash flows (receipts) occur at the beginning of each period turns this into an annuity due problem. The annuity due becomes $3,000(PVIFA$_{10\%,15}$)(1 + i) = $3,000(7.6061)(1+.10) = $25,100.13.

If the payments do not begin until five years from now, the present value of the retirement annuity would be $15,584.67 ([$25,100.13 x (PVIF$_{10\%,5}$ or 0.621]).

Sample Problem 16:

Congratulations. You just have just won the state lottery that will pay you $1,000,000 a year for 40 years. However, you also have the option of receiving a lump-sum payment of $9,000,000 today. If your required rate of return is 12%, which alternative should you choose?

Solution to Sample Problem 16:

The present value of receiving the annual payouts is $1,000,000(PFIVA$_{12\%,40}$) = $1,000,000(8.2438) = $8,243,800, which is considerably less than the $9,000,000. Take the $9,000,000 today.

Sample Problem: Deposits Needed to Accumulate Future Sum

Sample Problem 17:

You are hoping to purchase a $15,000 Harley-Davidson four years from now. To reach this goal, how much must you deposit each year into an account earning 8% per year?

Solution to Sample Problem 17:

Recall the formula for the future value of an annuity as FVA = PMT x (FVIFA$_{i,n}$). We adapt the equation to make it easier to find the unknown annual amount so that PMT = FVA/FVIFA$_{i,n}$. Given the future value of $15,000 and a FVIFA$_{8\%,4}$ of 4.5061, the annual payment becomes: PMT = 15,000 / 4.5061 = $3,328.82.

Sample Problem: Loan Amortization

Sample Problem 18:

What would be your monthly payment on a 2-year, $10,000 car loan if the interest rate were 12%?

Solution to Sample Problem 18:

$10,000 = PMT($PVIFA_{1\%,24}$). Recall this is a monthly loan so that the monthly interest rate is 12% / 12 = 1% and there are 24 periods for the loan (2 years x 12).

$10,000 = PMT(21.2434)
PMT = $10,000 / 21.2434 = $470.73

Sample Problem: Growth Rate

Sample Problem 19:

Your earnings for the past five years have been $15,000, $19,500, $16,000, $21,000, and $25,000. What is the average annual compound growth rate?

Solution to Sample Problem 19:

Disregarding the earnings for Years 2, 3, and 4, we are left with a beginning amount ($15,000 = PV), ending amount ($25,000 = FV), and number of growth periods (4).

$PV = FV(PVIF_{i,n})$
$15{,}000 = 25{,}000\ (PVIF_{i,4})$
$0.60 = (PVIF_{i,4})$

Look up the present value interest factor 0.60 across from 4 periods. The factor is between 13% and 14% so the annual growth rate is somewhere between 13% and 14%.

Study Tips

Once again, it cannot be emphasized enough that this chapter is critical to your success in the rest of the course. The methodology developed in this chapter forms the basis for what follows in later chapters. Make certain you can work the different types of problems, being especially certain you understand both how and why problems are solved in a particular way.

A particularly difficult aspect of this chapter is choosing the correct formula or equation to use in solving different types of problems. Some important rules of thumb that may prove to be beneficial include:

1. The majority of time value problems tend to deal with present value concepts. Use present value calculations to analyze investments and loan terms.

2. Future value calculations may be used to compute a future amount or the payments needed to achieve a particular future amount.

3. The annuity formulas and annuity factors are labor-savings devices that simplify the solving of long-term problems.

4. The use of a financial calculator to solve time value problems, although strongly recommended due to the time savings versus calculations by hand, does not eliminate the need to thoroughly understand time value concepts and formulas. The calculator is only helpful if you fully understand how to use it.

Sample Exam

True/False

T F 1. If the discount (or interest) rate is positive, the present value of an expected series of payments will always exceed the future value of the same series.

T F 2. If a bank uses quarterly compounding for savings accounts, the nominal rate will be greater than the effective annual rate.

T F 3. One of the potential benefits of investing early for retirement is that an investor can receive greater benefits from the compounding of interest.

T F 4. Time value of money is based on the belief that a dollar that will be received at some future date is worth more than a dollar today.

T F 5. Everything else being equal, the higher the interest rate, the higher the future value.

T F 6. The effective annual rate increases with increasing compounding frequency.

T F 7. The future value increases with increases in the interest rate or the period of time funds are left on deposit.

T F 8. The annual percentage rate (APR) is the nominal rate of interest, found by multiplying the periodic rate by the number of periods in one year.

T F 9. The annual percentage yield (APY) is the effective rate of interest that must be disclosed to customers by banks on their savings products because of "truth-in-savings laws."

T F 10. The effective rate of interest is the contractual rate of interest charged by a lender or promised by a borrower.

T F 11. An annuity due is an annuity for which the cash flow occurs at the beginning of each period.

T F 12. The Future Value Interest Factor for an Annuity (FVIFA) is the future value of a $1 ordinary annuity for *n* periods compounded at *i* percent.

T F 13. The future value of an annuity due is always greater than the future value of an otherwise identical ordinary annuity.

T F 14. Everything else being equal, the higher the discount rate, the higher the present value.

T F 15. Everything else being equal, for a single cash flow, the longer the period of time, the lower the present value.

Multiple Choice

1. Which of the following bank accounts would provide you with the highest effective rate of interest?
   a. Bank 1: 7.8 percent with quarterly compounding
   b. Bank 2: 8 percent with quarterly compounding
   c. Bank 3: 8 percent with annual compounding
   d. Bank 4: 7.8 percent with monthly compounding

2. What is the *future value* of a 5-year ordinary annuity with annual payments of $200, evaluated at a 15 percent interest rate?
   a. $670.43
   b. $842.91
   c. $1,169.56
   d. $1,348.48

3. What is the *present value* of a 5-year ordinary annuity with annual payments of $200, evaluated at a 15 percent interest rate?
   a. $670.43
   b. $842.91
   c. $1,169.56
   d. $1,348.48

4. Indicate which formula is correct to determine the future value of an annuity due.
   a. FV(annuity due) = Amount x $FVIFA_{i,n}$
   b. FV(annuity due) = Amount x [$FVIFA_{i,n}$ x (1 + i)]
   c. FV(annuity due) = Amount x [$FVIFA_{i,n}$/(1 + i)]
   d. FV(annuity due) = Amount x FVIFAi,n+1

5. You have the opportunity to buy a perpetuity that pays $1,000 annually. Your required rate of return on this investment is 15 percent. You should be essentially indifferent to buying or not buying the investment if it were offered at a price of
   a. $5,000.00.
   b. $6,000.00.
   c. $6,666.67.
   d. $7,500.00.

6. Assume that you will receive $2,000 a year in Years 1 through 5, $3,000 a year in Years 6 through 8, and $4,000 in Year 9, with all cash flows to be received at the end of the year. If you require a 14 percent rate of return, what is the present value of these cash flows?
   a. $9,851
   b. $11,714
   c. $15,129
   d. $17,353

7. If a 5-year ordinary annuity has a present value of $1,000, and if the interest rate is 10 percent, what is the amount of each annuity payment?
   a. $240.42
   b. $263.80
   c. $300.20
   d. $315.38

8. In 1958, the average tuition for one year at an Ivy League school was $1,800. Thirty years later, in 1988, the average cost was $13,700. What was the growth rate in tuition over the 30-year period?
   a. 12%
   b. 9%
   c. 7%
   d. 8%

9. South Fork Trucking is financing a new truck with a loan of $10,000 to be repaid in 5 annual end-of-year installments of $2,504.56. What annual interest rate is the company paying?
   a. 7%
   b. 8%
   c. 9%
   d. 10%

10. An annuity with an infinite life is called
   a. a perpetuity.
   b. a zero-coupon.
   c. an indefinite.
   d. a deep discount.

11. In future value or present value problems, unless stated otherwise, cash flows are assumed to be
   a. at the end of a time period.
   b. at the beginning of a time period.
   c. in the middle of a time period.
   d. spread out evenly over a time period.

12. You recently received a letter from Cut-to-the-Chase National Bank that offers you a new credit card that has no annual fee. It states that the annual percentage rate (APR) is 18 percent on outstanding balances. What is the effective annual interest rate? (Hint: Remember these companies bill you monthly.)
   a. 18.81%
   b. 19.56%
   c. 20.00%
   d. 18.00%

13. You are considering buying a new car. The sticker price is $15,000 and you have $2,000 to put toward a down payment. If you can negotiate a nominal annual interest rate of 10 percent and you wish to pay for the car over a 5-year period, what are your monthly car payments?
   a. $216.67
   b. $252.34
   c. $276.21
   d. $285.78

14. The future value of $200 received today and deposited at 8 percent compounded semiannually for three years is
   a. $380.
   b. $158.
   c. $253.
   d. $252.

15. $100 is received at the beginning of year 1, $200 is received at the beginning of year 2, and $300 is received at the beginning of year 3. If these cash flows are deposited at 12 percent, their combined future value at the end of year 3 is
    a. $1,536.
    b. $672.
    c. $727.
    d. $1,245.

16. Indicate which of the following is true about annuities.
    a. An ordinary annuity is an equal payment paid or received at the beginning of each period.
    b. An annuity due is a payment paid or received at the beginning of each period that increases by an equal amount each period.
    c. An annuity due is an equal payment paid or received at the beginning of each period.
    d. An ordinary annuity is an equal payment paid or received at the end of each period that increases by an equal amount each period.

17. $1,200 is received at the beginning of year 1, $2,200 is received at the beginning of year 2, and $3,300 is received at the beginning of year 3. If these cash flows are deposited at 12 percent, their combined future value at the end of year 3 is
    a. $6,700.
    b. $17,000.
    c. $12,510.
    d. $8,141.

18. Bill plans to fund his individual retirement account (IRA) with the maximum contribution of $2,000 at the end of each year for the next 20 years. If Bill can earn 12 percent on his contributions, how much will he have at the end of the twentieth year?
    a. $19,292
    b. $14,938
    c. $40,000
    d. $144,104

19. A college received a contribution to its endowment fund of $2 million. They can never touch the principal, but they can use the earnings. At an assumed interest rate of 9.5 percent, how much can the college earn to help its operations each year?
    a. $95,000
    b. $19,000
    c. $190,000
    d. $18,000

20. You have been offered a project paying $300 at the beginning of each year for the next 20 years. What is the maximum amount of money you would invest in this project if you expect a 9 percent rate of return on your investment?
    a. $2,738.70
    b. $2,985.18
    c. $15,347.70
    d. $6,000.00

Essay

1. Why do financial managers use present value techniques to evaluate investment opportunities?

2. Compare and contrast the terms discounting and compounding.

Chapter 5 Answer Key

True/False

1. F
2. F
3. T
4. F
5. T
6. T
7. T
8. T
9. T
10. F
11. T
12. T
13. T
14. F
15. T

Multiple Choice

1. B
2. D
3. A
4. B
5. C
6. B
7. B
8. C
9. B
10. A
11. A
12. B
13. C
14. C
15. C
16. C
17. D
18. D
19. C
20. B

Essay

1. Because most financial decisions are made today (at time zero), managers tend to rely on present value techniques. When evaluating projects or investments, financial managers must be able to determine what the future cash flows associated with the opportunity are worth in present-day dollars.

2. Compounding is associated with future value techniques which use compounding to find the future value of each cash flow at the end of the investment's life and then sum those values to find the investment's future value. Discounting is associated with present value techniques which use discounting to find the present value of each cash flow at time zero (the present time) and then sum these values to find the investment's value today.

RETURN AND RISK

Chapter Summary

Chapter 6 describes the key aspects of risk and return. It demonstrates techniques for assessing the risk of a single asset and of a portfolio of assets. It introduces the capital asset pricing model (CAPM) as a quantitative way to link return and risk using a beta coefficient.

LG 1 ***Understand the meaning and fundamentals of risk, return, and risk aversion.*** Risk is the chance that the actual return will differ from what is expected. Risks face both firms and investors. Firm-specific risks include business and financial risk; investor-specific risks include interest rate, liquidity, and market risks; and firms and investors face event, exchange rate, purchasing-power, and tax risks. Return is the current income plus any capital gain or loss during the period, expressed as a percentage of the beginning-of-period investment value. Most managers and investors are risk-averse: they generally prefer less risky alternatives, and they require higher expected returns as compensation for taking greater risk.

LG 2 ***Describe procedures for assessing the risk of a single asset.*** Sensitivity analysis and probability distributions can be used to assess risk. Sensitivity analysis uses several possible return estimates to assess the variability of outcomes. Probability distributions, both bar charts and continuous distributions, provide a more quantitative insight into an asset's risk.

LG 3 ***Discuss risk measurement for a single asset using the standard deviation and coefficient of variation.*** In addition to the range, which is the optimistic (best) outcome minus the pessimistic (worst) outcome, the standard deviation and the coefficient of variation can be used to measure risk. The standard deviation measures the dispersion around an asset's expected value; the coefficient of variation uses the standard deviation to measure dispersion on a relative basis.

LG 4 ***Understand the return and risk characteristics of a portfolio in terms of correlation and diversification, and the impact of international assets on a portfolio.*** The investor's goal and the financial manager's goal for the firm is to create an efficient portfolio, one that maximizes return for a given level of risk or minimizes risk for a given level of return. The risk of a portfolio of assets may be reduced through diversification.

New investments must be considered in light of their effect on the return and risk of the portfolio. Correlation, which is the statistical measure of the relationship between any two series of numbers, affects diversification: the more negative (or less positive) the correlation between asset returns, the greater the risk-reducing benefits of diversification. International diversification can be used to reduce a portfolio's risk further. With foreign assets come political risks and the risk of currency fluctuations.

Review the two types of risk and the derivation and role of beta in measuring the relevant risk of both an individual security and a portfolio. The total risk of a security consists of nondiversifiable and diversifiable risk. Nondiversifiable risk is the only relevant risk; diversifiable risk can be eliminated through diversification. Nondiversifiable risk is measured by the beta coefficient, which is a relative measure of the relationship between an asset's return and the market return. Beta is derived by finding the slope of the "characteristic line" that best explains the historical relationship between the asset's return and the market return. The beta of a portfolio is a weighted average of the betas of the individual assets that it includes.

Explain the capital asset pricing model (CAPM) and its relationship to the security market line (SML). The capital asset pricing model (CAPM) uses beta to relate an asset's risk relative to the market to the asset's required return. The graphical depiction of CAPM is the security market line (SML). Although it has some shortcomings, CAPM provides a useful conceptual framework for evaluating and linking return and risk.

Chapter Outline

Fundamental Concepts about Return and Risk

Every financial or investment decision presents certain return and risk characteristics that affect its valuation so a clear understanding of both return and risk is essential to making financial and investment decisions.

Definition of Return

The return on an investment is measured as the total gain or loss experienced on behalf of its owner over a given period of time. It is calculated by dividing the investment's current income plus any change in its value by its beginning-of-period investment value. The formula for calculating return is as follows:

$$k_t = \frac{C_t + (P_t - P_{t-1})}{P_{t-1}}$$

Where

k_t = rate of return during period t

C_t = current income (cash flow) received from the investment in the time period $t - 1$ to t

P_t = price (value) of investment at time t

P_{t-1} = price (value) of investment at time $t - 1$

Definition of Risk and Risk Preference

Risk is the chance that the actual return will differ from what is expected. Risks faced by financial managers include firm-specific risks such as business or operating risk and financial risk. Investors face investor-specific risks such as interest rate, liquidity, and market risks. Financial managers and investors both face event, exchange rate, purchasing-power, and tax risks.

Most managers and investors are risk-averse: they generally prefer less risky alternatives, and they require higher expected returns as compensation for taking greater risk. Few managers or investors are risk-indifferent, and fewer still are risk-seeking.

Measuring the Risk of a Single Asset

Sensitivity analysis uses multiple possible return estimates to assess the variability of outcomes. Although it does not actually measure the risk, it gives a feel for the risks involved.

Probability distributions provide a more quantitative insight into an asset's risk. Probability distributions can be shown as either bar charts, when there is a limited number of outcomes, and continuous distributions.

Standard Deviation and Coefficient of Variation

The most common statistical indicator of an asset's risk is the standard deviation, which measures the dispersion around an asset's expected value. The expected value of a return, $\bar{k}$, is the most likely return and is calculated as follows:

$$\bar{k} = \sum_{j=1}^{n} k_j \times \text{Pr}_j$$

Where

k_j	=	return for the jth outcome
Pr_j	=	probability of occurrence of the jth outcome
n	=	number of outcomes considered

The standard deviation, σ_k, is the calculated as:

$$\sigma_k = \sqrt{\sum_{j=1}^{n} \left(k_j - \bar{k}\right)^2 \times \mathbf{Pr}_j}$$

In general, the higher the standard deviation, the higher the risk. However, to be able to assess the relative risk of one asset against others, the return of the asset must also be considered. The coefficient of variation is used to compare the risk of assets that have different returns. It measures the risk per dollar of return and is calculated as:

$$CV = \frac{\sigma_k}{\bar{k}}$$

Return and Risk of a Portfolio

The risk of any single asset should not be viewed independently of other assets in a portfolio. The goal of both financial managers and investors is to create an efficient portfolio, one that maximizes return for a given level of risk or minimizes risk for a given level of return.

Portfolio return

The return of a portfolio is computed as the weighted average of the returns of each asset in the portfolio.

Portfolio risk

The risk of a portfolio depends not only on the risk of each asset in the portfolio but also on the correlation between each asset. Correlation is a statistical measure of the relationship between any two sets of numbers. The two sets of numbers can be:

1. Positively correlated, meaning they each move in the same direction.
2. Negatively correlated, meaning them move in opposite directions.
3. Uncorrelated, meaning there is no relationship between them.

The risk of a portfolio of assets may be reduced through diversification. New investments must be considered in light of their effect on the risk and return of the portfolio. The more negative (or less positive) the correlation between asset returns, the greater the risk-reducing benefits of diversification.

International diversification

Because the economies (and therefore currency values) of different countries do not always move together, the risk of a portfolio can typically be reduced by making international investments. However, the benefits from including foreign assets in a portfolio must be weighed against the investor's potential exposure to political risks and the risks of currency fluctuations.

Risk and Return: Beta and the Capital Asset Pricing Model (CAPM)

The overall risk of a security consists of nondiversifiable and diversifiable risk. Diversifiable risk (sometimes called unsystematic risk) arises from random firm-specific events; this risk can be eliminated through diversification. Nondiversifiable risk (sometimes called systematic risk) is attributable to market factors that affect all firms.

Nondiversifiable risk is the only relevant risk to an investor. It is measured by the beta coefficient, which is a relative measure of the relationship between an asset's return and the market return. Beta is derived by finding the slope of the "characteristic line" that best explains the historical relationship between the asset's return and the market return.

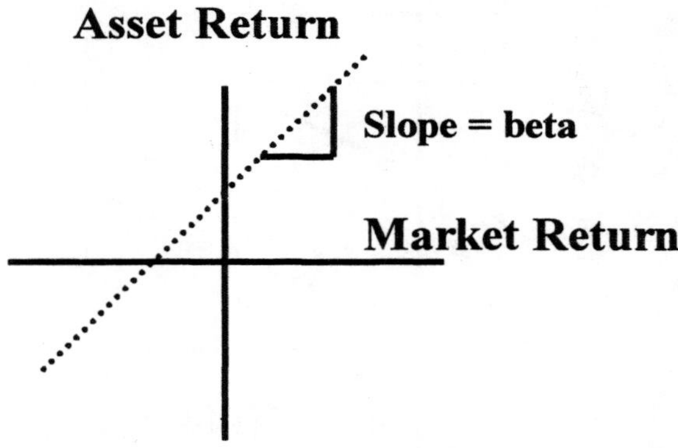

The beta of a portfolio is a weighted average of the betas of the individual assets that it includes.

$$b_p = \sqrt{\sum_{j=1}^{n} w_j \times b_j}$$

The Capital Asset Pricing Model (CAPM)

The capital asset pricing model (CAPM) uses beta to relate an asset's risk relative to the market to the asset's required return. The equation for the CAPM is as follows:

$$k_j = R_F + [b \times (k_m - R_F)]$$

Where

k_j	=	required return on asset *j*
R_F	=	risk-free rate of return, commonly measured by the return on a U.S. Treasury bill
b_j	=	beta coefficient or index of nondiversifiable risk for asset *j*
k_m	=	market return; return on the market portfolio of assets

The last portion of the equation (**k_m - R_F**) is called the market risk premium, because it represents the premium an investor must receive for taking the risk of the investment.

CAPM and the Security Market Line

When the required returns on all stocks are graphed against their corresponding betas, the result is the security market line (SML). The SML will be a straight line.

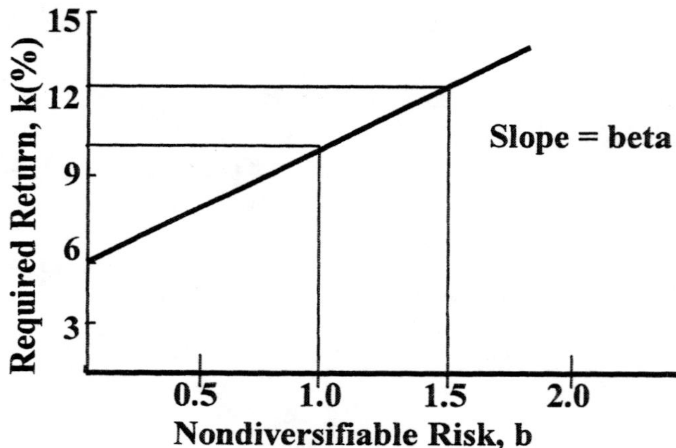

Although it has some shortcomings, the CAPM provides a useful conceptual framework for evaluating and linking risk and return.

Sample Problem Solutions

Sample Problem 1: Calculating Return

Calculate the return from holding one share of MicroApple stock if the stock rose in value from $30 to $40 and you received a dividend of $2 over the past year.

Solution to Sample Problem 1

$$k_{MicroApple} = \frac{\$2 + \$40 - \$30}{\$30} = \frac{\$12}{\$30} = 40\%$$

Sample Problem 2: Calculating Expected Value and Standard Deviation

For the stock listed in the following table, calculate its expected return, standard deviation, and coefficient of variation.

State of Economy	Probability	Stock Price	$k_j \times \mathrm{Pr}_j$	$(k_j - \bar{k}$	$(k_j - \bar{k})^2$	$(k_j - \bar{k})^2 \times \mathrm{Pr}_j$
Boom	0.30	$60				
Normal	0.50	30				
Depression	0.20	10				

Solution to Sample Problem 2

State of Economy	Probability	Stock Price	$k_j \times \mathrm{Pr}_j$	$(k_j - \bar{k}$	$(k_j - \bar{k})^2$	$(k_j - \bar{k})^2 \times \mathrm{Pr}_j$
Boom	0.30	$60	$18.00	25	625	187.50
Normal	0.50	30	15.00	-5	25	12.50
Depression	0.20	10	2.00	25	625	125.00
Exp. Return			$35.00			

$$\bar{k} = \$60 \times 30\% + \$30 \times 50\% + \$10 \times 20\% = \$35$$

$$\sigma_k = \sqrt{(187.50 + 12.50 + 125.00)} = 18.03$$

$$CV = \frac{18.03}{35} = .52$$

First, compute the expected value or mean of the stock prices. You should get $35 for the expected value. You next take each outcome (e.g., $60 for the boom), subtract the expected value ($35), square the difference, and then multiply by the probability of each outcome (e.g., $30% for the boom). Next, sum up the three outcomes and take the square root to calculate the standard deviation. Finally, the coefficient of variation is simply the standard deviation divided by the expected return.

Sample Problem 3: Risk Aversion

You currently own a stock that earns 13% and has a risk index of 8%. Reviewing the following information, determine which stock you would choose if you were a risk-averse investor.

Investment	Expected return	Expected Risk Index
Alpha Inc.	10%	8%
Beta Corp.	13%	10%
Gamma Enterprises	20%	6%

Solution to Sample Problem 3

A risk-averse investor would choose the investment that provided the most return for a given amount of risk or lowest risk for a given amount of return. Alpha is as risky as your current stock but promises a lower expected return. Beta provides the same expected return but at a higher level of risk. The risk-averse investor would choose Gamma since it is less risky and offers a higher expected return than your current stock.

Sample Problem 4: Portfolio Analysis

You are working on developing a stock portfolio and are evaluating the following four stocks.

Investment	Expected return	Beta
Asset A	6%	0.8
Asset B	10%	1.1
Asset C	16%	1.5
Asset D	20%	1.9

a. What would be the expected return and beta of your portfolio if you invested equally in each stock?

Solution to Sample Problem 4a

Expected return = 6% x 25% + 10% x 25% + 16% x 25% + 20% x 25% = 13%
Beta = 0.8 x 25% + 1.1 x 25% + 1.5 x 25% + 1.9 x 25% = 1.33

b. What would be the expected return and beta of your portfolio if you invested 15% in Stock A, 20% in Stock B, 35% in Stock C, and 30% in Stock D?

Solution to Sample Problem 4b

Expected return = 6% x 15% + 10% x 20% + 16% x 35% + 20% x 30% = 14.5%
Beta = 0.8 x 15% + 1.1 x 20% + 1.5 x 35% + 1.9 x 30% = 1.44

Sample Problem 5: Understanding the Capital Asset Pricing Model (CAPM)

a. If the risk-free rate of interest is 4% and the market return is 10%, what would be the required return for a security with a beta equal to 1.6?

Solution to Sample Problem 5a

k = 4% + [1.6(10% - 4%)]
k = 13.60%

b. If the required return for a security is 18%, and the risk-free rate of interest is 6% and the market return is 12%, what is the beta for the security?

Solution to Sample Problem 5b

15% = 6% + [b(12% - 6%)]
b = 1.50

c. If the required return for a security is 15%, it has a beta of 2.0, and the market return is 10%, what is the risk-free rate of interest?

Solution to Sample Problem 5c

15% = R_F + [2.0(10% - R_F)]
R_F = 5%

d. If the required return for a security is 20%, it has a beta of 1.4, and the risk-free rate of interest is 6%, what is the expected market return?

Solution to Sample Problem 5d

$$20\% = 6\% + [1.4(k_m - 6\%)]$$
$$k_m = 16\%$$

Study Tips

1. The CAPM provides a way of calculating the required return on a security. The required return is how much the investor must earn to be compensated for the risk of holding the security.

2. Be able to distinguish between diversifiable, or firm-specific risk, and nondiversifiable, or market, risk.

3. Remember that when examining an asset in a portfolio, the only risk that matters is market risk. If examined on its own, standard deviation and coefficient of variation are used to compare the risk of different securities.

Sample Exam

True/False

T F 1. The tighter the probability distribution of expected future returns, the smaller the risk of a given investment as measured by the standard deviation.

T F 2. The coefficient of variation is a better measure of risk than the standard deviation if the expected returns of the securities being compared differ significantly.

T F 3. Companies should deliberately increase their risk relative to the market only if the actions that increase the risk also increase the expected rate of return on the firm's assets by enough to completely compensate for the higher risk.

T F 4. According to the Capital Asset Pricing Model, investors are primarily concerned with portfolio risk, not the isolated risks of individual stocks. Thus, the relevant risk is an individual stock's contribution to the overall riskiness of the portfolio.

T F 5. Market risk refers to the tendency of a stock to move with the general stock market. A stock with above-average market risk will tend to be more volatile than an average stock, and it will definitely have a beta which is greater than 1.0.

T F 6. The slope of the SML is determined by the value of beta.

T F 7. Most managers are risk-averse, since for a given increase in risk they require an increase in return.

T F 8. The return on an asset is the change in its value plus any cash distribution over a given period of time, expressed as a percentage of its ending value.

T F 9. The risk of an asset can be measured by its variance, which is found by subtracting the worst outcome from the best outcome.

T F 10. The more certain the return from an asset, the less variability and therefore the less risk.

T F 11. An efficient portfolio is a portfolio that maximizes return for a given level of risk or minimizes risk for a given level of return.

T F 12. In general, the lower the correlation between asset returns, the greater the potential diversification of risk.

T F 13. When the U.S. currency gains in value, the dollar value of a foreign-currency-denominated portfolio of assets declines.

T F 14. The unsystematic risk can be eliminated through diversification.

T F 15. The slope of the SML reflects the degree of risk aversion. The steeper its slope, the greater the degree of risk aversion.

Multiple Choice

1. Which of the following statements is *incorrect*?
   a. The slope of the security market line is measured by beta.
   b. Two securities with the same stand-alone risk can have different betas.
   c. Company-specific risk can be diversified away.
   d. The market risk premium is affected by attitudes about risk.

2. Calculate the required rate of return for Mercury Inc., assuming that investors expect a 5 percent rate of inflation in the future. The real risk-free rate is equal to 3 percent and the market risk premium is 5 percent. Mercury has a beta of 2.0, and its realized rate of return has averaged 15 percent over the last 5 years.
   a. 15%
   b. 16%
   c. 17%
   d. 18%

3. AlphaBeta Company (ABC) has a required return of 11.3%. The risk-free rate is 5% and the return on the market is 10%. What is ABC's beta?
   a. 1.26
   b. 1.10
   c. 0.80
   d. 1.35

4. Assume that the risk-free rate is 5 percent, and that the market risk premium is 7 percent. If a stock has a required rate of return of 13.75 percent, what is its beta?
   a. 1.25
   b. 1.35
   c. 1.37
   d. 1.60

5. A stock has an expected return of 12.25 percent. The beta of the stock is 1.15 and the risk-free rate is 5 percent. What is the market risk premium?
   a. 1.30%
   b. 6.50%
   c. 15.00%
   d. 6.30%

6. ______ is the chance of loss or the variability of returns associated with a given asset.
   a. Return
   b. Value
   c. Risk
   d. Probability

7. Last year Mike bought 100 shares of Dallas Corporation common stock for $53 per share. During the year, he received dividends of $1.45 per share. The stock is currently selling for $60 per share. What rate of return did Mike earn over the year?
   a. 11.7 percent
   b. 13.2 percent
   c. 14.1 percent
   d. 15.9 percent

8. If a person requires greater return when risk increases, that person is said to be
   a. risk-seeking.
   b. risk-indifferent.
   c. risk-averse.
   d. risk-aware.

9. Since for a given increase in risk, most managers require an increase in return, they are
   a. risk-seeking.
   b. risk-indifferent.
   c. risk-free.
   d. risk-averse.

10. The ______ the coefficient of variation, the ______ the risk.
   a. lower; lower
   b. higher; lower
   c. lower; higher
   d. more stable; higher

11. A collection of assets is called
   a. a grouping.
   b. a portfolio.
   c. an investment.
   d. a diversity.

12. The goal of an efficient portfolio is to
   a. maximize risk for a given level of return.
   b. maximize risk in order to maximize profit.
   c. minimize profit in order to minimize risk.
   d. minimize risk for a given level of return.

13. In general, the lower (less positive and more negative) the correlation between asset returns,
   a. the less the potential diversification of risk.
   b. the greater the potential diversification of risk.
   c. the lower the potential profit.
   d. the less the assets have to be monitored.

14. Systematic risk is also referred to as
   a. diversifiable risk.
   b. economic risk.
   c. nondiversifiable risk.
   d. not relevant.

15. The beta of the market
    a. is greater than 1.
    b. is less than 1.
    c. is 1.
    d. cannot be determined.

16. Risk that affects all firms is called
    a. total risk.
    b. management risk.
    c. nondiversifiable risk.
    d. diversifiable risk.

17. Unsystematic risk is not relevant, because
    a. it does not change.
    b. it can be eliminated through diversification.
    c. it cannot be estimated.
    d. it cannot be eliminated through diversification.

18. The beta of a portfolio
    a. is the sum of the betas of all assets in the portfolio.
    b. is irrelevant, only the betas of the individual assets are important.
    c. does not change over time.
    d. is the weighted average of the betas of the individual assets in the portfolio.

19. In the capital asset pricing model, the beta coefficient is a measure of
    a. economic risk.
    b. diversifiable risk.
    c. nondiversifiable risk.
    d. unsystematic risk.

20. As risk aversion increases,
    a. a firm's beta will increase.
    b. investors' required rate of return would increase.
    c. a firm's beta will decrease.
    d. investors' required rate of return would decrease.

Essay

1. Explain what is meant by risk aversion.

2. Describe the components of the CAPM equation and how the equation is used to estimate the required return on an asset.

Chapter 6 Answer Key

True/False

1. T
2. T
3. T
4. T
5. T
6. F
7. T
8. F
9. F
10. T
11. T
12. T
13. T
14. T
15. T

Multiple Choice

1. A
2. D
3. A
4. A
5. D
6. C
7. D
8. C
9. D
10. A
11. B
12. D
13. B
14. C
15. C
16. C
17. B
18. D
19. C
20. B

Essay

1. Risk aversion refers to an investor preferring less risky alternatives, and requiring higher expected returns as compensation for taking greater risk.

2. The capital asset pricing model is used to find the required return on a stock. The required return is a function of the risk-free rate, the expected return on the stock market in general, and a stock's beta, which measures a stock's return relative to the market's. An increase in any of the variables results in an increase in the required return for a stock.

Chapter 7

VALUATION

Chapter Summary

Chapter 7 presents the key conceptual and computational procedures for use in valuation: determining the worth, or value, or an asset. Returns, timing, and risk are the three key inputs to the basic valuation model, which can be customized to value specific securities (bonds, preferred stock, and common stock).

LG 1 ***Describe the key inputs and basic model used in the valuation process.*** Key inputs to the valuation process include cash flows (returns), timing, and risk and the required return. The value, or worth, of any asset is equal to the present value of all future cash flows it is *expected* to provide over the relevant time period.

LG 2 ***Review the basic bond valuation model.*** The value of a bond is the present value of its interest payments plus the present value of its par value.

LG 3 ***Discuss bond value behavior, particularly the impact that required return and time to maturity have on bond value.*** The discount rate used to determine bond value is the required return, which may differ from the bond's coupon interest rate. A bond can sell at a discount, at par, or at a premium. The amount of time to maturity affects bond values. Even if required return remains constant, the value of a bond will approach its par value as the bond moves closer to maturity. The chance that interest rates will change and thereby change the required return and bond value is called interest rate risk. The shorter the amount of time until a bond's maturity, the less responsive is its market value to a given change in the required return.

LG 4 ***Explain yield to maturity, and the procedure used to value bonds that pay interest semiannually.*** Yield to maturity (YTM) is the rate of return investors earn if they buy a bond at a specific price and hold it until maturity. Bonds that pay interest semiannually are valued by using the same procedure used to value bonds paying annual interest except that the interest payments are one-half of the annual interest payments, the number of periods is twice the number of years to maturity, and the required return is one-half of the stated annual required return on similar-risk bonds.

LG 5 ***Perform basic common stock valuation using each of three models: zero-growth, constant-growth, and variable-growth.*** The value of a share of common stock is the present value of all future dividends it is expected to provide. Zero-growth, constant-growth, and variable-growth models of dividend growth can be considered in common stock valuation. The most widely cited model is the constant-growth (Gordon) model.

LG 6 ***Understand the relationships among financial decisions, return, risk, and stock value.*** In a stable economy, any action of the financial manager that increases the level of expected return without changing risk should increase share value, and any action that reduces the level of expected return without changing risk should reduce share value. Similarly, any action that increases risk (required return) will reduce share value, and any action that reduces risk will increase share value. Because most financial decisions affect both return and risk, an assessment of their combined effect on stock value must be part of the financial decision making process.

Chapter Outline

Valuation Fundamentals

Valuation is the process that links return and risk to determine the worth of an asset.

LG 1 The value of any asset depends on the cash flow(s) it is expected to provide over the ownership period.

In addition, the timing of the cash flows must be known. The combination of the cash flow and its timing fully defines the return expected from the asset. The level of risk associated with the cash flow can affect its value. In general, the greater the risk of a cash flow, the lower its value. Therefore, in the valuation process, the higher the risk, the greater the required return (discount rate).

Basic valuation model
The value, or worth, of any asset is equal to the present value of all future cash flows it is *expected* to provide over the relevant time period.

The basic valuation model for any asset is summarized as:

$$V_0 = \frac{CF_1}{(1+k)^1} + \frac{CF_2}{(1+k)^2} + \cdots + \frac{CF_n}{(1+k)^n}$$

$$= [CF_1 \times (PVIF_{k,1}) + CF_2 \times (PVIF_{k,2}) + \cdots + CF_n \times (PVIF_{k,n})$$

Where

V_0	=	value of the asset at time zero
CF_t	=	cash flow expected at the end of year t
k	=	appropriate required return (discount rate)
n	=	relevant time period

Bond Valuation

Bonds are long-term debt instruments used by business and government to raise large sums of money, typically from a diverse group of lenders. Most corporate bonds pay interest semiannually at a stated coupon interest rate, have an initial maturity of 10 to 30 years, and have a par value, or face value, of $1,000 that must be repaid at maturity.

The value of a bond is the present value of its interest payments plus the present value of its par value. The basic valuation model for a bond is as follows:

$$B_0 = I \times \left[\sum_{t=1}^{n} \frac{1}{(1+k_d)^t}\right] + M \times \left[\frac{1}{(1+k_d)^n}\right]$$

$$= I \times (PVIFA_{k_d,n}) + M \times (PVIF_{k_d,n})$$

Where

B_0	=	value of the bond at time zero
I	=	annual interest paid in dollars
n	=	number of years to maturity
M	=	par value in dollars
k_d	=	required return on a bond

Bond Value Behavior

The discount rate used to determine bond value is the required return, which may differ from the bond's coupon interest rate. The required return can change due to changes in economic conditions or from changes in the risk of the firm.

If not valued at its par value, a bond can sell at a discount (have a value less than par) or at a premium (have a value above par).

The amount of time to maturity affects bond values. Even if required return remains constant, the value of a bond will approach its par value as the bond moves closer to maturity.

The chance that interest rates will change and thereby change the required return and bond value is called interest rate risk. Rising interest rates are associated with falling bond prices. Since the market prices of shorter-maturity bonds are less responsive to a given change in the required return, they have less interest rate risk.

Yield to Maturity

Yield to maturity (YTM) is the rate of return investors earn if they buy a bond at a specific price and hold it until maturity. It is the discount rate k_d that equates the present value of the bond's cash flows to its current market value.

$$B_0 = I \times \left[\sum_{t=1}^{n} \frac{1}{(1+k_d)^t}\right] + M \times \left[\frac{1}{(1+k_d)^n}\right]$$

Although the yield to maturity can be found by trial and error, it is most often calculated using either a financial calculator or computer spreadsheet program.

Semiannual Interest Rates and Bond Values

Bonds that pay interest semiannually are valued by using the same procedure used to value bonds paying annual interest. The key differences are that the interest payments are one-half of the annual interest payments, the number of periods is twice the number of years to maturity, and the required return is one-half of the stated annual required return on similar-risk bonds.

Common Stock Valuation

The value of a share of common stock is the present value of all future benefits (dividends) it is expected to provide. Although a stockholder can earn capital gains by selling stock at a price above that originally paid, what is really sold is the right to the future dividends. The general formula for valuing common stock is directly related to the basic valuation model for all assets and is as follows:

$$P_0 = \frac{D_1}{(1+k_s)^1} + \frac{D_2}{(1+k_s)^2} + \cdots + \frac{D_\infty}{(1+k_s)^\infty}$$

Where

P_0 = value of common stock

D_t = per-share dividend expected at the end of year t

k_s = required return on common stock

There are three variations of the basic formula that can be made based upon the assumption of the growth of the dividends. The three models assume either zero-growth, constant-growth, or variable-growth in the expected dividends from the stock.

The valuation formula for a stock whose dividends are not expected to grow (the zero-growth model) is:

$$P_0 = \frac{D_1}{k_s}$$

The valuation formula for a stock whose dividends are expected to grow at some constant rate forever (the constant-growth or Gordon model) is:

$$P_0 = \frac{D_1}{k_s - g}$$

Where **g** = growth rate.

The valuation formula for a stock whose dividends are expected to grow at different rates is a bit more complex. We generally assume the simplest case in which there are only two growth rates, an initial growth rate, g_1, and a second growth rate, g_2, after the shift. The entire formula for a variable-growth stock under these circumstances can be written as:

$$P_0 = \sum_{t=1}^{N} \frac{D_0 \times (1+g_1)^t}{(1+k_s)^t} + \left[\frac{1}{(1+k_s)^N} \times \frac{D_{N+1}}{k_s - g}\right]$$

However, this formula can be broken down into two separate components: the calculation of the present value of the dividends during the first growth period and then the calculation of the price of the stock at the end of the initial growth period. This is accomplished in four steps.

1. Find the value of the cash dividends at the end of year using the formula

$$D_t = D_0(1+g_1)^t = D_0 \times FVIF_{g1,t}$$

2. Fine the present value of the cash dividends during the initial growth period as

$$\sum_{t=1}^{N} \frac{D_0 \times (1+g_1)^t}{(1+k_s)^t}$$

3. Find the value of the stock at the end of the initial growth period, *N*, and then find its present value. If the second growth rate is constant, the constant-growth rate

model can be used to value the stock at the end of the first growth period, and then the value of the stock is discounted to present day terms:

$$\frac{D_{N+1}}{k_s - g_2} \times \frac{1}{(1+k_s)^N} = \frac{D_{N+1}}{k_s - g_2} \times PVIF_{k_s,N}$$

4. The final step is to simply add together the present value terms found in steps 2 and 3.

Decision Making and Common Stock Value

LG 6

Stock valuation is based on expected returns and risk. Changes in these variables can cause the value of the firm to change.

In a stable economy, any action of the financial manager that increases the level of expected returns without changing risk should increase the share value of the firm and any action that decreases the level of expected returns should decrease the value.

Any management action that increases the risk (and therefore the required return) of the expected returns will reduce share value and any action that reduces risk will increase share value.

Because most financial decisions affect both return and risk, an assessment of their combined effect on stock value must be part of the financial decision making process.

Sample Problem Solutions

Sample Problem 1: Valuation of any asset

Calculate the value of some farm land you expect to sell for $200,000 in 10 years if the cost of capital is 15%.

Solution to Sample Problem 1

The value of any asset is found by calculating the present value of the cash flows the asset is expected to generate. In this case,

$PV_{farmland}$ = $200,000 x $PVIF_{15\%,10}$ = $49,440.00

Sample Problem 2: Valuation of any asset

You wish to invest in a commercial office building that is expected to generate cash flows of $235,000 per year for the next 25 years. What would you be willing to pay for this investment if you have a required return of 12%?

Solution to Sample Problem 2

A similar situation as above but now the expected cash flows are in the form of an annuity.

$$PV_{\text{office building}} = \$235{,}000 \times PVIFA_{12\%,25} = \$1{,}843{,}128.50$$

Sample Problem 3: Bond Valuation

Compute the value of a $1,000 par corporate bond that matures in five years and pays an 8% coupon annually. Assume a discount rate of 10%.

Solution to Sample Problem 3

At a coupon rate of 8%, the annual interest payment on the bond is $80. To value the bond, find the present value of the interest payments (a five-year annuity) and the present value of the par value of $1,000 (a single amount) to be received after five years.

$PV_{bond} = \$80 \times PVIFA_{10\%,5} + \$1{,}000 \times PVIF_{10\%,5} = \$80(3.7908) + \$1{,}000(.6209)$
$= \$924.16$

Alternatively, a financial calculator could be used, entering PMT = 80, FV = 1,000, N=5, and I = 10. The PV would then be computed (CPT) as $924.18.

Sample Problem 4: Bond Valuation

Compute the value of the bond in sample problem 3 assuming there are 20 years until the bond matures.

Solution to Sample Problem 4

$PV_{bond} = \$80 \times PVIFA_{10\%,20} + \$1{,}000 \times PVIF_{10\%,20} = \$80(8.5136) + \$1{,}000(.1486)$
$= \$829.69$

If a financial calculator is used, enter PMT = 80, FV = 1,000, N=20, and I = 10. The PV would equal $829.73.

Sample Problem 5: Bond Valuation

Compute the value of the bond in sample problem 3 assuming semiannual, rather than annual, coupon payments.

Solution to Sample Problem 5

With semiannual coupon payments, each payment is halved (i.e., $80 ÷ 2 = $40). The required return must also be halved (10% ÷ 2 = 5%) and the number of periods is doubled (5 x 2 = 10).

PV_{bond} = **$40** x $PVIFA_{5\%,10}$ + $1,000 x $PVIF_{5\%,10}$ = $40(7.7217) + $1,000(.6139) = $922.77

If a financial calculator is used, enter PMT = 40, FV = 1,000, N=10, and I = 5. The PV would then be computed (CPT) as $922.78.

Sample Problem 6: Stock Valuation–Zero-growth Model

Assume the current dividend on a share of stock is $2.00 and it is not expected to change. Using a discount rate of 15%, what would be the value (price) of a share of stock?

Solution to Sample Problem 6

Assuming no growth in the dividends, the zero-growth model can be used to value the stock. Therefore, the stock price (P_0) would be equal to D_1 / k_s = $2 / 0.15 = $13.33.

Sample Problem 7: Stock Valuation–Constant-growth Model

Assume instead that you expect the dividends from the stock in sample problem 6 to increase at 6% per year indefinitely. What would be the value of the stock in this situation?

Solution to Sample Problem 7

With the assumption of constantly growing dividends, the constant-growth, or Gordon growth, model can be used. Therefore, the stock price (P_0) would be equal to D_1 / (k_s – g) = $2(1 + .06) / (0.15 – 0.06) = $2.12 / 0.09 = $23.56.

Sample Problem 8: Stock Valuation–Variable-growth Model

Assume instead that you expect the dividends from the stock in sample problem 6 to increase by 20% per year for 3 years, followed by a constant 6% growth rate. What would be the value of the stock in this situation?

Solution to Sample Problem 8

This is probably a more realistic example than either the zero-growth or the constant-growth models. In addition, although the valuation of the stock appears very complex, if broken down into its four key components, the problem is not overly difficult to complete.

1. The first step is to find the value of the cash dividends expected at the end of each of the next three years. Given D_0 as $2.00,

$$D_1 = D_0(1 + g)^1 = \$2.00(1.20)^1 = \quad \$2.40$$
$$D_2 = D_0(1 + g)^2 = \$2.00(1.20)^2 = \quad \$2.88$$
$$D_3 = D_0(1 + g)^3 = \$2.00(1.20)^3 = \quad \$3.456$$

2. Find the present value of the cash dividends during the initial growth period discounted at the required rate of return of 15%.

$$D_1 = \$2.40 \text{ x } PVIF_{15\%,1} = \quad \$2.09$$
$$D_2 = \$2.88 \text{ x } PVIF_{15\%,2} = \quad 2.18$$
$$D_3 = \$3.456 \text{ x } PVIF_{15\%,3} = \quad \underline{2.27}$$
$$\$6.54$$

3. Find the value of the stock at the end of third year using the constant-growth model to value the expected dividends beyond Year 3.

$$P_3 = D_4 / (k_s - g) = 2.41 / (0.15 - .06) = \$26.78$$

Note that $D_4 = D_3\ (1 + g) = \$2.27(1.06) = \$2.41$

Next, find the present value of the stock you valued as of the end of Year 3.

$$P_0 = P_3 \text{ x } PVIF_{15\%,3} = 26.78 \text{ x } .6575 = \$17.61$$

4. Add the present value terms found in steps 2 and 3 to find the current value of the stock.

$6.54 + $17.61 = $24.15

Study Tips

1. Bond valuation can be checked using your understanding of bond discounts and premiums. If the market interest rate rises above the coupon rate of the bond, it must sell at a discount and the bond's present value will be less than $1,000. If the interest rate is below the coupon rate, it will sell at a premium above $1,000.

2. In valuing bonds with interest payments occurring more frequently than annual, remember that three components of the valuation equation must be changed. For example, for semiannual compounding, the size of the coupon payment is halved, the number of periods is doubled, and, the point most often forgotten, the discount rate is also halved.

3. The constant-growth (Gordon) model is a simple equation to lose, but often there are errors in using it. The model finds the value of a stock with constant growth one period before the time the dividend in the numerator occurs. For example, to find the value of a stock today (t = 0), we use the expected dividend for next year (t = 1). Similarly, the expected value of the stock three years from now can be found by using the expected dividend in the fourth year.

Sample Exam

True/False

T F 1. Because short-term interest rates are much more volatile than long-term rates, you would, in the real world, be subject to much more interest rate risk if you purchased a 30-day bond than if you bought a 30-year bond.

T F 2. For bonds, price sensitivity to a given change in interest rates generally *increases* as years remaining to maturity increases.

T F 3. The value of an asset depends on the historical cash flow(s) up to the present time.

T F 4. Valuation is the process that links risk and return to determine the worth of an asset.

T F 5. In the valuation process, the higher the risk, the greater the required return.

T F 6. Regardless of the exact cause, the important point is that when the required return is greater than the coupon interest rate, the bond value will be less than its par value.

T F 7. The required return on the bond is likely to differ from the stated interest rate for either of two reasons: 1) economic conditions have changed, causing a shift in the basic cost of long-term funds, or 2) the firm's risk has changed.

T F 8. The value of a bond with semiannual interest is greater than a bond with annual interest, everything else the same.

T F 9. Yield to maturity (YTM) is the rate investors earn if they buy the bond at a specific price and hold it until maturity.

T F 10. When the bond value differs from par, the yield to maturity will differ from the coupon interest rate.

T F 11. Because a rise in interest rates, and therefore the required return, results in an increase in bond value, bondholders are typically more concerned with dropping interest rates.

T F 12. The shorter the amount of time until a bond's maturity, the more responsive is its market value to a given change in the required return.

T F 13. Any action taken by the financial manager that increases risk will also increase the required return.

T F 14. In common stock valuation, any action taken by the financial manager that increases risk contributes toward an increase in value.

T F 15. In a stable economy, an action of the financial manager that increases the level of expected return without changing risk should reduce share value, and an action that reduces the level of expected return without changing risk should increase share value.

Multiple Choice

1. The key inputs to the valuation process include
   a. returns and risk.
   b. returns, timing, and risk.
   c. cash flows and discount rate.
   d. returns, discount rate, and risk.

2. The last dividend paid by Klein Company was $1.00. Klein's growth rate is expected to be a constant 5 percent forever. Klein's required rate of return on equity (k_s) is 12 percent. What is the current price of Klein's common stock?
   a. $8.75
   b. $14.29
   c. $15.00
   d. $20.00

3. You intend to purchase a 10-year, $1,000 face value bond that pays interest of $60 every 6 months. If your nominal annual required rate of return is 10 percent with semiannual compounding, how much should you be willing to pay for this bond?
   a. $826.31
   b. $1,086.15
   c. $957.50
   d. $1,124.62

4. Consider outstanding bonds with an annual 8 percent coupon. The bonds have a par value of $1,000 and a price of $865. The bonds will mature in 11 years. What is the yield to maturity of the bonds?
   a. 10.09%
   b. 11.13%
   c. 8.00%
   d. 9.89%

5. If the expected rate of return on a stock exceeds the required rate,
   a. the stock is experiencing supernormal growth.
   b. the stock should be sold.
   c. the company is probably not trying to maximize price per share.
   d. the stock is a good buy.

6. The Jones Company has decided to undertake a large project. Consequently, there is a need for additional funds. The financial manager plans to issue preferred stock with a perpetual annual dividend of $5 per share and a par value of $30. If the required return on this stock is currently 20 percent, what should be the stock's market value?
   a. $150
   b. $100
   c. $50
   d. $25

7. A share of preferred stock pays a quarterly dividend of $2.50. If the price of this preferred stock is currently $50, what is the nominal annual rate of return?
   a. 12%
   b. 18%
   c. 20%
   d. 23%

8. In the present value model, risk is generally incorporated into the
   a. cash flows.
   b. timing.
   c. discount rate.
   d. total value.

9. Thames Inc.'s most recent dividend was $2.40 per share (i.e., D_0 = $2.40). The dividend is expected to grow at a rate of 6 percent per year. The risk-free rate is 5 percent and the return on the market is 9 percent. If the company's beta is 1.3, what is the price of the stock today?
   a. $72.14
   b. $57.14
   c. $68.06
   d. $60.57

10. The process that links risk and return in order to determine the worth of an asset is termed
    a. evaluation.
    b. valuation.
    c. discounting.
    d. variable growth.

11. The less certain a cash flow, the ______ the risk, and the ______ the value of the cash flow.
    a. lower; higher
    b. lower; lower
    c. higher; lower
    d. higher; higher

12. The ______ value of a bond is also called its face value. Bonds that sell at less than face value are priced at a ______, while bonds that sell at greater than face value sell at a ______.
    a. discount; par; premium
    b. premium; discount; par
    c. par; discount; premium
    d. coupon; premium; discount

13. ______ in the beta coefficient normally causes ______ in the required return and therefore ______ in the price of the stock, all else remaining the same.
    a. An increase; an increase; an increase
    b. An increase; a decrease; an increase
    c. An increase; an increase; a decrease
    d. A decrease; a decrease; a decrease

14. The _____ is utilized to value preferred stock.
    a. constant growth model
    b. variable growth model
    c. zero-growth model
    d. Gordon model

15. A firm has an issue of preferred stock outstanding that has a stated annual dividend of $4. The required return on the preferred stock has been estimated to be 16 percent. The value of the preferred stock is _____.
    a. $64
    b. $16
    c. $25
    d. $50

16. A firm has an expected dividend next year of $1.20 per share, a zero growth rate of dividends, and a required return of 10 percent. The value of a share of the firm's common stock is ______.
    a. $120
    b. $10
    c. $12
    d. $100

17. In the Gordon model, the value of the common stock is the
    a. net value of all assets, which are liquidated for their exact, accounting value.
    b. actual amount each common stockholder would expect to receive if the firm's assets are sold, creditors and preferred stockholders are repaid, and any remaining money is divided among the common stockholders.
    c. present value of a non-growing dividend stream.
    d. present value of a constant, growing dividend stream.

18. A firm has experienced a constant annual rate of dividend growth of 9 percent on its common stock and expects the dividend per share in the coming year to be $2.70. The firm can earn 12 percent on similar risk involvements. The value of the firm's common stock is ______.
    a. $22.50/share
    b. $9/share
    c. $90/share
    d. $30/share

19. Calculate the value of a $1,000 bond that has 10 years until maturity and pays quarterly interest at an annual coupon rate of 12 percent. The required return on similar-risk bonds is 20 percent.
    a. $656.77
    b. $835.45
    c. $845.66
    d. $2,201.08

20. Calculate the value of a $1,000 bond that has 10 years until maturity with an annual coupon rate of 12 percent. The required return on similar-risk bonds is 8 percent.
    a. $1,273.55
    b. $3,735.55
    c. $1,268.40
    d. $1,000.00

Essay

1. Compute the value of a share of common stock of a company whose most recent dividend was $2.00 and is expected to grow at 3 percent per year for the next 2 years, after which the dividend growth rate will increase to 6 percent per year indefinitely. Assume 10 percent required rate of return.

2. Explain the relationship between changing interest rates and changing bond values.

Chapter 7 Answer Key

True/False

1. F
2. T
3. F
4. T
5. T
6. T
7. T
8. T
9. T
10. T
11. F
12. F
13. T
14. F
15. F

Multiple Choice

1. B
2. C
3. A
4. D
5. D
6. D
7. C
8. C
9. D
10. B
11. C
12. C
13. C
14. C
15. C
16. C
17. D
18. C
19. A
20. C

Essay

1. $D_1 = 2.00(1.03) = 2.06$ (discounted at 10% (k_s) for one year) = $1.87
   $D_2 = 2.06(1.03) = 2.12$ (discounted at 10% for two years) = $1.75

   $D_3 = 2.12(1.06) = 2.25$
   $P_2 = D_3/(k_s\text{-}g) = 2.25/(.10 - .06) = \$56.25$
   (discounted at 10% for two years) = $46.49
   Value of stock = $50.11

2. There is an inverse relationship between interest rates and bond values. Rising interest rates increase the required return for holding onto a bond. Thus, the expected cash flows from the bond are discounted at a higher rate, reducing the present value of the bond. Falling interest rates will lead to increasing bond values.

FINANCIAL STATEMENTS AND ANALYSIS

Chapter Summary

Chapter 8 reviews the contents of the stockholders' report by focusing on the four basic financial statements and discusses the use of ratios to examine the financial health of a firm. Ratios are useful for identifying the strengths and the weaknesses of a firm. On their own, ratios have little value. Their true usefulness is demonstrated when the ratios are compared over time or against ratios of similar firms. By the end of the chapter, you should have a greater familiarity and appreciation of the usefulness of financial statements and ratio analysis.

LG 1

Review the contents of the stockholders' report and the procedures for consolidating international financial statements. The annual stockholders' report, which publicly owned corporations are required to provide stockholders, documents the firm's financial activities during the past year. It includes the letter to stockholders and various subjective and factual information plus four key financial statements: the income statement, the balance sheet, the statement of retained earnings, and the statement of cash flows. Notes describing the technical aspects of the financial statements follow them. Financial statements of companies that have operations whose cash flows are denominated in one or more foreign currencies must be translated into dollars in accordance with *FASB Standard No. 52*.

LG 2

Understand who uses financial ratios, and how. Ratio analysis allows present and prospective stockholders, lenders, and the firm's management to evaluate the firm's financial performance. It can be performed on a cross-sectional or a time-series basis. Benchmarking is a popular type of cross-sectional analysis. Key cautions for applying financial ratios are: 1) Ratios with large deviations from the norm only indicate symptoms of a problem. 2) A single ratio does not generally provide sufficient information. 3) The ratios being compared should be calculated using financial statements dated at the same point in time during the year. 4) Audited financial statements should be used. 5) Data should be checked for consistency of accounting treatment. 6) Inflation and different asset ages can distort ratio comparisons.

Use popular ratios to analyze a firm's liquidity and activity. Liquidity, or the ability of the firm to pay its bills as they come due, can be measured by the current ratio and the quick (acid-test) ratio. Activity ratios measure the speed with which accounts are converted into sales or cash–inflows or outflows. The activity of inventory can be measured by its turnover, accounts receivable by the average collection period, and accounts payable by the average payment period. Total asset turnover measures the efficiency with which the firm uses its assets to generate sales.

LG 4 ***Discuss the relationship between debt and financial leverage and the ratios used to analyze a firm's debt.*** The more debt a firm uses, the greater its financial leverage, which magnifies both risk and return. Financial debt ratios measure both the degree of indebtedness and the ability to service debts. A common measure of indebtedness is the debt ratio. The ability to pay fixed charges can be measured by the times interest earned and fixed-payment coverage ratios.

LG 5 ***Use ratios to analyze a firm's profitability and its market value.*** The common-size income statement, which shows all items as a percentage of sales, can be used to determine gross profit margin, operating profit margin, and net profit margin. Other measures of profitability include earnings per share, return on total assets, and return on common equity. Market ratios include the price/earnings ratio and the market/book ratio.

LG 6 ***Use a summary of financial ratios and the DuPont system of analysis to perform a complete ratio analysis.*** A summary of all ratios–liquidity, activity, debt, profitability, and market–can be used to perform a complete ratio analysis using cross-sectional and time-series analysis approaches. The DuPont system of analysis is a diagnostic tool used to find the key areas responsible for the firm's financial performance. It allows the firm to break the return on common equity into three components: profit on sales, efficiency of asset use, and use of leverage. The DuPont system of analysis makes it possible to assess all aspects of the firm's activities in order to isolate key areas of responsibility.

Chapter Outline

The Stockholders' Report

LG 1 The annual stockholders' report, which publicly owned corporations are required to provide stockholders, documents the firm's financial activities during the past year. It includes a letter to the stockholders and various subjective and factual information plus four basic financial statements: the income statement; the balance sheet; the statement of retained earnings; and the statement of cash flows. Notes describing the technical aspects of the financial statements follow them. Financial statements of companies that have operations whose cash flows are denominated in one or more foreign currencies must be translated into dollars in accordance with *FASB Standard No. 52*.

Financial Statements

1. The income statement provides a financial summary of the firm's operating results during a specific period, usually one year. A firm's revenues minus its expenses provides the firm's net income for the period.

2. The balance sheet presents a summary statement of the firm's financial positions at a specific point in time. The balance sheet reports the firm's assets (what it owns) against its liabilities (what it owes) and the stockholder's equity (what money was provided by the owners of the firm).

3. The statement of retained earnings takes the net income for a firm and subtracts out the cash dividends paid during that period. The remaining amount is then added to the balance of retained earnings at the beginning of the period to produce a statement of retained earnings at the end of the period.

4. The statement of cash flows provides a summary of the firm's operating, investment, and financing cash flows and reconciles them with changes in its cash and marketable securities over a specific time period. The statement focuses on the sources and uses of cash for the firm.

Use of Financial Ratios

LG 2

Ratio analysis involves methods of calculating and interpreting financial ratios to analyze and monitor a firm's performance. Current and prospective shareholders use them to evaluate the firm's present and future levels of risk and returns, creditors evaluate the firm's ability to meet its financial obligations, and management evaluates the firm's overall financial situation and performance.

There are two types of ratio comparisons: cross-sectional and time-series.

1. **Cross-sectional analysis** involves the comparison of different firms' financial ratios at the same point in time.

2. **Time-series analysis** evaluates the performance of a firm over time.

Cautions about Ratio Analysis

1. Ratios with large deviations from the norm only indicate symptoms of a problem. Additional analysis is required to isolate the causes of the problem.

2. A single ratio does not generally provide sufficient information to judge the overall performance of a firm.

3. The financial ratios being compared should be calculated using statements dated at the same point in time during the year.

4. Audited financial statements should be used to ensure relevant financial information.

5. The financial data should be checked for consistency of accounting treatment.

6. Inflation and different asset ages can distort ratio comparisons, particularly for time-series analysis.

Liquidity Ratios

The liquidity of a firm is measured by its ability to satisfy its short-term obligations as they come due. The two basic measures of liquidity are the current ratio and the quick (acid-test) ratio.

The **current ratio** measures the firm's ability to meet its short-term obligations.

$$\textbf{Current Ratio} = \frac{\textbf{Current Assets}}{\textbf{Current Liabilities}}$$

The **quick (acid-test) ratio** is similar to the current ratio except that it excludes inventory, which is generally the least liquid current asset.

$$\textbf{Quick Ratio} = \frac{\textbf{Current Assets} - \textbf{Inventory}}{\textbf{Current Liabilities}}$$

Activity Ratios

The activity ratios measure the speed with which various accounts are converted into sales or cash inflows or outflows.

Inventory turnover measures the liquidity of a firm's inventory.

$$\textbf{Inventory Turnover} = \frac{\textbf{Cost of Goods Sold}}{\textbf{Inventory}}$$

The **average collection period**, or average age of accounts receivable, is useful in evaluating credit and collection policies.

$$\textbf{Average Collection Period} = \frac{\textbf{Accounts Receivable}}{\textbf{Average Sales per Day}}$$

$$= \frac{\textbf{Accounts Receivable}}{\textbf{Annual Sales} \div \textbf{360}}$$

The **average payment period**, or average age of accounts payable, is calculated in the same manner as the average collection period.

$$\textbf{Average Payment Period} = \frac{\textbf{Accounts Payable}}{\textbf{Average Purchases per Day}}$$

$$= \frac{\textbf{Accounts Payable}}{\textbf{Annual Purchases} \div \textbf{360}}$$

Total asset turnover indicates the efficiency with which the firm uses its assets to generate sales.

$$\textbf{Total asset turnover} = \frac{\textbf{Sales}}{\textbf{Total Assets}}$$

Debt Ratios

Creditors' claims must be satisfied before the earnings can be distributed to shareholders; so present and prospective shareholders pay close attention to the firm's ability to repay debts.

The more debt a firm uses, the greater its financial leverage. **Financial leverage** magnifies both the risk and return of a firm through its use of fixed-cost financing such as debt and preferred stock.

Financial debt ratios measure both the degree of indebtedness and the ability to service debts. A common measure of indebtedness is the debt ratio.

The **debt ratio** measures the proportion of total assets financed by the firm's creditors.

$$\textbf{Debt Ratio} = \frac{\textbf{Total Liabilities}}{\textbf{Total Assets}}$$

The ability to pay fixed charges can be measured by the times interest earned and fixed-payment coverage ratios.

The **times interest earned ratio** measures the firm's ability to make contractual interest payments.

$$\textbf{Times Interest Earned} = \frac{\textbf{Earnings Before Interest and Taxes}}{\textbf{Interest}}$$

The **fixed-payment coverage ratio** measures the firm's ability to meet all fixed-payment obligations, such as loan interest and principal, lease payments, and preferred stock dividends.

$$\textbf{Fixed Payment Coverage} = \frac{\textbf{Earnings Before Interest and Taxes} + \textbf{Lease Payments}}{\textbf{Interest} + \textbf{Lease Payments} + \{(\textbf{Principal Payments} + \textbf{Preferred Stock Dividends}) \times [1/(1-\textbf{T})]\}}$$

Profitability Ratios

LG 5

Measures of profitability allow the analyst to evaluate the firm's profits with respect to a given level of sales, a certain level of assets, or the owner's investment.

The common-sized income statement, which shows all items as a percentage of sales, can be used to determine gross profit margin, operating profit margin, and net profit margin.

The **gross profit margin** measures the percentage of each sales dollar remaining after the firm has paid for its goods.

$$\textbf{Gross profit margin} = \frac{\textbf{Sales} - \textbf{Cost of Goods Sold}}{\textbf{Sales}} = \frac{\textbf{Gross Profits}}{\textbf{Sales}}$$

The **operating profit margin** measures the percentage of each sales dollar remaining after all costs and expenses other than interest and taxes are deducted.

$$\textbf{Operating profit margin} = \frac{\textbf{Operating Profits}}{\textbf{Sales}}$$

The **net profit margin** measures the percentage of each sales dollar remaining after all costs and expenses, including interest, taxes, and preferred stock dividends, have been paid.

$$\textbf{Net profit margin} = \frac{\textbf{Earnings Available for Common Shareholders}}{\textbf{Sales}}$$

Other measures of profitability include earnings per share, return on total assets, and return on common equity.

The firm's **earnings per share** represents the number of dollars earned during the period on behalf of each outstanding share of stock.

$$\textbf{Earnings per share} = \frac{\textbf{Earnings Available for Common Shareholders}}{\textbf{Number of Shares of Common Stock Outstanding}}$$

The **return on total assets (ROA)**, often called the return on investment (ROI), measures the overall effectiveness of management in generating profits with its available assets.

$$\textbf{Return on total assets} = \frac{\textbf{Earnings Available for Common Shareholders}}{\textbf{Total Assets}}$$

The **return on common equity (ROE)** measures the return earned on the common stockholders' investment in the firm.

$$\textbf{Return on common equity} = \frac{\textbf{Earnings Available for Common Shareholders}}{\textbf{Common Stock Equity}}$$

Market Ratios

Market ratios relate the firm's market value, as measured by its current share price, to certain accounting values.

The **price/earnings (P/E) ratio** measures investor confidence in a firm's future performance as the amount investors are willing to pay for each dollar of a firm's current earnings.

$$\textbf{Price / earnings (P / E) ratio} = \frac{\textbf{Market Price per Share of Common Stock}}{\textbf{Earnings per Share}}$$

The **market/book (M/B) ratio** relates the market value of the firm's shares to their book (or strict accounting) value.

$$\textbf{Book value per share of common stock} = \frac{\textbf{Common Stock Equity}}{\textbf{Number of Shares Outstanding}}$$

$$\textbf{Market / Book (M / B) ratio} = \frac{\textbf{Market Price per Share of Common Stock}}{\textbf{Book Value per Share of Common Stock}}$$

A Complete Ratio Analysis

A summary of all ratios–liquidity, activity, debt, profitability, and market–can be used to perform a complete ratio analysis using cross-sectional or time-series analysis approaches.

The DuPont system of analysis is a diagnostic tool used to find the key areas responsible for the firm's financial performance. It allows the firm to break the return on common equity (ROE) into three components: net profit margin and total asset turnover, which together constitute return on total assets (ROA), plus the financial leverage multiplier, which is the ratio of total assets to total common equity.

1. The net profit margin (Net income ÷ Sales) measures the firm's profitability on sales
2. The total asset turnover (Sales ÷ Total Assets) indicates how efficiently the firm has used its assets to generate sales.
3. The financial leverage multiplier (Total Assets ÷ Total Common Equity) reflects the impact of financial leverage on the owners' return.

$$\textbf{ROA} = \frac{\textbf{Net income}}{\textbf{Total Assets}} = \frac{\textbf{Net income}}{\textbf{Sales}} \times \frac{\textbf{Sales}}{\textbf{Total Assets}}$$

$$\textbf{ROE} = \frac{\textbf{Net Income}}{\textbf{Common Equity}} = \frac{\textbf{Net income}}{\textbf{Total Assets}} \times \frac{\textbf{Total Assets}}{\textbf{Common Equity}}$$

Sample Problems and Solutions

Use the balance sheet and income statements for Badger Works, Inc. below to answer the sample problems.

Badger Works, Inc. **Income Statement** **Year Ending December 31, 2000**		
Net Sales Revenue		**$4,000,000**
Less: Cost of Goods Sold		**3,200,000**
Gross Profits		**800,000**
Less: Operating Expenses		
Selling Expenses	**$250,000**	
General and Administrative Expenses[a]	**100,000**	
Depreciation Expense	**50,000**	
Total Operating Expenses		**400,000**
Operating Profits		**$400,000**
Less: Interest Expense		**100,000**
Net Profits Before Tax		**300,000**
Less: Taxes (40%)		**120,000**
Net Profits After Tax (Net Income)		**$180,000**

[a]**Includes lease expense of $25,000**

Sample Problem 1: Ratio calculations

Calculate the ratios indicated using the financial statements provided above.

Ratio	Answer	Ratio	Answer
Current Ratio		**Times Interest Earned**	
Quick Ratio		**Fixed Payment Coverage**	
Inventory Turnover		**Gross Profit Margin**	
Avg. Collection Period		**Operating Profit Margin**	
Avg. Payment Period		**Net Profit Margin**	
Total Asset Turnover		**Earnings per share**	
Debt Ratio		**Return on Total Assets**	
		Return on Common Equity	

Solution to Sample Problem 1

Ratio	Answer	Ratio	Answer
Current Ratio	1,900,000/900,000 = 2.11	**Times Interest Earned**	400,000/100,000 = 4.00
Quick Ratio	1,900,000-1,000,000)/ 900,000 = 1.00	**Fixed Payment Coverage**	(400,000+25,000)/ (100,000+25,000+(100,000 +20,000)*(1/(1-.4))) = 1.31
Inventory Turnover	4,000,000/1,000,000 = 4.00	**Gross Profit Margin**	800,000/4,000,000 = 0.20
Avg. Collection Period	600,000/(4,000,000/ 360) = 54	**Operating Profit Margin**	400,000/4,000,000 = 0.10
Avg. Payment Period	300,000/(3,200,000/ 360) = 33.75	**Net Profit Margin**	180,000/4,000,000 = 0.045
Total Asset Turnover	4,000,000/3,000,000 = 1.33	**Earnings per share**	(180,000-20,000)/100,000 = 1.60
Debt Ratio	2,100,000/3,000,000 = 0.70	**Return on Total Assets**	(180,000-20,000)/4,000,000 = 0.04
		Return on Common Equity	(180,000-20,000)/800,000 = 0.20

Sample Problem 2: Common Size Income Statement

Prepare a common size income statement for Badger Works for the year ended 2000.

Badger Works, Inc. Income Statement Year Ending December 31, 2000		
Net Sales Revenue		
Less: Cost of Goods Sold		______
Gross Profits		______
Less: Operating Expenses		______
Selling Expenses	______	
General and Administrative Expenses	______	
Depreciation Expense	______	
Total Operating Expenses		
Operating Profits		______
Less: Interest Expense		______
Net Profits Before Tax		______
Less: Taxes (40%)		______
Net Profits After Tax (Net Income)		______
		______

Solution to Sample Problem 2

Badger Works, Inc. Income Statement Year Ending December 31, 2000		
Net Sales Revenue		**100.00%**
Less: Cost of Goods Sold		**80.00**
Gross Profits		**20.00%**
Less: Operating Expenses		
Selling Expenses	**6.25%**	
General and Administrative Expenses	**2.50**	
Depreciation Expense	**1.25**	
Total Operating Expenses		**10.00%**
Operating Profits		**10.00%**
Less: Interest Expense		**2.50**
Net Profits Before Tax		**7.50%**
Less: Taxes (40%)		**3.00**
Net Profits After Tax (Net Income)		**4.50%**

Sample Problem 3: Evaluating Ratios

Use the following ratios to evaluate the health of Banana Computers as compared against Pell Computers.

Time Series and Cross Section Ratios						
	2000		**1999**		**1998**	
Ratio	**Banana**	**Pell**	**Banana**	**Pell**	**Banana**	**Pell**
Current Ratio	2.77	1.72	2.43	1.45	1.88	1.66
Quick Ratio	2.75	1.64	2.38	1.36	1.64	1.51
Average Collection Period	40.0	41.3	57.9	43.4	52.6	41.9
Average Payment Period	65.9	61.0	58.0	61.6	43.2	61.4
Inventory Turnover	221.9	51.8	57.2	41.2	13.1	24.3
Total Asset Turnover	1.19	2.65	1.39	2.89	1.67	2.59
Debt Ratio	39.9%	66.2%	61.7%	69.7%	71.7%	73.1%
Times Interest Earned	15.4	(85.8)	6.3	(25.3)	(13.5)	(35.7)
Gross Profit Margin	27.6%	22.5%	24.9%	22.1%	19.3%	21.5%
Operating Profit Margin	11.8%	11.3%	6.6%	10.7%	-13.7%	9.2%
Net Profit Margin	9.8%	8.0%	5.2%	7.7%	-14.8%	6.7%
Return on Total Assets	11.6%	21.2%	7.2%	22.1%	-24.7%	17.3%
Return on Common Equity	19.4%	62.9%	18.8%	73.0%	-87.1%	64.3%

Solution to Sample Problem 3

There are many acceptable ways to conduct an analysis of a firm's financial ratios. One of the simplest yet most comprehensive methods is to separate the ratios into broad categories based on what they tell us. As is done in your textbook, review the liquidity ratios first, then the activity ratios, the debt ratios, and finally the profitability ratios. Assess the firm's ratios in each category, and then conclude with an overall assessment of the firm.

Liquidity: Banana's liquidity is considerably greater than Pell's and has been increasing. Given the small differences between the current and quick ratios we can also conclude that each firm holds only a very small amount of inventory. Be careful not to place too much value on the magnitude of the liquidity ratios, as there may be problems of having too much liquidity just as there are with not having enough.

Activity: With the exception of inventory turnover, Pell's activity ratios have been stable over the past three years. Banana's activity ratios, at least those dealing with current assets, have been steadily improving and are now comparable to Banana's. The inventory turnover numbers are quite high for both firms, indicating a conscious effort to minimize each firm's investment in inventories as was also seen in the liquidity ratios. The elimination of inventories is positive in that it frees up a firm's resources to make other, perhaps more profitable, investments but also increases the risk of running short of inventory. Another seemingly negative result of Banana improving its liquidity ratios is the reduction in its total asset turnover. Banana appears not to be generating enough revenues given its increased investment in current assets (other than inventory). However, as its overall financial performance has improved considerably over the past three years, this is a good example of why one should focus on more than one specific ratio (in this case total asset turnover) to make a complete assessment of a firm.

Debt: Again, Pell's debt management ratios have remained consistent over time. Given its unusual (and non meaningful negative) times interest earned numbers, we can conclude it uses very little debt financing, instead relying on current liabilities to finance its operations. Banana has steadily decreased its debt ratio, indicating an increased use of equity to fund its operations.

Profitability: Many analysts place additional emphasis on analyzing a firm's profitability ratios. Pell and Banana have both improved their profitability numbers with Banana recovering significantly from its losses in 1998. Most of the improvement in Banana's profitability seems to come from its gross profit margin numbers indicating an ability to sell its products at a considerable margin over the cost of the components. Pell's profit numbers, particularly its ROA and ROE, appear to be quite high, and rising.

Overall: Pell appears to have been a steady, and profitable, firm over the past three years. Investors have probably been very happy with its performance. During this same period, Banana has improved its financial numbers tremendously, although not to Pell's levels.

An investor or a potential creditor would need to analyze the firm more closely to better comprehend what it has done to improve its performance in the past and be cautious in assuming such improvements can continue. In a worst-case scenario these improvement could only be temporary, or purely illusionary, due to the use of different accounting methods or other window-dressing techniques.

Sample Problem 4: DuPont Analysis

Use the ratios given for Banana Computers and Pell Computers to perform a modified DuPont Analysis for the most recent year.

Solution to Sample Problem 4

	ROA = Net Profit Margin x Total Asset Turnover
For Banana in 2000:	ROA = 9.8% x 1.19 = 11.6%
For Pell in 2000:	ROA = 8.0% x 2.65 = 21.2%

	ROE = ROA x Financial Leverage Multiplier
For Banana in 2000:	ROE = 11.6% x 1.66 = 19.4%
For Pell in 2000:	ROE = 21.2% x 2.96 = 62.9%

The ROA and ROE for Banana are both less than for Pell. The DuPont analysis shows that although Banana had a higher profit margin on sales than Pell, Pell was much more efficient in the use of its asset investment and used its higher level of leverage to magnify the returns enjoyed by its shareholders.

Study Tips

1. If it has been a while since you studied accounting, this is a good time to review the basic financial statements you learned there. An assumption made throughout the book is that you are familiar with basic accounting methods.

2. Ratio analysis typically does not answer any questions; it only raises them. A firm's financial statements report the results of management and operating decisions made in the past so the ratios derived from such accounting data generally only report the *effects* of these decisions. Reviewing the ratios helps one focus analysis on better understanding the underlying *causes* for the figures to be what they are, why they may have changed, and why they may be different from other firms.

3. Do not put too much emphasis in cases where a firm's ratios deviate slightly over time or when they are compared with other firms. Look for longer-term trends that could indicate potential problems (or progress) rather than normal business cycle variations.

4. Do not focus on a single ratio (or set of ratios) in isolation. To get a clear view of a firm's financial situation, you must examine a wide variety of ratios.

Sample Exam

True/False

T F 1. Ratio analysis involves a comparison of the relationships between financial statement accounts so as to analyze the financial position and strength of a firm.

T F 2. The annual report contains four basic financial statements: the income statement; balance sheet; statement of cash flows; and statement of retained earnings.

T F 3. If a firm has high current and quick ratios, this is always a good indication that a firm is managing its liquidity position well.

T F 4. The inventory turnover ratio and average collection period are two ratios that can be used to assess how effectively the firm is managing its assets in consideration of current and projected operating levels.

T F 5. The degree to which the managers of a firm attempt to magnify the returns to owners' capital through the use of financial leverage is captured in debt management ratios.

T F 6. Price/earning and market/book ratios can provide management with a current assessment of how investors in the market view the firm's past performance and future prospects.

T F 7. Determining whether a firm's financial position is improving or deteriorating requires analysis of more than one set of financial statements. Trend analysis is one method of measuring a firm's performance over time.

T F 8. Retained earnings represents the cumulative total of all earnings retained and reinvested in the firm since its inception.

T F 9. The Financial Accounting Standards Board (FASB) Standard No. 52 mandates that U.S.-based companies translate their foreign-currency-denominated assets and liabilities into dollars using the current rate (translation) method.

T F 10. Ratio analysis merely directs the analyst to potential areas of concern; it does not provide conclusive evidence as to the existence of a problem.

T F 11. Both present and prospective shareholders are interested in the firm's current and future level of risk and return. These two dimensions directly affect share price.

T F 12. The use of differing accounting treatments–especially relative to inventory and depreciation–can distort the results of ratio analysis, regardless of whether cross-sectional or time-series analysis is used.

T F 13. Earnings per share represents the dollar amount earned and distributed to shareholders.

T F 14. The gross profit margin measures the percentage of each sales dollar left after the firm has paid for its goods and operating expenses.

T F 15. The financial leverage multiplier is the ratio of the firm's total assets to stockholders' equity.

Multiple Choice

1. Johnson Corporation has 100,000 shares of common stock outstanding. The firm's net income is $750,000 and its Price/Earning ratio is 8.0. What is the firm's stock price?
   a. $20.00
   b. $30.00
   c. $40.00
   d. $60.00

2. Operating profits are defined as
   a. earnings before depreciation and taxes.
   b. sales revenue minus depreciation expense.
   c. gross profits minus operating expenses.
   d. sales revenue minus cost of goods sold.

3. Retained earnings on the balance sheet represents
   a. net profits after taxes minus preferred dividends.
   b. the cumulative total of earnings reinvested in the firm.
   c. net profits after taxes.
   d. cash.

4. The statement of cash flows includes all of the following categories *except*
   a. financing flows.
   b. equity flows.
   c. operating flows.
   d. investment flows.

5. Cash flows directly related to production and sale of the firm's products and services are called
   a. financing flows.
   b. equity flows.
   c. operating flows.
   d. investment flows.

6. Present and prospective shareholders are mainly concerned with a firm's
   a. leverage.
   b. liquidity.
   c. risk and return.
   d. profitability.

7. In ratio analysis, a comparison to a standard industry ratio is made to isolate ________ deviations from the norm.
   a. any
   b. standard
   c. positive
   d. negative

8. The ________ of a business firm is measured by its ability to satisfy its short-term obligations as they come due.
   a. debt
   b. profitability
   c. activity
   d. liquidity

9. ________ ratios are a measure of the speed with which various accounts are converted into sales or cash.
   a. Debt
   b. Profitability
   c. Activity
   d. Liquidity

10. The three summary ratios basic to the DuPont system of analysis are
    a. net profit margin, total asset turnover, and financial leverage multiplier.
    b. net profit margin, financial leverage multiplier, and return on equity.
    c. net profit margin, total asset turnover, and return on investment.
    d. net profit margin, total asset turnover, and return on equity.

11. The ________ is a measure of liquidity that excludes ________, generally the least liquid asset.
    a. current ratio; inventory
    b. quick ratio; inventory
    c. current ratio; accounts receivable
    d. quick ratio; accounts receivable

12. The ________ is a popular approach for evaluating profitability in relation to sales by expressing each item on the income statement as a percent of sales.
    a. common-size income statement
    b. profit and loss statement
    c. retained earnings statement
    d. source and use statement

13. The ________ measures the overall effectiveness of management in generating profits with its available assets.
    a. return on equity
    b. return on total assets
    c. net profit margin
    d. price/earnings ratio

14. Examining the ratios of a particular firm against the same measures for a group of firms from the same industry, at a point in time, is an example of
    a. trend analysis.
    b. cross-sectional analysis.
    c. DuPont analysis.
    d. industry analysis.

The following financial statements apply to the next six sample exam questions.

March Madness Industries Balance Sheet
December 31, 2000
(Dollars in Thousands)

Cash	$400	Accounts payable	$410
Receivables	490	Notes payable	850
Inventory	1,250	Other current liabilities	230
Total current assets	$2,140	Total current liabilities	$1,490
Net fixed assets	2,400	Long-Term debt	840
		Common equity	2,210
Total assets	$4,540	Total liabilities and equity	$4,540

March Madness Industries Income Statement
Year Ended December 31, 20007
(Dollars in Thousands)

Sales	$4,800
Cost of goods sold	3,518
Gross profit	$1,282
Selling expenses	350
General and administrative expenses	432
Depreciation	150
Operating profit	$350
Less interest expense	70
Net profit before taxes	$280
Less taxes (40%)	112
Net income (Net profits after taxes)	$168

15. Calculate the liquidity ratios (i.e., the current ratio and the quick ratio).
    a. 1.20; 0.60
    b. 1.20; 0.80
    c. 1.44; 0.60
    d. 1.44; 0.80

16. Calculate the activity ratios (i.e., the inventory turnover ratio, total assets turnover, and average collection period).
    a. 2.81; 1.06; 35.25 days
    b. 2.81; 1.06; 34.10 days
    c. 2.81; 1.06; 36.75 days
    d. 2.81; 1.24; 34.10 days

17. Calculate the debt management ratios (i.e., the debt and times interest earned ratios).
    a. 0.51; 3.16
    b. 0.51; 5.00
    c. 0.39; 3.16
    d. 0.39; 5.00

18. Calculate the profitability ratios (i.e., the profit margin on sales, return on total assets, and return on common equity).
    a. 3.70%; 3.50%; 7.60%
    b. 3.50%; 4.25%; 7.60%
    c. 3.70%; 3.50%; 8.00%
    d. 3.50%; 3.70%; 7.60%

19. Calculate the market ratios (i.e., the price/earnings ratio and the market/book value ratios). March Madness had an average of 20,000 shares outstanding during 2000, and the stock price on December 31, 2000, was $80.00.
    a. 4.21; 0.72
    b. 4.76; 0.72
    c. 9.52; 1.38
    d. 9.52; 0.72

20. Use the extended DuPont equation to determine March Madness' return on equity.
    a. 6.90%
    b. 7.47%
    c. 7.60%
    d. 8.41%

Essay

1. What cautions must you exercise when you conduct ratio analysis?

2. What is the relationship between a firm's financial leverage and risk?

Chapter 8 Answer Key

True/False

1. T
2. T
3. F
4. T
5. T
6. T
7. T
8. T
9. T
10. T
11. T
12. T
13. F
14. F
15. T

Multiple Choice

1. D
2. C
3. B
4. B
5. C
6. C
7. A
8. D
9. C
10. A
11. B
12. A
13. B
14. B
15. C
16. C
17. B
18. D
19. D
20. C

Essay

1. a. Ratios with large deviations from the norm only indicate symptoms of a problem; additional analysis is required to isolate the causes.

   b. A single ratio does not generally provide sufficient information to judge the overall performance of a firm.

   c. The financial ratios being compared should be calculated using statements dated at the same point in time during the year

   d. Audited financial statements should be used, to ensure relevant financial information.

   e. The financial data should be checked for consistency of accounting treatment.

   f. Inflation and different asset ages can distort ratio comparisons, particularly for time-series analysis.

2. The more debt a firm uses, the greater its financial leverage and its perceived riskiness. The creditors of the firm must be satisfied before any earnings can be distributed to the shareholders so an increased use of debt reduces the chances that the shareholders will receive any of the firm's earnings. This increases the riskiness of their expected cash flows and the riskiness of their investment.

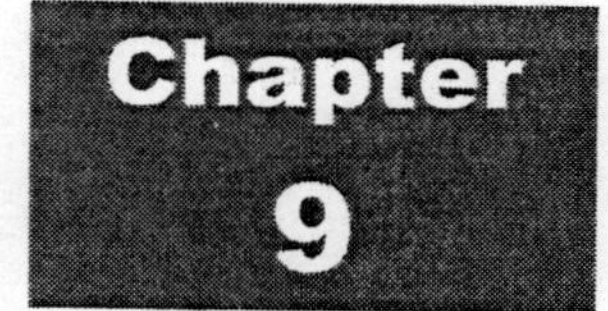

THE FIRM AND ITS ENVIRONMENT

Chapter Summary

Chapter 9 describes some of the key financial aspects of business firms and the environment in which they operate. Specific attention is given to the common forms of business organization, the financial management function, the goal of the firm, the agency issue, business taxation, depreciation, and cash flow.

LG 1 ***Review the common forms of business organization.*** The common forms of business organization are the sole proprietorship, the partnership, and the corporation. The corporation is dominant in terms of business receipts and net profits. The owners of a corporation are its stockholders, those who hold either common stock or preferred stock. Stockholders expect to earn a return by receiving dividends or by realizing gains through increases in share price.

LG 2 ***Describe the financial management function, its relationship to economics and accounting, and the financial manager's primary activities.*** All areas of responsibility within a firm interact with financial personnel and processes. In large firms, the financial management function may be handled by a separate department headed by the vice president of finance (CFO), to whom the treasurer and controller report; in small firms, the finance function is generally performed by the accounting department. The financial manager must understand the economic environment and relies heavily on the economic principle of marginal analysis when making decisions. Financial managers use accounting data but concentrate on cash flows and decision making. In addition to her or his ongoing involvement in financial analysis and planning, the primary activities of the financial manager are making investment decisions and making financing decisions.

LG 3 ***Explain the wealth maximization goal of the firm and the role of ethics in the firm.*** The goal of the financial manager is to maximize the owner's wealth, as evidenced by stock price, rather than profits. Profit maximization ignores the timing of returns, does not directly consider cash flows, and ignores risk, so it is an inappropriate goal. Both return and risk must be assessed by the financial manager when evaluating decision alternatives. The wealth-maximizing actions of financial managers should also consider the interests of stakeholders, groups who have a direct economic link to the firm. Positive ethical practices by the firm and its managers are believed to be necessary for achieving the firm's goal of maximizing owner wealth.

LG 4 ***Discuss the agency issue.*** An agency problem results when managers, as agents for owners, place personal goals ahead of corporate goals. Market forces, in the form of shareholder activism and the threat of takeover, tend to prevent or minimize agency problems. In addition, firms incur agency costs to monitor management behavior and provide incentives to management to act in the best interest of owners. Stock options and performance plans are examples of such agency costs.

LG 5 ***Review the fundamentals of business taxation of ordinary income and capital gains.*** Corporate income is subject to corporate taxes. Corporate tax rates are applicable to both ordinary income (after deduction of allowable expenses) and capital gains. The average tax rate paid by a corporation ranges from 15 to 35 percent. (For convenience, a 40 percent marginal tax rate is assumed in the textbook and this study guide.) Certain provisions in the tax code, such as intercorporate dividend exclusions and tax-deductible expenses, provide corporate taxpayers with opportunities to reduce their taxes.

LG 6 ***Understand the effect of depreciation on the firm's cash flows, the depreciable value of an asset, its depreciable life, and tax depreciation methods.*** Depreciation, the allocation of historical cost, is the most common type of noncash expenditure. To estimate cash flow from operations, depreciation and any other noncash charges are added back to net profits after taxes. Because they lower taxable income without an actual outflow of cash, noncash charges act as a source of funds to the firm. The depreciable value of an asset and its depreciable life are determined by using the modified accelerated cost recovery system (MACRS) standards of the federal tax code. MACRS groups assets into six property classes based on length of recovery period and can be applied using a schedule of yearly depreciation percentages for each period.

LG 7 ***Discuss the firm's cash flows, particularly the statement of cash flows.*** The statement of cash flows is divided into operating, investment, and financing flows. It can be developed using the income statement for the period, along with beginning- and end-of-period balance sheets. The statement reconciles changes in the firm's cash flows with changes in cash and marketable securities for the period. Interpreting the statement of cash flows requires an understanding of basic financial principles and involves both the major categories of cash flow and the individual items of cash inflow and outflow.

Chapter Outline

Three Basic Forms of Business

LG 1

The three basic forms of business organization are the sole proprietorship, the partnership, and the corporation.

A sole proprietorship is owned and operated by one individual. The profits from the sole proprietorship are taxed as the owner's personal income and the sole proprietor has unlimited liability to the creditors of the business.

A partnership consists of two or more owners doing business together for profit. Like the sole proprietorship, partnerships are taxed as the individual's personal income according to the percentage of ownership and the partners similarly face unlimited liability.

A corporation, the dominant form of business organization in terms of business receipts and net profits, is treated as a separate legal entity from the owners of the business. A corporation can sue and be sued, make and be party to contracts, and acquire property in its own name.

The owners of a corporation are its stockholders, those who hold either common stock or preferred stock. They have limited liability, meaning they cannot lose more than the amount they invest. Stockholders expect to earn a return by receiving dividends or by realizing gains through increases in the firm's share price. They elect a board of directors that has the ultimate authority to guide corporate affairs and make general policy. The board of directors, in turn, hire the president, or chief executive officer (CEO), to manage the firm's day-to-day operations and carry out the policies established by the board.

Relationships in Managerial Finance

All areas of responsibility within a firm interact with financial personnel and processes. In large firms, the financial management function may be handled by a separate department headed by the vice president of finance or chief financial officer (CFO), to whom the treasurer and controller report; in small firms the finance function is generally performed by the accounting department.

Finance is closely related to the field of economics in that financial managers must understand economic theory and the economic environment. Financial decision making relies heavily on the economic principle of marginal analysis, the principle that financial decisions should be made and actions taken when the added benefits exceed the added costs.

Finance is also closely related to the field of accounting in that financial managers make significant use of accounting data. The primary differences are that finance 1) concentrates more on cash flow analysis and 2) focuses on decision making based upon assessments of the accounting data.

Roles of the Financial Manager

The role of the financial manager can be broken down into three primary activities.

1. Conducting financial analysis and planning
2. Making investment decisions
3. Making financing decisions.

Goals of the Firm

The goal of the financial manager is not necessarily to maximize the profits of the firm, but to maximize the owner's wealth. The differences between the two goals include that fact that profit maximization:

1. Ignores the timing of returns. Dollars received sooner should be valued more than those received later.

2. Does not directly consider cash flows available to the shareholder either in the form of dividends or from potential gains to be realized from higher stock prices.

3. Disregards risk. The tradeoffs between return and risk must be assessed by the financial manager when evaluating decision alternatives.

One popular measure used by firms to determine whether an investment is contributing positively to the owner's wealth is economic value added. EVA is calculated by subtracting the cost of funds used to finance an investment from its after-tax operating profits. If positive, the investment is increasing owner wealth.

Employees, customers, suppliers, and creditors also have direct economic links to the firm. The interests of these stakeholders should also considered when making wealth-maximization decisions

Positive ethical practices by the firm and its managers are also believed to be necessary for achieving the firm's goal of maximizing owner wealth.

The Agency Problem

An agency problem results when managers, as agents for owners, place personal goals ahead of corporate goals. Two factors work to contain the agency problem.

1. By monitoring the activities of the managers, market forces, in the form of shareholder activism and the threat of takeover, tend to prevent or minimize agency problems.

2. In addition, firms incur agency costs to monitor management behavior and provide incentives to management to act in the best interest of owners. Stock options and performance plans are examples of such agency costs.

Business Taxation

LG 5

The ordinary income and capital gains of corporations are subject to corporate taxes at tax rates different from those for individuals.

Ordinary income is the income earned through the sales of goods or services. Any interest received by the corporation is also included in ordinary income. Dividends received on common or preferred stock of another corporation in which the firm has less than 20% ownership are subject to a 70% exclusion. In other words, only 30% of these dividends received are included in ordinary income.

A capital gain occurs when the selling price of an asset is greater than its initial price. Currently there is no difference in the corporate tax rates for ordinary income and capital gains.

It is important to distinguish between the average tax rate paid by a firm and its marginal tax rate. The average tax rate is calculated by dividing the amount of taxes by the firm's taxable income. The marginal tax rate is the rate at which any additional income is taxed. For convenience, a 40 percent marginal tax rate is assumed in the textbook and this study guide.

Depreciation

Depreciation is the allocation of historical cost of an asset over time. It is the most common type of noncash expenditure. Noncash expenses are deductible from income but do not involve an actual outlay of cash during the period. Because of this, when estimating a firm's cash flow from operations, depreciation and any other noncash charges are added back to net profits after taxes. Since depreciation lowers taxable income without an actual outflow of cash, noncash charges act as a source of funds to the firm.
The depreciable value of an asset and its depreciable life are determined by using the modified accelerated cost recovery system (MACRS) standards of the federal tax code.

1. The depreciable value is the full cost of the asset, including outlays for installation.

2. The depreciable life is determined by which one of six MACRS property classes (3, 5, 7, 10, 15, or 20 years) the asset falls into.

The amount of depreciation charged each year is determined by multiplying the yearly depreciation percentages taken from the MACRS schedule times the asset's depreciable value.

Cash Flow

A firm's cash flows can be divided into operating, investment, and financing flows.

1. Operating flows are cash flows directly related to the production and sale of the firm's products and services.

2. Investment flows are cash flows associated with the purchase and sale of both fixed assets and business interests.

3. Financing flows result from debt and equity financing transactions.

The statement of cash flows summarizes the sources and uses of cash for the firm. It can be developed using the income statement for the period, along with beginning- and end-of-period balance sheets.

The statement reconciles changes in the firm's cash flows with changes in cash and marketable securities for the period. Besides the cash flows generated by the net income and depreciation charges for the firm,

1. the decrease in any asset account represents a source of cash and the increase represents a use of cash; and

2. the increase in any liability represents a source of cash and the decrease represents a use of cash.

Interpreting the statement of cash flows requires an understanding of basic financial principles. This involves analyzing the major categories of cash flow as well as the individual items of cash inflow and outflow.

Sample Problem Solutions

Sample Problem 1: Average and Marginal Tax Rates

Murray Industries earned $225,000 in 1999. What are the taxes due on this amount? What are the average tax rate and the marginal tax rate?

Solution to Sample Problem 1

Based upon the current tax schedule, the total taxes payable would be:

15% x $50,000	=	$7,500
25% x $25,000 ($75,000 – $50,000)	=	6,250
34% x $25,000 ($100,000 – $75,000)	=	8,500
39% x $125,000 ($225,000 – $100,000)	=	48,750
		$71,000

The average tax rate is equal to $71,000 ÷ $225,000 = 31.6%.
The marginal tax rate is the tax rate paid on the last dollar of income. In this example, the rate applied to the last $125,000 is 39%.

Sample Problem 2: MACRS Depreciation

A new milling machine costs $80,000 plus an additional $6,000 to place it into service. The machine is expected to have a life of five years. Compute the MACRS annual depreciation.

Solution to Sample Problem 2

Depreciable cost: $80,000 + $6,000 = $86,000

Year	Percentage	Depreciation
1	20%	$17,200
2	32%	27,520
3	19%	16,340
4	12%	10,320
5	12%	10,320
6	5%	4,300

Annual depreciation amount: MACRS percentage x $86,000

Sample Problem 3: Sources and Uses of Cash

Classify each of the following as a source (S) or use (U) of cash. Designate the cash flow as (N) if it is neither a source nor use of cash.

Item	Change ($)	Type	Item	Change ($)	Type
Cash	+200		Accounts receivable	+300	
Inventory	-500		Fixed assets	+500	
Accounts payable	-600		Notes payable	+200	
Long-term debt	-800		Common stock	+100	
Net income	+200		Cash dividends	+100	

Solution to Sample Problem 3

Item	Change ($)	Type	Item	Change ($)	Type
Cash	+200	S	Accounts receivable	+300	U
Inventory	-500	S	Fixed assets	+500	U
Accounts payable	-600	U	Notes payable	-200	U
Long-term debt	+800	S	Common stock	+100	S
Net income	+200	S	Cash dividends	+100	U

1. Increases in assets (Cash, Accounts Receivable, Fixed Assets) are uses of cash.
2. Decreases in assets (Inventory) are sources of cash.
3. Increases in liabilities and common equity (Long-term debt, Common Stock, Net Income*) are sources of cash.
4. Decreases in liabilities and common equity (Accounts payable, Notes payable, Cash Dividends*) are uses of cash.

*Net income is a source of cash because it increases a firm's retained earnings. The payment of cash dividends is a use of cash because it decreases retained earnings.

Study Tips

1. Realize that the main differences between accounting and finance are two-fold.

   a. Accountants use the accrual approach to determine income, while financial managers focus on cash flows.

   b. Accountants deal with collecting and reporting data, while financial managers use the data to help them make decisions.

2. Remember the goal of financial managers is to maximize shareholder wealth as measured by the firm's stock price. To do this well, financial managers must pay attention to the timing, the risk, and the size of the firm's cash flows.

3. Understand the costs of the actions firms take (agency costs) to reduce the likelihood that managers will maximize their wealth rather than the shareholders.

4. Be careful to avoid two common errors in computing depreciation using the MACRS method.

   a. While expected salvage value is used in calculating straight-line depreciation, it is not considered with MACRS.

   b. Because only half of a year's depreciation is allowed in the first year, the other half occurs in the year after the of the asset's depreciable life. That is, a three-year asset is depreciated for four years, a five-year asset is depreciated over six years, etc.

5. Remember that financial managers focus on cash flows, so it is important to understand how a firm measures its cash inflows and cash outflows.

Sample Exam

True/False

T F 1. The major advantage of a regular partnership or a corporation as a form of business is the fact that both offer their owners limited liability, whereas proprietorships do not.

T F 2. If a firm's stock price falls during the year, this indicates that the firm's managers are not acting in the shareholders' best interest.

T F 3. An agency relationship exists when one or more persons hire another person to perform some service but withhold decision making authority from that person.

T F 4. Studies show, and most executives agree, that unfortunately, there is a negative correlation between being ethical and long-run corporate profitability.

T F 5. In a partnership, owners have unlimited liability and may have to cover debts of other less financially sound partners.

T F 6. The board of directors is responsible for managing day-to-day operations and carrying out the policies established by the chief executive officer.

T F 7. High cash flow is generally associated with a higher share price whereas higher risk tends to result in a lower share price.

T F 8. The wealth of corporate owners is measured by the share price of the stock.

T F 9. Economic value added (EVA) is calculated by subtracting the cost of funds used to finance an investment from its after-tax operating profits.

T F 10. The profit-maximization goal ignores the timing of returns, does not directly consider cash flows, and ignores risk.

T F 11. When considering each financial decision alternative or possible action in terms of its impact on the share price of the firm's stock, financial managers should accept only those actions that are expected to increase share price.

T F 12. The likelihood that managers may place personal goals ahead of corporate goals is called the agency problem.

T F 13. The marginal tax rate represents the rate at which additional income is taxed.

T F 14. Noncash charges are expenses that involve an actual outlay of cash during the period but are not deducted on the income statement.

T F 15. Given the financial manager's preference for faster receipt of cash flows, a longer depreciable life is preferred to a shorter one.

Multiple Choice

1. Which of the following actions are likely to reduce agency conflicts between stockholders and managers?
   a. Paying managers a large fixed salary.
   b. Increasing the threat of corporate takeover.
   c. Placing restrictive covenants in debt agreements.
   d. All of the above.

2. Which of the following statements is most correct?
   a. Bond covenants are a good way to resolve agency conflicts between stockholders and managers.
   b. Hostile takeovers tend to reduce the value of a company's stock.
   c. Corporations have limited liability.
   d. All of the above.

3. The depreciable value of an asset, under MACRS, is
   a. the original cost (purchase price) only.
   b. the original cost minus salvage value.
   c. the original cost plus installation costs.
   d. the original cost plus installation costs, minus salvage value.

4. Which of the following is not a source of cash?
   a. A decrease in accounts receivable
   b. Net profits after taxes
   c. The payment of dividends
   d. An increase in accruals

5. Which of the following is not a use of cash?
   a. An increase in inventory
   b. A decrease in cash
   c. The payment of dividends
   d. A decrease in notes payable

6. Which of the following is not a financing cash flow?
   a. The issuance of stock
   b. The payment of stock dividends
   c. Increasing debt
   d. Repurchasing stock

7. Which of the following is not an operating cash flow?
   a. Net profit after taxes
   b. Increases or decreases in current liabilities
   c. Increases or decreases in fixed assets
   d. Depreciation expense

8. Which of the following legal forms of organization's income is not taxed under individual income tax rate?
   a. Sole proprietorships
   b. Partnerships
   c. Limited partnership
   d. Corporation

9. The responsibility for managing day-to-day operations and carrying out corporate policies belongs to the
   a. board of directors.
   b. chief executive officer.
   c. stockholders.
   d. creditors.

10. Which of the following legal forms of organization is characterized by limited liability?
    a. Sole proprietorship
    b. Partnership
    c. Corporation
    d. Professional partnership

11. A "legal entity" which can sue and be sued, make and be party to contracts, and acquire property in its own name is
    a. a sole proprietorship.
    b. a partnership.
    c. a corporation.
    d. a professional partnership.

12. The primary emphasis of the financial manager is the use of
    a. accrued earnings.
    b. cash flow.
    c. organization charts.
    d. profit incentives.

13. The primary goal of the financial manager is
    a. minimizing risk.
    b. maximizing profit.
    c. maximizing wealth.
    d. minimizing return.

14. Marginal analysis states that financial decisions should be made and actions taken only when
    a. demand equals supply.
    b. benefits equal costs.
    c. added benefits exceed added costs.
    d. added benefits are greater than zero.

15. Corporate owner's receive realizable return through
    a. earnings per share and cash dividends.
    b. increase in share price and cash dividends.
    c. increase in share price and earnings per share.
    d. profit and earnings per share.

16. Wealth maximization as the goal of the firm implies enhancing the wealth of
    a. the board of directors.
    b. the firm's employees.
    c. the federal government.
    d. the firm's stockholders.

17. The goal of profit maximization would result in priority for
    a. cash flows available to stockholders.
    b. risk of the investment.
    c. earnings per share.
    d. timing of the returns.

18. The key variables in the owner wealth maximization process are
    a. earnings per share and risk.
    b. cash flows and risk.
    c. earnings per share and share price.
    d. profits and risk.

19. Financial managers evaluating decision alternatives or potential actions must consider
    a. only risk.
    b. only return.
    c. both risk and return.
    d. risk, return, and the impact on share price.

20. The difference between the cost of funds used to finance an investment and its after-tax operating profits is called
    a. earnings per share.
    b. dividend.
    c. economic value added.
    d. retained earnings.

Essay

1. Why is a shorter depreciable life on an asset beneficial to a corporation?

2. Why is the statement of cash flows important to the financial manager?

Chapter 9 Answer Key

True/False

1. F
2. F
3. F
4. F
5. T
6. F
7. T
8. T
9. T
10. T
11. T
12. T
13. T
14. F
15. F

Multiple Choice

1. B
2. C
3. C
4. C
5. B
6. B
7. C
8. D
9. B
10. C
11. C
12. B
13. C
14. C
15. B
16. D
17. C
18. B
19. D
20. C

Essay

1. A shorter depreciable life means that a larger portion of the depreciation is charged in earlier years. This reduces income taxes paid and increases cash inflows.

2. Financial managers are concerned with the amount of cash available to the firm. The statement of cash flows allows financial managers to analyze past and future cash flows available to the firm. Using this information, financial managers can make better decisions concerning the future financial projects and the financial policies of the firm.

CAPITAL BUDGETING: CASH FLOW PRINCIPLES

Chapter Summary

Chapter 10 describes the capital budgeting decision process and the procedures used to estimate the relevant cash flows associated with a proposed capital expenditure. Specific attention is given to the three components of a proposed project's cash flows–the initial investment, the operating cash flows, and the terminal cash flow.

LG 1 ***Understand the key capital expenditure motives and the steps in the capital budgeting process.*** Capital budgeting is the process used to evaluate and select capital expenditures consistent with the firm's goal of maximizing owner wealth. Capital expenditures are long-term investments made to expand, replace, or renew fixed assets or to obtain some other less tangible benefit. The capital budgeting process includes five distinct but interrelated steps: proposal generation, review and analysis, decision making, implementation, and follow-up.

LG 2 ***Define the basic capital budgeting terminology.*** Capital expenditure proposals may be independent or mutually exclusive. Typically, firms have only limited funds for capital investments and must ration them among carefully selected projects. The two basic approaches to capital budgeting decisions are the accept-reject approach and the ranking approach. Conventional cash flow patterns consist of an initial outflow followed by a series of inflows; any other pattern is nonconventional.

LG 3 ***Discuss the major components of relevant cash flows, expansion versus replacement cash flows, and international capital budgeting and long-term investments.*** The relevant cash flows for capital budgeting decisions are the initial investment, the operating cash flows, and the terminal cash flow. For replacement decisions, these flows are found by determining the difference between the cash flows of the new asset and the old asset. In international capital budgeting, currency risks and political risks can be minimized through careful planning.

Calculate the initial investment associated with a proposed capital expenditure. The initial investment is the initial outflow required, taking into account the installed cost of the new asset, the after-tax proceeds from the sale of the old asset, and any change in net working capital. Finding the after-tax proceeds from the sale of the old asset, which reduces the initial investment, involves cost, depreciation, and tax data. The book value of an asset is its accounting value, which is used to determine what taxes are owed as a result of its sale. Any of three forms of taxable income–capital gain, recaptured depreciation, or a loss–can result from the sale of an asset. The form of taxable income that applies depends on whether the asset is sold for 1) more than its initial purchase price, 2) more than book value but less than what was initially paid, 3) book value, or 4) less than book value. The change in net working capital is the difference between the change in current assets and the change in current liabilities expected to accompany a given capital expenditure.

LG 5 ***Determine relevant operating cash inflows using the income statement format.*** The operating cash inflows are the incremental after-tax cash inflows expected to result from a project. The income statement format involves adding depreciation back to net profits after taxes, and gives the operating cash flows associated with the proposed and present projects. The relevant (incremental) cash inflows are the difference between the operating cash inflows of the proposed project and those of the present project.

LG 6 ***Find the terminal cash flow.*** The terminal cash flow represents the after-tax cash flow, exclusive of operating cash inflows, that is expected from liquidation of a project. It is calculated by finding the difference between the after-tax proceeds from sale of the new and the old asset at project termination and then adjusting this difference for any change in net working capital. Sale price and depreciation data are used to find the taxes and the after-tax sale proceeds on the new and old assets. The change in net working capital typically represents the reversion of any initial investment in net working capital.

Chapter Outline

The Capital Budgeting Decision Process

LG 1 Capital budgeting is the process used to evaluate and select capital expenditures consistent with the firm's goal of maximizing owner wealth. Capital expenditures are long-term investments typically made to expand, replace, or renew fixed assets. These assets are often referred to as earning assets since they provide the basis for the firm's earning power and value.

The capital budgeting process includes five distinct but interrelated steps that are summarized below.

Step	Description
Proposal Generation	Proposals are made at all levels within a business organization and are reviewed at a high level. Proposals that require large outlays are more carefully scrutinized than less costly ones.
Review and Analysis	Formal review and analysis assess the appropriateness of proposals and evaluate their economic viability. Once the analysis is complete, a summary report is submitted to decision makers.
Decision Making	Firms typically delegate capital expenditure decision making on the basis of dollar limits. Generally, the board of directors must authorized expenditures beyond a certain amount. Often plant managers are given authority to make decisions necessary to keep the production line moving.
Implementation	Following approval, expenditures are made and projects implemented. Often expenditures for a large project occur in phases.
Follow-up	Results are monitored, and actual costs and benefits are compared with those that were expected. Action may be required if actual outcomes differ from projected ones.

Basic Terminology

LG 2

Independent projects are projects where cash flows are unrelated or independent of one another; the acceptance of one does not eliminate the others from further consideration.

Mutually exclusive projects are projects that compete with one another, so that the acceptance of one eliminates the others from further consideration.

If a firm has unlimited funds for investment, all independent projects providing an acceptable return will be accepted. Most firms do not have unlimited funds so instead operate under capital rationing. Under capital rationing, the various project proposals must compete for the fixed number of dollars available.

There are the two basic approaches to making capital budgeting decisions. The accept-reject approach evaluates proposals to determine whether they meet the firm's minimum acceptance criterion. Under the ranking approach, all acceptable projects are ranked based on some predetermined measure, such as rate of return.

Conventional cash flow patterns consist of an initial outflow followed by a series of inflows; any other pattern is nonconventional and can cause difficulties in evaluating the projects.

Relevant Cash Flows

The relevant cash flows are the incremental cash outflow (investment) and resulting subsequent inflows associated with a proposed capital expenditure. Incremental cash flows are the additional cash flows (outflows and inflows) expected to result from the proposed capital expenditure.

The major cash flow components for a project are:

1. The initial investment, or the cash outflow for a proposed project at time zero.

2. The operating cash flows, or the incremental after-tax cash inflows from implementation of a project during its life.

3. The terminal cash flow, or the after-tax nonoperating cash flow (if any) occurring in the final year of a project that is usually attributed to liquidation of the project.

Expansion versus replacement cash flows

For expansion decisions, the relevant cash flows are merely those associated with the proposed project. Replacement decisions are more complex, since the relevant flows must be found by determining the difference between the cash flows of the new asset and the old asset.

International capital budgeting

The assessment of international projects is more complicated because their cash inflows and outflows typically occur in a foreign currency and the investment entails potentially significant political risks. Through careful planning, these currency risks and political risks can be minimized.

Finding the Initial Investment

The initial investment for a proposed project is the initial outflow required. This takes into account 1) the installed cost of the new asset, 2) the after-tax proceeds from the sale of the old asset, and 3) any change in net working capital.

The installed cost, also its depreciable value, is the cost of the new asset plus its installation costs.

The after-tax proceeds from the sale of the old asset reduces the initial investment. The proceeds equal the difference between the old asset's sale price and any applicable taxes or tax refunds related to its sale, net of any removal or cleaning costs. The tax on the sale of the old asset depends on its sale price, its initial purchase price and current book value, and existing government tax rules.

The book value of an asset is its accounting value, equal to its original installed cost less the accumulated depreciation on the asset.

Any of three forms of taxable income–capital gain, recaptured depreciation, or a loss–can result from the sale of an asset. The form of taxable income depends on the relationship of the sales price of the asset and its initial purchase price and current book value. The four possible situations are summarized below.

Situation	Tax Consequence
The sales price is more than the original purchase price.	Two components: 1) A capital gain on the amount above the asset's initial purchase price; and 2) recaptured depreciation on the remaining amount above the asset's book value. Both components are taxed as ordinary income.
The sales price is less than its original purchase price but greater than the asset's book value.	No capital gains but recaptured depreciation, taxes as ordinary income, on the amount above the asset's book value.
The sales price is equal to the asset's book value.	No tax consequences.
The sales price is less than the asset's book value.	This results in a loss and (usually) a tax refund based on the amount of loss and the ordinary income tax rate.

Net working capital is the amount by which a firm's current assets exceed its current liabilities. Changes in net working capital often accompany capital expenditures and need to be accounted for in the capital budgeting process. The change in net working capital is the difference between the change in current assets and the change in current liabilities expected to accompany a given capital expenditure. If positive, it would represent an additional cash outflow associated with the initial investment; if negative, it would represent a cash inflow.

Finding the Operating Cash Inflows

LG 5

The operating cash inflows are the incremental after-tax cash inflows expected to result from a project. The benefits provided by a proposed project are measured on a cash flow basis, rather than accounting profits, since only cash can be used to pay the firms obligations. This typically involves adding depreciation charges back to net profits after taxes (known as the income statement approach), which gives the operating cash flows associated with the proposed and present projects.

The relevant (incremental) cash inflows are the difference between the operating cash inflows of the proposed project and those of the present project. These cash flows must be measured on an after-tax basis to ensure consistency and fairness when evaluating competing projects.

Finding the Terminal Cash Flow

For expansion projects, the terminal cash flow, if any, represents the after-tax cash flow, exclusive of operating cash inflows, that is expected from liquidation of a project. It is typically represented by the after-tax proceeds from the sale of the asset, plus the reversion of any initial investment in net working capital.

For replacement projects, it is calculated by finding the difference between the after-tax proceeds from the sale of the new and the old asset at project termination and then adjusting this difference for any change in net working capital. The components for calculating the terminal cash flow under these circumstances are described below.

After-tax proceeds from the sale of new asset =
Proceeds from sale of new asset ±Tax on sale of new asset
– After-tax proceeds from the sale of old asset =
Proceeds from sale of old asset ± Tax on sale of old asset
± Change in net working capital
= Terminal cash flow

Sample Problem Solutions

Sample Problem 1: Expansion Project

Consider the following expansion plan for Walworth, Inc. The initial cost of the new equipment is $300,000 plus $20,000 in installation costs. Net working capital is expected to increase by $40,000. The new facility will be depreciated over 5-years using MACRS depreciation. Revenues generated by the new facility are expected to be $150,000 per year and operating expenses are expected to be $50,000 per year. The firm has a tax rate of 40%. After five years, Walworth expects to sell the used equipment for $40,000. What are the initial investment, annual operating cash flows, and terminal cash flow for the project?

Solution to Sample Problem 1

a. The initial investment for an expansion project typically involves three components: the purchase price ($300,000), installation costs ($20,000), and incremental effects on net working capital (increase of $40,000) for a total of $360,000.

Initial investment	
Purchase price	$300,000
Installation	20,000
Installed cost	320,000
Increase in net working capital	40,000
Net investment	$360,000

b. Finding the operating cash flows involves four steps components.

Step 1: The revenues and operating costs from the proposed project are estimated.

Step 2: The depreciation expense is calculated. The annual depreciation charge is equal to the relevant MACRS percentage times the depreciable cost (installed cost) of the asset. For example, the first year's depreciation equals 20% x $320,000 = $64,000.

Step 3: Taxes are subtracted (added in the case of a loss) from the operating profits of the proposed project to arrive at earnings after tax.

Step 4: The depreciation expense is added back to the after-tax earnings to arrive at net cash flow for each year.

Annual Cash Flows					
	Year 1	**Year 2**	**Year 3**	**Year 4**	**Year 5**
Revenues	$150,000	$150,000	$150,000	$150,000	$150,000
- Oper costs	50,000	50,000	50,000	50,000	50,000
- Depr	64,000	102,400	60,800	38,400	38,400
EBT	36,000	-2,400	39,200	61,600	61,600
± Tax	-14,400	+960	-15,680	-24,640	-24,640
EAT	21,600	-1,440	23,520	36,960	36,960
+ Depr	64,000	102,400	60,800	38,400	38,400
Net cash flow	$84,600	$100,960	$84,320	$75,360	$75,360

c. The terminal value involves three components: the sales price of the equipment at termination ($40,000), the tax effect associated with the sale ($9,600), and the return of the original investment in net working capital ($40,000) for a total of $70,400.

Note: The tax on the sale of the equipment at termination is equal to the gain on the sale (sale price minus book value) times the tax rate. The book value of the equipment equals the initial investment minus the accumulated depreciation or $16,000 ($320,000 - $64,000 - $102,400 - $60,800 - $38,400 - $38,400). The tax on the gain is therefore $9,600 [($40,000 sales price - $16,000 book value) x 40%].

Terminal Cash Flow	
Sales price	$40,000
Tax on sale of asset	-9,600
Net sales proceeds	30,400
Return of net working capital	40,000
Terminal cash flow	$70,400

Sample Problem 2: Replacement Project

Assume the same situation as the first problem except that instead of expanding the facilities, Walworth is simply proposing to replace existing equipment. The existing equipment was purchased 3 years ago for $200,000 and is being depreciated following the MACRS five-year schedule. If replaced, the existing equipment could be sold today for $80,000. This equipment is expected to last an additional five years after which it could be sold for scrap for $6,000. Walworth is currently generating revenues of $80,000 and operating costs of $30,000 per year with the existing equipment. What are the initial investment, annual operating cash flows, and terminal cash flow for the project?

Solution to Sample Problem 2

a. For a replacement project, the installed cost of the new equipment remains the same ($320,000) but the initial investment is reduced by the net proceeds from selling the existing equipment ($71,200). The proceeds equal the selling price less the tax paid on the gain on the sale with the gain equal to the difference between the sale price and the book value of the equipment.

The book value of the equipment equals the initial investment minus the accumulated depreciation, which is equal to $58,000.

Original price	$200,000	
Year 1 depreciation	(40,000)	$200,000 x 20%
Year 2 depreciation	(64,000)	$200,000 x 32%
Year 3 depreciation	(38,000)	$200,000 x 19%
Book value	$58,000	

The tax on the gain is equal to ($80,000 – $58,000) x 40%, or $8,800.
The after-tax proceeds on the sale are therefore $71,200 ($80,000 - $8,800).

Initial investment	
Purchase price	$300,000
Installation	20,000
Installed cost	320,000
Less: After-tax proceeds from sale of existing equipment	(71,200)
Plus: Increase in net working capital	40,000
Net investment	$288,800

b. For a replacement project, only the incremental cash flows are relevant. To calculate the incremental cash flows, two sets of operating cash flows must be constructed, one with the new equipment, the other with the existing equipment. The resulting differences in annual cash flows between the two sets of cash flows become the relevant, or incremental, cash flows.

The operating cash flows associated with the new equipment is the same as for the expansion project discussed in problem 1.

	Annual Cash Flows (new equipment)				
	Year 1	**Year 2**	**Year 3**	**Year 4**	**Year 5**
Revenues	$150,000	$150,000	$150,000	$150,000	$150,000
- Oper costs	50,000	50,000	50,000	50,000	50,000
- Depr	64,000	102,400	60,800	38,400	38,400
EBT	36,000	-2,400	39,200	61,600	61,600
± Tax	-14,400	+960	-15,680	-24,640	-24,640
EAT	21,600	-1,440	23,520	36,960	36,960
+ Depr	64,000	102,400	60,800	38,400	38,400
Net cash flow	$84,600	$100,960	$84,320	$75,360	$75,360

	Annual Cash Flows (existing equipment)				
	Year 1	**Year 2**	**Year 3**	**Year 4**	**Year 5**
Revenues	$80,000	$80,000	$80,000	$80,000	$80,000
- Oper costs	30,000	30,000	30,000	30,000	30,000
- Depr	24,000	24,000	10,000	0	0
EBT	26,000	26,000	40,000	50,000	50,000
± Tax	-10,400	-10,400	-16,000	-20,000	-20,000
EAT	15,600	15,600	24,000	30,000	30,000
+ Depr	24,000	24,000	10,000	0	0
Net cash flow	$39,600	$39,600	$34,000	$30,000	$30,000

Note: Since the existing equipment has already been operated and depreciated for three years, the depreciation charges above (Years 1, 2, and 3) reflect the remaining three years of depreciation.

Depreciable value $200,000	
Year 1 depreciation = 24,000	$200,000 x 12% (4th year)
Year 2 depreciation = 24,000	$200,000 x 12% (5th year)
Year 3 depreciation = 10,000	$200,000 x 5% (6th year)

Annual Cash Flows (new - existing equipment)					
	Year 1	**Year 2**	**Year 3**	**Year 4**	**Year 5**
NCF (new)	$84,600	$100,960	$84,320	$75,360	$75,360
- NCF (old)	39,600	39,600	34,000	30,000	30,000
Net cash flow	$45,000	61,360	50,320	45,360	45,360

c. For replacement projects, the terminal cash flow is calculated by finding the difference between the after-tax proceeds from the sale of the new and the old equipment at project termination and then adjusting this difference for the return of the net working capital. It is the after-tax proceeds from the sale of the new equipment ($30,400–same as for the expansion project in problem 1) minus the after-tax proceeds from the sale of the old equipment and minus the return of the net working capital ($40,000).

The proceeds from the sale of the existing equipment is the selling price ($6,000) less the tax paid on the gain on the sale. Since the equipment is fully depreciated, the entire $6,000 is taxable so the net proceeds would equal $3,600 ($6,000 - $6,000 x 40).

Terminal Cash Flow – Replacement Project	
Net proceeds from new equipment	$30,400
Net proceeds from old equipment	-3,600
Net sales proceeds	26,800
Return of net working capital	40,000
Net terminal cash flow	$66,800

Study Tips

1. Review finding the book value of an asset. The book value is equal to the original book value minus accumulated depreciation. Alternatively, if using the MACRS system, you can find the book value as the undepreciated value of the asset. For example, if a five-year asset is sold after four years, 17% of its original book value is undepreciated (100 – 20% - 32% - 19% - 12% = 17%), or, reading from the bottom of the MACRS schedule 5% + 12% = 17%.

2. Understand the difference between an expansion and a replacement project. Replacement projects are more difficult because you are, in effect, calculating three capital budgets: the costs and benefits of using the new asset, the costs and benefits of continuing with the old asset, and then the incremental differences between the two.

3. Conducting cash flow estimates is ideally suited for computer spreadsheets. Try to use a spreadsheet to work out your homework assignments. The initial investment in time and effort to set up a capital budgeting example will be rewarded with ease in adapting the spreadsheet to future problems as well as ease of correcting mistakes, which can be quite time-consuming if done by hand.

Sample Exam

True/False

T F 1. Since the focus of capital budgeting is on cash flows rather than on net income, changes in noncash balance sheet accounts such as inventory are not relevant in the analysis.

T F 2. When calculating the cash flows for a project, you should include interest payments.

T F 3. Any cash flow that can be classified as incremental is relevant in a capital budgeting project analysis.

T F 4. Net incremental cash flow is calculated by adding back the change in depreciation to the change in net income.

T F 5. The capital budgeting technique is used to evaluate the firm's fixed asset investments that provide the basis for the firm's earning power and value.

T F 6. A capital expenditure is an outlay of funds invested only on fixed assets and is expected to produce benefits over a period of time greater than one year.

T F 7. Capital expenditure proposals are reviewed to assess their appropriateness in light of the firm's overall objectives and plans, and to evaluate their economic validity.

T F 8. If a firm has unlimited funds to invest, all the mutually exclusive projects that meet its minimum investment criteria can be implemented.

T F 9. Mutually exclusive projects are projects whose cash flows are unrelated to one another; the acceptance of one does not eliminate the others from further consideration.

T F 10. The relevant cash flows for a proposed capital expenditure are the incremental after-tax cash outflows and resulting subsequent inflows.

T F 11. International capital budgeting differs from the domestic version because 1) cash inflows and outflows occur in a foreign currency, and 2) foreign investments potentially face significant political risk.

T F 12. Sunk costs are cash outlays that have already been made and therefore have no effect on the cash flows relevant to the current decision. As a result, sunk costs should not be included in a project's incremental cash flows.

T F 13. The book value of an asset is equal to its depreciable value minus the accumulated depreciation.

T F 14. Capital gain is the portion of the sale price that is in excess of the initial purchase price.

T F 15. The change in net working capital–regardless of whether an increase or decrease–is not taxable because it merely involves a net build-up or reduction of current accounts.

Multiple Choice

1. ______ is the process of evaluating and selecting long-term investments consistent with the firm's goal of owner wealth maximization.
   a. Recapitalizing assets
   b. Capital budgeting
   c. Ratio analysis
   d. Restructuring debt

2. The final step in the capital budgeting process is
   a. implementation.
   b. follow-up monitoring.
   c. re-evaluation.
   d. education.

3. The first step in the capital budgeting process is
   a. review and analysis.
   b. implementation.
   c. decision making.
   d. proposal generation.

4. Which of the following does not define a capital expenditure?
   a. An outlay made for the earning assets of the firm
   b. An outlay expected to produce benefits over a period of time greater than one year
   c. An outlay for current asset expansion
   d. An outlay commonly used to expand the level of operations

5. Which pattern of cash flow stream is the most difficult to use when evaluating projects?
   a. Mixed stream
   b. Conventional flow
   c. Nonconventional flow
   d. Annuity

6. The cash flow pattern where a $25,000 investment produces cash inflows of $8,000 a year for 5 years may be characterized as
   a. an annuity and conventional cash flow.
   b. a mixed stream and nonconventional cash flow.
   c. an annuity and nonconventional cash flow.
   d. a mixed stream and conventional cash flow.

7. ______ projects have the same function; the acceptance of one ______ the others from consideration.
   a. Capital; eliminates
   b. Independent; does not eliminate
   c. Mutually exclusive; eliminates
   d. Replacement; does not eliminate

8. A nonconventional cash flow pattern associated with capital investment projects consists of an initial
   a. outflow followed by a series of cash inflows and outflows.
   b. inflow followed by a series of cash inflows and outflows.
   c. outflow followed by a series of inflows.
   d. inflow followed by a series of outflows.

9. Projects that compete with one another, so that the acceptance of one eliminates the others from further consideration, are called
   a. independent projects.
   b. mutually exclusive projects.
   c. replacement projects.
   d. None of the above.

10. When making replacement decisions, the development of relevant cash flows is complicated when compared to expansion decisions, due to the need to calculate ______ cash inflows.
   a. conventional
   b. nonconventional
   c. incremental
   d. initial

11. When evaluating a capital budgeting project, the change in net working capital must be considered as part of
    a. the operating cash inflows.
    b. the initial investment.
    c. the incremental operating cash inflows.
    d. the operating cash outflows.

12. The change in net working capital when evaluating a capital budgeting decision is
    a. current assets minus current liabilities.
    b. the increase in current assets.
    c. the increase in current liabilities.
    d. the change in current assets minus the change in current liabilities.

13. An important cash inflow in the analysis of initial cash flows for a replacement project is
    a. taxes.
    b. the cost of the new asset.
    c. installation cost.
    d. the sale value of the old asset.

14. The tax treatment regarding the sale of existing assets which are sold for more than the book value and more than the original purchase price results in
    a. an ordinary tax benefit.
    b. no tax benefit or liability.
    c. recaptured depreciation taxed as ordinary income.
    d. a capital gain tax liability and recaptured depreciation taxed as ordinary income.

15. In evaluating the initial investment for a capital budgeting project,
    a. an increase in net working capital is considered a cash inflow.
    b. a decrease in net working capital is considered a cash outflow.
    c. an increase in net working capital is considered a cash outflow.
    d. net working capital does not have to be considered.

16. Benefits expected from proposed capital expenditures must be on an after-tax basis because
    a. taxes are cash outflows.
    b. no benefits may be used by the firm until tax claims are satisfied.
    c. there may also be tax benefits to be evaluated.
    d. it is common, accepted practice to do so.

17. One basic technique used to evaluate after-tax operating cash flows is to
    a. add noncash charges to net income.
    b. subtract depreciation from operating revenues.
    c. add cash expenses to net income.
    d. subtract cash expenses from noncash charges.

18. A corporation is considering expanding operations to meet growing demand. With the capital expansion, the current accounts are expected to change. Management expects cash to increase by $20,000, accounts receivable by $40,000, and inventories by $60,000. At the same time, accounts payable will increase by $50,000, accruals by $10,000, and long-term debt by $100,000. The change in net working capital is
    a. an increase of $120,000.
    b. a decrease of $40,000.
    c. a decrease of $120,000.
    d. an increase of $60,000.

19. A corporation is selling an existing asset for $1,000. The asset, when purchased, cost $10,000, was being depreciated under MACRS using a five-year recovery period, and has been depreciated for four full years. If the assumed tax rate is 40 percent on ordinary income and capital gains, the tax effect of this transaction is
    a. $0 tax liability.
    b. $1,100 tax liability.
    c. $3,600 tax liability.
    d. $280 tax benefit.

20. A corporation has decided to replace an existing asset with a newer model. Two years ago, the existing asset originally cost $70,000 and was being depreciated under MACRS using a five-year recovery period. The existing asset can be sold for $30,000. The new asset will cost $80,000 and will also be depreciated under MACRS using a five-year recovery period. If the assumed tax rate is 40 percent on ordinary income and capital gains, the initial investment is
    a. $48,560.
    b. $44,360.
    c. $49,240.
    d. $27,600.

Problem

Cheeseheads, Inc. must develop the relevant cash flows for a replacement capital investment proposal. The proposed asset costs $50,000 and has installation costs of $3,000. The asset will be depreciated using a five-year recovery schedule. The existing equipment, which originally cost $25,000 and will be sold for $10,000, has been depreciated using an MACRS five-year recovery schedule and three years of depreciation has already been taken. The new equipment is expected to result in incremental before-tax net profits of $15,000 per year. The firm has a 40 percent tax rate.

1. What is the initial cash outflow for this project?

2. What are the incremental cash flows for years 1 to 5?

Chapter 10 Answer Key

True/False		Multiple Choice			
1.	F	1.	B	16.	B
2.	F	2.	B	17.	A
3.	T	3.	D	18.	D
4.	T	4.	C	19.	D
5.	T	5.	C	20.	A
6.	F	6.	A		
7.	T	7.	C		
8.	F	8.	A		
9.	F	9.	B		
10.	T	10.	C		
11.	T	11.	B		
12.	T	12.	D		
13.	T	13.	D		
14.	T	14.	D		
15.	T	15.	C		

Problem

1. The initial cash outflow for the project is $44,100 as calculated below:

Purchase price	$50,000
Installation	3,000
Installed cost	$53,000
Less: After-tax proceeds from sale of existing equipment	
10,000 – [(10,000 - 25,000 (.29))(.40)]	8,900
Net investment	$44,100

2. The incremental cash flows for years 1 to 5 are calculated below:

	Year 1	Year 2	Year 3	Year 4	Year 5
Before-tax profits	$15,000	$15,000	$15,000	$15,000	$15,000
- Tax	6,000	6,000	6,000	6,000	6,000
Earnings after tax	9,000	9,000	9,000	9,000	9,000
+ Depr (new)	10,600	16,960	10,070	6,360	6,360
- Depr (old)	3,000	3,000	1,250	0	0
Net cash flow	$16,600	$22,960	$17,820	$15,360	$15,360

Chapter 11

CAPITAL BUDGETING TECHNIQUES: CERTAINTY AND RISK

Chapter Summary

Chapter 11 presents the three most popular capital budgeting techniques–the payback period, net present value (NPV), and internal rate of return (IRR), first assuming certainty and then considering risk. Each has specific strengths and weaknesses. The behavioral approaches for dealing with risk–sensitivity analysis and scenario analysis and simulation–are described and demonstrated, as is a detailed discussion of the risk-adjusted discount rate (RADR).

LG 1

Calculate, interpret, and evaluate the payback period. The payback period is the amount of time required for the firm to recover its initial investment, as calculated from cash inflows. Shorter payback periods are preferred. The payback period's strengths include consideration of cash flows, the implicit consideration given to timing, and its ability to measure risk exposure. Its weaknesses include its lack of linkage to the wealth maximization goal, its failure to consider time value explicitly, and the fact that it ignores cash flows that occur after the payback period.

LG 2

Apply net present value (NPV) and internal rate of return (IRR) to relevant cash flows to choose acceptable capital expenditures. Sophisticated capital budgeting techniques use the cost of capital to consider the time factor in the value of money. Two such techniques are net present value (NPV) and internal rate of return (IRR). Both NPV and IRR yield the same accept-reject decisions but often provide conflicting ranks.

LG 3

Use net present value profiles to compare NPV and IRR techniques in light of conflicting rankings. Net present value profiles are useful in comparing projects, especially when conflicting rankings exist between NPV and IRR. On a purely theoretical basis, NPV is preferred over IRR, because NPV assumes reinvestment of intermediate cash inflows at the cost of capital and does not exhibit the mathematical problems that often occur when IRRs are calculated for nonconventional cash flows. In practice, however, the IRR is more commonly used because it is consistent with the general preference toward rates of return.

LG 4 ***Recognize sensitivity and scenario analysis and simulation as behavioral approaches for dealing with project risk.*** Risk in capital budgeting is the chance that a project will prove unacceptable or, more formally, the degree of variability of cash flows. Sensitivity analysis and scenario analysis are two behavioral approaches for dealing with project risk that capture the variability of cash inflows and NPVs. Simulation is a statistically based behavioral approach that results in a probability distribution of project returns. It usually requires a computer and allows the decision maker to understand the risk-return tradeoffs involved in a proposed investment.

LG 5 ***Discuss the unique risks that multinational companies face.*** Although the basic capital budgeting techniques are the same for purely domestic and multinational companies, firms that operate in several countries must also deal with both exchange rate and political risks, tax law differences, transfer pricing, and a strategic rather than a strict financial viewpoint.

LG 6 ***Understand how to determine and use risk-adjusted discount rates.*** Risk-adjusted discount rates (RADRs) are a popular risk-adjustment technique that uses a market-based adjustment of the discount rate to calculate the NPV. The logic underlying the RADR is closely linked to the capital asset pricing model (CAPM). Most firms subjectively adjust the RADR up or down depending on whether the proposed project is more or less risky than the average risk of the firm. RADRs are commonly used in practice, because decision makers prefer rates of return and find RADRs easy to estimate and apply.

Chapter Outline

Capital Budgeting Techniques

Capital budgeting techniques are used by firms to evaluate projects that will increase shareholder's wealth. The preferred techniques combine time value procedures, return and risk considerations, and valuation concepts to select capital expenditures that are most consistent with the firm's goals. The three most popular capital budgeting techniques are the payback period, net present value, and internal rate of return.

Payback Period

The payback period is the amount of time required for the firm to recover its initial investment, as calculated from cash inflows. If the payback period is less than the maximum period allowable, a project is accepted; if not, it is rejected. Shorter payback periods are preferred.

The payback period's strengths include consideration of cash flows, the implicit consideration given to timing, and its ability to measure risk exposure. It is also popular because it is easy to calculate and offers a simple intuitive appeal. However, as an unsophisticated technique it has perceived weaknesses including its lack of linkage to the wealth maximization goal, its failure to consider time value explicitly, and the fact that it ignores cash flows that occur after the payback period.

Net Present Value (NPV)

Sophisticated capital budgeting techniques use the cost of capital to consider the time factor in the value of money. Two such techniques are net present value (NPV) and internal rate of return (IRR).

The NPV is found by subtracting the project's initial investment from the present value of its cash inflows. The formula to calculate NPV is as follows:

$$\mathbf{NPV} = \sum_{t=1}^{n} \frac{\mathbf{CF_t}}{(1+k)^t} - \mathbf{CF_0}$$

If the NPV is greater than \$0, the project is accepted; if it is less than \$0, it is rejected.

Internal Rate of Return

The IRR is probably the most widely used of the sophisticated capital budgeting techniques. It is defined as the discount rate that causes the NPV to equal \$0. It is also the compound annual rate of return the firm will earn if it invests in the project and receives the given cash inflows. Mathematically, the IRR is the value of *k* in the NPV formula that causes the NPV to equal \$0:

$$\$0 = \sum_{t=1}^{n} \frac{CF_t}{(1+IRR)^t} - CF_0$$

or

$$CF_0 = \sum_{t=1}^{n} \frac{CF_t}{(1+IRR)^t}$$

If the IRR is greater than the firm's cost of capital, the project is accepted; if it is less than the cost of capital, it is rejected.

Calculating the IRR by hand involves a complex trial-and-error technique. Fortunately, most financial calculators and computer spreadsheet programs are preprogrammed with IRR functions. To use a financial calculator, enter each of the cash flows and then depress the IRR button to find the internal rate of return.

Both NPV and IRR provide the same accept-reject decisions but often provide conflicting ranks.

Comparing NPV and IRR techniques

Net present value profiles are useful in comparing projects, especially when conflicting rankings exist between NPV and IRR. NPV profiles are graphical depictions of a project's NPV at various discount rates.

NPV and IRR often rank projects differently because the implicit assumption of each technique with regard to the reinvestment of intermediate cash flows – cash inflows received prior to termination of the project. NPV assumes reinvestment of intermediate cash flows at the cost of capital while IRR assumes the cash flows are reinvested at a rate equal to the project's IRR. This leads to different conclusions about projects whenever projects differ by size (scale) or the timing of the cash flows. Higher reinvestment rates (k) tend to favor 1) smaller projects because more funds are available to invest at the higher rate of return and 2) projects with faster paybacks because there are more cash flows available early for reinvestment.

On a theoretical basis, NPV is preferred over IRR because the cost of capital (discount rate) tends to be a more realistic reinvestment rate for the intermediate cash flows. In addition, NPV does not suffer from mathematical problems that can occur when calculating IRRs for nonconventional cash flows.

In practice, IRR is more commonly used because it is consistent with the general preference of businesspeople toward rates of return rather than actual dollar return.

Behavioral Approaches for Dealing with Risk

Risk in capital budgeting is concerned with either the chance that a project will prove unacceptable or, more formally, the degree of variability of expected cash inflows. There are several approaches for dealing with risk in capital budgeting.

Sensitivity analysis is a behavioral approach that uses multiple possible values for a given variable to assess its impact on the firm's return. A common approach is to estimate the NPVs associated with pessimistic (worst), most likely (expected), and optimistic (best) estimates of cash flows.

Scenario analysis is similar but broader in scope. Rather than singling out the change in one variable, scenario analysis evaluates the impact on returns of simultaneous changes in multiple variables.

Simulation is a statistically based behavioral approach that applies predetermined profitability distributions and random numbers to estimate the probability distribution of project returns. It usually requires a computer and allows the decision maker to understand the continuum of risk-return tradeoffs involved in a proposed investment.

International Risk Considerations

Although the basic capital budgeting techniques are the same for purely domestic and multinational companies, firms that operate in several countries must deal with other issues. Among these are:

1. Exchange rate risk because the dollar value of expected cash inflows and outflows might change as exchange rates change.

2. Political risks because political interference may put future expected cash flows at risk.

3. Taxes because earnings may be taxed by both the foreign government and the U.S. government.

4. Transfer pricing or the ability to charge or allocate different prices among different affiliates and subsidiaries of the corporation.

5. Strategic rather than strict financial perspectives dominating the investment analysis.

Risk-Adjusted Discount Rates (RADRs)

LG 6

Due to risk considerations, sometimes it may be necessary to adjust the present value of the expected cash flows. This can be accomplished by adjusting the cash inflows, a highly subjective technique, or, preferably, adjusting the discount rate.

Risk-adjusted discount rates (RADR) are a popular risk-adjustment technique that use a market-based adjustment of the discount rate to calculate the NPV as seen below:

$$\text{NPV} = \sum_{t=1}^{n} \frac{\text{CF}_t}{(1+\text{RADR})^t} - \text{CF}_0$$

The logic underlying the RADR is closely linked to the capital asset pricing model (CAPM) in that riskier projects should be compensated for with higher expected returns. Most firms subjectively adjust the RADR up or down depending on whether the proposed project is more or less risky than the average risk of the firm.

RADRs are commonly used in practice because decision makers prefer rates of return and find them easier to estimate and apply.

Sample Problem Solutions

Sample Problem 1: Payback

Suppose you are planning to invest in a $300,000 project that you expect to provide cash inflows of $100,000 the first year, $150,000 in the second year, and $80,000 for the final three years of the project. What is the payback period?

Solution to Sample Problem 1

The payback period is the time it takes to recover your initial investment. It is found by summing the cumulative cash flows from the project.

Year	Cash flow	Cumulative cash flow
0	($300,000)	($300,000)
1	100,000	(200,000)
2	140,000	(60,000)
3	80,000	20,000

After two years, $240,000 of the $300,000 investment has been recovered. Three-quarters through the third year ($60,000 / $80,000), the entire investment will be recovered. Thus, the payback period is 2 3/4 years.

Sample Problem 2: Net Present Value

Assuming your cost of capital is 12%, what is the Net Present Value for the project in sample problem 1?

Solution to Sample Problem 2

To find the Net Present Value, calculate the present value of all the cash inflows and subtract out the initial investment cash flow.

Year	(a) Cash Flow	(b) $PVIF_{12\%,t}$	(a x b) PV-Cash Flow
0	($300,000)	1.0000	($300,000)
1	100,000	0.8929	89,290
2	140,000	0.7972	111,608
3	80,000	0.7118	56,944
4	80,000	0.6355	50,840
5	80,000	0.5674	45,392
NPV			$54,074

Alternatively, a financial calculator can be used, by first entering the cash flows (CF_0 = -300000, CF_1 = 100000, CF_2 = 140000, and $CF_{3\text{-}5}$ = 80000). Next, depress the NPV key, enter the discount rate (12%) prompted for, and then compute (CPT) the NPV = $54,071.

Sample Problem 3: Internal Rate of Return

Find the Internal Rate of Return for the project in sample problem 1.

Solution to Sample Problem 3

Although the Internal Rate of Return can be found through a complex trial-and-error method, financial calculators and computer spreadsheet programs have IRR functions preprogrammed into them. Assuming the cash flows from problem 2 are still in the memory of your calculator (if not, you will need to reenter them), find the IRR by pressing the IRR key (and CPT if necessary); the result should be 19.61%.

Sample Problem 4: NPV, IRR, and NPV profiles

You are asked to evaluate two mutually exclusive projects, X and Y. The cash flows for each are listed below. The firm's cost of capital is 15%.

Year	X	Y
0	-$120,000	-$200,000
1	60,000	100,000
2	50,000	90,000
3	70,000	100,000

a. Calculate the NPV of each project, and assess its acceptability.

b. Calculate the IRR of each project, and assess its acceptability.

c. Draw the NPV profiles for both projects on the same set of axes.

d. Evaluate and discuss the rankings of the two projects.

Solution to Sample Problem 3

a.

Year	Cash Flow (X) (a)	Cash Flow (Y) (b)	$PVIF_{15\%,t}$ (c)	PV(X) (a) x (c)	PV(Y) (b) x (c)
0	($120,000)	($200,000)	1.0000	($120,000)	($200,000)
1	60,000	100,000	0.8696	52,176	86,960
2	50,000	90,000	0.7561	37,805	68,049
3	70,000	100,000	0.6575	46,025	65,750
NPV				$16,006	$20,759

NPV for X = $16,006. With a financial calculator, NPV = $16,007.
NPV for Y = $20,759. With a financial calculator, NPV = $20,761.

Both NPVs are positive (greater than $0), so each project is acceptable. However, since the projects are mutually exclusive, project Y would be preferred because it has a higher NPV.

b. Using a financial calculator, the IRR for X = 22.70% and Y = 21.18%. The IRR for each project is greater than the firm's cost of capital of 15%, so each is acceptable. However, since they are mutually exclusive, project X would be preferred because it has a higher IRR.

c. The NPV profiles are found by calculating the NPV for each project at different discount rates. The discount rates you choose are not too important so long as you use at least one discount rate that causes the NPVs to become negative. The NPVs for each project at different discount rates is summarized below.

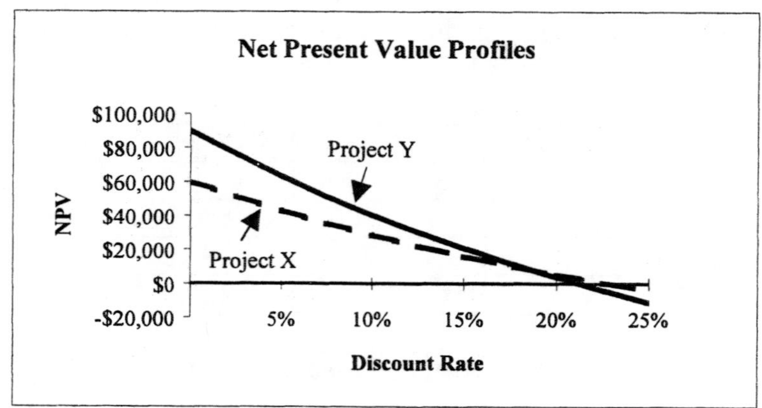

Discount Rate	NPV(X)	NPV(Y)
0%	$60,000	$90,000
5%	$42,963	$63,255
10%	$28,460	$40,421
15%	$16,007	$20,761
20%	$5,231	$3,704
25%	-$4,160	-$11,200

d. With mutually exclusive projects, NPV and IRR often lead to conflicting results. The IRR for Project X (22.70%) is higher than for Project Y (21.18%) yet at a cost of capital of 15%, Project Y is preferred over X because it has a larger NPV.

Because of the assumptions about the reinvestment rate of the intermediate cash flows, NPV is generally preferred over IRR on a purely theoretical basis so Project Y should be chosen. However, managers generally prefer IRR so they would likely choose Project X instead.

Study Tips

1. Be sure to know the advantages and disadvantages of using the payback period, net present value, and internal rate of return methods to evaluate capital investment opportunities.

2. Be careful to note when risk adjustments may be required. Incorporating risk, such as the use of risk-adjusted discount rates, may change the accept/reject decision or the ranking of different investment alternatives.

Sample Exam

True/False

T F 1. One advantage of the payback period method of evaluating fixed asset investment possibilities is that it provides a rough measure of a project's liquidity and risk.

T F 2. The internal rate of return is that discount rate which equates the present value of the cash outflows (or costs) with the present value of the cash inflows.

T F 3. If a project's NPV exceeds the project's IRR, then the project should be accepted.

T F 4. In the case of annuity cash inflows, the payback period can be found by dividing the initial investment by the annual cash inflow.

T F 5. One weakness of payback is its failure to recognize cash flows that occur after the payback period.

T F 6. Net present value is considered a sophisticated capital budgeting technique since it gives explicit consideration to the time value of money.

T F 7. If the net present value of a project is greater than zero, the firm will earn a return greater than its cost of capital. Such a project should enhance the wealth of the firm's owners.

T F 8. The net present value is found by subtracting a project's initial investment from the present value of its cash inflows discounted at a rate equal to the project's internal rate of return.

T F 9. The internal rate of return (IRR) is defined as the discount rate that equates the net present value with the initial investment associated with a project.

T F 10. For conventional projects, both NPV and IRR techniques will always generate the same accept-reject decision, but differences in their underlying assumptions can cause them to rank projects differently.

T F 11. On a purely theoretical basis, NPV is a better approach to capital budgeting than IRR because NPV implicitly assumes that any intermediate cash inflows generated by an investment are reinvested at the firm's cost of capital.

T F 12. In capital budgeting, risk refers to the chance that a project has a high degree of variability of the initial investment.

T F 13. Sensitivity analysis is a behavioral approach that uses a number of possible values for a given variable to assess its impact on a project's return.

T F 14. The danger that an unexpected change in the exchange rate between the dollar and the currency in which a project's cash flows are denominated can increase the market value of that project's cash flow.

T F 15. The higher the risk of a project, the higher its risk-adjusted discount rate and thus the lower the net present value for a given stream of cash inflows.

Multiple Choice

1. The ______ is the exact amount of time it takes the firm to recover its initial investment.
   a. average rate of return
   b. internal rate of return
   c. net present value
   d. payback period

2. Which of the following is not a reason many firms use the payback period as a guideline in capital investment decisions?
   a. It gives an implicit consideration to the timing of cash flows.
   b. It recognizes cash flows that occur after the payback period.
   c. It is a measure of risk exposure.
   d. It is easy to calculate.

3. A firm is evaluating a proposal that has an initial investment of $50,000 and has cash flows of $15,000 per year for five years. The payback period of the project is
   a. 1.5 years.
   b. 2 years.
   c. 3.3 years.
   d. 4 years.

4. A firm would accept a project with a net present value of zero because
   a. the project would maintain the wealth of the firm's owners.
   b. the project would enhance the wealth of the firm's owners.
   c. the return on the project would be positive.
   d. the return on the project would be zero.

5. The ______ is the discount rate that equates the present value of the cash inflows with the initial investment.
   a. payback period
   b. average rate of return
   c. cost of capital
   d. internal rate of return

6. A firm is evaluating two independent projects utilizing the internal rate of return technique. Project X has an initial investment of $80,000 and cash inflows at the end of each of the next five years of $25,000. Project Z has an initial investment of $120,000 and cash inflows at the end of each of the next four years of $40,000. The firm should
   a. accept both if their cost of capital is 15% at the maximum.
   b. accept only Z if their cost of capital is 15% at the maximum.
   c. accept only X if their cost of capital is 15% at the maximum.
   d. reject both if their cost of capital is 12% at the maximum.

7. When the net present value is negative, the internal rate of return is _____ the cost of capital.
   a. greater than
   b. greater than or equal to
   c. less than
   d. equal to

8. The underlying cause of conflicts in ranking for projects by internal rate of return and net present value methods is
   a. the reinvestment rate assumption regarding intermediate cash flows.
   b. that neither method explicitly considers the time value of money.
   c. the assumption made by the IRR method that intermediate cash flows are reinvested at the cost of capital.
   d. the assumption made by the NPV method that intermediate cash flows are reinvested at the internal rate of return.

9. Comparing net present value and internal rate of return analysis
   a. always results in the same ranking of projects.
   b. always results in the same accept/reject decision.
   c. may give different accept/reject decisions.
   d. is only necessary on mutually exclusive projects.

10. In comparing the internal rate of return and net present value methods of evaluation,
    a. internal rate of return is theoretically superior, but financial managers prefer net present value.
    b. net present value is theoretically superior, but financial managers prefer to use internal rate of return.
    c. financial managers prefer net present value, because it is presented as a rate of return.
    d. financial managers prefer net present value, because it measures benefits relative to the amount invested.

11. ______ measure(s) the risk of a capital budgeting project by estimating the NPVs associated with the optimistic, most likely, and pessimistic cash flow estimates.
    a. Certainty equivalents
    b. Risk-adjusted discount rates
    c. Sensitivity analysis
    d. Multiple regression analysis

12. Risk in a capital budgeting project can best be adjusted for by
    a. ignoring it.
    b. adjusting the discount rate downward for increasing risk.
    c. adjusting the discount rate upward for increasing risk.
    d. reducing the net present value by 10 percent for risky projects.

13. The advantage of using simulation in the capital budgeting process is
    a. ease of calculation.
    b. the availability of a continuum of risk-return trade-offs, which may be used as the basis for decision-making.
    c. dependability of predetermined probability distributions.
    d. that it generates a continuum of risk-return trade-offs rather than a single-point estimate.

14. Which of the following is not a weakness of the payback period?
    a. Its disregard for cash flows after the payback period
    b. Its implicit consideration of the timing of cash flows
    c. Its difficulty in specifying the appropriate payback period
    d. Its use of cash flows, not accounting profits.

15. Sophisticated capital budgeting techniques do not
    a. examine the size of the initial outlay.
    b. use net profits as a measure of return.
    c. explicitly consider the time value of money.
    d. take into account an unconventional cash flow pattern.

16. The minimum return that must be earned on a project in order to leave the firm's value unchanged is
    a. the internal rate of return.
    b. the interest rate.
    c. the discount rate.
    d. the compound rate.

17. In the context of capital budgeting, risk refers to
    a. the degree of variability of the cash inflows.
    b. the degree of variability of the initial investment.
    c. the chance that the net present value will be greater than zero.
    d. the chance that the internal rate of return will exceed the cost of capital.

18. The theoretical basis from which the concept of risk-adjusted discount rates is derived is
    a. the Gordon model.
    b. the capital asset pricing model.
    c. simulation theory.
    d. the basic cost of money.

19. Which of the following is not an argument to justify the use of risk-adjusted discount rates?
    a. Certainty equivalents are complex to develop.
    b. RADRs are consistent with the general disposition of financial decision makers toward rates of return.
    c. RADRs are easily estimated and applied to risky projects.
    d. The market risk-return function is easily determined.

20. ______ measure(s) the risk of a capital budgeting project by estimating the NPVs associated with the optimistic, most likely, and pessimistic cash flow estimates.
    a. Certainty equivalents
    b. Risk-adjusted discount rates
    c. Sensitivity analysis
    d. Multiple regression analysis

Problem

A firm is considering investment in a capital project with an initial investment of $1,000,000 followed by four years of cash inflows of $350,000. It uses a discount rate of 14% for capital budgeting decisions.

a. Calculate the payback period. If the minimum acceptable payback period were three years, would the project be acceptable?

b. Calculate the net present value. Would the project be acceptable?

c. Calculate the internal rate of return. Would the project be acceptable?

d. Assume that because of the risk of the project, a risk-adjusted discount rate of 16% is used. Would the project be acceptable?

Chapter 11 Answer Key

True/False

1. T
2. T
3. F
4. T
5. T
6. T
7. T
8. F
9. T
10. T
11. T
12. F
13. T
14. F
15. T

Multiple Choice

1. D
2. B
3. C
4. A
5. D
6. C
7. C
8. A
9. B
10. B
11. C
12. C
13. D
14. C
15. B
16. C
17. A
18. B
19. D
20. C

Problem

a. Payback period = $1,000,000 ÷ 350,000 = 2.86 years < 3 years so the project is acceptable.

b. NPV = 350,000($PVIFA_{14\%,4}$) – 1,000,000 = 1,019,800 – 1,000,000 = $19,800 > $0 so the project is acceptable.

c. IRR = 14.96% > 14% so the project is acceptable.

d. NPV = 350,000($PVIFA_{16\%,4}$) – 1,000,000 = 979,363 – 1,000,000 = -$20,637 < $0 so the project is no longer acceptable.

Notice that a similar conclusion could also be arrived at by comparing IRR = 14.96 < RADR = 16.00%.

COST OF CAPITAL

Chapter Summary

Chapter 12 focuses on the concepts and procedures related to estimation of a firm's cost of capital. The cost of capital is an extremely important financial concept. It acts as a major link between the firm's long-term investment decisions and the wealth of the owners. The costs of long-term debt, preferred stock, and common stock equity, both retained earnings and new common stock, are needed to find the firm's weighted average cost of capital (WACC). The WACC is used to develop the weighted marginal cost of capital (WMCC), which is then used in combination with the investment opportunity schedule (IOS) to determine the optimum capital budget.

LG 1 ***Understand the basic concept of cost of capital and the specific sources of capital it includes.*** The cost of capital is the rate of return that a firm must earn on its investments to maintain its market value and attract needed funds. To capture the interrelatedness of financing, a weighted average cost of capital should be used to find the expected average future cost of funds over the long run. The specific costs of the basic sources of capital (long-term debt, preferred stock, retained earnings, and common stock) can be calculated individually.

LG 2 ***Determine the cost of long-term debt and the cost of preferred stock.*** The cost of long-term debt is the after-tax cost today of raising long-term funds through borrowing. Cost quotations, calculation (using either a trial-and-error technique or a financial calculator), or an approximation can be used to find the before-tax cost of debt, which must then be tax-adjusted. The cost of preferred stock is the ratio of the preferred stock dividend to the firm's net proceeds from the sale of preferred stock.

LG 3 ***Calculate the cost of common stock equity and convert it into the cost of retained earnings and the cost of new issues of common stock.*** The cost of common stock equity can be calculated by using the constant-growth valuation model or the CAPM. The cost of retained earnings is equal to the cost of common stock equity. An adjustment in the cost of common stock equity to reflect underpricing and flotation costs is required to find the cost of new issues of common stock.

Find the weighted average cost of capital. The firm's WACC reflects the expected future cost of funds over the long run. It can be determined by combining the cost of specific types of capital after weighting each of them by their proportion in the firm's capital structure.

LG 5

Describe the procedures used to determine break points and the weighted average marginal cost of capital (WMCC). As the volume of total new financing increases, the costs of the various types of financing will increase, raising the firm's WACC. The WMCC is the firm's WACC associated with its next dollar of total new financing. Break points represent the level of new financing at which the cost of one of the financing components rises, causing an upward shift in the WMCC.

LG 6

Explain how the weighted marginal cost of capital can be used with the investment opportunity schedule (IOS) to make the firm's financing/investment decisions. The IOS presents a ranking of currently available investments from best (highest return) to worst (lowest return). It is used in combination with the WMCC to find the level of financing/investment that maximizes owner wealth. The firm accepts projects up to the point at which the marginal return on its investment equals its weighted marginal cost of capital.

Chapter Outline

Overview of the Cost of Capital

LG 1

The cost of capital is the rate of return that a firm must earn on its project investments to maintain its market value. It can also be thought of as the rate of return required by the market suppliers of capital to attract their funds to the firm. The four basic sources of capital typically available to firms are long-term debt, preferred stock, retained earnings, and common stock.

Although firms tend to raise funds in lumps, the costs of the different sources of capital are interrelated with the others. To capture the interrelatedness of financing, a weighted average cost of capital is used to find the expected average future cost of funds over the long run.

The weights within the capital structure tend to reflect some optimal mix of the different sources of capital. The specific cost of each source of capital is the after-tax cost of obtaining that source of financing today, not what it had cost the firm in the past.

The Cost of Long-Term Debt

The cost of long-term debt is the after-tax cost today of raising long-term funds through borrowing. For convenience, we assume that firms raise long-term debt in the form of bonds that pay interest on an annual basis. The net proceeds from selling bonds are the funds actually received by the firm, after subtracting out the costs of issuing and selling the bonds.

Before-tax cost of debt

The before-tax cost of debt, k_d, can be found in one of three ways: 1) cost quotations, 2) calculation, and 3) approximation.

When the net proceeds from selling the bond equal its face or par value, the coupon interest rate can be used for the firm's before-tax cost of debt. In addition, if the yield to maturity (YTM) on similar-risk bonds is available, the YTM can be used for the firm's before-tax cost.

If the net proceeds do not equal the par value, it is necessary to either calculate or approximate the cost. The calculation of the before-tax cost of the bond involves finding the bond's internal rate of return using either a trial-and-error technique or a financial calculator.

To approximate the before-tax cost of debt, the following equation (for a $1,000 par value bond) can be used:

$$\mathbf{k_d = \frac{I + \frac{\$1{,}000 - N_d}{n}}{\frac{N_d + \$1{,}000}{2}}}$$

Where:

I = annual interest in dollars
N_d = net proceeds from the sale of debt (bond)
n = number of years to the bond's maturity

After-tax cost of debt

The interest the firm pays on its debt is tax-deductible so the after-tax cost of debt must be found. The formula for calculating the after-tax cost of debt is as follows:

$$k_i = k_d \times (1 - T)$$

Where:

k_i = after-tax cost of debt
k_d = before-tax cost of debt
T = corporate tax rate

The Cost of Preferred Stock

Preferred stock is a special type of ownership interest in the firm because its dividends must be paid before any dividends are distributed to the common stockholders. Most preferred stock dividends are stated as a dollar amount but some are stated as a percentage of the stock's value. Before the cost of preferred stock is calculated, any dividends stated as percentages should be converted to annual dollar dividends.

The cost of preferred stock is the ratio of the preferred stock dividend to the firm's net proceeds from the sale of preferred stock. There is no tax adjustment to the cost because preferred stock dividends are paid out of the after-tax earnings of the firm. The formula for calculating the cost of preferred stock is as follows:

$$\mathbf{k_p = \frac{D_p}{N_p}}$$

Where:

k_p = cost of preferred stock
D_p = annual dollar dividend
N_p = net proceeds from the sale of preferred stock

The Cost of Common Stock

The cost of common stock is the return required on the stock by investors in the marketplace. There are two forms of common stock financing: retained earnings and new issues of common stock. The cost of common stock equity can be calculated by using the constant-growth valuation model or the CAPM.

Using the Constant-Growth Model

The constant-growth (Gordon) model was discussed in Chapter 7 as a way to determine the current price of a stock. The formula is restated below.

$$\mathbf{P_0 = \frac{D_1}{k_s - g}}$$

Where:

P_0 = value of common stock
D_1 = per-share dividend expected at the end of Year 1
k_s = required return on common stock
g = constant growth rate of dividends

Rearranging terms, we find the required rate of return, or cost of common stock equity:

$$k_s = \frac{D_1}{P_0} + g$$

Using the Capital Asset Pricing Model

The capital asset pricing model (CAPM) can also be used to estimate the cost of common stock equity. The CAPM describes the relationship between the required return, or the cost of common equity, and the nondiversifiable risk of the firm as measured by its beta coefficient. The following formula represents the basic CAPM:

$$k_s = R_F + [b \times (k_m - R_F)]$$

Where:
R_F = risk-free rate of return
b = beta coefficient
k_m = market return

The Cost of Retained Earnings

If earnings were not retained, dividends would be considered the equivalent of retained earnings and these retained earnings would be paid out as cash to the common stockholders. Consequently, retaining earnings (not paying out dividends) is equivalent to issuing additional common stock. Therefore, the cost of retained earnings, k_r, is the same as the cost of common stock equity.

$$k_r = k_s$$

The Cost of New Issues of Common Stock

An adjustment in the cost of common stock equity to reflect underpricing and flotation costs is required to find the cost of new issues of common stock. Besides the flotation costs paid for issuing and selling a new issue of common stock, the common stock is also often underpriced–sold at a price below its current market price. These two factors increase the cost of issuing new common stock, k_n, as reflected in the following equation:

$$k_n = \frac{D_1}{N_n} + g$$

Where:
k_n = cost of new issue of common stock
N_n = net proceeds from the sale of the new issue

The Weighted Average Cost of Capital (WACC)

The firm's WACC reflects the expected future cost of funds over the long run. It can be determined by combining the cost of specific types of capital after weighting each of them by its proportion in the firm's capital structure. The formula for WACC is as follows:

$$k_a = (w_i \times k_i) + (w_p \times k_p) + (w_s \times k_{rorn})$$

Where:

k_a = weighted average cost of capital
w_i = proportion of long-term debt in the firm's capital structure
w_p = proportion of preferred stock in the firm's capital structure
w_s = proportion of common stock equity in the firm's capital structure

The Marginal Cost and Investment Decisions

LG 5

The firm's weighted average cost of capital is a key input to the decision making process so it is important to understand that as the volume of total new financing increases, the costs of the various types of financing will increase, raising the firm's WACC. The weighted marginal cost of capital (WMCC) is simply the firm's WACC associated with its next dollar of total new financing.

Finding breaking points

To calculate the WMCC, the breaking points must be found. Break points represent the level of total new financing at which the cost of one of the financing components rises, causing an upward shift in the WMCC. The general formula for break points is as follows:

$$\mathbf{BP_j = \frac{AF_j}{w_j}}$$

Where:

BP_j = break point for financing source *j*
AF_j = amount of funds available from financing source *j* at a given cost
w_j = capital structure weight (stated in decimal form) for financing source *j*

Once the break points have been calculated, the WACC over different ranges must be determined. When these different ranges are grouped together, they are used to prepare a WMCC schedule, which is a graph that relates the firm's WACC to the level of total new financing.

The Investment Opportunity Schedule (IOS)

The IOS presents a ranking of currently available investments from best (highest return) to worst (lowest return). As long as a project's internal rate of return is greater than the weighted marginal cost of new financing, the firm should accept the project.

The IOS is used in combination with the WMCC to find the level of financing/investment that maximizes owner wealth. If a project's return is above the WMCC, the project should be accepted. If the project falls below the WMCC, the project should be rejected.

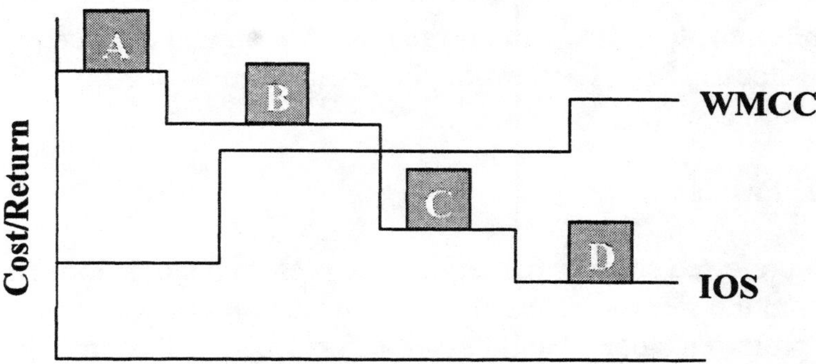

In the above graph, the four different investments available to the firm are represented by letters A through D and ranked in descending order by their internal rates of return. This is the IOS schedule. The WMCC schedule shows the cost of capital for different amounts of investment. The firm would accept projects up to the point at which the marginal return on its investment equals its marginal cost of capital, which is the point of intersection between the WMCC and IOS schedules. In the above example, Projects A and B would be accepted and Projects C and D would be rejected.

Sample Problem Solutions

Sample Problem 1: Cost of Long-Term Debt

Find the cost of debt for a bond that is selling for $960, has 10 years to maturity, and has a coupon interest rate of 8%. Assume a tax rate of 40%.

Solution to Sample Problem 1

The before-tax cost of debt is usually found by either calculating or approximating the bond's yield to maturity. Using a financial calculator, the YTM is found by entering N =10, PV = -960, FV = 1000, PMT = 80, and computing (CPT) the interest rate I = 8.61%. The after-tax cost, k_i, is equal to 8.61 x (1 - .4) = 5.17%.

Sample Problem 2: Cost of Preferred Stock

Find the cost of preferred stock financing if the promised annual dividend is $8 and the current market price of the stock is $80. There would be flotation costs of $2 per share if the firm issued new preferred stock.

Solution to Sample Problem 2

The cost of preferred stock is the ratio of the preferred stock dividend to the firm's net proceeds from the sale of preferred stock. The net proceeds would be $78 ($80 - $2) so the cost of preferred stock would be $8 / $78 = 10.26%. Preferred stock dividends are not tax-deductible so there are no tax adjustments to make to the cost.

Sample Problem 3: Cost of Common Stock

Find the cost of equity if the firm's beta is 1.2, the risk-free rate of interest is 4%, and the return on the market is 9%.

Solution to Sample Problem 3

Given the information available, the CAPM equation can be used to find the cost of equity.

$$k_s = R_F + b\,[k_m - R_F]$$

so

$$k_s = 4\% + 1.2\,[9\% - 4\%] = 10\%$$

Sample Problem 4: Cost of Common Stock

Find the cost of equity if common stock is selling for $50, the growth rate is expected to be 6%, and next year's dividend is expected to be $2.

Solution to Sample Problem 4

Given the information available, the only model that can be used is the constant-growth model. By rearranging the terms, we find that:

$$k_s = D_1 / P_0 + g$$

so

$$k_s = \$2 / \$50 + 6\% = 10\%$$

Sample Problem 5: Cost of Common Stock

Assume the same information as in problem 4 but if new stock is sold, flotation costs are expected to be 10% of the current market price of the stock.

Solution to Sample Problem 5

With flotation costs, the cost of common stock equity rises because, although the firm will pay out the same amount in dividends, it receives a lesser amount for the stock. The constant-growth model must be adjusted to account for the net price of $45 ($50 x (1 – 0.10)) that new shares of stock would bring into the firm.

$$k_s = D_1 / P_n + g$$

so

$$k_s = \$2 / \$45 + 6\% = 10.44\%$$

Sample Problem 6: Weighted Average Cost of Capital

Compute the weighted average cost of capital given a target capital structure of 30% debt, 10% preferred stock, and 60% common stock equity. The after-tax cost of debt is 8%, the cost of preferred stock is 12%, and the cost of common stock equity is 16%.

Solution to Sample Problem 6

$$WACC = 0.30(0.08) + 0.10(0.12) + 0.60(0.16) = 0.138 = 13.20\%$$

Sample Problem 7: Weighted Marginal Average Cost of Capital

Assume a target capital structure of 30% debt, 10% preferred stock, and 60% common stock equity. The after-tax cost of debt is 8%, but only $10 million can be raised at 8%. Beyond $10 million, the after-tax cost of debt rises to 11%. The cost of preferred stock is 12% and can be issued in unlimited amounts. The cost of common stock equity is 16%, but the firm only expects to have $15 million available from retained earnings. Any new common stock financing would cost 18%. Calculate the weighted marginal cost of capital schedule.

Solution to Sample Problem 7

This may seem to be a difficult problem because there are so many steps. However, if completed in a systematic fashion, the problem becomes less complex. First, determine the initial weighted average cost of capital. Second, find the break points where the costs of capital change. Third, compute the weighted average cost of capital at each break point. Finally, you can graph the results.

1. Compute the initial WACC.
   $WACC_1 = 0.30(0.08) + 0.10(0.12) + 0.60(0.16) = 0.138 = 13.20\%$

2. Determine the break points.
   Debt break point = $10 ÷ 0.3 = $33.33
   Retained earnings break point = $15 ÷ 0.6 = $25.00

3. Compute the WACCs after each break point.
   After retained earnings break point ($25)
   $WACC_2 = 0.30(0.08) + 0.10(0.12) + 0.60(0.18) = 0.138 = 14.40\%$

   After debt break point ($33.33)
   $WACC_3 = 0.30(0.11) + 0.10(0.12) + 0.60(0.18) = 0.138 = 15.30\%$

4. Therefore, for raising $0 to $25 million, the weighted average cost of capital is 13.20%, from $25 million to $33.33 million the cost is 14.40%, and beyond $33.33 million the cost is 15.30%. Graphically, the WMCC curve looks like the following:

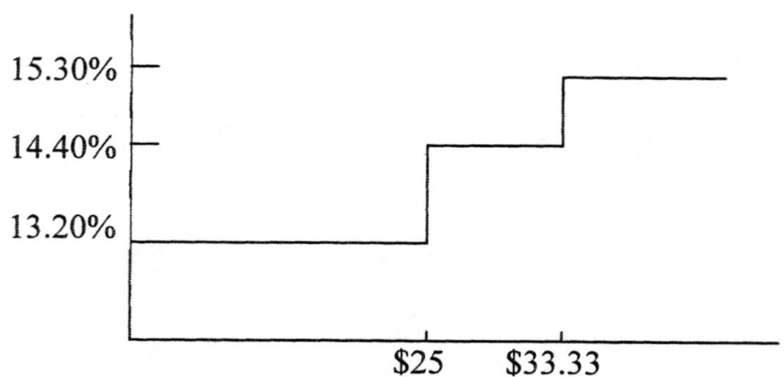

Total Dollars Invested

Study Tips

1. In calculating the costs of capital, recall there is only one method for finding the cost of debt (yield to maturity), one for finding the cost of preferred stock (zero-growth model), but more than one for finding the cost of common stock (constant-growth model and CAPM).

2. Be sure to use the after-tax cost of debt. Some problems may provide this number but most will require you to find this amount by taking the before-tax or nominal interest rate and multiplying by (1 – tax rate).

3. Calculating the weighted average cost of capital involves three steps: 1) finding the cost of each component of capital, 2) finding the relative weight of each component in the firm's capital structure, and 3) multiplying the costs by the weights.

4. In determining the marginal weighted average cost of capital, be careful in calculating and interpreting the breakpoints. The breakpoints represent the total amount of money raised before there is an increase in the cost of the particular cost of capital. For example, if debt occupies 20% of the capital structure and if there is $100,000 of debt available at one price, then a total of $500,000 can be raised before there will be an increase in the marginal cost of capital. The debt ($100,000) represents 20% of the total with other sources of financing (preferred and common stock) comprising the remaining 80% ($400,0000).

Sample Exam

True/False

T F 1. The component costs of capital are market-determined variables in as much as they are based on investors' required returns.

T F 2. The *before-tax* cost of debt, which is lower than the *after-tax* cost, is used as the component cost of debt for purposes of developing the firm's WACC.

T F 3. The cost of issuing preferred stock by a corporation must be adjusted to an after-tax figure because of the 70 percent dividend exclusion provision for corporations holding other corporations' preferred stock.

T F 4. The cost of common stock is the rate of return stockholders require on the firm's common stock.

T F 5. Funds acquired by the firm through retaining earnings have no cost because there are no dividend or interest payments associated with them, but capital raised by selling new stock or bonds does have a cost.

T F 6. The cost of capital should reflect the average cost of the various sources of long-term funds a firm uses to support its assets.

T F 7. The firm's cost of external equity capital is the same as the required rate of return on the firm's outstanding common stock.

T F 8. A break point will occur in the MCC schedule whenever the cost of one of the capital components rises.

T F 9. The target capital structure is the desired optimal mix of debt and equity financing that most firms attempt to achieve and maintain.

T F 10. The cost of capital can be thought of as the rate of return required by the market suppliers of capital in order to attract their funds to the firm.

T F 11. The cost of preferred stock is typically higher than the cost of long-term debt (bonds) because the cost of long-term debt (interest) is tax deductible.

T F 12. The cost of common stock equity may be measured using either the constant growth valuation model or the capital asset pricing model.

T F 13. The weighted marginal cost of capital schedule is a graph that relates the firm's weighted average cost of capital to the level of total new financing.

T F 14. While the return will increase with the acceptance of more projects, the weighted marginal cost of capital will increase because greater amounts of financing will be required.

T F 15. According to the firm's owner wealth maximization goal, the firm should accept projects up to the point where the marginal return on its investment is equal to its weighted marginal cost of capital.

Multiple Choice

1. Which of the following is *not* considered a capital component for calculating the weighted average cost of capital as it applies to capital budgeting?
   a. Long-term debt.
   b. Common stock.
   c. Short-term debt used to finance seasonal current assets.
   d. Preferred stock.

2. The ______ is the rate of return required by the market suppliers of capital in order to attract their funds to the firm.
   a. yield to maturity
   b. internal rate of return
   c. cost of capital
   d. gross profit margin

3. The firm's optimal mix of debt and equity is called its
   a. optimal ratio.
   b. target capital structure.
   c. maximum wealth.
   d. maximum book value.

4. The before-tax cost of debt for a firm that has a 40 percent marginal tax rate is 12 percent. The after-tax cost of debt is
   a. 4.8 percent.
   b. 6.0 percent.
   c. 7.2 percent.
   d. 12 percent.

5. When determining the after-tax cost of a bond, the face value of the issue must be adjusted to the net proceeds amounts by considering
   a. the risk.
   b. the flotation costs.
   c. the approximate returns.
   d. the taxes.

6. A firm has common stock with a market price of $25 per share and an expected dividend of $2 per share at the end of the coming year. The growth rate in dividends has been 5 percent. The cost of the firm's common stock equity is
   a. 5 percent.
   b. 8 percent.
   c. 10 percent.
   d. 13 percent.

7. The approximate before-tax cost of debt for a 10-year, 8 percent, $1,000 par value bond selling at $1,150 is
   a. 6 percent.
   b. 8.3 percent.
   c. 8.8 percent.
   d. 9 percent.

8. Debt is generally the least expensive source of capital. This is primarily due to
   a. fixed interest payments.
   b. its position in the priority of claims on assets and earnings in the event of liquidation.
   c. the tax deductibility of interest payments.
   d. the secured nature of a debt obligation.

9. A firm has determined it can issue preferred stock at $115 per share par value. The stock will pay a $12 annual dividend. The cost of issuing and selling the stock is $3 per share. The cost of the preferred stock is
   a. 6.4 percent.
   b. 10.4 percent.
   c. 10.7 percent.
   d. 12 percent.

10. The cost of new common stock financing is higher than the cost of retained earnings due to
    a. flotation costs and underpricing.
    b. flotation costs and overpricing.
    c. flotation costs and commission costs.
    d. commission costs and overpricing.

11. The constant growth valuation model (the Gordon model) is based on the premise that the value of a share of common stock is
    a. the sum of the dividends and expected capital appreciation.
    b. determined based on an industry standard P/E multiple.
    c. determined by using a measure of relative risk called beta.
    d. equal to the present value of all expected future dividends.

12. A firm has a beta of 1.2. The market return equals 14 percent and the risk-free rate of return equals 6 percent. The estimated cost of common stock equity is
    a. 6 percent.
    b. 7.2 percent.
    c. 14 percent.
    d. 15.6 percent.

13. Since retained earnings are viewed as a fully subscribed issue of additional common stock, the cost of retained earnings is
    a. less than the cost of new common stock equity.
    b. equal to the cost of new common stock equity.
    c. greater than the cost of new common stock equity.
    d. not related to the cost of new common stock equity.

14. Generally, the order of cost, from the least expensive to the most expensive, for long-term capital of a corporation is
    a. new common stock, retained earnings, preferred stock, long-term debt.
    b. common stock, preferred stock, long-term debt, short-term debt.
    c. preferred stock, retained earnings, common stock, new common stock.
    d. long-term debt, preferred stock, retained earnings, new common stock.

15. When discussing weighing schemes for calculating the weighted average cost of capital, the preferences can be stated as
    a. market value weights are preferred over book value weights and target weights are preferred over historic weights.
    b. book value weights are preferred over market value weights and target weights are preferred over historic weights.
    c. book value weights are preferred over market value weights and historic weights are preferred over target weights.
    d. market value weights are preferred over book value weights and historic weights are preferred over target weights.

16. The ______ is the level of total financing at which the cost of one of the financing components rises.
    a. weighted average cost of capital
    b. weighted marginal cost of capital
    c. target capital structure
    d. breaking point

17. As a source of financing, once retained earnings have been exhausted, the weighted average cost of capital will
    a. increase.
    b. remain the same.
    c. decrease.
    d. change in an undetermined direction.

18. The wealth-maximizing investment decision for a firm occurs when
    a. the cost of capital equals the return on the project.
    b. the weighted marginal cost of capital is less than the investment opportunity schedule.
    c. the weighted cost of capital exceeds the marginal cost of capital.
    d. the weighted marginal cost of capital equals the investment opportunity schedule.

19. A firm expects to have available $500,000 of earnings in the coming year that it will retain for reinvestment purposes. It has a target capital structure of 40% debt, 10% preferred stock, and 50% common stock equity. At what level of total new financing will retained earnings be exhausted?
    a. $500,000
    b. $800,000
    c. $1,000,000
    d. $1,500,000

20. In utilizing the investment opportunity schedule and the weighted marginal cost of capital, a capital project will be .
    a. acceptable as long as the marginal return equals or exceeds the average cost of capital over all levels of needed funding.
    b. unacceptable if the marginal return equals the weighted marginal cost of capital.
    c. unacceptable if the marginal return equals or exceeds the weighted marginal cost of capital.
    d. acceptable as long as the marginal return equals or exceeds the weighted marginal cost of capital.

Problem

Columbus Corporation is estimating its WACC. Its target capital structure is 20 percent debt, 20 percent preferred stock, and 60 percent common equity. Its bonds have a 12 percent coupon, paid semiannually, a current maturity of 20 years, and sell for $1,000. The firm could sell, at par, $100 preferred stock that pays a 12 percent annual dividend, but flotation costs of 5 percent would be incurred. Columbus' beta is 1.2, the risk-free rate is 10 percent, and the market risk premium is 5 percent. Columbus is a constant-growth firm that just paid a dividend of $2.00, sells for $27.00 per share, and has a growth rate of 8 percent. The firm's marginal tax rate is 40 percent.

a. What is Columbus' component cost of debt?

b. What is Columbus' cost of preferred stock?

c. What is Columbus' cost of common stock (k_s) using the CAPM approach?

d. What is Columbus' cost of common stock (k_s) using the constant-growth model approach?

e. What is Columbus' WACC?

Chapter 12 Answer Key

True/False

1. T
2. F
3. F
4. T
5. F
6. T
7. F
8. T
9. T
10. T
11. T
12. T
13. T
14. T
15. T

Multiple Choice

1. C
2. C
3. B
4. C
5. B
6. D
7. A
8. C
9. C
10. A
11. D
12. D
13. A
14. D
15. A
16. D
17. A
18. D
19. C
20. D

Problem

a. $k_i = 0.12(1 - 0.4) = 0.072 = 7.20\%$

b. $k_{ps} = 12/(100 - 5) = 12.63\%$

c. $k_s = 0.10 + 1.2\,(0.05) = 16.00\%$

d. $k_s = 2(1.08)/27 + 0.08 = 2.16/27 + 0.08 = 16.00\%$

e. $k_a = 0.20(7.20\%) + 0.20(12.63\%) + 0.60(16.00\%) = 13.57\%$

CAPITAL STRUCTURE AND DIVIDENDS

Chapter Summary

Chapter 13 describes the key aspects of a firm's capital structure and its dividend policy. The discussion of capital structure is centered on the EBIT-EPS approach to capital structure and some procedures for selecting the wealth-maximizing rather than EPS-maximizing capital structure. Dividend fundamentals include the residual theory of dividends and dividend irrelevance/relevance arguments, dividend policy, and forms of dividends other than cash.

LG 1 ***Describe the basic types of capital, external assessment of capital structure, capital structure of non-U.S. firms, and the optimal capital structure.*** Two basic types of capital–debt capital and equity capital–make up a firm's capital structure. Capital structure can be externally assessed by using the debt ratio and the times-interest-earned ratio. Non-U.S. companies tend to have much higher degrees of indebtedness than their U.S. counterparts do, primarily because U.S. capital markets are much better developed.

The zero-growth valuation model can be used to define the firm's value as its after-tax EBIT divided by its weighted average cost of capital (WACC). Assuming a constant EBIT, the value of the firm is maximized by minimizing its WACC. The optimal capital structure is the one that minimizes the WACC. Graphically, the firm's WACC exhibits a U-shape, whose minimum value defines the optimum capital structure that maximizes owner wealth.

LG 2 ***Discuss the EBIT-EPS approach to capital structure.*** The EBIT-EPS approach evaluates capital structures in light of the returns they provide the firm's owners and their degree of financial risk. Under the EBIT-EPS approach, the preferred capital structure is the one that is expected to provide maximum EPS over the firm's expected range of EBIT. Graphically, this approach reflects risk in terms of the financial breakeven point and the slope of the capital structure line. The major shortcoming of the EBIT-EPS analysis is that it concentrates on maximizing earnings rather than owners' wealth.

LG 3 ***Review the return and risk of alternative capital structures, their relationship to market value, and other important capital structure considerations.*** The best capital structure can be selected by using a valuation model to link return and risk factors. The preferred capital structure would be the one that results in the highest estimated share value, not the highest EPS. Other important nonquantitative factors, such as revenue stability, cash flow, contractual obligations, management preferences, control, external risk assessment, and timing, must also be considered when making capital structure decisions.

LG 4 ***Explain cash dividend payment procedures, dividend reinvestment plans, the residual theory of dividends, and the key arguments with regard to dividend irrelevance or relevance.*** The cash dividend decision is normally made by the board of directors, which establishes the record and payment dates. Generally, the larger the dividend charged to retained earnings and paid in cash, the greater the amount of financing that must be raised externally. Some firms offer dividend reinvestment plans that allow stockholders to acquire shares in lieu of cash dividends.

The residual theory suggests that dividends should be viewed as the earnings left after all acceptable investment opportunities have been undertaken. Miller and Modigliani argue in favor of dividend irrelevance, using a perfect world wherein information content and clientele effects exist. Gordon and Lintner advance the theory of dividend relevance, basing their argument on the uncertainty-reducing effects of dividends, supported by their bird-in-the-hand argument. The actions of financial managers and stockholders tend to support the belief that dividend policy does affect sock value.

LG 5 ***Understand the key factors involved in formulating a dividend policy and the three basic types of dividend policies.*** A firm's dividend policy should provide for sufficient financing and maximize the wealth of its owners. Dividend policy is affected by certain legal, contractual, and internal constraints, as well as growth prospects, owner considerations, and market considerations.

With a constraint-payout ratio dividend policy, the firm pays a fixed percentage of earnings to owners each period; dividends move up and down with earnings, and no dividend is paid when a loss occurs. Under a regular dividend policy, the firm pays a fixed-dollar dividend each period; it increases the amount of dividends only after a proven increase in earnings has occurred. The low-regular-and-extra dividend policy is similar to the regular dividend policy, except that it pays an "extra dividend" in periods when the firm's earnings are higher than normal. The regular and the low-regular-and-extra dividend policies are generally preferred because their stable patterns of dividends reduce uncertainty.

LG 6 ***Evaluate the key aspects of stock dividends, stock splits, and stock repurchases.*** The payment of stock dividends involves a shifting of funds between capital accounts rather than a use of funds. Shareholders receiving stock dividends receive nothing of value; the market value of their holdings, their proportion of ownership, and their share of the total earnings remain unchanged. However, the firm may use stock dividends to satisfy owners and retain its market value without having to use cash.

Stock splits are used to enhance trading activity of a firm's shares by lowering or raising the market price. A stock split merely involves accounting adjustments; it has no effect on the firm's cash or on its capital structure. Stock repurchases can be made in lieu of cash dividend payments to retire outstanding shares. They reduce the number of outstanding shares and thereby increase earnings per share and the market price per share. They also delay the tax burden of shareholders.

Chapter Outline

The Firm's Capital Structure

LG 1

Capital structure refers to the mix of long-term debt and equity maintained by the firm. The two basic type of capital are debt capital and equity capital.

Debt capital includes all long-term financing for the firm. It is cheaper than equity capital for three reasons because

1. Debt holders have a higher priority claim against the firm's earnings or assets.
2. Debt holders can exert stronger legal pressure.
3. Interest payments on debt are tax deductible.

Equity capital includes all long-term funds provided by the owner's. The two basic sources of equity capital are preferred stock and common stock equity, which includes the common stock and retained earnings. In order of cost, common stock is the most expensive form of equity, followed by retained earnings and preferred stock, respectively.

External Assessment of Capital Structure

Financial leverage results from the use of fixed-cost financing, such as debt and preferred stock, to magnify return and risk. Capital structure can be externally assessed by using the debt ratio, which measures the relative amount of debt, or financial leverage, used by the firm, with higher debt ratios indicating greater use of financial leverage. Another measure is the times interest earned (TIE) ratio, which measures the firm's ability to meet contractual payments associated with the debt. Smaller TIE ratios indicate higher use of financial leverage.

Non-U.S. companies tend to have much higher degrees of indebtedness than do their U.S. counterparts, primarily because U.S. capital markets are much better developed.

The Optimal Capital Structure

Although there are debates over whether it truly exists or not, most managers behave as if there were an optimal capital structure, a mixture of debt and equity that maximizes the value of the firm.

Different weighted average cost of capital (WACC) figures can be found by examining the relative costs of debt and equity capital at different levels of debt. The cost of debt remains relatively low due to its tax advantages, but increases as leverage increases to compensate lenders for increasing risk. The cost of equity also rises but more rapidly, because the shareholders will demand higher returns for the higher degree of financial risk they assume with increased leverage.

This is shown graphically below by assuming a zero-growth valuation model that defines the firm's value as its after-tax operating earnings (EBIT) divided by its weighted average cost of capital. Assuming EBIT is constant, the value of the firm is maximized by minimizing its WACC. The firm's WACC thus exhibits a U-shape whose minimum value defines the optimum capital structure that maximizes owner wealth.

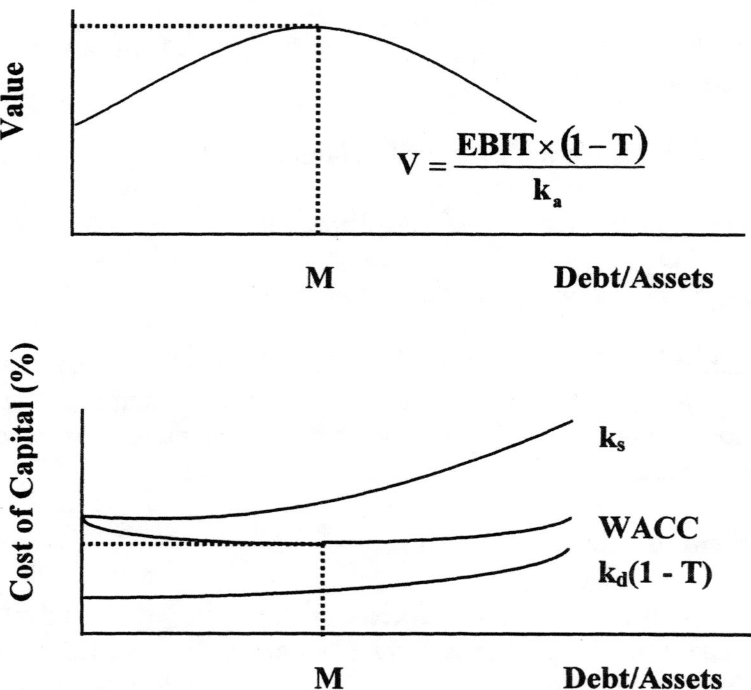

The EBIT-EPS Approach to Capital Structure

The EBIT-EPS approach evaluates capital structures in light of the returns they provide the firm's owners and their degree of financial risk. Under the EBIT-EPS approach, the preferred capital structure is the one that is expected to provide maximum EPS over the firm's expected range of EBIT.

Graphically, the EBIT-EPS approach reveals that over certain ranges of expected EBIT, an optimal capital structure exists that maximizes EPS. The graph reflects risk in terms of the financial breakeven point and the slope of the capital structure line. The steeper the slope, the greater the financial risk of that capital structure that is caused by increased leverage.

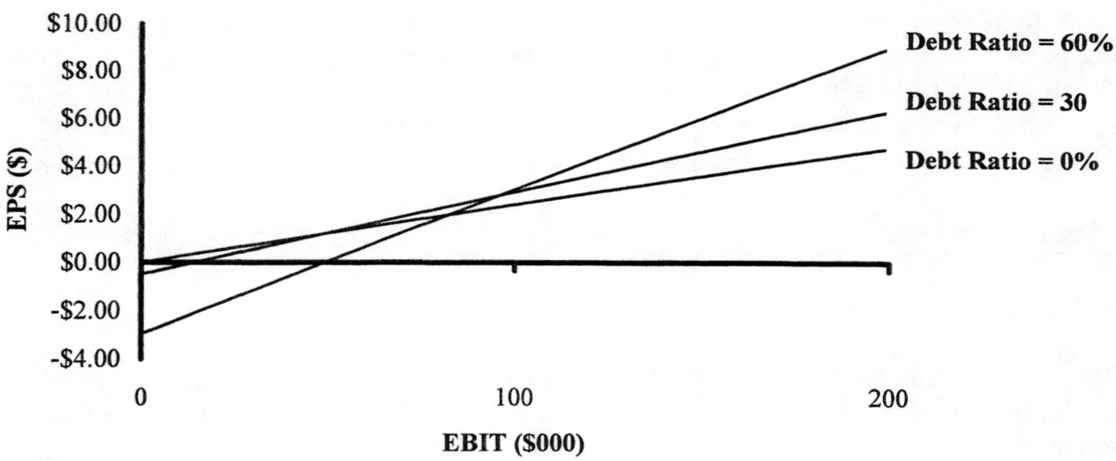

The major shortcoming of the EBIT-EPS analysis is that it concentrates on maximizing earnings rather than owners' wealth. There may be a positive relationship between these two objectives, but the EBIT-EPS approach ignores risk, which plays a major role in determining owner's wealth.

Choosing the Optimal Capital Structure

The best capital structure can be selected by using a valuation model to link return and risk factors. The preferred capital structure would be the one that results in the highest estimated share value, not the highest EPS.

One approach for linking the return and risk associated with alternative capital structures is to estimate the beta for each alternative capital structure and use the CAPM framework to calculate the required return, k_s. A second approach involves linking the financial risk associated with each capital structure alternative directly to the required return. For example, the required returns could be estimated for different levels of risk as measured by the coefficient of variation for EPS.

Other important nonquantitative factors, such as revenue stability, cash flow, contractual obligations, management preferences, control, external risk assessment, and timing, must also be considered when making capital structure decisions.

Dividend Fundamentals

Because retained earnings–earnings that are not distributed as dividends–are a form of internal financing, the dividend decision can affect the firm's external financing requirements. Generally, the larger the dividend charged to retained earnings and paid in cash, the greater the amount of financing that must be raised externally.

The cash dividend decision is normally made by the board of directors, which establishes the record and payment dates. Every person whose name is recorded as a shareholder on the specified date of record receives the declared dividend at a specified date, usually a few weeks after the record date. Due to bookkeeping delays when stock is traded, the stock begins selling without the right to the dividend (or ex-dividend) two business days prior to the date of record.

Declaration Date	Ex-date	Record date	Payment date
June 7	June 28	July 1	August 1

As an alternative to cash dividends, some firms offer dividend reinvestment plans (DRPs) that allow stockholders to acquire additional shares, even fractional or part shares, at little or no transaction costs.

Residual Theory of Dividends

The residual theory of dividends suggests that dividends should be viewed as the earnings left after all acceptable investment opportunities have been undertaken. This implies that as long as a firm has additional investment opportunities requiring financing, a firm should not pay out any dividends. This view of dividends suggests that the required return of investors, k_s, is not influenced by the firm's dividend policy, which in turn suggests that dividend policy is irrelevant.

Dividend Irrelevance

Dividend irrelevance is argued by Miller and Modigliani (M & M) using a perfect world (certainty, no taxes, no transaction costs, and no other market imperfections) in which a firm's value is based solely on the earning power and risk of its assets and in which it does not matter how the earnings are split between dividends and retained earnings.
M & M argue that dividends merely act as a signal (information) to investors regarding management expectations about future earnings. An increase in dividends is viewed as a positive signal, causing investors to bid up the share price. Similarly, a clientele effect may exist in that investors in a firm are attracted to its dividend payment pattern, thus the shareholders receive the dividends they expect.

Dividend Relevance

On the other hand, Gordon and Lintner suggest that there is a relationship between dividend policy and firm value. Dividends are relevant because investors view current dividends as less risky than future dividends or capital gains. They argue that current dividend payments reduce investor uncertainty, causing investors to discount future earnings at a lower rate and thereby place a higher value of the firm's stock.

Although there is no conclusive evidence, the actions of financial managers and stockholders tend to support the belief that dividend policy does affect stock value.

Dividend Policy

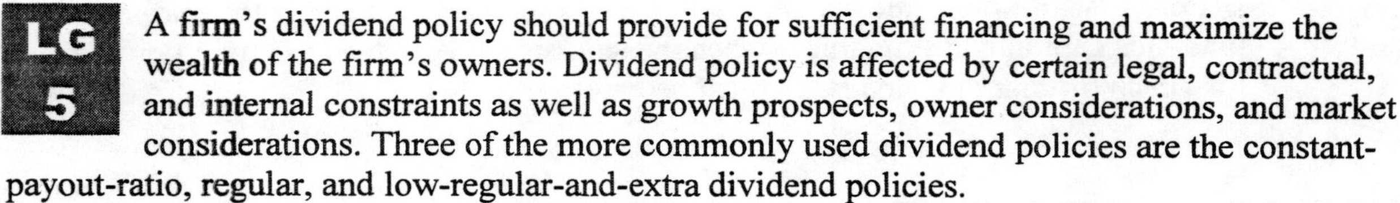

LG 5 A firm's dividend policy should provide for sufficient financing and maximize the wealth of the firm's owners. Dividend policy is affected by certain legal, contractual, and internal constraints as well as growth prospects, owner considerations, and market considerations. Three of the more commonly used dividend policies are the constant-payout-ratio, regular, and low-regular-and-extra dividend policies.

1. With a constraint-payout ratio dividend policy, the firm pays a fixed percentage of earnings to owners each period; dividends move up and down with earnings, and no dividend is paid when a loss occurs.

2. Under a regular dividend policy, the firm pays a fixed-dollar dividend each period; it increases the amount of dividends only after a proven increase in earnings has occurred.

3. The low-regular-and-extra dividend policy is similar to the regular dividend policy, except that it pays an "extra dividend" in periods when the firm's earnings are higher than normal.

The regular and the low-regular-and-extra dividend policies are generally preferred because their stable patterns of dividends reduce uncertainty.

Other Forms of Dividends

Stock dividends, stock splits, and stock repurchases can be viewed as alternatives to the payment of cash dividends to owners.

1. The payment of <u>stock dividends</u> is an accounting adjustment that involves a shifting of funds between capital accounts rather than a use of funds. Shareholders receiving stock dividends receive nothing of value; the market value of their holdings, their

proportion of ownership, and their share of the total earnings remain unchanged. However, the firm may use stock dividends to satisfy owners and retain its market value without having to use cash.

2. Although not a type of dividend, stock splits (or reverse splits) are used to enhance trading activity of a firm's shares by lowering or raising the market price of the stock by increasing or decreasing the number of shares belonging to each shareholder. Like stock dividends, a stock split merely involves accounting adjustments; it has no effect on either the firm's cash or its capital structure.

3. Stock repurchases can be made in lieu of cash dividend payments to retire outstanding shares. Stock repurchases are also used for acquisitions and to have shares available for employee stock option plans. They reduce the number of outstanding shares and thereby increase earnings per share and the market price per share. They also delay the tax burden of shareholders by increasing the market price (and thus capital gains treatment when the stock is sold) instead of paying dividends, for which ordinary income taxes must be paid.

Sample Problem Solutions

Sample Problem 1: Expansion Project

Calloway Industries is planning to raise $4 million of new capital. They currently have $2 million of 5% debt outstanding together with 200,000 shares of common stock. They can raise the additional funds by issuing 10% debt or by issuing additional 100,000 shares at $40 per share. The marginal tax rate is 40%. Assuming EBIT of both $1 million and $2 million, find the EBIT-EPS coordinates for each capital structure and graph the results. If EBIT were expected to be $1.5 million, which financing would be preferred?

Solution to Sample Problem 1

	Debt Financing		Equity Financing	
EBIT	$1,000,000	$2,000,000	$1,000,000	$2,000,000
Interest*	500,000	500,000	100,000	100,000
EBT	500,000	1,500,000	900,000	1,900,000
Taxes	200,000	600,000	360,000	760,000
Net income	$300,000	$900,000	$540,000	$1,140,000
Shares	200,000	200,000	300,000	300,000
EPS	$ 1.50	$ 4.50	$ 1.80	$ 3.80

*Interest currently is 5% x $2,000,000 = $100,000. If additional debt financing is used, total interest payments will be $100,000 + $4,000,000 x 10% = $500,000.

To present a graphical representation of the two differing capital structures, find the coordinates for EPS for capital structures at both $100,000 and $200,000, and any other points (for example, EBIT = $0) that may be relevant.

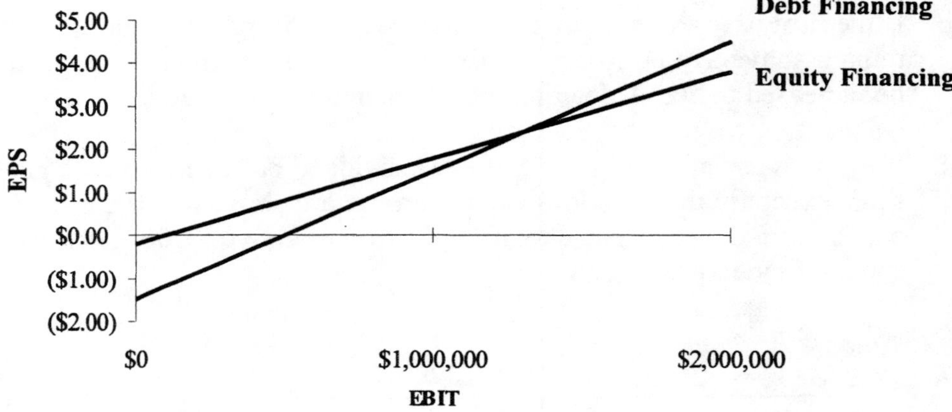

As the following table shows, financing the firm with additional debt will produce a higher level of EPS than would additional equity, at an EBIT level of $1,500,000.

	Debt	**Equity**
EBIT	$1,500,000	$1,500,000
Interest	500,000	100,000
EBT	1,000,000	1,400,000
Taxes	400,000	560,000
Net income	$600,000	$840,000
Shares	200,000	300,000
EPS	$ 3.00	$ 2.80

Sample Problem 2: Dividend Policy

Webb Corporation has had the following earnings per share over the 1990–1999 period:

Year	Earnings per share
1990	$1.00
1991	$0.80
1992	$0.00
1993	-$0.50
1994	$0.60
1995	$1.20
1996	$1.50
1997	$1.50
1998	$0.90
1999	$1.20

a. If the firm uses a constant-payout-ratio policy and has set the level at 50%, determine the annual dividend paid each year.

b. If the firm uses a regular dividend policy of $0.50 per share until per-share earnings remain above $1.000 for two consecutive periods at which time the dividend would be increased to $0.60, determine the annual dividend paid each year.

c. If the firm use a low-regular-and-extra dividend policy in which it pays $0.25 per share except in those periods when earnings are above $1.00 during which they pay out an extra dividend equal to 50% of earnings above $1.00, determine the total annual dividend paid each year.

Solution to Sample Problem 2

Year	EPS	(a)	(b)	(c)
1990	$1.00	$0.50	$0.50	$0.25
1991	$0.80	$0.40	$0.50	$0.25
1992	$0.00	$0.00	$0.50	$0.25
1993	-$0.50	$0.00	$0.50	$0.25
1994	$0.60	$0.30	$0.50	$0.25
1995	$1.20	$0.60	$0.50	$0.35
1996	$1.50	$0.75	$0.60	$0.50
1997	$1.50	$0.75	$0.60	$0.75
1998	$0.90	$0.45	$0.60	$0.25
1999	$1.20	$0.60	$0.60	$0.35

a. The dividend per share is simply 50% of the earnings per share, except in 1993 when no dividend is paid because the firm suffered a loss.

b. The dividend per share is $0.50 per share until earning rose above $1.00 per share for two years (in 1996) after which the dividend was increased to $0.60 per share.

c. The regular dividend per share is $0.25 per share. The extra dividend is 50% of all earning above $1.00 per share. For example, in 1995, the extra dividend was $0.10 (50% x ($1.20 - $1.00)) for a total dividend of $0.35.

Study Tips

1. Remember, the goal of optimizing a firm's capital structure is to maximize the value of the firm. However, in optimizing their capital structure, each firm will have a unique mix of debt and equity because each faces different bankruptcy and agency costs.

2. Be sure to understand the key advantages and disadvantages of the different dividend policies.

Sample Exam

True/False

T F 1. Whenever a firm goes into debt, it is using financial leverage.

T F 2. In a world with no taxes, Miller and Modigliani show that the capital structure of a firm does not affect the value of the firm. However, when taxes are considered, M & M show a positive relationship between debt and value.

T F 3. The optimal dividend policy for a firm strikes a balance between payment of current dividends and retention of earnings for future growth, and results in the maximization of stock price.

T F 4. Miller and Modigliani's dividend irrelevance theory says that dividend policy does not affect a firm's value but can affect its cost of capital.

T F 5. Generally, increases in leverage result in increased return and risk.

T F 6. If a firm adopts a residual dividend policy, dividends are determined as a residual item. Therefore, the better the firm's investment opportunities, the lower its dividend payments should be.

T F 7. A firm's capital structure is the mix of the debt and equity maintained by the firm.

T F 8. Effective capital structure decisions can lower the cost of capital, resulting in higher NPVs and more acceptable projects, thereby increasing the value of the firm.

T F 9. The cost of equity increases with increasing financial leverage in order to compensate the stockholders for the higher degree of financial risk.

T F 10. The EBIT-EPS approach to capital structure involves selecting the capital structure that maximizes earnings before interest and taxes (EBIT) over the expected range of earnings per share (EPS).

T F 11. Purchasers of a stock selling ex-dividend receive the current dividend.

T F 12. Because retained earnings are a form of internal financing, the dividend decision can significantly affect the firm's external financing requirements.

T F 13. The clientele effect is the argument that a firm attracts shareholders whose preferences with respect to the payment and stability of dividends corresponds to the payment pattern and stability of the firm itself.

T F 14. According to the bird-in-the-hand argument, current dividend payments reduce investor uncertainty and result in a higher value for the firm's stock.

T F 15. The stock repurchase can be viewed as a cash dividend.

Multiple Choice

1. Fixed financial charges include
   a. common stock dividends and bond interest expense.
   b. common stock dividends and preferred stock dividends.
   c. bond interest expense and preferred stock dividends.
   d. stock repurchase expense.

2. In the real world, we find that dividends
   a. usually exhibit greater stability than earnings.
   b. fluctuate more widely than earnings.
   c. are usually changed every year to reflect earnings changes.
   d. are usually set as a fixed percentage of earnings.

3. Gordon and Lintner believe that the required return on equity increases as the dividend payout ratio is decreased. Their argument is based on the assumption that

   a. investors are indifferent between dividends and capital gains.
   b. capital gains are taxed at a higher rate than dividends.
   c. investors view dividends as being less risky than potential future capital gains.
   d. investors value a dollar of expected capital gains more highly than a dollar of expected dividends because of the lower tax rate on capital gains.

4. Which of the following statements is most correct?
   a. If a company puts in place a 2-for-1 stock split, its stock price should roughly double.
   b. Share repurchases are taxed less favorably than dividends; this explains why firms are more likely to pay cash dividends than engage in stock repurchase plans.
   c. On average, a company's stock price tends to rise when it announces that it is initiating a share repurchase program.
   d. All of the statements are correct.

5. Through the effects of financial leverage, as EBIT increases, earnings per share
   a. increases.
   b. decreases.
   c. remains unchanged.
   d. changes in an undetermined direction.

6. The payment of cash dividends to corporate stockholders is decided by the
   a. management.
   b. stockholders.
   c. SEC.
   d. board of directors.

7. The information content of dividends refers to
   a. nonpayment of dividends by corporations.
   b. dividend changes as indicators of a firm's future.
   c. a stable and continuous dividend.
   d. a dividend paid as a percent of current earnings.

8. Gordon's "bird-in-the-hand" argument suggests that
   a. dividends are irrelevant.
   b. firms should have a 100 percent payout policy.
   c. shareholders are generally risk-averse and attach less risk to current dividends.
   d. the market value of the firm is unaffected by dividend policy.

9. ______ results from the use of fixed-cost assets or funds to magnify returns to the firm's owners.
   a. Long-term debt
   b. Equity
   c. Leverage
   d. Capital structure

10. The firm's ______ is the mix of long-term debt and equity utilized by the firm, which may significantly affect its value by affecting return and risk.
    a. dividend policy
    b. capital budget
    c. capital structure
    d. working capital

11. The long-term debt in a firm's capital structure is relatively inexpensive because
    a. the equity holders are the true owners of the firm.
    b. equity capital has a fixed return.
    c. creditors have a higher position in the priority of claims.
    d. dividend payments are tax-deductible.

12. The optimal capital structure is the one that balances
    a. return and risk factors in order to maximize profits.
    b. return and risk factors in order to maximize earnings per share.
    c. return and risk factors in order to maximize market value.
    d. return and risk factors in order to maximize dividends.

13. In theory, the firm should maintain financial leverage consistent with a capital structure that
    a. meets the industry standard.
    b. maximizes the earnings per share.
    c. maximizes the owner's wealth.
    d. maximizes dividends.

14. In the EBIT-EPS approach to capital structure, a constant level of EBIT is assumed
    a. to ease the calculations of owners' equity.
    b. to isolate the impact on returns of the financing costs associated with alternative capital structures.
    c. to emphasize the relationship between interest expenses and taxes.
    d. to concentrate on the effect of revenue and expense on capital structure decisions.

15. A stock split has ______ effect on the firm's capital structure.
    a. little
    b. no
    c. a measurable
    d. a detrimental

16. Which of the following is not a reason why debt capital is considered the least risky source of capital?
    a. It has a high priority claim against assets and earnings.
    b. It has a strong legal position.
    c. It is a low cost source of capital because interest payments are tax deductible.
    d. It does not normally have to be repaid at a specific future date.

17. Enhancement of shareholder value through stock repurchase is achieved by
    a. reducing the number of shares outstanding and thereby raising earnings per share.
    b. sending a positive signal to investors in the marketplace that management believes that the stock is undervalued.
    c. providing a temporary floor for the stock price that may have been declining.
    d. All of the above.

18. According to the traditional approach to capital structure, the value of the firm will be maximized when
    a. the financial leverage is maximized.
    b. the cost of debt is minimized.
    c. the weighted average cost of capital is minimized.
    d. the dividend payout is maximized.

19. Which of the following is NOT a key difference between debt and equity capital?
    a. Voice in management
    b. Maturity
    c. Tax treatment
    d. Effect on operating leverage

20. Modigliani and Miller suggest that the value of the firm is not affected by the firm's dividend policy, due to
    a. the relevance of dividends.
    b. the clientele effect.
    c. the informational content.
    d. the optimal capital structure.

Essay

1. What is the implication for a firm following a residual dividend policy if it finds more investment opportunities?

2. Describe the importance of operating at a firm's optimal capital structure.

Chapter 13 Answer Key

True/False

1. T
2. T
3. T
4. F
5. T
6. T
7. T
8. T
9. T
10. F
11. F
12. T
13. T
14. T
15. T

Multiple Choice

1. C
2. A
3. C
4. C
5. A
6. D
7. B
8. C
9. C
10. C
11. C
12. C
13. C
14. B
15. B
16. D
17. D
18. C
19. D
20. B

Essay

1. If a firm follows a residual dividend policy, it pays as dividends all funds remaining after financing wealth-generating projects. If more wealth-generating investment opportunities arise, there will be less funds remaining to be paid out as dividends.

2. A firm operating at its optimal capital structure minimizes its weighted average cost of capital. Because this is the rate used to discount cash flows, more capital expenditures will become profitable; that is, more capital expenditure projects will have net present values greater than zero. This increases the wealth of the shareholders. In fact, minimizing the weighted average cost of capital is synonymous to maximizing the value of the firm.

FINANCIAL PLANNING

Chapter Summary

Chapter 14 describes key aspects of financial planning. The financial planning process begins with long-term (strategic) planning that guides short-term (operating) plans and budgeting. Cash planning focuses primarily on preparation and evaluation of cash budgets. Profit planning, with particular emphasis on the preparation and interpretation of pro forma income statements and balance sheets, is also an important aspect of financial planning.

LG 1 ***Understand the financial planning process, including long-term (strategic) financial plans and short-term (operating) financial plans.*** The two key aspects of the financial planning process are cash planning and profit planning. Cash planning involves the cash budget or cash forecast. Profit planning relies on the pro forma income statement and balance sheet. Long-term (strategic) financial plans act as a guide for preparing short-term (operating) financial plans. Long-term plans tend to cover periods ranging from 2 to 10 years. Short-term plans most often cover a 1- to 2-year period.

LG 2 ***Discuss cash planning, sales forecasts, and the procedures for preparing the cash budget.*** The cash planning process uses the cash budget, based on a sales forecast, to estimate short-term cash surpluses and shortages. The sales forecast may be based on external or internal data or on a combination of the two. The cash budget is typically prepared for a 1-year period divided into months. It nets cash receipts and disbursements for each period to calculate net cash flow. Ending cash is estimated by adding beginning cash to the net cash flow. By subtracting the desired minimum cash balance from the ending cash, the financial manager can determine required total financing (typically notes payable) or the excess cash balance (typically held as marketable securities).

LG 3 ***Describe how the cash budget is evaluated and the procedures for coping with uncertainty in the cash budget.*** The cash budget indicates whether the firm is likely to have cash surpluses and allows the firm to arrange for adequate borrowing to meet forecasted cash shortages. To cope with uncertainty in the cash budget, sensitivity analysis (preparation of several cash budgets) or computer simulation can be used.

LG 4

Prepare a pro forma income statement using both the percent-of-sales method and a breakdown of costs and expenses into their fixed and variable components. A pro forma income statement can be developed by calculating past percentage relationships between certain cost and expense items and the firm's sales and then applying these percentages to forecast sales. Because this approach implies that all costs and expenses are variable, it tends to understate profits when sales are increasing and overstate profits when sales are decreasing. This problem can be avoided by breaking down costs and expenses into fixed and variable components. In this case, only the variable costs and expenses are forecast on a percent-of-sales basis.

LG 5

Explain the procedures used to develop a pro forma balance sheet using the judgmental approach and an external financing required figure. Under the judgmental approach, the values of certain balance sheet accounts are estimated, frequently based on their relationship to sales, and the firm's external financing is used as a balancing, or "plug," figure. A positive value for "external financing required" means that the firm must raise funds externally, by using debt and/or equity financing or by reducing dividends; a negative value indicates that funds are available for use in repaying debt, repurchasing stock, or increasing dividends.

LG 6

Cite the weaknesses of the simplified approaches to pro forma preparation and the common uses of pro forma statements. Simplified approaches for pro forma statement preparation, although popular, can be criticized for assuming that the firm's past condition is an accurate predictor of the future and that certain variables can be forced to taken on desired values. Pro forma statements are commonly used to forecast and analyze the firm's level of profitability and overall financial performance so that adjustments can be made to planned operations in order to achieve short-term financial goals.

Chapter Outline

The Financial Planning Process

Financial planning guides, coordinates, and controls the firm's actions to achieve its objectives. The two key aspects of the financial planning process are cash planning and profit planning. Cash planning involves the cash budget or cash forecast. Profit planning relies on the pro forma income statement and balance sheet.

The financial planning process begins with long-term, or strategic, financial plans that lay out a company's planned financial actions and the anticipated impact of those actions over periods ranging from two to ten years.

The strategic financial plans in turn guide the formulation of short-term, or operating, plans and budgets. These plans specify short-term financial actions and the anticipated impact of those actions over a period of one to two years. They center on key inputs, such as sales and other operational and financial forecasts, and key outputs, such as operating budgets, the cash budget, and pro forma financial statements.

Cash Planning: Cash Budgets

The cash planning process uses the cash budget, or cash forecast, based on a sales forecast, to estimate monthly and annual cash surpluses and shortages. The sales forecast may be based on internal data, typically generated by the firm's marketing department, on external economic data that affect the firm's sales, or a combination of the two.

It nets cash receipts (cash sales, collection of accounts receivable, etc.) and disbursements (cash purchases, payment of accounts payable and operating expenses, etc.) for each period to calculate net cash flow. Ending cash is estimated by adding beginning cash to the net cash flow. By subtracting the desired minimum cash balance from the ending cash, the financial manager can determine required total financing (typically notes payable) or the excess cash balance (typically held as marketable securities).

The general format for the cash budget is presented below:

	Jan.	Feb.	...	Nov.	Dec.
Cash receipts					
Less: Cash disbursements					
Net cash flow					
Add: Beginning cash					
Ending cash					
Less: Minimum cash balance					
Excess (short*) cash balance					

*A shortage indicates the extent to which external financing is necessary.

Evaluating the Cash Budget

The cash budget indicates whether a cash shortage or surplus is expected in each of the months covered by the forecast. Excess cash can be invested in marketable securities, while adequate borrowing can be arranged to meet forecasted cash shortages.

In evaluating the cash budget, a level of uncertainty does exits. There are two ways to cope with the uncertainty. The financial manager could first conduct sensitivity (what-if) analysis by preparing several cash budgets based on different assumptions. A more sophisticated approach is to conduct a computer simulation, in which the level of sales and other uncertain events are simulated, leading to a probability distribution of ending cash flows.

Profit Planning: Pro Forma Statements

Profit planning focuses on the preparation of pro forma (projected or forecasted) balance sheets and income statement. The two key inputs required for preparing pro forma statements are 1) the financial statements for the preceding year, and 2) the sales forecast for the coming year.

Pro Forma Income Statement

A pro forma income statement can be developed by calculating past percentage relationships between certain cost and expense items (such as cost of goods sold and operating expenses) and the firm's sales. These percentages are then applied to forecasted sales.

This approach implies that all costs and expenses are variable, so it tends to understate profits when sales are increasing and to overstate profits when sales are decreasing. This problem can be avoided by breaking down costs and expenses into fixed and variable components. In this case, only the variable costs and expenses are forecast on a percent-of-sales basis.

Pro Forma Balance Sheet

The most popular method for developing a pro forma balance sheet is the judgmental approach. This approach is based on estimating the value of certain balance sheet accounts, frequently on the basis of their relationship to sales, and calculating other accounts.

The firm's external financing is then used as a balancing, or "plug," figure. A positive value for "external financing required" means that the firm must raise funds externally using debt and/or equity financing, or by reducing dividends. A negative "external financing required" value indicates that funds are available for use in repaying debt, repurchasing stock, or increasing dividends.

Evaluation of Pro Forma Statements

The percent-of sales and judgmental approaches for preparing pro forma financial statements, although popular, have critical weaknesses. First, these simplified techniques assume that the firm's past condition is an accurate predictor of its future.

Second, they assume that certain variables, such as cash or other working capital amounts, can be forced to take on desired values. Despite the shortcomings, pro forma statements are commonly used to forecast and analyze the firm's level of profitability and overall financial performance so that adjustments can be made to planned operations in order to achieve short-term financial goals.

Sample Problem Solutions

Sample Problem 1: Cash Budget

Prepare a cash budget for the first quarter given the following data. Management has compiled its sales results for December 2000 and projected total and credit sales for the first three months of 2001 as follows:

Month	Dec. 2000	Jan. 2001	Feb. 2001	Mar. 2001
Total Sales	$900,000	$600,000	$700,000	$800,000
Credit Sales	$850,000	$560,000	$670,000	$780,000

Based on historical data, 60% of the credit sales are collected in the month the sales were made; the other 40% are collected the next month. Purchases are estimated to be 50% of next month's total sales, but are paid for in the month following the order. This means that the expenditure for inventory in each month is 50% of that month's sales. The beginning and target cash balance is $50,000. Other projected disbursements are as follows:

Month	Jan. 2001	Feb. 2001	Mar. 2001
Wages	$200,000	$250,000	$300,000
Rent	$30,000	$30,000	$30,000
Other Expenses	$10,000	$15,000	$20,000
Taxes	$80,000		
Dividends			$50,000
Capital Expenditures	$50,000	$100,000	

Solution to Sample Problem 1

CASH BUDGET			
	January 2001	February 2001	March 2001
SALES	$600,000	$700,000	$800,000
RECEIPTS			
Cash Sales	$40,000	$30,000	$20,000
Collections	676,000	626,000	736,000
Total Cash Receipts	$716,000	$656,000	$756,000
DISBURSEMENTS			
Payments of A/P	$300,000	$350,000	$400,000
Wages	200,000	250,000	300,000
Rent	30,000	30,000	30,000
Other Expenses	10,000	15,000	20,000
Taxes	80,000		
Dividends			50,000
Capital Expenditures	50,000	100,000	
Total Cash Disbursements	$670,000	$745,000	$800,000
Beginning cash	$50,000	$96,000	$7,000
Cash in (out)	$46,000	($89,000)	($44,000)
Ending Cash	$96,000	$7,000	($51,000)
Target Balance	$50,000	$50,000	$50,000
Excess Cash / (Financing Needed)	**$46,000**	**($43,000)**	**($101,000)**

40%(850,000) + 60%(560,000)

50%(600,000)

Total cash receipts – total expenditures

96,000 - 50,000 Excess (shortage) of cash

Sample Problem 2: Pro Forma Financial Statements

StarTrek Enterprises plans to use the percent-of-sales method to prepare its 2001 pro forma financial statements. Use the following operating information and the current income statement and balance sheet data to prepare the pro forma statements.

1. The firm has estimated sales for 2001 to be $7,000.
2. The firm expects to pay $300 in cash dividends in 2001.
3. All assets and current liabilities are will change as a percentage-of-sales except for taxes payable, which will equal 25% of the tax liability on the pro forma income statement.

StarTrek Enterprises Income Statement For Year Ended December 31, 2000	
Net Sales	$5,000
Less: Cost of Goods Sold	3,500
Gross Profit	$1,500
Less: Operating Expenses	800
Profits Before Taxes	$700
Less: Taxes (40%)	280
Net Profits After Taxes	$420
Less: Cash Dividend	200
Increase in Retained Earnings	$220

StarTrek Enterprises Balance Sheet December 31, 2000			
Assets		**Liabilities and Owners' Equity**	
Cash	$60	Accounts Payable	$600
Marketable Securities	100	Taxes Payable	100
Accounts Receivable	400	Other Current Liabilities	80
Inventory	800	Total Current Liabilities	$780
Total Current Assets	$1,360	Long-Term Debt	300
Net Fixed Assets	640	Common Stock	200
		Retained Earnings	720
Total Assets	$2,000	Total Liabilities and Equity	$2,000

Solution to Sample Problem 2

StarTrek Enterprises Pro Forma Income Statement For Year Ended December 31, 2001	
Net Sales	$7,000
Less: Cost of Goods Sold	4,900
Gross Profit	$2,100
Less: Operating Expenses	1,120
Profits Before Taxes	$980
Less: Taxes (40%)	392
Net Profits After Taxes	$588
Less: Cash Dividend	300
Increase in Retained Earnings	$288

3,500/5,000 = .70
.70 x 7,000 = 4,900

800/5,000 = .16
.16 x 7,000 = 1,120

Add this figure to 2000 retained earnings to find 2001 retained earnings.

StarTrek Enterprises
Pro Forma Balance Sheet
December 31, 2001

Assets		Liabilities and Owners' Equity	
Cash	$84	Accounts Payable	$840
Marketable Securities	140	Taxes Payable	98
Accounts Receivable	560	Other Current Liabilities	112
Inventory	1,120	Total Current Liabilities	$1,050
Total Current Assets	$1,904	Long-Term Debt	300
Net Fixed Assets	896	Common Stock	200
		Retained Earnings	1,008
		External Funds Required	242
Total Assets	$2,800	Total Liabilities and Equity	$2,800

60/5,000 = .012
.012 x 7,000 = 84
Each balance is found the same way.

392 x .25 = 98

Only assets and current liabilities are assumed to fluctuate with sales

720 + 288 = 1,008

Plug external funds required to balance total liabilities and equity to total assets

Study Tips

1. Be sure to understand both the mechanics of the percentage-of-sales forecasting method and its weaknesses. Despite the insights gained by the technique, assuming that past conditions are accurate indicators of future performance and that specific variables (for example, current assets) can be forced to take specific values may reduce the value of such a forecasting method.

2. Because of key uncertainties such as future sales, sensitivity analysis is an important tool for determining the right level of external financing. However, in the end, it is the financial manager's experience, intuition, and risk tolerance that dictates the type and extent of borrowing the firm employs.

Sample Exam

True/False

T F 1. A typical sales forecast, though concerned with future events, will usually be based on recent historical trends and events as well as on forecasts of economic prospects.

T F 2. One of the key steps in the development of pro forma financial statements is to identify those assets and liabilities that increase spontaneously with net income.

T F 3. The first, and most critical, step in constructing a set of pro forma financial statements is the sales forecast.

T F 4. The financial planning process begins with short-run, or operating, plans and budgets that in turn guide the formulation of long-run, or strategic, financial plans.

T F 5. The cash budget is a statement of the firm's planned inflows and outflows of cash that is used to estimate its long-term cash requirement.

T F 6. Cash planning involves the preparation of the firm's cash budget. Without adequate cash, regardless of the level of profits, any firm could fail.

T F 7. Cash budgets and pro forma statements are useful not only for internal financial planning but also are routinely required by the Internal Revenue Service (IRS).

T F 8. The cash budget gives the financial manager a clear view of the timing of the firm's expected profitability over a given period.

T F 9. An internal sales forecast can be based on the relationships that can be observed between the firm's sales and certain key economic indicators such as the gross domestic product, new housing starts, or disposable personal income.

T F 10. In cash budgeting, the impact of depreciation is reflected in the level of cash outflow represented by the tax payments.

T F 11. Required financing and excess cash are typically viewed as short term. Therefore, required financing may be represented by notes payable and excess cash is assumed invested in a liquid, interest-paying vehicle such as marketable securities.

T F 12. The required total financing figures in the cash budget refer to the monthly changes in borrowing.

T F 13. The financial manager may cope with uncertainty and make more intelligent short-term financial decisions by preparing several cash budgets, each based on differing assumptions.

T F 14. If the net cash flow is less than the minimum cash balance, financing is required.

T F 15. One basic weakness of the simplified pro-forma approaches lies in the assumption that the firm's past financial condition is an accurate indicator of its future.

Multiple Choice

1. The financial planning process begins with _____ financial plans that in turn guide the formation of _____ plans and budgets.
   a. short-run; long-run
   b. short-run; operating
   c. long-run; strategic
   d. long-run; short-run

2. The key output(s) of the short-run financial planning process are a(n)
   a. cash budget, pro forma income statement, and pro forma balance sheet.
   b. cash budget, sales forecast, and income statement.
   c. sales forecast and cash budget.
   d. income statement, balance sheet, and source and use statement.

3. Pro forma statements are used for
   a. cash budgeting.
   b. credit analysis.
   c. profit planning.
   d. leverage analysis.

4. Key inputs to short-term financial planning are
   a. operating budgets.
   b. economic forecasts.
   c. sales forecasts, and operating and financial data.
   d. leverage analysis.

5. The key input to any cash budget is
   a. the sales forecast.
   b. the production plan.
   c. the pro forma balance sheet.
   d. the current tax laws.

6. The _____ is a financial projection of the firm's short-term cash surpluses or shortages.
   a. operating financial plan
   b. cash budget
   c. strategic financial journal
   d. capital assets journal

7. _____ consider proposed fixed-asset outlays, research and development activities, marketing and product development actions, and both the mix and major sources of financing.
   a. Short-term financial plans
   b. Long-term financial plans
   c. Pro-forma statements
   d. Cash budgets

8. Once sales are forecasted, _____ must be generated to estimate a variety of operating costs.
   a. a production plan
   b. a cash budget
   c. an operating budget
   d. a pro forma statement

9. The firm's final sales forecast is usually a function of
   a. economic forecasts.
   b. a salesperson's estimates of demand.
   c. internal and external factors in combination.
   d. accounts receivable experience.

10. A firm has projected sales in May, June, and July of $100, $200, and $300, respectively. The firm makes 20 percent of sales for cash and collects the balance one month following the sale. The firm's total cash receipts in July
   a. are $220.
   b. are $200.
   c. are $180.
   d. cannot be determined with the information provided.

11. In the month of August, a firm had total cash receipts of $10,000, total cash disbursements of $8,000, depreciation expense of $1,000, a minimum cash balance of $3,000, and a beginning cash balance of $500. The excess cash balance, or required financing, for August is
   a. required total financing of $500.
   b. excess cash balance of $5,500.
   c. excess cash balance of $500.
   d. required total financing of $2,500.

12. The most common components of cash receipts are
    a. dividend income, cash sales, and accounts payable.
    b. cash sales, receivable collections, and miscellaneous receipts.
    c. accrual collections, cash sales, and interest income.
    d. retained earnings, dividends, and cash sales.

13. The most common cash disbursement are
    a. dividend income, cash sales, and accounts payable.
    b. cash purchases, dividends, and interest income.
    c. cash purchases, dividends, and accounts payable.
    d. cash sales, rent, and accounts payable.

14. One way a firm can reduce the amount of cash it needs in any one month is to
    a. slow down the payment of receivables.
    b. delay the payment of wages.
    c. accrue taxes.
    d. speed up payment of accounts payable.

15. In April, a firm had an ending cash balance of $35,000. In May, the firm had total cash receipts of $40,000 and total cash disbursements of $50,000. The minimum cash balance required by the firm is $25,000. At the end of May, the firm had
    a. an excess cash balance of $25,000.
    b. an excess cash balance of $0.
    c. required financing of $10,000.
    d. required financing of $25,000.

16. A weakness of the percent-of-sales method to preparing a pro forma income statement is
    a. the assumption that the values of certain accounts can be forced to take on desired levels.
    b. the assumption that the firm faces linear total revenue and total operating cost functions.
    c. the assumption that the firm's past financial condition is an accurate predictor of its future.
    d. ease of calculation and preparation.

17. The key inputs for preparing pro forma income statements using the simplified approaches are the
    a. sales forecast for the preceding year and financial statements for the coming year.
    b. sales forecast for the coming year and the cash budget for the preceding year.
    c. sales forecast for the coming year and financial statements for the preceding year.
    d. cash budget for the coming year and sales forecast for the preceding year.

18. Under the judgmental approach for developing a pro forma balance sheet, the "plug" figure required to bring the statement into balance may be called the
    a. cash balance.
    b. retained earnings.
    c. external financing required.
    d. accounts receivable.

19. A projected excess cash balance for the month may be
    a. financed with short-term securities.
    b. financed with long-term securities.
    c. invested in marketable securities.
    d. invested in long-term securities.

20. The weakness of the judgmental approach to preparing a pro forma balance sheet is
    a. the assumption that the values of certain accounts can be forced to take on desired levels.
    b. the assumption that the firm faces linear total revenue and total operating cost functions.
    c. the assumption that the firm's past financial condition is an accurate predictor of its future.
    d. ease of calculation and preparation.

Problem

Jo's Hair Salon had the following balance sheet last year:

Cash	$800	Accounts payable	$350
Accounts receivable	450	Accrued wages	150
Inventory	950	Notes payable	2,000
Net fixed assets	34,000	Mortgage	26,500
		Common stock	3,200
		Retained earnings	4,000
Total assets	$36,200	Total liabilities and equity	$36,200

One of Jo's major competitors has recently retired so she expects this will cause her sales to double from $10,000 to $20,000, increasing her net income to $1,000. She feels that she can handle the increase without adding any fixed assets.

Assuming she does not pay any dividends, how much, if any, external financing will Jo need?

Chapter 14 Answer Key

True/False		Multiple Choice			
1.	T	1.	D	16.	C
2.	F	2.	A	17.	C
3.	T	3.	C	18.	C
4.	F	4.	C	19.	C
5.	T	5.	A	20.	A
6.	T	6.	B		
7.	F	7.	B		
8.	F	8.	C		
9.	T	9.	C		
10.	T	10.	A		
11.	T	11.	A		
12.	F	12.	B		
13.	T	13.	C		
14.	T	14.	B		
15.	T	15.	B		

Problem

Cash	$1,600	Accounts payable	$700
Accounts receivable	900	Accrued wages	300
Inventory	1,900	Notes payable	2,000
Net fixed assets	34,000	Mortgage	26,500
		Common stock	3,200
		Retained earnings	5,000
		External funds	**700**
Total assets	$38,400	Total liabilities and equity	$38,400

On the asset side, cash, accounts receivable, and inventory double because of doubling of sales. On the liability side, accounts payable and accrued wages double. Retained earnings increased from $4,000 to $5,000 due to expected net income of $1,000. The difference ($700) is the external financing needed to support the increase in sales.

SHORT-TERM FINANCIAL MANAGEMENT

Chapter Summary

Chapter 15 focuses on the most important topics related to short-term financial management. The cash conversion cycle provides a framework for linking the key aspects of short-term financial management–inventory, receivables, and disbursements–to the goal of minimizing the firm's reliance on negotiated liabilities. The short-term financing of the firm is represented by its current liabilities, both spontaneous and negotiated.

LG 1

Describe the scope of short-term financial management and the cash conversion cycle. Short-term financial management is focused on managing each of the firm's current assets (cash, marketable securities, accounts receivable, and inventory) and current liabilities (accruals, accounts payable, and notes payable) in a manner that positively contributes to the firm's value. The cash conversion cycle represents the amount of time a firm's resources are tied up. It has three components: 1) the average age of inventory, 2) the average collection period, and 3) the average payment period. The length of the cash conversion cycle determines the amount of time resources are tied up in the firm's day-to-day operations.

LG 2

Explain the funding requirements of the cash conversion cycle and the strategies for minimizing negotiated liabilities. The firm's investment in short-term assets often consists of both permanent and seasonal funding requirements. Cyclical or seasonal firms have operating peaks and valleys that cause their level of operating assets to fluctuate and that therefore create seasonal funding requirements. These seasonal requirements can be financed using either a low-cost, high-risk aggressive financing strategy or a high-cost, low-risk conservative financing strategy. The firm's funding decision for its cash conversion cycle ultimately depends on management's disposition toward risk and the strength of its banking relationships. To minimize its reliance on negotiated liabilities, the financial manager seeks to 1) turn over inventory as quickly as possible, 2) collect accounts receivable as quickly as possible, 3) manage mail, processing, and clearing time, and 4) pay accounts payable as slowly as possible. Use of these strategies should minimize the cash conversion cycle.

Understand inventory management: differing views, common techniques, and international concerns. The viewpoints of marketing, manufacturing, and purchasing managers about the appropriate levels of inventory tend to cause higher inventories than those deemed appropriate by the financial manager. Four commonly used techniques for effectively managing inventory to keep its level low are: 1) the ABC system, 2) the economic order quantity (EOQ) model, 3) the materials requirement planning (MRP) system, and 4) the just-in-time (JIT) system. International inventory managers place greater emphasis on making sure that sufficient quantities of inventory are delivered where they are needed, and in the right condition, than on ordering the economically optimal quantities.

LG 4 ***Explain the key aspects of accounts receivable management, including credit selection and standards, credit terms, and credit monitoring.*** Credit selection and standards are concerned with applying techniques for determining which customers' creditworthiness is consistent with the firm's credit standards. Two popular credit selection techniques are the Five C's of Credit and credit scoring. Changes in credit standards can be evaluated mathematically by assessing the effects of a proposed change on profits on sales, the cost of accounts receivable investment, and bad-debt costs. Changes in credit terms, particularly the initiation of, or a change in, the cash discount, can be quantified in a way similar to that for changes in credit standards. Credit monitoring, the ongoing review of customer payment of accounts receivable, frequently involves use of 1) the average collection period and 2) the aging of accounts receivable. A number of popular collection techniques are used by firms.

LG 5 ***Review the management of receipts and disbursements, including float, speeding collections, slowing payments, cash concentration, and zero-balance accounts.*** Float is the amount of time that elapses between when a payment is mailed by the payer and when the payee has spendable funds. The components of float are mail time, processing time, and clearing time. Float occurs in both the average collection period and the average payment period. One technique for speeding up collections to reduce collection float is a lockbox system. A popular technique for slowing payment to increase payment float is controlled disbursing, which involves strategic use of mailing points and bank accounts. The goal for managing operating cash is to balance the opportunity cost of nonearning balances against the transaction cost of temporary investments. Firms commonly use depository transfer checks (DTCs), ACH transfers, and wire transfers to transfer lockbox receipts to the concentration banks quickly. Zero-balance accounts (ZBAs) can be used to eliminate nonearning cash balances in corporate checking accounts.

LG 6 ***Discuss current liability management, including spontaneous liabilities, unsecured short-term financing, and secured short-term financing.*** Spontaneous liabilities include accruals and accounts payable. The objective of accounts payable management is to pay accounts as slowly as possible without damaging the firm's credit rating. This is accomplished by paying on the last day of the credit period. If a supplier offers a cash discount, the firm in need of short-term funds must compare the cost of not availing itself of the discount to its least-cost alternative financing source in order to decide whether to decline the discount or take it and borrow elsewhere.

Unsecured short-term financing can be obtained from a bank at a rate tied to the prime rate of interest by using a single-payment note, a line of credit, or a revolving credit agreement. Large firms with high credit standing may issue commercial paper to obtain unsecured short-term financing. International transactions that expose the firm to exchange rate risk can be financed using a letter of credit, by borrowing in the local market, or through dollar-denominated loans from international banks.

Secured short-term financing requires collateral–typically accounts receivable or inventory–and is more costly because the collateral does not reduce the risk of default. Both pledging and factoring accounts receivable can be used to obtain needed short-term funds. Inventory can be used as short-term loan collateral under a floating lien, a trust receipt loan, or a warehouse receipt loan.

Chapter Outline

Scope of Short-Term Financial Management

Short-term financial management is focused on managing each of the firm's current assets (cash, marketable securities, accounts receivable, and inventory) and current liabilities (accruals, accounts payable, and notes payable) in a manner that positively contributes to the firm's value.

Operating Cycle and Cash Conversion Cycle

A firm's operating cycle is the time from the beginning of the production process to the point in time when cash is collected from the sale of the finished product. It is calculated as the sum of the average age of the inventory and the average collection period.

The cash conversion cycle represents the amount of time a firm's resources are tied up. It has three components: 1) the average age of inventory, 2) the average collection period, and 3) the average payment period. The length of the cash conversion cycle determines the amount of time resources are tied up in the firm's day-to-day operations.

Funding Requirements of the Cash Conversion Cycle

The firm's investment in short-term assets often consists of both permanent and seasonal funding requirements. Cyclical or seasonal firms have operating peaks and valleys that cause their level of operating assets to fluctuate and create seasonal funding requirements.

These seasonal requirements can be financed using either a low-cost, high-risk aggressive financing strategy or a high-cost, low-risk conservative financing strategy.

1. An aggressive financing strategy results in a firm financing its seasonal needs with short-term funds. Short-term funds are typically less expensive than long-term funds due to the typical upward-sloping yield curve. However, relying on short-term funds subjects the firm to the increased risks of refinancing at potentially higher interest rates as well as difficulties in obtaining financing quickly when the need arises.

2. A conservative financing strategy results in a firm financing all its operating needs with long-term funds. Long-term financing is typically more expensive but allows the firm to avoid the risks associated with the aggressive strategy.

The firm's funding decision for its cash conversion cycle ultimately depends on management's disposition toward risk and the strength of its banking relationships.

Although many of the short-term needs can be covered by spontaneous liabilities, such as accrued expenses and accounts payable, firms also often rely on negotiated liabilities (bank loans and other forms of debt) to finance the difference. To minimize its reliance on negotiated liabilities, the financial manager seeks to

1. turn over inventory as quickly as possible without stockouts that result in lost sales.

2. collect accounts receivable as quickly as possible without losing sales from high-pressure collection techniques.

3. manage mail, processing, and clearing time to reduce them when collecting payments from customers and to increase them when paying suppliers.

4. pay accounts payable as slowly as possible without damaging the firm's credit rating.

Inventory Management

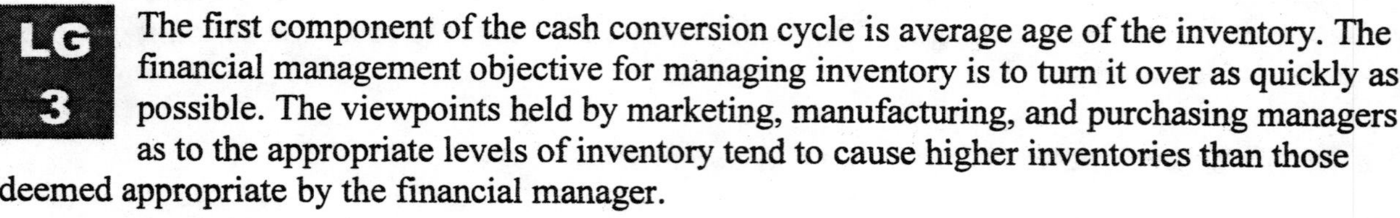

LG 3

The first component of the cash conversion cycle is average age of the inventory. The financial management objective for managing inventory is to turn it over as quickly as possible. The viewpoints held by marketing, manufacturing, and purchasing managers as to the appropriate levels of inventory tend to cause higher inventories than those deemed appropriate by the financial manager.

1. Marketing managers are concerned with sales so they prefer larger inventories of finished goods to avoid stockouts and lost sales.

2. Manufacturing managers are concerned with efficient production so they prefer larger in-process inventories to avoid production delays and lower per unit production costs.

3. Purchasing managers are concerned with buying the raw materials required in production as inexpensively as possible so they prefer larger ordering quantities to get quantity discounts.

Techniques for Managing Inventory

Four commonly used techniques for effectively managing inventory to keep its level low are the ABC system, the economic order quantity (EOQ) model, the materials requirement planning (MRP) system, and the just-in-time (JIT) system.

1. The ABC system divides inventory into three groups. The A group is made up of the most expensive inventory items which are actively controlled and managed, often verified on a daily basis. The B group consists of the next most expensive items controlled on a weekly or monthly basis. The C group consists of mainly inexpensive items monitored by less sophisticated techniques.

2. The EOQ model determines an inventory item's optimal order quantity that minimizes the total costs of ordering and carrying it in inventory. The formula for the EOQ is:

$$\mathbf{EOQ} = \sqrt{\frac{\mathbf{2 \times S \times O}}{\mathbf{C}}}$$

Where:

EOQ = order quantity in units
S = usage in units per period
O = order cost per order
C = carrying cost per unit per period

Once the firm has determined its economic order quantity, it must determine when to place orders. Assuming a constant usage rate for inventory, the reorder point can be determined by the following equation:

Reorder point = Days of lead time × Daily usage

Because of the difficulty of precisely forecasting lead times and daily usage rates, many firms maintain safety stocks, extra inventories on hand to meet greater than expected demand.

3. Materials requirement planning (MRP) uses EOQ concepts and computer simulation to compare production needs to available inventory balances. A MRP system determines when orders should be placed for various items (bill of materials) that go into making the finished product.

4. The objective of a just-in-time (JIT) system is to have material inputs arrive at exactly the time they are needed in the production process.

International Inventory Management

The complexities of exporting and importing inventory items makes international inventory management more complicated. Therefore, international inventory managers typically place greater emphasis on making sure that sufficient quantities of inventory are delivered where and when they are needed, and in the right condition than on ordering the economically optimal quantities.

Accounts Receivable Management

The second component of the cash conversion cycle is the average collection period. The goal is to collect accounts receivable as quickly as possible without losing sales from high-pressure collection techniques. There are three components to accomplishing this goal: credit selection and standards, credit terms, and credit monitoring.

Credit Selection and Standards

Credit selection and standards are concerned with applying techniques for determining which customers' creditworthiness is consistent with the firm's credit standards. Two popular credit selection techniques are 1) the Five C's of Credit and 2) credit scoring.

1. The Five C's of Credit provides a framework for analyzing credit. It consists of analyzing credit applications using five criteria.

   Character–the applicant's record of meeting past obligations.

   Capacity–the applicant's ability to repay the requested credit.

   Capital–the financial strength of the applicant as reflected by its equity position.

   Collateral–the amount of assets the applicant has available for use in securing the credit.

   Conditions–the current economic and business conditions and any unique circumstances surrounding a specific transaction.

2. Credit scoring is a procedure resulting in a score reflecting an applicant's overall credit strength, derived from weighting specific scores on key financial and credit characteristics. The resulting score is used to make accept or reject decisions for granting the applicant credit.

Changing Credit Standards

Firms occasionally examine changing their credit standards in order to improve returns or to create greater value for its owners. Changes in credit standards can be evaluated mathematically by comparing profits on sales, the cost of accounts receivable investment, and bad debt costs attributable to a proposed change.

1. Relaxing credit standards should increase sales profitability, but will also add costs by increasing the investment in accounts receivable and the amount of bad debt.

2. Tightening credit standards should decrease sales profitability, but will reduce the investment in accounts receivable and the amount of bad debts.

Determining the Values of Key Variables

1. Profit contribution from sales

   Since fixed costs are generally unaffected by changes in sales, the relevant costs are the variable costs. The profit contribution is the difference between the sales price per unit and its variable cost per unit multiplied by the increase (or decrease) in sales that result from the change in credit standards.

2. Cost of marginal investment in accounts receivable

   The marginal cost is the difference in the cost of carrying the receivables under the two different credit standards. This cost is found by calculating the difference in the average amount of investment in accounts receivable under each standard multiplied by the firm's cost of capital. The average investment in accounts receivable is calculated using the following formula:

$$\textbf{Average investment in accounts receivable} = \frac{\textbf{Total variable cost of annual sales}}{\textbf{Turnover of account receivable}}$$

   Where:
   Total variable cost of annual sales = Variable cost per unit x annual sales
   Turnover of accounts receivable = 360 ÷ average collection period

3. Cost of marginal bad debts

   The cost of marginal bad debts is found by taking the difference between the level of bad debts before and after the change in credit standards.

Making the Credit Standard Decision

To decide whether to relax (or tighten) its credit standards, the firm must compare the additional (reduced) profit contribution from sales to the increased (decreased) costs of the marginal investment in accounts receivable and marginal bad debts. If the additional profits are greater than the increased costs (or the decreased costs greater than the decreased profits), the credit standards should be changed.

Managing International Credit

Credit management is usually more difficult for firms that operate internationally because international operations typically expose a firm to exchange rate risk. There are also dangers and delays involved in shipping goods long distances and across international borders.

Credit Terms

Credit terms specify the repayment requirements that a firm places on its credit customers. Credit terms typically involve three items: a cash discount, the cash discount period, and the total credit period. They are often written in a type of shorthand, such as 2/10, net 30. In this example, the firm is offering a 2% cash discount to customers paying within 10 days; otherwise, the entire amount must be received within 30 days after the beginning of the credit period.

Changes in credit terms, particularly the initiation or change in the cash discount, can be assessed quantitatively in a way similar to that for changes in credit standards.

Credit Monitoring

Credit monitoring is an ongoing review of the firm's accounts receivable to determine if customers are paying according to the stated credit terms.

Two popular techniques for monitoring accounts receivable are the calculation of the average collection period and the creation of an aging schedule of accounts receivable.

1. The average collection period is comprised of the time from the sale until the customer makes a payment plus the time to receive, process, and collect (convert) the payment into cash. Calculating the average collection period allows the firm to determine if there is a general problem in collecting accounts receivable.

2. The aging schedule allows the firm to determine if any problems with collecting accounts receivable are attributable to specific accounts. The schedule breaks down the accounts receivable into the length of time (typically on a month-by-month basis) they have been outstanding.

The final component in credit monitoring is collecting overdue accounts. A number of different collection techniques are used by firms.

Management of Receipts and Disbursements

LG 5

As mentioned earlier, the second component of the cash conversion cycle is the average collection period, which is comprised of the time from the sale until the customer makes a payment plus the time to receive, process, and collect (convert) the payment into cash. The third component, the average payment period, also has two parts: the time from purchase of goods on account until the firm makes payment plus the time for the supplier to receive, process, and collect (convert) the payment into cash. Management of accounts receivable and accounts payable thus also involves managing the cash receipts and disbursements system.

Float

Float is the amount of time that elapses between when a payment is mailed by the payer and when the payee has spendable funds. It occurs in both the average collection period and the average payment period. The components of float are:

1. *Mail time*–the delay between when payment is placed in the main and when the payment is received.

2. *Processing time*–the delay between the receipt of the payment and its deposit into the firm's account.

3. *Clearing time*–the delay between deposit of the payment and when spendable funds become available to the firm.

Managing Float

Speeding up collections reduces customer collection float time and thus reduces the firm's average collection period. One technique for speeding up collections to reduce collection float is a **lockbox system**, a procedure that can reduce all three components of float. A lockbox system involves customers making payments to a nearby post office box that is regularly emptied, with the payments immediately processed and deposited.

A popular technique for slowing payment to increase payment float is **controlled disbursing**, which involves the strategic use of mailing points, to lengthen mail time, and bank accounts, to lengthen clearing time.

Managing Cash Balances

The goal for managing operating cash is to balance the opportunity cost of non-earning balances against the transaction cost of temporary investments.

Firms commonly use depository transfer checks (DTCs), automated clearinghouse (ACH) transfers, and wire transfers to quickly transfer lockbox receipts to the concentration banks. By concentrating cash collection efforts, firms can benefit from reduced transaction costs, improved tracking and internal control of its cash, and enhanced ability to implement more efficient payment strategies, such as zero-balance accounts (ZBAs).

ZBAs are disbursement accounts that always have an end-of-day balance of zero. They are used to eliminate non-earning cash balances in corporate checking accounts by allowing the firm to transfer any funds remaining in its disbursement account into an interest-bearing account.

Current Liability Management

The short-term financing of the firm is represented on its balance sheet by its current liabilities. The source of the financing may be **spontaneous** (arising in the normal course of the firm's operations) such as accruals and accounts payable or **negotiated** (non-spontaneous) forms of secured or unsecured debt.

Accounts Payable

Accounts payable are a major source of short-term financing and a key component of the cash conversion cycle. The objective of accounts payable management is to pay accounts as slowly as possible without damaging the firm's credit rating. This is accomplished by paying on the last day of the credit period.

If a supplier offers a cash discount, the firm incurs a cost by not taking the discount. The cost of giving up a cash discount can be found by using the following equation:

$$k_{discount} = \frac{d}{(1-d)} \times \frac{360}{(CP - DP)}$$

Where

$k_{discount}$	=	the annual interest cost of not taking a cash discount
d	=	percent discount (in decimal form)
CP	=	credit period
DP	=	cash discount period

A firm in need of short-term funds must compare the cost of the discount to its least-cost alternative financing cost in order to choose between not taking the discount and borrowing.

Unsecured Short-Term Financing

Unsecured short-term financing can be obtained from a bank at a rate typically tied to the prime rate of interest. The prime rate is the lowest rate of interest charged by banks on business loans to their most important business borrowers.

The major of type of loan made by banks to businesses is the short-term, self-liquidating loan in which the borrowed money is used to provide the mechanism through which the loan is repaid.

There are three basic ways a bank lends unsecured short-term funds to businesses:

1. A single-payment note is a short-term, one-time loan that is payable as a single amount at its maturity.

2. A line of credit is an agreement between the bank and the borrower specifying the amount of funds available to the firm over a given period of time. It is not a guaranteed loan but indicates the maximum amount the firm can borrow, assuming the bank has sufficient funds available to make the loan.

3. A revolving credit agreement is a guaranteed line of credit. Because the bank guarantees the availability of funds, it normally charges a commitment fee on the unused portion of the loan.

Commercial Paper

Commercial paper is a form of financing that consists of short-term, unsecured promissory notes issued by large firms with high credit standing. From the firm's perspective, the cost of commercial paper is normally much less expensive than borrowing from a bank.

International Loans

The key difference between international and domestic financing transactions is that payments are often made or received in a foreign currency and thus expose the firm to exchange rate risk. Specialized techniques for financing international trade transactions include:

1. Letters of credit, in which a bank guarantees payment of the transaction if the underlying agreements are met.

2. Borrowing in the local financial market to meet local financing needs.

3. Obtaining dollar-denominated loans (Eurocurrency loans) from international banks.

Secured short-term financing

Once a firm has exhausted its unsecured sources of short-term financing, it may be able to obtain additional short-term loans on a secured basis. Secured short-term financing has specific assets, typically accounts receivable or inventory, as collateral. However, because the collateral does not reduce the risk of default, the cost of the loans is not reduced.

To obtain needed short-term funds, accounts receivable may be pledged, used as collateral to secure the financing, factored, or sold at a discount to a financial institution.
Inventory can also be used as short-term loan collateral in one of three ways.

1. Floating lien–the lender has a claim against the entire inventory of the firm.

2. Trust receipt–the lender has a claim against specific inventory items, identifiable by a serial number.

3. Warehouse receipt–the lender obtains control of the pledged inventory collateral with the inventory stored by a designated agent on the lender's behalf.

Sample Problem Solutions

Sample Problem 1: Cash Conversion Cycle

Lupi Engines has an average age of inventory of 85 days, an average collection period of 58 days, and an average payment period of 50 days. Compute its cash conversion cycle.

Solution to Sample Problem 1

Cash conversion cycle = 85 + 58 – 50 = 93 days.

Sample Problem 2: EOQ Model

Early Bird Corporation sells 200,000 widgets per year with sales constant throughout the year. It can purchase and receive new widgets in 18 days. EBC has analyzed its inventory costs and has found that its order cost is $400 per order and the carrying cost is $10 per widget per year.

a. Calculate the EOQ for the firm's widgets.

b. Calculate the firm's reorder point in terms of widgets.

Solution to Sample Problem 2

a. To calculate the EOQ for the firm's widgets, the values of S = 200,000 units, O = $500, and C = $10 are substituted into the EOQ formula.

$$\mathbf{EOQ} = \sqrt{\frac{2 \times S \times O}{C}} = \sqrt{\frac{(2)(200{,}000)(400)}{10}} = \mathbf{4{,}000\ widgets}$$

b. The reorder point is calculated as the lead time times the daily usage of widgets.
18 days x 200,000/360 = 10,000 widgets.

Sample Problem 3: Sales Profitability from Credit Policy Change

Harrison Wheels sold 20,000 off-road bicycles last year, but based on proposed changes in credit terms, the firm anticipates that sales will increase by 5%, to 21,000 bicycles, in the coming year. The firm's total fixed cost is $400,000, its variable cost per bicycle is $120, and the sale price per bike is $200. The firm expects the costs and sales price to remain unchanged in the coming year.

a. Calculate the average cost per bike under both the present and the proposed plans.

b. Calculate the additional profit contribution from sales expected to result from implementation of the proposed plan.

Solution to Sample Problem 3

a. Present plan: Total cost = $400,000 + 20,000($120) = $2,800,000
Average cost = $2,800,000 ÷ 20,000 = $140

Proposed plan: Total cost = $400,000 + 21,000($120) = $2,920,000
Average cost = $2,920,000 ÷ 21,000 = $139.05

b. The additional profit can be calculated by multiplying the added units of sales by their per-unit profit contribution, which is found by subtracting the variable cost per unit from the sale price per unit.

Additional profit = (21,000 – 20,000) x ($200 - $120) = $80,000

Sample Problem 4: Marginal Cost of Accounts Receivable from Credit Policy Change

Assume that under both the present and the proposed plans in sample problem 3 that Harrison makes all sales on credit. Under the present plan, the average collection period is 30 days; under the proposed plan, it would be 60 days. The firm's required return on investment is 16%.

a. Calculate the firm's average investment in accounts receivable under both the present and the proposed plans.

b. Determine the firm's cost of the marginal investment in accounts receivable.

c. If bad debts are unaffected by the proposal, would you recommend the plan?

Solution to Sample Problem 4

a. The average investment in accounts receivable is equal to the total variable cost of annual sales divided by the annual turnover of accounts receivable.

Present: Total variable cost of sales = 20,000 units x \$120/unit = \$2,400,000
Turnover of accounts receivables = 360 ÷ 30 = 12
Average investment in A/R = 2,400,000 ÷ 12 = \$200,000

Proposed: Total variable cost of sales = 21,000 units x \$120/unit = \$2,520,000
Turnover of accounts receivables = 360 ÷ 60 = 6
Average investment in A/R = 2,520,000 ÷ 6 = \$420,000

b. The cost of the marginal investment is found by multiplying the marginal investment in accounts receivable by the firm's required return.

Marginal investment = \$420,000 - \$200,000 = \$220,000

Cost of marginal investment = \$220,000 x 16% = \$35,200

c. The proposal would be acceptable because the additional contribution to profits from the sales increase of \$80,000 exceeds the marginal cost of the accounts receivable of \$35,200.

Sample Problem 5: Marginal Cost of Bad Debts from Credit Policy Change

Assume that Harrison currently has bad debt expenses of 2% but expects bad debts of 3% under the proposed plan. Calculate the cost of the marginal bad debts associated with implementing the proposed plan. Would this additional information change the decisions reached in sample problem 4?

Solution to Sample Problem 5

The cost of the marginal bad debts is found by calculating the cost of bad debts under each plan and then taking the difference.

Proposed:	(.03)(21,000)(\$200) =	\$126,000
Present:	(.02)(20,000)(\$200) =	80,000
Marginal Cost		\$46,000

Adding the cost of marginal bad debts (\$46,000) to the cost of the marginal investment in accounts receivable (\$35,200) results in total costs to the proposed plan equaling \$81,200. The total costs now exceed the benefits of \$80,000 so the plan would no longer be acceptable.

Sample Problem 6: Cost of Giving Up Cash Discounts

Determine the cost of giving up the cash discount under each of the following credit terms from three different suppliers.

Supplier A: 2/10, net 30
Supplier B: 1/15, net 45
Supplier C: 3/10, net 60

If the firm can borrow from the bank at 15%, which, if any, of the cash discounts should you take?

Solution to Sample Problem 6

The formula to calculate the cost of each alternative is given as

$$k_{discount} = \frac{d}{(1-d)} \times \frac{360}{(CP-DP)}$$

Supplier A: (.02/.98) x (360/(30-10)) = 36.37%
Supplier B: (.01/.99) x (360/(45-15)) = 12.12%
Supplier C: (.03/.97) x (360/(60-10)) = 22.27%

The cost of giving up the cash discounts from Suppliers A and C exceeds the cost of borrowing from the bank so, if necessary, the firm should borrow from the bank to pay Suppliers A and C to take advantage of the discounts. You should not borrow from the bank to take advantage of the cash discounts from Supplier B because the cost of borrowing (15%) exceeds the benefits (12.12%) of taking the discount.

Study Tips

1. Short-term financial management is one of the financial manager's most important and time-consuming activities. You should not underestimate its importance.

2. Remember that there is a trade-off between the profitability and the risk associated with different short-term financial management strategies.

3. The decision to give up the cash discount should be the result of an analysis of the cost of not taking the discount relative to the cost of borrowing short-term funds to make the payment.

4. Cash management techniques exist to take advantage of float and certain imperfections in the collections and payment system. Cash needs can be reduced by speeding up collections and slowing down disbursements.

5. Inventory and accounts receivable often involve large investments of a firm's resources and therefore require careful management attention to minimize the size of that investment.

6. Credit policies should be evaluated by estimating the effects of changing credit standards or practices on the key variables of sales, average investment in accounts receivable, and bad debt expense.

7. Do not overlook the affect changing levels of sales have on the cost of those sales. Increases in sales lead to increases in the cost of goods sold; decreases in sales lead to decrease in the cost of goods sold.

Sample Exam

True/False

T F 1. Determination of a firm's investment in current assets and how that investment is financed are elements of working capital policy.

T F 2. For a firm that makes heavy use of float, being able to forecast its collections and disbursement check clearings is essential.

T F 3. Lockbox arrangements are one way for a firm to speed up its collection of payments from customers.

T F 4. The average accounts receivables balance is determined jointly by the volume of credit sales and the average collection period.

T F 5. The central goal of inventory management is to provide sufficient incentives to ensure that the firm never suffers a stockout (i.e., runs out of an inventory item).

T F 6. Accruals represent a source of "free" financing in the sense that no explicit interest is paid on these funds.

T F 7. The principal goal of most inventory management systems is to balance the costs of ordering, shipping, and receiving goods with the cost of carrying those goods, while simultaneously meeting the firm's policy with respect to avoiding running short of stock and disrupting production schedules.

T F 8. When deciding whether or not to take a trade discount, the cost of borrowing funds should be compared to the cost of trade credit to determine if the cash discount should be taken.

T F 9. Trade credit and accrual accounts are always costless sources of spontaneous financing for the firm.

T F 10. Short-term financing may be riskier than long-term financing because during periods of tight credit, the firm may not be able to rollover (renew) its debt.

T F 11. A line of credit and a revolving credit agreement are similar except that a line of credit creates a legal obligation for the bank.

T F 12. Factoring involves the outright sale of accounts receivable.

T F 13. The economic order quantity (EOQ) is that order quantity which results in the minimum ordering cost and the minimum carrying cost; that is, the EOQ minimizes both of these cost components.

T F 14. The aggressive strategy operates with minimum net working capital since only the permanent portion of the firm's current assets is being financed with long-term funds.

T F 15. The risk to a U.S. importer with foreign-currency-denominated accounts payable is that the dollar will depreciate.

Multiple Choice

1. A lockbox plan is
   a. a method for safe-keeping of marketable securities.
   b. used to identify inventory safety stocks.
   c. a system for slowing down the collection of checks written by a firm.
   d. a system for speeding up a firm's collection of checks received.

2. Inventory financing can take the form of a
   a. blanket lien.
   b. trust receipt.
   c. warehouse receipt.
   d. All of the above.

3. If Hot Tubs Inc. had sales of $2 million per year (all credit) and its average collection period was equal to 35 days, what was its average amount of accounts receivable outstanding (assume a 360-day year)?
   a. $194,444
   b. $57,143
   c. $5,556
   d. $97,222

4. Firms generally choose to finance temporary assets with short-term debt because
   a. matching the maturities of assets and liabilities reduces risk.
   b. short-term interest rates have traditionally been more stable than long-term interest rates.
   c. a firm that borrows heavily long-term is more apt to be unable to repay the debt than the firm that borrows heavily short-term is.
   d. sales remain constant over the year, and financing requirements also remain constant.

5. Calculate the economic ordering quantity given the following information:

Sales	= 15,000 units per year
Sales price	= $10.00 per unit
Purchase price	= $5.00
Carrying cost	= $1.25 per unit
Fixed cost per order	= $1,000

   a. 3,464 units
   b. 4,899 units
   c. 346 units
   d. 490 units

6. Which of the following is not a basic strategy for managing a firm's cash?
   a. Paying accounts payable as late as possible (without damaging the firm's credit rating)
   b. Turning over inventory as quickly as possible, while avoiding stockouts
   c. Operating in a fashion that requires maximum cash
   d. Collecting accounts receivable as quickly as possible (without damaging customer rapport)

7. The ______ of a firm is the amount of time that elapses from the point when the firm makes an outlay to purchase raw materials to the point when cash is collected from the sale of the finished good.
   a. cash turnover
   b. cash conversion cycle
   c. average age of inventory
   d. average collection period

8. In working capital management, risk is measured by the probability that a firm will become
   a. liquid.
   b. technically insolvent.
   c. unable to meet long-term obligations.
   d. less profitable.

9. The purpose of managing current assets and current liabilities is to
   a. achieve as low a level of current assets as possible.
   b. achieve as low a level of current liabilities as possible.
   c. achieve a balance between profitability and risk that contributes to the firm's value.
   d. achieve as high a level of current liabilities as possible.

10. A decrease in the current liabilities to total assets ratio has the effects of ______ on profits and ______ on risk.
   a. an increase; an increase
   b. an increase; a decrease
   c. a decrease; a decrease
   d. a decrease; an increase

11. The aggressive financing strategy results in the firm financing its short-term needs with ______ funds and its long-term needs with ______ funds.
   a. long-term; short-term
   b. short-term; long-term
   c. permanent; seasonal
   d. seasonal; permanent

12. The conservative financing strategy results in financing all projected funds requirements with ______ funds and use of ______ funds in the event of an unexpected cash outflow.
   a. long-term; short-term
   b. short-term; long-term
   c. permanent; seasonal
   d. seasonal; permanent

13. A risk of the ______ financing strategy is unpredictable interest expense.
   a. aggressive
   b. conservative
   c. permanent
   d. seasonal

14. Accruals and accounts payable are ______ sources of short-term financing.
   a. negotiated, secured
   b. negotiated, unsecured
   c. spontaneous, secured
   d. spontaneous, unsecured

15. If the firm decides to take the cash discount that is offered on goods purchased on credit, the firm should
    a. pay as soon as possible.
    b. pay on the last day of the credit period.
    c. take the discount no matter when the firm actually pays.
    d. pay on the last day of the discount period.

16. A firm is offered credit terms of 2/10 net 45 by most of its suppliers but frequently does not have the cash available to take the discount. The firm has a credit line available at a local bank at an interest rate of 12 percent. The firm should
    a. give up the cash discount, financing the purchase with the line of credit.
    b. take the cash discount and pay on the 45th day after the date of sale.
    c. take the cash discount and pay on the first day of the cash discount period.
    d. take the cash discount and finance the purchase with the line of credit, the cheaper source of funds.

17. The cost of giving up a cash discount under the terms of sale 1/10 net 60 (assume a 360-day year) is
    a. 7.2 percent.
    b. 6.1 percent.
    c. 14.7 percent.
    d. 12.2 percent.

18. A letter written by a company's bank to the company's foreign supplier, stating that the bank will guarantee payment of an invoiced amount if all the underlying agreements are met, is called
    a. a letter of invoice.
    b. a letter of intent.
    c. a letter of credit.
    d. None of the above.

19. A ______ guarantees the borrower that a specified amount of funds will be available regardless of the tightness of money.
    a. revolving credit agreement
    b. line of credit
    c. short-term self-liquidating loan
    d. single payment note

20. _____ are the major source of unsecured short-term financing for business firms.
    a. Accounts receivable
    b. Accruals
    c. Notes payable
    d. Accounts payable

Problem

Gateway Corporation expects to have sales this year of $15 million under its current credit policy. The present terms are net 30; the average collection period is 60 days; and the bad debt loss percentage is 5 percent. In addition, Gateway's cost of capital is 15 percent, and its variable costs total 60 percent of sales. Since Gateway wants to improve its profitability, a proposal has been made to offer a 2 percent discount for payment within 10 days; that is, change the credit terms to 2/10, net 30. The consultants predict that sales would increase by $500,000, and that 50 percent of *all* customers would take the discount. The new average collection period would be 30 days, and the bad debt loss percentage on all sales would fall to 4 percent.

a. What would be the cost to Gateway of the discounts taken?

b. What would be the incremental bad debt losses if the change were made?

c. What would be the incremental cost of carrying receivables if the change were made?

d. What are the incremental pre-tax profits from this proposal?

Chapter 15 Answer Key

True/False

1. T
2. T
3. T
4. T
5. F
6. T
7. T
8. T
9. F
10. T
11. F
12. T
13. F
14. F
15. T

Multiple Choice

1. D
2. D
3. A
4. A
5. B
6. C
7. B
8. B
9. C
10. C
11. D
12. A
13. A
14. D
15. D
16. A
17. C
18. A
19. D
20. D

Problem

a. New policy: $15,500,000 x 50% x 2% discount		$155,000
Old policy:		0
Incremental cost		$155,000
b. New policy: $15,500,000 x 4% loss rate		$620,000
Old policy: $15,000,000 x 5% loss rate		750,000
Incremental gain		$130,000
c. New policy: $15,500,000/360 x 30 days x .60 x 15%		$116,250
Old policy: $15,000,000/360 x 60 days x .60 x 15%		225,000
Incremental gain		$108,750
d. Incremental Costs: Cash discounts		$155,000
Incremental Gains:		
Bad debts		130,000
Finance Accounts Receivable		108,750
Increase in sales	500,000	
Less: increase in cost of sales (60%)	300,000	200,000
Total incremental gains		$438,750
Incremental pre-tax profits ($438,750 - $155,000)		$283,750

Chapter 16

INVESTMENT INFORMATION AND TRANSACTIONS

Chapter Summary

Chapter 16 describes the type of information used by investors to make investments, how financial markets facilitate the investment transactions, and the types of transactions requested by investors.

LG 1 ***Review background material on investing.*** Investments are made by individual and institutional investors. The investment decisions made by investors will determine the annual return on investment portfolios and therefore, the accumulated value of those portfolios.

LG 2 ***Describe the economic, industry, global, and market information sources used to make investment decisions.*** Investors rely on information sources such as the Federal Reserve and Bloomberg to conduct economic analyses; Standard and Poor's, Moody's, and Value Line to conduct industry analyses; and the *International Financial Statistics* and international financial newspapers to conduct global analyses.

LG 3 ***Describe the firm-specific information sources used to make relevant investment decisions.*** For firm-specific information, investors rely on the annual report or other financial reports provided by the firm, as well as information provided by investment service companies such as Moody's, Standard and Poor's, and Value Line.

LG 4 ***Identify the main U.S. and foreign securities exchanges in the U.S. that facilitate the investing process.*** The main securities exchanges are the organized exchanges (including the New York Stock Exchange and the American Stock Exchange) and the over-the-counter exchange. Organized exchanges act as secondary markets for securities. The over-the-counter exchange facilitates trading of securities in the secondary market and of new issues in the primary market.

LG 5 ***Describe the types of securities transactions requested by investors, and explain how these transactions are accommodated by brokerage firms.*** Investors can place a market order, a limit order, or a stop order. A market order is executed at the prevailing market price. A limit order imposes a limit on the price at which investors are willing to buy or sell a stock. Stop orders are orders to execute a transaction when the stock price reaches a specified level. A buy stop order represents an order for the brokerage firm to buy a stock for the investor when the price reaches a specified level (above the prevailing price). Conversely, a sell stop order is an order for the brokerage firm to sell a stock when the price reaches a specified level (below the prevailing price).

Investors can also purchase stocks on margin, financing part of the investment with borrowed funds. Buying stocks on margin results in a higher potential return on investment, but it also results in higher risk. Investors can also make short sale transactions, in which they borrow a stock that they sell in the market. They hope to purchase that stock in the market in the future (when they will return the stock to the investor from whom it was borrowed) at a lower price than the price they paid for it. They consider short sale transactions for stocks that they expect will experience a decline in price.

Chapter Outline

Background on Investing

Investments are made by individual and institutional investors. Institutional investors include the portfolio managers of financial institutions, mutual funds, and pension funds, who invest funds on behalf of their employers or the clients they are serving.

The investment decisions made by investors will determine the return on their future wealth of their investment portfolios, and therefore will determine the future wealth of those portfolios. Decisions are made based on the same return and risk tradeoffs that face financial managers. Common investment decisions include:

1. How much to invest in securities.

2. How to allocate funds between different types of securities (such as stocks versus bonds).

3. Which specific securities to purchase as investments.

Such decisions are made based on several factors including the anticipated earnings of the investor, an understanding of how the securities market function, and thorough analysis of relevant economic and business information.

General Information Used to Make Investment Decisions

Information important for making investment decisions can be segmented according to whether the information pertains to economic conditions, industry conditions, global conditions, market conditions, or the financial condition of the issuer of the security.

To conduct economic analysis, investors rely on both governmental information sources such as the Federal Reserve and private firms such as Bloomberg. To conduct industry analysis, including industry ratios and forecasts, the private sector, such as Standard and Poor's, Moody's, and Value Line, is generally consulted. Sources of information to conduct global analysis include the *International Financial Statistics*, published by the International Monetary Fund, and international financial newspapers such as the *Financial Times*.

Firm-Specific Information

For firm-specific information, investors rely on information in the annual reports or other financial reports provided by the firm. Investors use the balance sheet to determine how the firm has obtained funds (liabilities and stockholders' equity) and how it has invested funds (assets). They use the income statement to determine the firm's flow of revenues and expenses. The statement of cash flow can be used as a base to estimate the firm's future cash flows. Other important sources of information, required by the Securities and Exchange Commission, include the firm's security prospectus, which contains detailed financial information about the firm, and disclosures of purchases and sales of the firm's financial managers and other insiders.

Investors also rely on information provided by investment service companies such as Value Line, Moody's, and Standard and Poor's. In addition, securities firms often employ analysts who may develop recommendations (buy, sell, or hold) about the securities.

Other important information may be found by carefully examining a firm's financial decisions and other activities.

1. Positive signals may include announcements about increases in dividends, higher-than-expected earnings levels, the firm being acquired by another firm, and repurchases of the firm's stock.

2. Negative signals include decreases or omissions of dividends, earnings lower than expected, the firm acquiring another firm (if investors believe it is paying too much for the acquisition) and new (secondary) stock offerings.

Securities Exchanges

The main organized securities exchanges are the New York Stock Exchange and the American Stock Exchange. In addition, there is an over-the-counter market, linked through the National Association of Securities Dealers Automated Quote (NASDAQ)

System, that serves as an intangible market for the purchase and sale of securities not listed on the organized exchanges and the primary market for selling all new public issues.

There are also many foreign securities exchanges where U.S. investors can purchase foreign stocks. U.S. investors can also invest in foreign stocks by purchasing American depository receipts (ADRs). ADRs are certificates representing shares of foreign stocks that trade on the OTC exchange. Increased availability of information about foreign securities and foreign market conditions are making foreign stock more attractive to U.S. investors.

Investor Transactions

To buy or sell stock, investors can request a market order, a limit order, or a stop order.

1. A market order is executed at the prevailing market price.
2. A limit order places a limit on the price at which investors are willing to buy or sell a stock.
3. Stop orders are orders to execute a transaction when the stock price reaches a specified level. For example, a buy stop order represents an order for the brokerage firm to buy a stock for the investor when the price reaches a specified level (above the prevailing price). Conversely, a sell stop order is an order for the brokerage firm to sell as stock when the price reaches a specified level (below the prevailing price).

Investing on Margin

Investors can also purchase stocks on margin, in which they finance part of the investment with borrowed funds. Buying stocks on margin results in a higher potential return on investment, but also results in higher risk. The following equation is used to find the total return from investing in stocks on margin:

$$R = \frac{SP - II + D - LP}{II}$$

Where:

R = the return from investing in a stock
SP = the proceeds from selling the stock at the end of the investment period
II = the initial investment necessary to make the investment at the beginning of the investment period.
D = the dividends received over the investment period.
LP = the loan payment made back to the broker after selling the stock at the end of the investment period.

Short Sales

Investors can also make short sale transactions, in which they borrow a stock that they sell in the market. They hope to purchase the stock in the market in the future (when they will provide the stock back to whom they borrowed it from) at a lower price than the price they paid for it. They consider short sale transactions for stocks that they expect will experience a decline in price. The risk of a short sale is the possibility that the stock price will increase and the investor will have to buy the stock at a price higher than that at which the stock was initially sold.

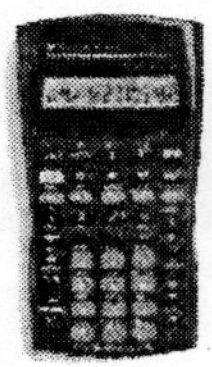

Sample Problem Solutions

Sample Problem 1: Buying Stock on Margin

Shares of ComDot.Com are currently $50 and you expect it to rise in the future. You purchase 100 shares on margin from your broker at a margin interest rate of 10%.

a. What would be your return if a ComDot.Com stock rose to $80 per share at the end of one year?

b. What would be your return if a ComDot.Com stock fell to $30 per share at the end of one year?

c. How would your results in (a) and (b) differ if you had not bought the stock on margin?

Solution to Sample Problem 1

The total return on the investment is equal to the proceeds earned from the investment after paying off any loans used to make the investment divided by the initial amount of funds invested by the investor. The equation to calculate the return is: (SP – II + D – LP) ÷ II.

a. If the stock rises to $80 per share,
SP = $80 x 100 = $8,000
II = ($50 x 100) x 50% = $2,500
D = $0
LP = $5,000 x 50% = $2,500 + 10% cost ($250) = $2,750

Return = ($8,000 - $2,500 + $0 - $2,750) ÷ $2,500 = 110%

b. If the stock falls to $30 per share,
   SP = $30 x 100 = $3,000
   II = $50 x 100 x 50% = $2,500
   D = $0
   LP = $5,000 x 50% = $2,500 + 10% cost ($250) = $2,750

   Return = ($3,000 - $2,500 + $0 - $2,750) ÷ $2,500 = -90%

c. If the stock had not been purchase on margin, the differences would be a higher initial investment (the full price of $5,000) and $0 loan proceeds.

   At a stock price of $80 per share,
   SP = $80 x 100 = $8,000
   II = $50 x 100 = $5,000
   D = $0
   LP = $0

   Return = ($8,000 - $5,000 + 0 - 0) ÷ $5,000 = 60%

   At a stock price of $30 per share,
   SP = $30 x 100 = $3,000
   II = $50 x 100 = $5,000
   D = $0
   LP = 0

   Return = ($3,000 - $5,000 + $0 - $0) ÷ $5,000 = -40%

   By purchasing the stock on margin, the potential returns from rising stock prices are magnified by using margin (110% versus 60%) but so are the potential risks from falling stock prices (-90% versus -40%).

Study Tips

1. Understand that investment decisions should be based on an analysis of all relevant information about the firm and there is a wide variety of sources for this information.

2. Although their titles are descriptive, be sure to know the difference between a market and a limit order.

Sample Exam

True/False

T F 1. Investment decisions should not be made based on the investor's current earnings or wealth.

T F 2. Even with access to the same information, investors make may make different investment decisions because they have different preferences for risk.

T F 3. Day traders are called that because their investment horizon is measured in days rather than years.

T F 4. The Federal Reserve banks provide a great deal of economic information useful for making investment decisions.

T F 5. Because little information is available on-line, it is difficult to get timely economic or market information.

T F 6. A good source of firm-specific information is its annual report.

T F 7. Value Line provides a great deal of firm-specific information.

T F 8. Any insider trading activity must be reported to the Securities and Exchange Commission.

T F 9. An announcement of increased dividends often leads to an increase in the price of a stock.

T F 10. Acquisitions of one firm by another are always viewed the same way. The value of the stock of both firms either increases or decreases by a similar percentage.

T F 11. The Nasdaq and the New York Stock Exchange have recently merged.

T F 12. American Depository Receipts (ADRs) are certificates representing shares of U.S. stocks traded on foreign stock exchanges.

T F 13. A market order is an order to buy or sell a stock at the prevailing market price.

T F 14. Electronic trading of securities has been growing in recent years.

T F 15. Investors cannot sell shares of securities they do not own.

Multiple Choice

1. The over-the-counter market is
   a. the New York Stock Exchange.
   b. an organized stock exchange.
   c. a place where securities are bought and sold.
   d. an intangible market for unlisted securities.

2. The ______ stock exchange is a primary market where new public issues are sold.
   a. regional
   b. American
   c. New York
   d. over-the-counter

3. ________ are an indirect way U.S. investors can invest in foreign companies.
   a. ADRs
   b. IRAs
   c. SDRs
   d. none of the above

4. Initial margin requirements on stocks are set by
   a. the Federal Deposit Insurance Corporation.
   b. the Federal Reserve.
   c. the New York Stock Exchange.
   d. the Securities and Exchange Commission.

5. Restrictions on trading involving insider information apply to
   a. corporate officers and directors.
   b. major stockholders.
   c. relatives of corporate directors and officers.
   d. All of the above.

6. You purchased XYZ stock at $50 per share. The stock is currently selling at $65. Your gains could be protected by placing a
   a. limit-buy order.
   b. limit-sell order.
   c. market order.
   d. stop-loss order.

7. Borrowing a security from your broker in order to sell it, with the intention of repurchasing it later when the price is lower, is called
   a. post-purchasing.
   b. pre-selling.
   c. short-selling.
   d. reverse-investing.

8. Assume you purchased 200 shares of XYZ common stock on margin at $60 per share from your broker. If the initial margin is 60%, the amount you borrowed from the broker is
   a. $4,000.
   b. $4,800.
   c. $6,000.
   d. $7,200.

9. You purchased 300 shares of common stock on margin for $60 per share. The initial margin is 60% and the stock pays no dividend. Your rate of return would be _______ if you sell the stock at $40 per share. Ignore interest on margin.
   a. 33%
   b. -33%
   c. -44%
   d. -56%

10. _______ center on the trade-off between the return the investor wants and how much risk the investor is willing to assume.
   a. Investment constraints
   b. Investment objectives
   c. Investment policies
   d. None of the above

Essay

1. Describe a short sale of securities.

2. What sources of information are available for making investment decisions?

Chapter 16 Answer Key

True/False		Multiple Choice	
1.	F	1.	D
2.	T	2.	D
3.	F	3.	A
4.	T	4.	B
5.	F	5.	D
6.	T	6.	B
7.	T	7.	C
8.	T	8.	D
9.	T	9.	B
10.	F	10.	B
11.	F		
12.	F		
13.	T		
14.	T		
15.	F		

Essay

1. In a short sale, an investor borrows stock from a broker and sells in the market. The investor hopes to purchase the stock in the market in the future (when he returns the stock he borrowed) at a lower price than the price he paid for it, profiting from a decline in the stock's price. The risk of a short sale is the possibility that the stock price will increase and the investor will have to buy the stock at a price higher than that at which the stock was initially sold.

2. There are many sources of information available to help investors make investment decisions. To conduct economic analysis, there is information available from government sources such as the Federal Reserve and from private firms such as Bloomberg. To conduct industry analysis, including industry ratios and forecasts, the private sector, such as Standard and Poor's, Moody's, and Value Line, is generally consulted. Sources of information to conduct global analysis include the *International Financial Statistics*, published by the International Monetary Fund, and international financial newspapers such as the *Financial Times*.

HOW EXTERNAL FORCES AFFECT FIRM VALUE

Chapter Summary

Chapter 17 explains how a firm's cash flows and required rate of return (and therefore its value) can be affected by economic conditions. The impact of economic factors, government policies, industry conditions, and global conditions are discussed. Managers and investors may be able to anticipate changes in the firm's value by monitoring changes in economic conditions over time.

LG 1 ***Identify economic conditions that affect a firm's value, and explain how those conditions can do so.*** The main economic conditions that affect a firm's value are economic growth, interest rates, and inflation. Economic growth can affect the demand for a firm's products and therefore affect its cash flows. Interest rate movements can affect the volume of purchases of particular products that are supported by credit and therefore can affect the cash flows of firms that sell these types of products. They can also affect a firm's cash inflows indirectly by affecting the general level of economic growth. Interest rate movements also affect the rate of return required by investors who invest in firms. Inflation can affect a firm's cash outflows through its impact on the firm's cost of labor and materials used to produce products. It may also affect the firm's cash inflows if the firm changes the prices it charges for its products. In general, high economic growth, low interest rates, and low inflation have a favorable impact on a firm's value. In some periods, one or more economic conditions exert a favorable effect on firm value, while others exert an unfavorable impact.

LG 2 ***Identify government policies that affect a firm's value, and explain how those policies can do so.*** The main government policies that affect a firm's value are monetary policy and fiscal policy. Monetary policy can affect firm value by affecting interest rates, which influence the cash flows of firms, and the rate of return required by investors who invest in firms. Low interest rates tend to enhance the expected cash flows and to lower the rate of return required by investors, which increases a firm's value. Higher interest rates tend to reduce expected cash flows and to increase the rate of return required by investors, and therefore reduce a firm's value.

LG 3 ***Identify industry conditions that affect a firm's value, and explain how those conditions can do so.*** A firm's value can be affected by demand in its industry, as some industries experience shifts in demand over time in response to changes in consumer behavior. Firms generally benefit from such an increase in their industry demand. An increase in competition within an industry tends to reduce a firm's value, as firms lose market share or need to reduce their prices (resulting in lower cash inflows) to maintain market share. Firms can be adversely affected by industry labor conditions such as strikes and by government regulations.

LG 4

Identify global conditions that affect a firm's value, and explain how those conditions can do so. Global conditions can affect a firm with international business. Exporters and importers are affected by foreign economic conditions and exchange rates. Strong economic growth normally has a favorable effect on the firm's cash flows. Appreciation of a foreign currency tends to increase the demand for a U.S. exporter's products (and therefore increases its cash flows); depreciation of a foreign currency has the opposite effect. Firms with direct foreign investment are affected by these conditions, as well as by political risk. An increase in political risk in a foreign country can result in a reduction in dollar cash flows to the U.S. firm.

Chapter Outline

Economic Factors and Firm Value

A firm's value is the present value of its expected cash flows, based on the required rate of return of investors. Economic forces that affect either the cash flows or the required rate of return will affect the firm's value. The main economic conditions that affect firm value are economic growth, interest rates, and inflation.

Economic Growth

Economic growth represents the change in the level of economic activity over a particular period. It is commonly measured as the change in the U.S. gross domestic product (GDP). Changes in growth can affect the demand for a firm's products, either upward or downward, directly affecting its cash inflows. Cash outflows can be affected as firm's make fixed asset and inventory investment decisions based upon expected changes in economic growth.

Interest Rate Movements

Interest rate movements can affect the volume of purchases of particular products that are supported by credit, and therefore affect the cash flows of firms that sell these types of products. Lower interest rates tend to increase demand for products financed with credit; higher interest rates decrease demand. A firm's cash flows may also be indirectly affected, as interest rate movements tend to affect the general level of economic growth with lower interest rates encouraging growth and higher rates discouraging growth. Interest rate movements also affect the required rate of return by investors who invest in firms; lower interest rates reduce the required rate of return, whereas higher rates increase it.

Inflation

Inflation is the increase in the general level of prices of products and services. It can affect a firm's cash outflows through its impact on the firm's cost of labor and materials used to produce products with higher prices resulting in higher cash outflows. It may also affect the firm's cash inflows if the firm changes prices charged for its products with higher prices resulting in higher cash inflows. A firm's cash flows and investors required rate of return might also be affected as expected changes in inflation influence changes in interest rates.

In general, high economic growth, low interest rates, and low inflation have a favorable impact on firm value. In some periods, one or more economic conditions exert a favorable effect on firm value, while others exert an unfavorable impact.

Government Policies and Firm Value

LG 2

The main government policies that affect firm value are monetary policy and fiscal policy.

Monetary policy is conducted by the U.S. Federal Reserve System (the Fed). The Fed adjusts interest rates in the economy by increasing or decreasing the supply of funds available to commercial banks. Through the activities of the Federal Open Market Committee, U.S. treasury securities are bought from and sold to the banks. When the FOMC buys government securities, the supply of funds available increases. When it sells government securities, the supply decreases.

Monetary policy can affect firm value by affecting interest rates, which affects cash flows of firms, and the required rate of return by investors who invest in firms. Low interest rates tend to enhance the expected cash flows and lower the required rate of return by investors, which increases a firm's value. Higher interest rates tend to reduce expected cash flows, increase the required rate of return by investors, and therefore reduce a firm's value.

Fiscal Policy

Fiscal policy represents the means by which the federal government imposes taxes and allocates funds to the public. Reducing (increasing) personal income taxes increases (decreases) disposable income for consumers and their demand for products and services, which affects corporate cash inflows. Reducing (increasing) corporate income taxes or excise taxes reduces (increases) corporate cash outflows.

Government spending policies can also affect the cash flows of firms. Increases (decreases) in government expenditures increase (decrease) the expected cash flows of those firms from whom the government is buying. If the government increases its borrowing to finance these expenditures (or decreases its debt from reductions in spending), the demand for funds in the economy is affected, leading to changes in interest rates, which can affect the value of firms.

Industry Conditions and Firm Value

A firm's value can change in response to changes in industry conditions surrounding the firm. Key factors affecting firm value include overall industry demand, competition within the industry, and labor and regulatory conditions affecting the industry.

Industry Demand

A firm's value can be affected by its respective industry demand, as some industries experience shifts in demand over time in response to consumer behavior. Firms generally benefit from an increase in their respective industry demand.

Industry Competition

An increase in competition within an industry tends to reduce a firm's value, as firms lose market share or need to reduce their prices (resulting in lower cash inflows) to maintain market share.

Labor and Regulatory Conditions

Firms can be adversely affected by industry labor conditions such as strikes, as some firms in the industry may benefit at the expense of the firms suffering labor difficulties. Changes in government regulations can also affect firms if the changes lead to expectations of either higher or lower cash flows.

Global Conditions and Firm Value

Global conditions can affect a firm with international business. Exporters and importers are mostly affected by foreign economic conditions and exchange rates. The global factors with the strongest influence on a firm's value are foreign economic growth, foreign interest rates, foreign inflation, exchange rate fluctuations, and political risk.

Foreign Economic Growth

Strong economic growth normally has a favorable effect on the cash flows of firms conducting business in a given country as demand for the firm's products and services are expected to rise. Weak or negative growth (recession) has the opposite effect. Firms attempt to reduce their exposure to specific foreign economies by diversifying their business across countries.

Foreign Interest Rates

Changes in foreign interest rates affect foreign consumers just as domestic rates affect domestic consumers. Higher interest rates tend to decrease the demand for products and services of firms conducting business in the country, lower rates tend to increase the demand. Higher foreign interest rates also increase the cost of firms financing in those countries, while lower interest rates reduce financing costs.

Exchange Rate Fluctuations

Appreciation of a foreign currency relative to the U.S. dollar tends to increase the demand for a U.S. exporter's products because the local price for the products will fall. This increased demand will increases the firm's cash flows; depreciation of a foreign currency has the opposite effect. U.S. importers face the reverse situation in that they benefit from purchasing goods in currencies that are depreciating and hurt from purchases in appreciating currencies.

Appreciating and depreciating currencies can also affect a firm's expected cash flows after the purchase or sale is made. Cash flows from accounts receivable (from foreign sales) increase as the currency in which the receivables are denominated appreciates; cash flows decrease as the currency depreciates. Similarly, cash flows from accounts payable (from foreign purchases) increase as the currency in which the payables are denominated depreciates; cash flows decrease as the currency appreciates.

Exchange rate fluctuations can also affect the value of firms not engaged in international business if they face foreign competition. Changing exchange rates may cause consumers to shift purchases from U.S. firms to foreign firms.

The value of direct foreign investments made by U.S. firms is also affected by exchange rate fluctuations, as well as political risk. An increase in political risk in a foreign country can result in a reduction in dollar cash flows to the U.S. firm. Exposure to political risk can occur due to:

- Consumer preferences for domestic products over foreign products.
- Differential tax treatment between domestic and foreign companies.
- Government restrictions on cash flow transfers.
- Government bureaucracy.

Study Tips

1. Although the specific impact of a given change in economic conditions, government policies, industry or global conditions is usually clear, keep in mind that such changes usually do not occur in isolation. A given change may have a greater impact than expected if other factors work to magnify the change. Another change may have little or no impact if it is offset by other forces.

Sample Exam

True/False

T F 1. Because they are out of the control of a firm, changes in the economic environment do not have any direct effects on the firm's cash flows.

T F 2. All firms face the same level of exposure to changes in general economic conditions.

T F 3. Because their cost of funds rises, firms are concerned about rising interest rates.

T F 4. When the Fed wishes to lower interest rates, it buys Treasury securities from commercial banks.

T F 5. Only firms that conduct business with the Federal government need be concerned with fiscal policy.

T F 6. Increased industry competition usually results in increased sales for all firms in an industry.

T F 7. Only firm's engaged in international business need be concerned with global economic conditions.

T F 8. Changes in global economic conditions can either increase or decrease a firm's cash flows.

T F 9. U.S. exporters and importers are both hurt by an increase in the value of the U.S. dollar.

T F 10. Monetary policy refers to the U.S. Treasury issuing new Treasury bonds.

Multiple Choice

1. If economic conditions were such that very slow growth is expected in the near future, one would want to invest in industries with _______ sensitivity to economic conditions.
   a. below average
   b. average
   c. above average
   d. None of the above

2. The gross domestic product (GDP) measures
   a. the economy's total production of goods and services.
   b. total goods and services consumed domestically.
   c. excess goods and services produced domestically and sold in foreign countries.
   d. excess goods and services sold domestically, but produced in foreign countries.

3. Which of the following is not an example of fiscal policy?
   a. Social Security spending
   b. Medicare spending
   c. Government purchases of Treasury securities
   d. Changes in the tax rate

4. A decrease in the federal government deficit should _______ the level of interest rates.
   a. increase
   b. decrease
   c. sometimes increase and sometimes decrease
   d. have no effect on

5. If the U.S. dollar is depreciating, this should _______ U.S. exports and _______ U.S. imports.
   a. stimulate; stimulate
   b. stimulate; discourage
   c. discourage; stimulate
   d. discourage; discourage

6. _______ the rate at which the general level of prices for goods and services is rising.
   a. The exchange rate is
   b. The gross domestic product is
   c. The inflation rate is
   d. None of the above

7. If interest rates increase, business investment expenditures are likely to _______ and consumer durable expenditures are likely to _______.
   a. increase; increase
   b. increase; decrease
   c. decrease; increase
   d. decrease; decrease

8. Increases in the money supply will cause demand for investment and consumption goods to _______ in the short run and cause prices to _______ in the long run.
   a. increase; increase
   b. increase; decrease
   c. decrease; increase
   d. decrease; decrease

Essay

1. How can an increase in the value of the U.S. dollar affect a U.S. corporation?

2. Why are firms concerned with rising inflation rates?

Chapter 17 Answer Key

True/False

1. F
2. F
3. T
4. T
5. F
6. F
7. T
8. T
9. F
10. F

Multiple Choice

1. A
2. A
3. C
4. B
5. B
6. C
7. D
8. C

Essay

1. An increase in the value of the dollar will affect U.S. firms differently depending on their international activities. Appreciation of the U.S. dollar will make U.S. goods more expensive for foreign buyers so U.S. exporters will be hurt. On the other hand, U.S. firms purchasing foreign goods will find that their costs decline. Foreign investments will also become cheaper; however, the value of U.S. investments overseas is also reduced.

2. Firms are concerned with rising inflation rates for a variety of reasons. It can affect a firm's cash outflows through its impact on the firm's cost of labor and materials used to produce products with higher prices resulting in higher cash outflows. It may also affect the firm's cash inflows if the firm changes prices charged for its products with higher prices resulting in higher cash inflows.

   A firm's cash flows and investors' required rate of return may also be affected as increased inflation puts upward pressure on interest rates. Higher interest rates can reduce demand for products supported by credit and may reduce the general level of economic growth.

INVESTING IN STOCKS

Chapter Summary

Chapter 18 explains how s firm's stock can be valued, how a stock's performance can be evaluated, and the meaning of market efficiency as related to valuation.

LG 1 ***Explain how stocks can be valued using valuation models that are alternatives to the dividend discount model.*** The price/earnings (P/E) method estimates the price as the product of the respective industry P/E ratio and the firm's expected annual earnings. The industry P/E ratio is based on a composite of comparable firms with characteristics similar to those of the firm being valued. The P/E method is subject to error because of the possibility of using an improper mix of comparable firms or using a poor forecast of the firm's earnings.

The market/book (M/B) is the market price per share of common stock divided by the book value per share. The industry M/B ratio is based on a composite of comparable firms. The price/revenue (P/R) value method estimates the firm's stock price as the product of the respective industry P/R ratio and the annual revenue of the firm. The use of these types of multiples to value firms is subject to error because of the possibility of using an improper mix of comparable firms to derive the multiple.

LG 2 ***Explain the valuation of the stock market.*** The stock market is valued as the weighted sum of the values of firms within that market. Therefore, any factors that influence the firms that constitute the market will affect the general stock market conditions. Very favorable stock market conditions in the mid- and late-1990s were attributed to strong economic growth (which increased the expected growth of firms), advances in technology (which increased efficiency), and a reduction in interest rates (which reduced the rate of return required by investors). It has also been argued that these favorable stock market conditions cannot be completely explained and that they partially reflect a speculative bubble that will burst someday.

Describe the valuation and performance of initial public offering (IPO) stocks. Stocks can be valued at the time of an IPO by applying multiples, such as the price/earnings multiple, the market/book multiple, and the price/revenue multiple. Some IPO stocks have experienced very high performance during the first day of trading but generally have not performed well over periods of one year or longer. They are normally subject to more uncertainty than other stocks because they have not been valued by the market in the past.

LG 4

Identify benchmarks commonly used for assessing investment performance. Stock market indexes are commonly used to assess investment performance. Each index reflects a specific market or sector. If investors are effective at selecting investments, their performance should exceed that of a corresponding index in the same sector. Stock market quotations are used to assess investment performance of individual firms.

LG 5

Describe the forms of stock market efficiency. Stock market efficiency takes three forms. Weak-form efficiency suggests that stock prices fully reflect historical price, volume, and other market-related information. Semistrong-form efficiency suggests that stock prices fully reflect all publicly available information, including market-related information and other information about the firm. Strong-form efficiency suggests that stock prices fully reflect all information, including information that is not publicly available. Evidence generally supports weak-form and semistrong-form efficiency. However, there are some exceptions including a size effect and a P/E effect in some periods. There is also evidence that refutes the notion of strong-form efficiency.

LG 6

Describe the valuation, performance measurement, and efficiency of foreign stocks. Foreign stock values are commonly measured by using the dividend discount model or the price/earnings multiple. The dividend discount model is used by investors to derive cash flow estimates. U.S. investors who use this method are most concerned with the dividends from a U.S. perspective. Thus, they must convert the dividends into dollars, based on forecasted exchange rates in the future periods, and this creates an additional source of uncertainty. The price/earnings multiple is usually based on a composite of comparable foreign firms in the same country, because each country's P/E ratios can be affected by country-specific accounting rules.

Chapter Outline

Alternative Stock Valuation Models

The basic stock valuation method values a share of stock as equal to the present value of all future dividends the stock is expected to provide. As an equation, the dividend discount model appears as follows:

$$P_0 = \frac{D_1}{(1+k_s)^1} + \frac{D_2}{(1+k_s)^2} + \cdots + \frac{D_\infty}{(1+k_s)^\infty}$$

The dividend discount model is not directly applicable to valuing firms that have low or zero dividends so investors use various alternative valuation methods.

Price-Earning Multiples

The P/E method estimates the price of a firm's stock as the product of the respective industry P/E ratio and the firm's expected annual earnings. The industry P/E ratio is based on a composite of comparable firms with characteristics that are similar to the firm being valued. The expected annual earnings figure may be taken from outside sources such as Value Line or the Institutional Brokerage Estimate System (IBES) or estimated from pro forma income statements. The P/E method can be used as a complement or a substitute for the dividend discount model. Some investors are more confident calculating earning than cash flows.

The P/E method has limitations as it is subject to error. It depends on forecasts of the firm's earnings, which could be inaccurate, and the determination of an industry P/E ratio, which might be constructed with firms not directly comparable to the firm being valued.

Book Value Multiples

The market-book (M/B) is the market price per share of common stock divided by the book value per share. The market/book (M/B) value method estimates the firm's stock price as the product of the respective industry M/B ratio and the book value of the firm. It also has limitations due to inappropriate firms included in the industry ratio and the issue that book values do not reflect information regarding a firm's potential for growth.

Revenue Multiples

The price-to-revenue (P/R) value method estimates the firm's stock price as the product of the respective industry P/R ratio and the annual revenue of the firm. The use of these types of multiples to value firms is also subject to error because of the possible improper mix of comparable firms used to derive the multiple.

Valuing the Stock Market

The value of the stock market is the weighted sum of the values of firms within that market. Therefore, any factors that influence the firms that comprise the market will affect the general stock market conditions.

Very favorable stock market conditions in the mid- and late-1990s were attributed to strong economic growth (which increased the expected growth of firms), advances in technology (which increased efficiency), and a reduction in interest rates (which reduced the rate of return required by investors). It has also been argued that the favorable stock market conditions cannot be completely explained. The alternative explanation is that there has been overly optimistic and irrational speculation in the market, causing a speculative bubble that will burst someday.

Valuation and Performance of IPO Stocks

An initial public offering (IPO) represents the first offering of stock to the public by a particular firm. Stocks can be valued at the time of an IPO by applying multiples, such as the price/earnings, market/book, or price/revenue multiples.

Some IPO stocks have experienced very high performance during the first day of trading, but generally have not performed well over periods of one year or longer. They are normally subject to more uncertainty than other stocks because they have not been valued by the market in the past.

Stock Performance Benchmarks for Investors

Stock market indexes are commonly used to assess investment performance. Each index reflects a specific market or sector. The most popular indexes followed by investors include:

- Dow Jones Industrial Average, a weighted average of stock prices of 30 large U.S. companies.
- Standard & Poor's 500, a weighted average of stocks prices of 500 large U.S companies.
- New York Stock Exchange Composite Index, the average price of all stocks traded at the NYSE.
- Nasdaq Composite, the price of stocks traded in the Nasdaq market.
- Sector indexes representing stocks in particular industry sectors, such as utilities, Internet firms, and telecommunications firms.

The ability of investors to select stocks can be measured by comparing the performance to that of a related index. If investors are effective at selecting investments, their performance should exceed that of a corresponding index in the same sector.

Stock Price Quotations

Stock price information can be readily found in financial newspapers, like the *Wall Street Journal*, and through the Internet. Individual stock quotations include current and historical price information (shown either in fraction or decimal form), dividend information, and price-earnings multiples. Price data on market and sector indexes is also available, as well as price quotations on publicly traded stock indexes like the Standard & Poor's Depository Receipt (SPDR, or Spider) which are baskets of stocks matched to the index, enabling investors to take positions in the index by purchasing shares.

Stock Market Efficiency

Given the continuous workings of the stock markets and the nearly instantaneous response of stock prices to new information, the stock markets are referred to as efficient. An inefficient market is one in which stock prices do not fully reflect all information that is available to investors and in which undervalued or overvalued stocks can therefore be found.

Stock market efficiency is classified into three forms: weak-form, semistrong-form, and strong-form.

1. Weak-form efficiency suggests that stock prices fully reflect historical price, volume, and other market-related information. Therefore, investors cannot profit from analyzing recent trends in stock prices.

2. Semistrong-form efficiency suggests that stock prices fully reflect all publicly available information, including market-related information and other information about the firm. Therefore, investors cannot gain by researching annual reports to fund undervalued stocks.

3. Strong-form efficiency suggests that stock prices fully reflect all public information as well as private (insider) information.

Evidence of Inefficiencies

In general, there is evidence that generally supports weak-from and semistrong-form efficiency, although some exceptions exist. There is also evidence that refutes the notion of strong-form efficiency. Specific examples of inefficiencies include

1. The January effect, in which stocks tend to increase in value in January, after falling in November and December.

2. The Monday, or weekend effect, in which stock prices are lower on Mondays than on the previous Friday.

3. Size effects, in which smaller firms have larger risk-adjusted returns than larger firms.

4. Price/earnings effects, in which stocks with low P/E ratios outperform those with higher P/E ratios.

Despite these apparent inefficiencies, it is difficult to exploit the discrepancies because the gains from trading are reduced or eliminated by having to pay trading commissions and taxes on any remaining gain.

Foreign Stock Valuation, Performance, and Efficiency

As with domestic stocks, foreign stocks are commonly measured using the dividend discount model or price-earning multiple with adjustments made for exchange rate changes.

The dividend discount model is used to derive cash flow estimates to the investors. U.S. investors who use this method are most concerned with the dividends from a U.S. perspective. Thus, they must convert the dividends to dollars, based on forecasted exchange rates in the future periods, which creates an additional source of uncertainty.

The price/earnings multiple is usually based on a composite of comparable foreign firms in the same country, as each country's P/E ratios can be affected by country-specific accounting rules.

Foreign stock market indexes can be used to assess the performance of investments in particular countries.

As trading in foreign markets has increased, so too has the level of stock market efficiency.

Sample Problem Solutions

Sample Problem 1: Alternative Stock Valuation Methods

You are attempting to value the stock of HighFlying Inc. The firm has never paid dividends so you are unable to use the dividend discount model. However, you have been researching the firm and its industry and have collected the following information.

Expected 2001 revenues:	$5,000,000
Expected 2001 earnings:	$1,000,000
Current book value of firm:	$6,000,000
Number of share outstanding:	500,000

Industry P/E ratio = 20
Industry M/B ratio = 4.0
Industry P/R ratio = 2.5

How much should a share of HighFlying stock be worth using the P/E, M/B, and P/R methods?

Solution to Sample Problem 1

The firm has expected earnings per share of \$2 (\$1,000,000 ÷ 500,000). With an industry P/E ratio of 20, one share of stock would be valued at \$40 (20 x \$2).

The firm has a book value of \$6,000,000. At the industry M/B ratio of 2.5, the market value of the firm's stock should be \$15,000,000 (\$6,000,000 x 2.5). Each share of stock would therefore be valued at \$30 (\$15,000,000 ÷ 500,000).

The firm has expected revenue per share of \$10 (\$5,000,000 ÷ 500,000). With an industry P/R ratio of 2.5, one share of stock would be valued at \$25 (2.5 x \$10).

Study Tips

1. Understand that not all firms' stock can be valued using either the Gordon growth or CAPM models. For firms that do not pay dividends or for which betas cannot be calculated, other methods such as price-earning or market/book ratios may be more appropriate.

2. Know the difference between the three forms of market efficiency. Weak-form implies current stock prices incorporate all historical price information; semistrong-form implies current stock prices incorporate all publicly available information about the stock; and strong-form implies current stock prices incorporate all information, public and private, about the stock.

Sample Exam

True/False

T F 1. One of the strengths of the constant-growth (Gordon) model is that it readily applies to the valuation of any stock.

T F 2. The price/earnings multiple estimate for valuing a firm's stock is based on the stock prices and earnings of comparable firms.

T F 3. The market/book multiple is the ratio of the current value of the stock market (as measured by the Standard & Poor's 500 to the book value of a firm).

T F 4. The Dow Jones Industrial Average is the weighted average of the stock prices of all industrial companies traded in the United States.

T F 5. Besides broad stock market indexes such as the Dow Jones Industrial Average and the Nasdaq Composite, there are indexes called sector indexes representing stocks in particular industry sectors such as utilities and telecommunications.

T F 6. Besides current prices, a wide range of information regarding the trading of a firm's stock (dividend information, volume of trading) can be found in most financial newspapers like the *Wall Street Journal*.

T F 7. If a stock market were truly efficient, it would not matter in which stocks one invested.

T F 8. Weak-form efficiency means that the evidence for proving stock market efficiency is weak.

T F 9. The January effect says that because of the Super Bowl, the volume of stock market trading falls, particularly late in the month.

T F 10. Because foreign stock markets are not as well developed as those in the United States, market indexes do not exist outside of the United States.

Multiple Choice

1. The use of the ______ is helpful in valuing firms that are not publicly traded.
   a. liquidation value
   b. book value
   c. P/E multiple
   d. present value of the dividends

2. According to the efficient market theory,
   a. stock prices can be undervalued or overvalued in an efficient market and bear searching out.
   b. stock prices can only be undervalued in an efficient market.
   c. stock prices do not differ from their true values in an efficient market.
   d. stock prices can only be overvalued in an efficient market.

3. The current price of DEF Corporation stock is $26.50 per share. Earnings next year should be $2 per share and it should pay a $1 dividend. The P/E multiple is 15 times on average. What price would you expect for DEF's stock in the future?
   a. $13.50
   b. $15.00
   c. $26.50
   d. $30.00

4. Which of the following is not true with respect to the theory of efficient markets?
   a. Securities are typically in equilibrium, meaning they are fairly priced and their expected returns equal their required returns.
   b. The Warren Buffetts of the market have proven that stocks are not fully and fairly priced, so investors should spend time searching for mispriced stocks.
   c. At any point in time, security prices fully reflect all public information available about the firm and its securities, and these prices react swiftly to new information.
   d. Since stocks are fully and fairly priced, it follows that investors should not waste their time trying to find and capitalize on mispriced securities.

5. If you believe in the _______ form of market efficiency, you believe that stock prices reflect all publicly available information but not information that is available only to insiders.
   a. semistrong
   b. strong
   c. weak
   d. Any of the above

6. If you believe in the _______ form of the market efficiency, you believe that stock prices reflect all relevant information including information that is available only to insiders.
   a. semistrong
   b. strong
   c. weak
   d. any of the above

7. If studies suggest that domestic securities markets are efficient at the semistrong level, this implies that all foreign securities markets are efficient at the ________ level.
   a. weak
   b. semistrong
   c. strong
   d. None of the above.

8. The industry market/book ratio is 4.0. The book value of World Industries is $1,000,000 and it has 100,000 shares of common stock outstanding. What should be the market price for one share of stock?
   a. $40.00
   b. $2.50
   c. $4.00
   d. Not enough information to determine the market price.

9. The Dow Jones Industrial Average is
   a. the weighted average of stock prices of 500 large U.S. industrial companies.
   b. the weighted average of stock prices of industrial firms trading in the Nasdaq market.
   c. the weighted average of stock prices of 30 large U.S. companies.
   d. the average price of stocks of all industrial firms traded at the New York Stock Exchange.

10. Weyerhaeuser Incorporated has a balance sheet that lists $70 million in assets, $45 million in liabilities, and $25 million in common shareholders' equity. It has 1,200,000 common shares outstanding. The replacement cost of its assets is $85 million. Its share price in the market is $49. Its book value per share is
    a. $16.67.
    b. $20.83.
    c. $37.50.
    d. $40.83.

11. Which of the following statements is most correct?
    a. Semistrong-form market efficiency implies that all private and public information is rapidly incorporated into stock prices.
    b. Market efficiency implies that all stocks should have the same expected return.
    c. Weak-form market efficiency implies that recent trends in stock prices would be of no use in selecting stocks.
    d. None of the above is correct.

12. Which of the following statements is most correct?
    a. If a market is strong-form efficient, this implies that the returns on bonds and stocks should be identical.
    b. If a market is weak-form efficient, this implies that all public information is rapidly incorporated into market prices.
    c. If your aunt earns a return higher than the overall stock market, this means the stock market is inefficient.
    d. None of the above is correct.

Essay

1. What do the theories and evidence say about stock market efficiency in the United States?

2. What factors are important in valuing foreign stocks?

Chapter 18 Answer Key

True/False

1. F
2. T
3. F
4. F
5. F
6. T
7. F
8. F
9. F
10. F

Multiple Choice

1. C
2. C
3. D
4. B
5. A
6. B
7. D
8. A
9. C
10. B
11. C
12. D

Essay

1. The theory of weak-form efficiency suggests that stock prices fully reflect historical price, volume, and other market-related information. Therefore, investors cannot profit from analyzing recent trends in stock prices. The evidence generally supports the theory.

   The theory of semistrong-form efficiency suggests that stock prices fully reflect all publicly available information, including market-related information and other information about the firm. Therefore, investors cannot gain by researching annual reports to fund undervalued stocks. Again, the evidence supports the theory although some exceptions exist.

   The theory of strong-form efficiency suggests that stock prices fully reflect all public information as well as private (insider) information. There is some evidence that refutes the notion of strong-from efficiency.

2. Foreign stocks are generally valued like domestic stock using dividend discount models or price/earning multiples. However, adjustments need to be made because the expected dividends must be converted into U.S. dollars, which requires the forecasting of exchange rates. The need to forecast exchange rates creates an additional source of uncertainty in the valuation models.

Chapter 19

INVESTING IN BONDS

Chapter Summary

Chapter 19 provides a background on bonds, including the types, quotations, measurement of bond yields, risk, factors that affect bond prices, and different bond investment strategies.

List the different types of bonds. Bonds are distinguished by the type of issuer. They are issued by the U.S. Treasury, municipalities, federal agencies, and corporations. There are also international bonds that are issued by government agencies or corporations in other countries.

LG 2

Explain how investors use bond quotations. Investors use bond quotations to monitor the prices of individual bonds or of particular types of bonds. Quotations are provided by financial newspapers on individual corporate bonds, Treasury bonds, municipal bonds, and federal agency bonds. In addition, quotations are provided for indexes representing corporate bonds, Treasury bonds, federal agency bonds, municipal bonds, and global bonds with various maturities.

LG 3

Describe how yields and returns are measured for bonds. A bond's yield to maturity represents the annualized return that is earned by the bondholder over the remaining life of the bond. The yield to maturity does not include transaction costs associated with issuing the bond. For investors who hold the bond until maturity, the yield to maturity represents their annualized yield. Investors who do not anticipate holding the bonds until maturity normally estimate the holding period yield that they will earn, based on the expected selling price of the bond at a future point in time.

LG 4

Describe the risks that investing in bonds entail. Bonds can expose investors to a wide variety of risks such as price risk, default risk, reinvestment rate risk, purchasing power risk, call (prepayment) risk, and liquidity risk. Investors focus on price risk when monitoring day-to-day changes in the values of bonds, because bond prices are very sensitive to interest rate movements. The degree of a bond's sensitivity to interest rate movements is dependent on the bonds' coupon rate and its remaining time to maturity. Bonds with higher coupon payments and shorter remaining times to maturity are less sensitive to interest rate movements.

Identify the factors that affect bond prices over time. Bond prices are inversely related to interest rate movements. Economic growth affects bond prices by influencing the default risk of the bonds and by influencing interest rates. Inflation affects bond prices by influencing interest rates.

Describe the strategies commonly used for investing in bonds. Investors can use a variety of strategies to invest in bonds. The passive strategy represents the investment in a diversified portfolio of bonds on a long-term basis, without frequent changes in the investment positions. The matching strategy is intended to generate, from the investments, cash inflows to cover expected cash outflows. The laddered strategy allocates investments across bonds with different maturities. The barbell strategy divides an investment in bonds between those with short time periods remaining until maturity (for liquidity purposes) and long-term bonds (where the expected return is higher). The interest rate strategy is to allocate bonds to capitalize on interest rate expectations. When interest rates are expected to increase, the allocation would focus on bonds with a short term to maturity to reduce exposure to interest rate risk. When interest rates are expected to decrease, the allocation would focus on bonds with a long term to maturity that would benefit the most from a reduction in interest rates.

Chapter Outline

Background on Bonds

Bonds are long-term debt securities that are issued by government agencies or corporations. The issuer of a bond is obligated to pay interest (coupon) payments periodically (such as annually or semiannually) and the par value at maturity. Most bonds have maturities of 10 to 30 years.

Bonds can be valued as the present value of its future cash flows. Anything that affects the expected coupon or principal payments or the investors required rate of return could influence the value of the bond.

Bonds are distinguished by the type of issuer. They are issued by the U.S. Treasury, municipalities, federal agencies, and corporations.

Treasury bonds are issued by the federal government and are perceived to be free from default risk. Some Treasury bonds are stripped, meaning that bonds have been partitioned into two separate securities, one paying only the coupon payments, the other only the principal. Inflation-indexed Treasury bonds are also issued, in which the principal of the bond is adjusted for changes in inflation.

Municipal bonds are issued by state and local government agencies. They may be attractive to investors because the income earned on them is exempt from federal income taxes.

Federal agency bonds are issued by federal agencies and may be backed by the federal government (for example, the Government National Mortgage Association, or Ginnie Mae, Federal Housing Administration and Veteran's Administration). Other similar bonds not backed by the federal government include those of the Federal Home Loan Mortgage Association (Freddie Mac) and Federal National Mortgage Association (Fannie Mae).

Corporate bonds are issued by large firms. Since they offer varying amounts of risk, investors have a wide selection of corporate bonds to choose from based upon their return and risk preferences. The highest risk bonds, and consequently those offering the highest returns, are usually referred to as junk bonds.

In addition, foreign governments and corporations issue bonds, often denominated in a foreign currency, available for investment by U.S. investors. Investors may invest in international bonds to take advantage of higher yields and potential gains from currency gains. However, the higher expected returns come with both higher degrees of default risk and exchange rate risk.

Bond Quotations

Bond quotations are used by investors to monitor the prices of individual bonds or of particular types of bonds. Quotations are provided by financial newspapers on individual corporate bonds, Treasury bonds, municipal bonds, and federal agency bonds.

Corporate bond quotations indicate the coupon rate and maturity of the particular bond, the current yield (annual coupon rate divided by current price), and its current price, quoted as a percentage of par. For example, a quote of 92¼ indicates a $1,000 par value bond would be priced at $922.25 (92¼% x $1,000).

Treasury bonds and Federal agency bond quotations list the coupon rate and maturity of each bond, the bid price (price at which bond dealer will buy a bond) and asked price (price at which bond dealer will sell a bond) quoted in fractions of 32nds. For example, a quote of 102:24 means the price of the bond is 102 24/32% for every $100 of par value so a $1,000 bond would be priced at $1,027.50. The bond's yield to maturity is also given.

In addition, quotations are provided for indexes representing corporate bonds, Treasury bonds, federal agency bonds, municipal bonds, and global bonds with various maturities.

Bond Yields and Returns

The bond's yield to maturity is the annualized yield that will be paid to investors over the life of the bond. For issuers, the yield to maturity at the time of the issue represents the cost of financing. For investors who hold the bond until maturity, the yield to maturity represents their annualized yield.

Investors who do not anticipate holding the bonds until maturity will normally estimate the holding period yield that they will earn, based on the expected selling price of the bond at a future point in time. The formula for measuring the expected holding period yield is as follows:

$$E(HPR) = \frac{E(P_{t+1}) - P_t + Coup}{P_t}$$

Where:

$E(HPR)$	= expected return on the bond during period t
$E(P_{t+1})$	= expected price of the bond at the time it is sold
P_t	= price of bond at beginning of period t
$Coup$	= coupon payments received during period t

For international bonds, the expected holding period return must be adjusted to account for exchange rate fluctuations over the holding period. The forecasted exchange rate on each coupon payment date and at the time the bond is to be sold are used to convert the expected cash flows from holding the bond into dollar terms.

Bond Risk

Bonds can expose investors to a wide variety of risks such as price risk, default risk, reinvestment risk, purchasing-power risk, call risk, and liquidity risk. Investors focus on price risk when monitoring day-to-day movements in the values of bonds, as bond prices are very sensitive to interest rate movements.

The degree of a bond's sensitivity to interest rate movements is dependent on the bonds' coupon rate and its term to maturity. Bonds with higher coupon payments and shorter terms to maturity are less sensitive to interest rate movements than those with lower coupon payments and longer terms to maturity.

Factors that Affect Bond Prices Over Time

The value of a bond is the present value of its interest payments plus the present value of its par value. The basic valuation model for a bond is as follows:

$$B_0 = I \times \left[\sum_{t=1}^{n} \frac{1}{(1+k_d)^t}\right] + M \times \left[\frac{1}{(1+k_d)^n}\right]$$
$$= I \times (PVIFA_{k_d,n}) + M \times (PVIF_{k_d,n})$$

Where

B_0 = value of the bond at time zero
I = annual interest paid in dollars
n = number of years to maturity
M = par value in dollars
k_d = required return on a bond

The equation shows that the value of a bond is determined by the coupon payments offered by the bond issue, and the required rate of return by investors. Once a bond is issued, its coupon payments do not change so any change in its value occur in response to changes in the required rate of return.

Bond Values and Changes in the Required Rate of Return

The required rate of return is primarily composed of the risk-free rate and the default risk premium of the particular bond. Any factors that affect the risk-free rate or default risk premium can affect the required rate of return on the bond, and therefore affect its value. There is an inverse relationship between bond prices and interest rate movements and default risk premiums.

Factors Affecting the Risk-Free Rate

The risk-free rate is affected by the monetary policy actions of the Fed, by inflation, and by economic growth. A tightening of the money supply, rising inflation, or increasing economic growth will place upward pressure on interest rates, and therefore downward pressure on bond prices.

Factors Affecting the Default Risk Premium

Similarly, the default risk premium is affected by economic growth and changes in a firm's financial condition. Decreases in economic growth and or the deterioration of a firm's financial health will put upward pressure on a firm's default risk premium, and downward pressure on the price of its bonds.

Bond Market Indicators

Investors actively monitor the factors that can affect the value of their bonds. Inflation is monitored by assessing changes in the consumer price index, producer price index, or prices on key resources such as steel or oil. Economic growth is monitored by assessing changes in personal income, employment, and various production indexes. A firm's default risk is monitored by assessing changes in its financial condition such as its financial leverage, debt ratio, or times interest earned ratio.

Bond Investment Strategies

LG 6

Investors can use a variety of strategies to invest in bonds.

A passive strategy is represented by an investment in a diversified portfolio of bonds on a long-term basis, without frequent changes in investment positions. This reduces trading costs and likely results in a return similar to a bond index comprised of similar bond investments.

A matching strategy is intended to generate cash inflows from the investments that cover expected cash outflows. Once the outflows are estimated, bond investments are made so that the coupon and principal payments are sufficient to cover the outflows.

A laddered strategy allocates investments across bonds with different maturities. By diversifying maturities, the adverse effects of rising interest rates are reduced.

The barbell strategy allocates some investment in bonds with short terms remaining until maturity for liquidity purposes, and some investment in long-term bonds where the expected return is higher. The interest rate strategy is to allocate bonds to capitalize on interest rate expectations. When interest rates are expected to increase, the allocation would focus on bonds with a short term to maturity to reduce exposure to interest rate risk. When interest rates are expected to decrease, the allocation would focus on bonds with a long term to maturity that would benefit the most from a reduction in interest rates.

Sample Problem Solutions

Sample Problem 1: Expected Holding Period Return

You are considering purchasing bonds that have a par value of $10,000 and a coupon rate of 10%. The current price of the bonds is $9,800. You plan to sell the bonds in one year at which time you expect that there is a 50% chance they will be worth $9,900, a 35% chance they will be worth $10,000 and a 15% chance they will be worth $9,600. What is your expected holding period return?

Solution to Sample Problem 1

The formula for finding the expected holding period return is

$$E(HPR) = \frac{E(P_{t+1}) - P_t + Coup}{P_t}$$

There is a 50% chance the return will equal:
($9,900 - $9,800 + $1,000)/ $9,800 = 11.22%

There is a 35% chance the return will equal:
($10,000 - $9,800 + $1,000)/ $9,800 = 12.24%

There is a 15% chance the return will equal:
($9,600 - $9,800 + $1,000)/ $9,800 = 8.16%

Study Tips

1. Know the difference between yield to maturity and holding period yield. The expected yield to maturity is known with certainty–if the bond is held to maturity–but the expected holding period yield must be estimated using a forecast of the price of the bond when it will be sold.

2. Remember there are many different risks associated with bond investments depending on market and issuer-specific factors. Investors tend to focus on two: price risk (the risk that rising interest rates will reduce the value of the bond) and default risk (the risk that the declining financial condition of the firm will reduce the value of the bond by increasing the likelihood of default).

3. Remember that prices of Treasury bonds are quoted differently from most other bonds. Most bonds are quoted in fractional terms (e.g., ¼) or their decimal equivalent (0.25). Treasury bonds are priced in 32nds so that a quote of 101-8 means the bond is valued at 101 and 8/32 percent of par.

Sample Exam

True/False

T F 1. A quote of 105-24 means a Treasury bond is priced at 105.24% of its par value.

T F 2. Ginnie Mae, Fannie Mae, and Freddie Mac are all different types of government agency bonds.

T F 3. Because of exchange rate and political risks, foreign bonds have a higher return than domestic bonds.

T F 4. A bond's yield to maturity is the annualized yield that will be paid to investors over the life of the bond.

T F 5. Investors not anticipating holding a bond until maturity need to estimate the expected holding period yield they will earn. This is a simple adjustment to the basic yield to maturity formula.

T F 6. Because short-term interest rates tend to be more volatile, shorter-term bonds are more price sensitive to changes in interest rates than longer-term bonds.

T F 7. The price of a bond may be affected by changes in the risk-free interest rate or changes in the default risk premium of a bond.

T F 8. An increase in the default risk premium for a bond is determined solely by the deterioration of the financial health of a firm.

T F 9. A passive bond investment strategy is represented by a portfolio of bond investments that does not change frequently.

T F 10. Bond investors wanting to match cash inflows to cover expected outflows would likely follow a barbell strategy.

Multiple Choice

1. Interest rate risk and the time to maturity have a relationship that is best characterized as
   a. constant.
   b. varying.
   c. direct.
   d. inverse.

2. The ABC Company has two bonds outstanding that are the same except for the maturity date. Bond D matures in 4 years, while Bond E matures in 7 years. If the required return changes by 15 percent,
   e. Bond D will have a greater change in price.
   f. Bond E will have a greater change in price.
   g. the price of the bonds will be constant.
   h. the price change for the bonds will be equal.

3. When valuing a bond, the characteristics of the bond that remain fixed are all of the following EXCEPT the
   a. coupon rate.
   b. price.
   c. face value.
   d. interest payment.

4. For an investor who plans to purchase a bond maturing in one year, the primary consideration should be
   a. interest rate risk.
   b. changes in the risk of the issue.
   c. yield to maturity.
   d. coupon rate.

5. Generally, an increase in risk will result in ______ required return or interest rate.
   a. a lower
   b. a higher
   c. an unchanged
   d. an undetermined

6. Which of the following is not a true statement regarding municipal bonds?
   a. A municipal bond is a debt obligation issued by state or local governments.
   b. A municipal bond is a debt obligation issued by the Federal Government.
   c. The interest income from a municipal bond is exempt from federal income taxation.
   d. Municipal bonds typically have lower yields than corporate bonds of the same maturity.

7. The bid price of a Treasury bond is
   a. the price at which the dealer in Treasury bonds is willing to sell the bond.
   b. the price at which the dealer in Treasury bonds is willing to buy the bond.
   c. greater than the ask price of the Treasury bonds expressed in dollar terms.
   d. the price at which the investor can buy the Treasury bond.

8. The price quotations of Treasury bonds in the *Wall Street Journal* show an ask price of 104:08 and a bid price of 104:04. As a buyer of the bond you expect to pay
   a. $1,041.25.
   b. $1,042.50.
   c. $1,044.00.
   d. $1,048.00.

9. If you purchase a bond for $1,000, expect to receive interest of $60, and expect to sell the bond at the end of the year for $1,100, what is your expected holding period yield?
   a. 5%
   b. 10%
   c. 16%
   d. 18%

10. Consider two bonds, A and B. Both bonds presently are selling at their par value of $1,000. Each pay interest of $120 annually. Bond A will mature in 5 years while Bond B will mature in 6 years. If the yields to maturity on the two bonds change from 12% to 14%,
   a. both bonds will increase in value but Bond A will increase more than Bond B.
   b. both bonds will increase in value but Bond B will increase more than Bond A.
   c. both bonds will decrease in value but Bond A will decrease more than Bond B.
   d. both bonds will decrease in value but Bond B will decrease more than Bond A.

11. Yields on municipal bonds are generally lower than yields on similar corporate bonds because of differences in
   a. marketability.
   b. risk.
   c. taxation.
   d. call protection.

Essay

1. Describe the relationship between the price sensitivity of a bond to changes in interest rates and 1) the bond's maturity, and 2) the bond's coupon rate.

2. Describe some of the commonly used strategies for investing in bonds.

Chapter 19 Answer Key

True/False

1. F
2. T
3. F
4. T
5. F
6. F
7. T
8. F
9. T
10. F

Multiple Choice

1. C
2. B
3. B
4. D
5. B
6. B
7. B
8. B
9. C
10. D
11. C

Essay

1. Because of the nature of discounting the expected cash flows to determine the value of a bond, the value of bonds with lower coupon payments is more sensitive to a given change in interest rates. Similarly, the value of bonds with longer terms to maturity is more sensitive to interest rate movements.

2. Among the different types of bond investment strategies are the passive, matching, laddered, barbell, and interest rate strategies. A passive strategy is associated with a diversified portfolio of bonds with few changes in investment positions. A matching strategy is intended to generate cash inflows from bond investments that cover expected cash outflows. A laddered strategy allocates investments across bonds with different maturities. By diversifying maturities, the adverse effects of rising interest rates are reduced. The barbell strategy allocates some investment in bonds with short terms remaining until maturity for liquidity purposes, and some investment in long-term bonds where the expected return is higher. The interest rate strategy allocates bonds to capitalize on interest rate expectations. When interest rates are expected to increase, the focus is on short-term bonds to increase current income; if rates are expected to decrease, the focus is on long-term bonds to capitalize on capital gains.

MUTUAL FUNDS AND ASSET ALLOCATION

Chapter Summary

Chapter 20 provides a background on mutual funds, including the operations of stock funds, bond funds, and money market funds. It also explains the factors that affect asset allocation among different types of investments.

LG 1 ***Describe the operations of stock mutual funds, and explain how these funds are used by investors.*** Stock mutual funds sell shares to investors and use the proceeds to invest in stocks for those investors. Stock mutual funds allow investors to invest in a diversified stock portfolio even if they have only a small amount of money to invest, and investors in such funds can rely on the professional expertise of stock portfolio managers. Open-end mutual funds stand ready to issue new shares upon demand by investors, and they repurchase shares that investors sell. By contrast, closed-end funds are closed to new investors, and shares held by investors can be sold on an exchange. Load mutual funds charge an initial fee to investors investing in the fund, whereas no-load funds do not charge a fee. All funds incur administrative and management expenses that they pass on to shareholders, but some funds incur much higher expenses than others do. Each stock mutual fund attempts to satisfy a particular investment objective, such as income, growth, Internet emphasis, or investment in international stocks.

LG 2 ***Describe the operations of bond mutual funds, and explain how these funds are used by investors.*** Bond mutual funds sell shares to investors and use the proceeds to invest in bonds for those investors. They enable even small investors to invest in a diversified bond portfolio, and they offer the professional expertise of bond portfolio managers. Like stock mutual funds, bond mutual funds are classified according to whether there is an initial fee (load versus no-load) and are also distinguished as open-end or closed-end. Each bond mutual fund attempts to satisfy a particular investment objective that reflects the degree of interest rate risk and the degree of default risk that investors are willing to tolerate.

LG 3 ***Describe the operations of money market mutual funds, and explain how these funds are used by investors.*** Money market mutual funds sell shares to investors and use the proceeds to invest in money market securities. Although money market funds provide relatively low returns (compared to stock and bond mutual funds), they offer liquidity. Thus, most investors maintain a money market fund for liquidity while investing additional money in other investments. Money market funds are distinguished by the average maturity of their security holdings (which affects interest rate risk) and by the type of issuer of the securities they purchased (which affects the default risk of the fund's portfolio).

LG 4

Explain the meaning of asset allocation and the factors that influence a particular investor's asset allocation decision. An investor's asset allocation decision involves determining what proportion of funds should be invested in each type of financial asset. This decision is affected by the investor's profile (stage in life and willingness to tolerate risk) and by the investor's expectations of future performance of different types of assets.

Chapter Outline

Stock Mutual Funds

Stock mutual funds sell shares to investors and use the proceeds to invest in stocks for those investors. They allow investors to invest in a diversified stock portfolio with a small amount of funds, and investors can rely on the professional expertise of stock portfolio managers.

At the end of each day, the market value of all assets (stocks plus cash) of a stock mutual fund is determined. Any interest or dividends earned are added to the market value of the assets, and any liabilities of the fund or any dividends distributed are deducted from the market value of the assets. This amount is divided by the number of shares outstanding to determine the fund's net asset value (NAV). As the prices of the stocks in a mutual fund rise, so does the fund's NAV and the investor's proportionate share.

Open-end mutual funds stand ready to issue new shares upon demand by investors, and they repurchase shares sold by investors. Conversely, closed-end funds are closed to new investors, and shares held by investors can be sold on an exchange.

Load mutual funds charge an initial fee to investors investing in the fund, while no-load funds do not charge a fee. All funds incur administrative and management expenses that they pass on to shareholders, but some funds incur much higher expenses than others do.

Each stock mutual fund attempts to satisfy a particular investment objective, such as income, growth, or Internet emphasis. There are also funds focusing on foreign stocks (international funds) or a mixture of U.S. and foreign stocks (global funds). Mutual funds that mirror particular stock indexes are also available.

Stock Fund Quotations

Mutual fund quotations are found in the financial press and on the Internet. Mutual funds are usually grouped by families, associated with the institutional investor or investment bank that operates the fund and other types of mutual funds. The NAV is the quoted price of open-end mutual funds. Closed-end fund quotations include both their NAV and their price, which may be more or less that its NAV due to the market demand for shares in the fund.

Bond Mutual Funds

Bond mutual funds sell shares to investors and use the proceeds to invest in bonds for those investors. They allow investors to invest in a diversified bond portfolio, and offer the professional expertise of bond portfolio managers.

Like stock mutual funds, bond mutual funds are classified according to whether there is an initial fee (load versus no-load) and are also distinguished as open-end or closed-end. Each bond mutual fund attempts to satisfy a particular investment objective that relates to the degree of interest rate risk (for example, intermediate-term or long-term bond funds) and the degree of default risk (for example, Treasury bond or GNMA bond fund, high-yield/junk bond fund, or international/global bond fund) that investors are willing to tolerate.

Money Market Mutual Funds

Money market mutual funds sell shares to investors and use the proceeds to invest in money market securities. While money market funds provide relatively low returns (compared to stock and bond mutual funds), they offer liquidity for investors. Thus, most investors maintain a money market fund for liquidity while investing additional money in other investments.

Money market funds are distinguished by the average maturity of their security holdings, which affects interest rate risk and by the type of issuer (for example, Treasury or municipal money market funds) of the securities they purchased, which affects the default risk of the fund's portfolio.

Asset Allocation

An investor's asset allocation decision involves determining the proportion of funds that should be invested in each type of financial asset. This decision is influenced by the investor's profile (stage in life and willingness to tolerate risk) and by the investor's expectations (of future performance of different types of assets).

Investor Profile and Expectations

Investors expecting to need funds in the near future tend to allocate more of their funds in relatively safe and liquid financial assets. Those with a longer time horizon tend to allocate more of their funds in riskier financial assets with a high potential for growth. Besides their stage of life, investors also make investment decisions based on their degree of risk tolerance. Some are more conservative, while others are more willing to tolerate higher levels of risk.

Financial assets are also allocated according to investor expectations about the future performance of each type of asset. Investors allocate larger proportions of their funds in assets expected to achieve high performance, and reduce or eliminate investments in assets expected to underperform.

Study Tips

1. Be sure to understand the differences between load and no-load mutual funds and the difference between closed-end and open-end.

2. Realize that an individual's asset allocation is based on the investor's profile and expectations of future performance of different types of assets.

Sample Exam

True/False

T F 1. The net asset value for a mutual fund is determined just like any other asset: by the demand for and supply of shares in the mutual fund.

T F 2. Load mutual funds may charge fees to investors investing in the fund.

T F 3. All stock mutual funds have the same investment objective, namely, growth or capital appreciation.

T F 4. Bond mutual funds are similar to stock mutual funds; only the particular type of asset invested in changes.

T F 5. Most money market mutual funds invest in the same types of money market instruments so they are generally indistinguishable from one another.

T F 6. Asset allocation refers to decisions that determine the proportion of funds invested in each type of financial asset.

T F 7. Investors nearing retirement tend to invest in riskier assets than other investors do.

T F 8. Not all investors at a specific stage in life share the same degree of risk tolerance.

T F 9. Once an asset allocation has been made, changing investor expectations about the future performance of different types of assets may cause changes in the allocation.

T F 10. A preference for liquidity is typically the primary factor in determining an investor's asset allocation.

Multiple Choice

1. Asset allocation refers to the
   a. allocation of the investment portfolio across broad asset classes.
   b. analysis of the value of securities.
   c. choice of specific assets within each asset class.
   d. None of the above.

2. Mutual funds perform the function of _______ for their shareholders.
   a. diversification
   b. professional management
   c. record keeping and administration
   d. All of the above.

3. The primary measurement unit used for assessing the value of one's stake in an investment company is
   a. net asset value.
   b. average asset value.
   c. gross asset value.
   d. total asset value.

4. Investors who wish to liquidate their holdings in a closed-end fund may
   a. sell their shares back to the fund at a discount.
   b. sell their shares back to the fund at net asset value.
   c. sell their shares on the open market.
   d. None of the above.

5. Assume that you have just purchased some shares in an investment company reporting $300 million in assets, $20 million in liabilities, and 10 million shares outstanding. What is the Net Asset Value (NAV) of these shares?
   a. $30
   b. $28
   c. $18
   d. $14.50

6. _______ fund is one where there is a sales commission charged on either buying or exiting the fund.
   a. A load
   b. A no-load
   c. An index
   d. All of the above

7. Which of the following is a false statement regarding open-end mutual funds?
   a. They offer investors a guaranteed rate of return.
   b. They offer investors a well-diversified portfolio.
   c. They redeem shares at their net asset value.
   d. None of the above.

8. An official description of a particular mutual fund's planned investment policy can be found in the fund's
   a. prospectus.
   b. indenture.
   c. investment statement.
   d. All of the above.

9. Investors tend to become _______ as they approach retirement.
   a. greedier
   b. less interested in investments
   c. more risk averse
   d. more risk tolerant

10. The term "asset allocation" refers to the process of allocating funds between
    a. individual security issues.
    b. investment and current consumption.
    c. major asset categories such as stocks, bonds, real estate, etc.
    d. short-term and long-term investments.

11. The stage an individual is in his/her life cycle will affect his/her
    a. return requirements.
    b. risk tolerance.
    c. Both a and b.
    d. Neither a nor b.

12. When used in the context of investment decision making, the term "liquidity" refers to
    a. the ease and speed with which an asset can be sold.
    b. an aspect of fiscal policy.
    c. an aspect of monetary policy.
    d. the proportion of short-term to long-term investments held in an investor's portfolio.

13. A mutual fund that attempts to hold quantities of shares in proportion to their representation in the market is called a(n) _______ fund.
    a. stock
    b. index
    c. hedge
    d. money market

14. The two most important factors in describing an individual's investment objectives are
    a. income level and age.
    b. income level and risk tolerance.
    c. age and risk tolerance.
    d. return requirement and risk tolerance.

Essay

1. Describe some of the benefits of investing in mutual funds rather than directly in stocks or bonds.

2. How might an investor's profile or expectations affect his or her asset allocation?

Chapter 20 Answer Key

True/False

1. F
2. T
3. F
4. T
5. F
6. T
7. F
8. T
9. T
10. F

Multiple Choice

1. A
2. D
3. A
4. C
5. B
6. A
7. A
8. A
9. C
10. C
11. C
12. A
13. B
14. D

Essay

1. Mutual funds allow investors to invest in a diversified stock portfolio with only a small amount of funds. In addition, investors can rely on the professional expertise of stock and bond portfolio managers rather than making investment decisions by themselves.

2. Investors, such as those nearing retirement age, expecting to need funds in the near future tend to allocate more of their funds in relatively safe and liquid financial assets. Those with a longer time horizon tend to allocate more of their funds in riskier financial assets with a high potential for growth. Besides their stage of life, investors also make investment decisions based on their degree of risk tolerance. Some are more conservative, while others are more willing to tolerate higher levels of risk.

   Financial assets are also allocated according to investor expectations about the future performance of each type of asset. Investors allocate larger proportions of their funds in assets expected to achieve high performance, and reduce or eliminate investments in assets expected to underperform.

DERIVATIVE SECURITIES

Chapter Summary

Chapter 21 explains how investors can use call options, put options, and financial futures to hedge their existing investment positions. These derivative securities are used to help investors manage changes in the underlying financial assets.

LG 1 ***Explain how call options are used by investors.*** Call options are commonly used by investors to capitalize on expectations of an increase in the price of the underlying stock. Investors pay a premium for the right to buy the stock at a specified exercise price. They consider purchasing a call option if they expect that the price of the stock will exceed the exercise price by an amount that more than covers the premium paid. Some investors who expect the stock price to remain stable or to decline consider selling call options.

LG 2 ***Explain how put options are used by investors.*** Put options are commonly used by investors to capitalize on expectations of a decrease in the price of the underlying stock. Investors pay a premium for the right to sell the stock at a specified exercise price. They consider purchasing a put option if they expect that the price of the stock will be lower than the exercise price by an amount that more than covers the premium paid. Some investors who expect the stock price to remain stable or to increase consider selling put options.

LG 3 ***Explain how financial futures are used by investors.*** Buying a financial futures contract locks in the price at which one can purchase a specified instrument (such as Treasury bonds or a stock index) as of the future settlement date. Thus, investors consider purchasing financial futures contracts that represent securities or indexes whose values they expect to rise. Selling a financial futures contract locks in the price at which one can sell a specified instrument as of the future settlement date. Thus, investors consider selling financial futures contracts that represent securities or indexes whose values they expect to decline.

Chapter Outline

Background on Derivatives

Derivative securities are securities whose values are derived from the values of other related securities. They are neither debt nor equity but derive their characteristics from underlying financial assets.

Two of the most popular types of derivative securities are options and financial futures. Options are contracts that give the investor the opportunity to purchase or sell a specified asset (typically stock) under specified conditions. Stock options typically trade at an exchange such as the Chicago Board Options Exchange. Financial futures are agreements between two parties for one to sell and the other to buy a specified financial instrument on a specified future settlement date. Financial futures are traded on exchanges such as the Chicago Mercantile Exchange and the Chicago Board of Trade.

Call Options

Call options are commonly used by investors to capitalize on expectations of an increase in the price of the underlying stock. Investors pay a premium for the right to buy the stock at a specified exercise price by a specified expiration date.

Options can be either American-style, which allows the holder to exercise the option throughout the life of the option, or European-style, which can be exercised only on the option's expiration date.

Call options may also be classified as in-, at-, or out-of-the-money. A call option is in-the-money when the prevailing stock price is above the exercise price, and therefore possible to exercise. A call option is at-the-money when the stock price is equal to the exercise price and out-of-the-money when the stock price is below the exercise price.

Investors consider purchasing a call option if they expect that the price of the stock will exceed the exercise price by an amount that more than covers the premium paid. Some investors who expect the stock price to remain stable or to decline consider selling call options.

Factors Affecting the Call Option Premium

The premium of a call option is determined by the number of market participants wishing to purchase the option (demand) and the number wishing to sell (supply). The premium is primarily influenced by three factors: the price of the stock, the time to maturity, and the volatility of the stock price.

1. The higher a stock price relative to the exercise price specified in the call option, the more desirable it is and the higher its value.

2. The longer the time to maturity, the greater the potential benefits for investors holding the option, so the higher its value.

3. The more volatile the price of the underlying stock, the greater the potential benefits for investors holding the option, so the higher its value.

Put Options

Put options are commonly used by investors to capitalize on expectations of a decrease in the price of the underlying stock. Investors pay a premium for the right to sell the stock at a specified exercise price by a specified expiration date.

Put options may be classified as in-, at-, or out-of-the-money. A put option is in-the-money when the prevailing stock price is below the exercise price, and therefore possible to exercise. A put option is at-the-money when the stock price is equal to the exercise price and out-of-the-money when the stock price is above the exercise price.

Investors consider purchasing a put option if they expect that the price of the stock will be lower than the exercise price by an amount that more than covers the premium paid. Some investors who expect the stock price to remain stable or to increase consider selling put options.

The premium of a put option is determined by the number of market participants wishing to purchase the option (demand) and the number wishing to sell (supply). The premium is primarily influenced by three factors: the price of the stock, the time to maturity, and the volatility of the stock price.

1. The lower a stock price relative to the exercise price specified in the put option, the more desirable it is and the higher its value.

2. The longer the time to maturity, the greater the potential benefits for investors holding the option, so the higher its value.

3. The more volatile the price of the underlying stock, the greater the potential benefits for investors holding the option, so the higher its value.

Financial Futures

The purchase of a financial futures contract locks in the price at which one can purchase the specified instrument (such as Treasury bonds or a stock index) as of the future settlement date. Thus, investors consider purchasing financial futures contracts representing securities or indexes whose values they expect to rise.

The sale of a financial futures contract locks in the price at which one can sell a specified instrument as of the future settlement date. Thus, investors consider selling, or shorting, financial futures contracts representing securities or indexes whose values they expect to decline.

Although there is no premium for entering a future contract, as is the case for options, investors are required to maintain a deposit, called a margin, to back any loss that might result from the futures position.

Many investors use financial futures to hedge an existing investment position. This usually involves taking a position in financial future contracts that will incur a gain to offset a loss in their existing investment portfolio. For example, investors can sell stock index futures to protect against a fall in the value of their stock portfolios or Treasury bond futures to protect against a fall in the value of their bond portfolios.

Sample Problem Solutions

Sample Problem 1: Call Option

You expect shares of Live Enterprises to rise considerably in the near future. You could either purchase 100 shares of stock at $50 per share or a call option for $5 that allows you to purchase 100 shares of stock at an exercise price of $50. What would be your profit (or loss), in both dollar and percentage terms, from a) investing in the stock today and selling at the future expected price, or b) purchasing and exercising the stock option if the price of the future stock becomes (1) $45, (2) $50, (3) $55, (4) $60, or (5) $65.

Solution to Sample Problem 1

a. The profit (loss) from purchasing stock is calculated by subtracting the selling proceeds from the cost of purchasing the stock. For example, at $45, the loss is $500 ($45 x 100 shares - $50 x 100 shares), and at $60, the gain is $1,000 ($60 x 100 - $50 x 100). The percentage gain (loss) is calculated as the total gain (loss) divided by the amount invested. At $45, the percentage loss is 10% (-$500 ÷ $5,000), and at $60, it is 20% ($1,000 ÷ $5,000).

b. The profit (loss) from purchasing the option is the calculated by subtracting the cost of the option ($500 = $5 x 100 shares) from the profit upon exercising the option ([Stock price – exercise price] x 100 shares). For example, at $45, the loss is $500, the cost of the option because it will not be exercised. At $60, the gain is $500 ([($60 - $50) x 100] - $500). The percentage gain (loss) is calculated as the total gain (loss) divided by the cost of the option. At $45, the percentage loss is 100% (-$500 ÷ $500), and at $60, it is 100% ($500 ÷ $500).

Future price of stock	Profit (loss) from stock		Profit (loss) from option	
$45	($500)	-10%	($500)	-100%
$50	$0	0%	($500)	-100%
$55	$500	10%	$0	0%
$60	$1,000	20%	$500	100%
$65	$1,500	30%	$1,000	200%

Study Tips

1. Understand that derivative securities have become a very important part of the corporate finance, investments, and the financial markets. Derivatives are used as investment securities and as hedging instruments. Thus, they can be used to either increase returns or reduce risk.

2. Remember that the same factors affect the value of call and put options. Both are positively related to the volatility of the underlying asset and the time to maturity. Where they differ is the relationship of the strike price to the market price of the underlying asset. Higher market prices make call options more valuable and increase their price; put options become less valuable and their price decreases.

Sample Exam

True/False

T F 1. An option is a contract that gives its holder the right to buy or sell an asset at a predetermined price within a specified period of time.

T F 2. An American-style option can only be exercised at its expiration date.

T F 3. A call option is in the money when the prevailing stock price is above the exercise price.

T F 4. The price of an option is determined by its demand and supply.

T F 5. Factors influencing the price of an option are the price of the underlying stock, the volatility of the stock price, and time to maturity of the option.

T F 6. Put options are bought by investors expecting a rise in the price of the underlying stock.

T F 7. The exercise price of a put option is the price paid to acquire the option contract.

T F 8. A futures contract gives the holder the right, but not the obligation, to buy or sell the underlying assets.

T F 9. The price, or premium, for a futures contract is determined by the same factors that pertain to option premiums.

T F 10. Investors can use stock index futures to protect against the fall in the value of their stock portfolios.

Multiple Choice

1. An option which gives the holder the right to sell a stock at a specified price at some time in the future is called a(n)
   a. call option.
   b. put option.
   c. out-of-the-money option.
   d. futures contract.

2. The value of an option depends on the stock's price, the risk-free rate, and the
   a. exercise price.
   b. variability of the stock price.
   c. option's time to maturity.
   d. All of the above.

3. Which of the following events is likely to *decrease* the value of call options on the common stock of GCC Company?
   a. An increase in GCC's stock price.
   b. An increase in the exercise price of the option.
   c. An increase in the amount of time until the option expires.
   d. GCC's stock price becomes more risky (higher variance).

4. A ______ gives its holder the right to buy an asset for a specified exercise price on or before a specified expiration date.
   a. call option
   b. futures contract
   c. put option
   d. None of the above.

5. The purchase of a futures contract involves
   a. the right to buy an item at a specified price.
   b. the right to sell an item at a specified price.
   c. the obligation to buy an item at a specified price.
   d. the obligation to sell an item at a specified price.

6. The price which the owner of a call option must pay in order to purchase the stock named in the option contract is called the
   a. purchase price.
   b. exercise price.
   c. premium.
   d. futures price.

7. The term "hedge" refers to an investment which
   a. is entered into primarily for tax purposes.
   b. is entered into to mitigate specific financial risks.
   c. is entered into to conceal one's true investment strategy from other market participants.
   d. None of the above answers is correct.

8. An American-style put option gives its holder the right to
   a. buy the underlying asset at the exercise price on or before the expiration date.
   b. buy the underlying asset at the exercise price only at the expiration date.
   c. sell the underlying asset at the exercise price on or before the expiration date.
   d. sell the underlying asset at the exercise price only at the expiration date.

9. The writer or seller of a put option
   a. agrees to sell shares at a set price.
   b. agrees to buy shares at a set price.
   c. acquires the opportunity to buy shares at a set price.
   d. acquires the opportunity to sell shares at a set price.

10. Each stock option contract provides for the right to buy or sell _____ shares of stock.
   a. 1
   b. 10
   c. 100
   d. 1,000

11. Call options on IBM stock options are
   a. created by investors.
   b. issued by IBM Corporation.
   c. issued by the Federal Reserve.
   d. All of the above.

12. A put option on Snapple Beverage has an exercise price of $30. The current stock price of Snapple Beverage is $24.25. The put option is
   a. at the money.
   b. in the money.
   c. out of the money.
   d. None of the above.

13. A call option on Brocklehurst Corp. has an exercise price of $30. The current stock price of Brocklehurst Corp. is $32. The call option is
   a. at the money.
   b. in the money.
   c. out of the money.
   d. None of the above.

14. Futures are widely used for
   a. hedging the purchase price of assets.
   b. hedging the sale price of assets.
   c. speculation.
   d. All of the above.

15. If you expect a market downturn, one potential defensive strategy would be to
   a. buy stock index futures.
   b. sell stock index futures.
   c. buy stock index options.
   d. sell foreign exchange futures.

16. A futures contract
    a. is a contract to be signed in the future by the buyer and the seller of an asset.
    b. is an agreement to buy or sell a specified amount of an asset at a predetermined price on the expiration date of the contract.
    c. is an agreement to buy or sell a specified amount of an asset at the market price on the expiration date of the contract.
    d. gives the buyer the right, but not the obligation, to buy an asset some time in the future.

17. An investor would want to ________ to exploit an expected fall in interest rates.
    a. buy S&P 500 index futures
    b. sell treasury bond futures
    c. buy (take a long position in) treasury bond futures
    d. buy (take a long position in) wheat futures

Essay

1. How do the price and volatility of a stock and the time to maturity affect the value of a call option?

2. How can a stock index futures contract protect an investor's stock portfolio?

Chapter 21 Answer Key

True/False

1. T
2. F
3. T
4. T
5. T
6. F
7. F
8. F
9. F
10. T

Multiple Choice

1. B
2. D
3. B
4. A
5. C
6. B
7. B
8. C
9. A
10. C
11. A
12. B
13. B
14. D
15. B
16. B
17. C

Essay

1. The higher a stock price relative to the exercise price specified in the call option, the more desirable it is and the higher its value. The longer the time to maturity, the greater the potential benefits for investors holding the option, so the higher its value. The more volatile the price of the underlying stock, the greater the potential benefits for investors holding the option, so the higher its value.

2. Investors can sell stock index futures to protect against a fall in the value of their stock portfolios. They could also sell Treasury bond futures to protect against a fall in the value of their bond portfolios.

CORPORATE CONTROL AND GOVERNANCE

Chapter Summary

Chapter 22 describes the potential conflicts between managers and investors. It explains how the firm's board of directors can exert control over a firm's managers and how investors can do so. It also describes the market for corporate control, as reflected in the threat of takeover of underperforming firms.

LG 1 ***Describe the relationship between mangers and investors, and explain the potential conflict in goals.*** Managers serve as agents of the firm by managing the firm in a manner that is supposed to maximize the value of the firm's stock. However, managers may themselves benefit more directly by making decisions that are intended to serve their own interests rather than the interests of shareholders.

LG 2 ***Explain how a firm's board of directors can control the managers of the firm.*** A board is normally expected to be more effective in exerting control over managers if it is dominated by outside directors, allows an outside director to serve as chair of the board, compensates the directors with stock instead of cash payments, and has a relatively small number of directors. The board may initiate restructuring that is more aligned with shareholder interests. It may alter the compensation of the CEO and other high-level managers to ensure their managerial decisions are aligned with shareholder interests. It also has the power to fire a CEO who does not attempt to serve shareholder interests.

LG 3 ***Explain how investors in the firm's stock can control the managers of the firm.*** Investors can sell the firm's stock if the firm's managers do not serve shareholder interests. Alternatively, they may be able to communicate to the firm's board of directors that they are displeased with the firm's management. They can also attempt to sue the board of directors if it is not living up to its responsibility of serving shareholder interests.

LG 4 ***Explain how the market for corporate control can ensure that managers of firms serve their firms' respective shareholders.*** If managers of a firm do not serve shareholder interests, the stock price will be lower than the price that would exist if shareholder interests were served. This firm may become a takeover target because its

stock can be purchased at a relatively low price. Other firms could acquire this firm at a low price and restructure it so that the business can be more efficiently managed as it is merged with the acquiring firm's existing business.

LG 5 ***Describe the relationship between managers and creditors.*** If managers make specific decisions that temporarily maximize the value of the stock by increasing the potential return, they may increase the perceived risk of the firm. This could adversely affect the value of existing debt securities held by creditors. To prevent such actions, creditors normally demand restrictive covenants in the loan or bond indenture.

LG 6 ***Describe the relationship between mutual fund management and investors.*** Mutual fund management is supposed to serve the interests of shareholders. However, the management may sometimes make decisions that do not serve their shareholders' interests. For example, some mutual funds charge a relatively high level of expenses that cannot be justified given their operations. Each mutual fund has a board of directors that is responsible for monitoring the management, but some boards do not effectively force mutual fund managers to act in the interests of shareholders.

Chapter Outline

Relationship Between Firm's Managers and Investors

LG 1 Managers serve as agents of the firm by managing the firm in a manner that is supposed to maximize the value of the firm's stock.

The separation of ownership and control of the firm introduces conflicts, which lead to agency problems. For example, managers may benefit directly more from making decisions that are intended to serve their own interests rather than the interests of shareholders.

Furthermore, there is a problem of asymmetric information in that the managers have information about the firm that is not available to the shareholders. This complicates any attempt from the shareholders to monitor the firm's managers to ensure that they are serving shareholder interests.

Control by the Board of Directors

The shareholders elect the board of directors, which oversees the key management decisions of a firm. The board members may include both inside directors (including the firm's CEO) who are employed by the firm, and outside directors, who are not employed by the firm.

The board of directors is responsible for monitoring the managers on behalf of the shareholders. Several factors associated with the effectiveness of a board to exert control over the managers include:

1. Relevant strength on the board of outside (independent) directors including having an outside director serve as chair of the board

2. Compensation of the directors with stock instead of cash payments

3. Relative size of board with smaller boards being more effective.

How the Board Aligns Manager and Investor Interests

The board may initiate various activities to better align managerial decisions with the interests of the shareholders. Three common techniques include:

1. Reducing or restricting free cash flow (that is, extra cash available and not designated for specific purposes) available to the managers.

2. Forcing the firm's CEO and other high-level managers to invest in the stock of the firm that they manage so they benefit directly from making decisions that maximize the stock price.

3. Compensating the CEO and other high-level managers based on their ability to maximize the value of the firm for the shareholders.

Control by Investors

If the firm's board of directors is ineffective, the investors may need to become involved personally to ensure that the firm's managers serve shareholder interests. The relative influence of the shareholders is greatest when the ownership is not widely spread and when there is a significant proportion of institutional ownership because institutional investors typically have the resources to better monitor managerial activities.

Investors who are displeased with the manner in which the managers are managing the firm have several options. Besides doing nothing and hoping for the best, investors can sell the firm's stock if they believe the firm's managers are not serving shareholder interests. Alternatively, they can possibly communicate with the firm's board of directors if they are displeased with the firm's management. They can also attempt to sue the board of directors if the board is not performing its responsibility of serving shareholder interests.

Market for Corporate Control

LG 4

If managers of a firm do not serve shareholder interests, the stock price will be lower that the potential price that would exist if shareholder interests were served. Underperforming firms may become a takeover target, because their stock can be purchased at a relatively low price. Other firms could acquire this firm at a low price, and restructure it so that the business can be more efficiently managed as it is merged with their existing business.

Barriers to Corporate Control

The power of corporate control to eliminate agency problems is limited due to barriers that make it costly for firms to acquire underperforming firms. Such barriers include:

1. Anti-takeover amendments in the corporate charter, such as requiring a two-thirds approval by shareholders to prevent hostile takeovers.

2. Poison pills, such as instantaneous special allocations of new stock to all existing shareholders, which increase the cost of a potential takeover.

3. Golden parachutes, such as additional compensation to managers in the event of a loss of their jobs or a change in the control of the firm, which also increases the cost of a potential takeover.

4. Government intervention, particularly in cases of international takeovers, which increase the cost or even eliminate the possibility of takeover.

Monitoring and Control by Creditors

Like shareholders, creditors must monitor a firm's managers. If managers make specific decisions that temporarily maximize the value of the stock by increasing the potential return, they may increase the perceived risk of the firm. This could adversely affect the value of existing debt securities held by creditors.

To prevent such actions, creditors normally demand protective covenants in loan or bond indentures. One example of a protective covenants would be a restriction on exceeding a specific maximum debt-to-equity ratio.

Conflict between Managers and Mutual Fund Investors

LG 6 Mutual fund management is supposed to serve the interests of the shareholders. However, the management may sometimes make decisions that do not serve their shareholders' interests. For example, some mutual funds may not account for transactions that are advantageous to the shareholders from a tax perspective. Others may charge a relatively high level of expenses that cannot be justified given their operations.

Each mutual fund has a board of directors that is responsible for monitoring the management, but some boards do not effectively force mutual fund managers to serve shareholder interest. The agency problem in mutual funds is quite pronounced.

Study Tips

1. The agency problem can be defined as the likelihood that managers may place personal goals ahead of corporate goals. It is generally controlled by actions of the board of directors working on behalf of the shareholders. If not satisfied, shareholders can become more active in voicing their displeasure with management or the board.

2. Also, recall that a second type of agency relationship exists between the creditors and the managers. Creditors attempt to put restrictions on managers who may attempt to maximize their personal wealth or the wealth of the shareholders at the expense of the bondholders.

Sample Exam

True/False

T F 1. Agency problems arise from the separation of the ownership and the control of a firm.

T F 2. Asymmetric information means that managers and shareholders have the same information about the firm.

T F 3. The chief executive officer (CEO) is usually chosen by the firm's shareholders.

T F 4. The board of directors is responsible for monitoring the managers on behalf of the shareholders.

T F 5. One method of ensuring that managers work towards maximizing the value of the firm is to offer them a large fixed salary.

T F 6. The existence of institutional investors usually makes it easier for the shareholders to exert influence on the management of the firm.

T F 7. The board of directors of a corporation cannot be sued by the shareholders.

T F 8. Golden parachutes refer to executive compensation tied to the value of the firm. If the value of the firm increases, the manager receives more pay.

T F 9. Creditors often demand protective covenants in loan or bond indentures to stop managers from increasing the risk of the firm and thereby reducing the value of the bondholders investment.

T F 10. Agency problems are much less common with mutual fund managers than with corporate managers.

Multiple Choice

1. Which of the following actions help managers defend against hostile takeovers?
   a. Establishing a poison pill provision.
   b. Granting lucrative golden parachutes to senior managers.
   c. Establishing a super-majority provision in the company's bylaws, which raises the percentage of the board of directors that must approve an acquisition from 50 percent to 75 percent.
   d. All of the answers above are correct.

2. A proxy battle is the attempt by
   a. the creditors of a bankrupt firm to seize assets.
   b. the management to dismiss the board of directors.
   c. a nonmanagement group to gain control of the management of a firm through the solicitation of a sufficient number of corporate votes.
   d. the employees to unionize.

3. Which of the following does not represent an agency cost?
   a. Management reports to stockholders
   b. Performance incentives paid to managers
   c. The cost of monitoring management behavior
   d. Purchasing insurance against management misconduct

4. The conflict between the goals of a firm's owners and the goals of its nonowner managers is
   a. the agency problem.
   b. incompatibility.
   c. serious only when profits decline.
   d. of little importance in most large U.S. firms.

5. One way often used to insure that management decisions are in the best interest of the stockholders is to
   a. threaten to fire managers who are seen as not performing adequately.
   b. remove management's perquisites.
   c. tie management compensation to the performance of the company's common stock price.
   d. tie management compensation to the level of earnings per share.

6. Which of the following is not a trend resulting from the agency problem?
   a. Compensating managers with stock and stock options rather than a large fixed salary
   b. Restructuring through leveraged buyouts
   c. Management by active investors
   d. Prohibiting managers from maintaining an ownership interest

7. Reducing the free cash flow available to managers
   a. is one method of aligning manager and investor interests.
   b. is an example of a typical restrictive covenant.
   c. reduces the ability of managers to maximize the value of the firm.
   d. is often done in lieu of offering stock options.

8. Which of the following is not a barrier making it costly for investors to acquire an underperforming firm?
   a. Poison pills
   b. Golden parachutes
   c. Government intervention
   d. Free cash flow

9. Which of the following is not a potential agency problems associated with mutual funds?
   a. Mutual fund managers accounting for transactions that are disadvantageous to the shareholders
   b. Mutual funds charging a relatively high level of expenses that can not be justified given their operations
   c. Mutual fund managers investing contrary to the stated investment objective of the fund
   d. Mutual fund investment returns significantly lower than other funds with the same investment objective

10. One example of a protective debt covenant is specifying
    a. the form of compensation offered to managers.
    b. a maximum debt-to-equity ratio for the firm.
    c. a restriction on the countries to which the firm's products can be exported.
    d. the interest rate on the loan or bond.

Essay

1. Explain the potential agency problem between managers and creditors.

2. Explain the role of golden parachutes and poison pills in protecting against potential corporate takeovers.

Chapter 22 Answer Key

True/False

1. T
2. F
3. F
4. T
5. F
6. T
7. F
8. F
9. T
10. F

Multiple Choice

1. D
2. C
3. A
4. A
5. D
6. D
7. C
8. D
9. D
10. A

Essay

1. There is a possibility that managers may make specific decisions that temporarily maximize the value of the stock by increasing the potential return and likewise, the perceived risk of the firm. This could adversely affect the value of existing debt securities held by creditors. To prevent such actions, creditors normally demand protective covenants in loan or bond indentures.

2. The threat of takeover as a means of eliminating agency problems is limited due to barriers that make it costly for firms to acquire underperforming firms. Such barriers include poison pills (instantaneous special allocations of new stock to all existing shareholders) and golden parachutes (additional compensation to managers in the event of a loss of their jobs or a change in the control of the firm). Both of these measures increase the cost of a potential takeover.

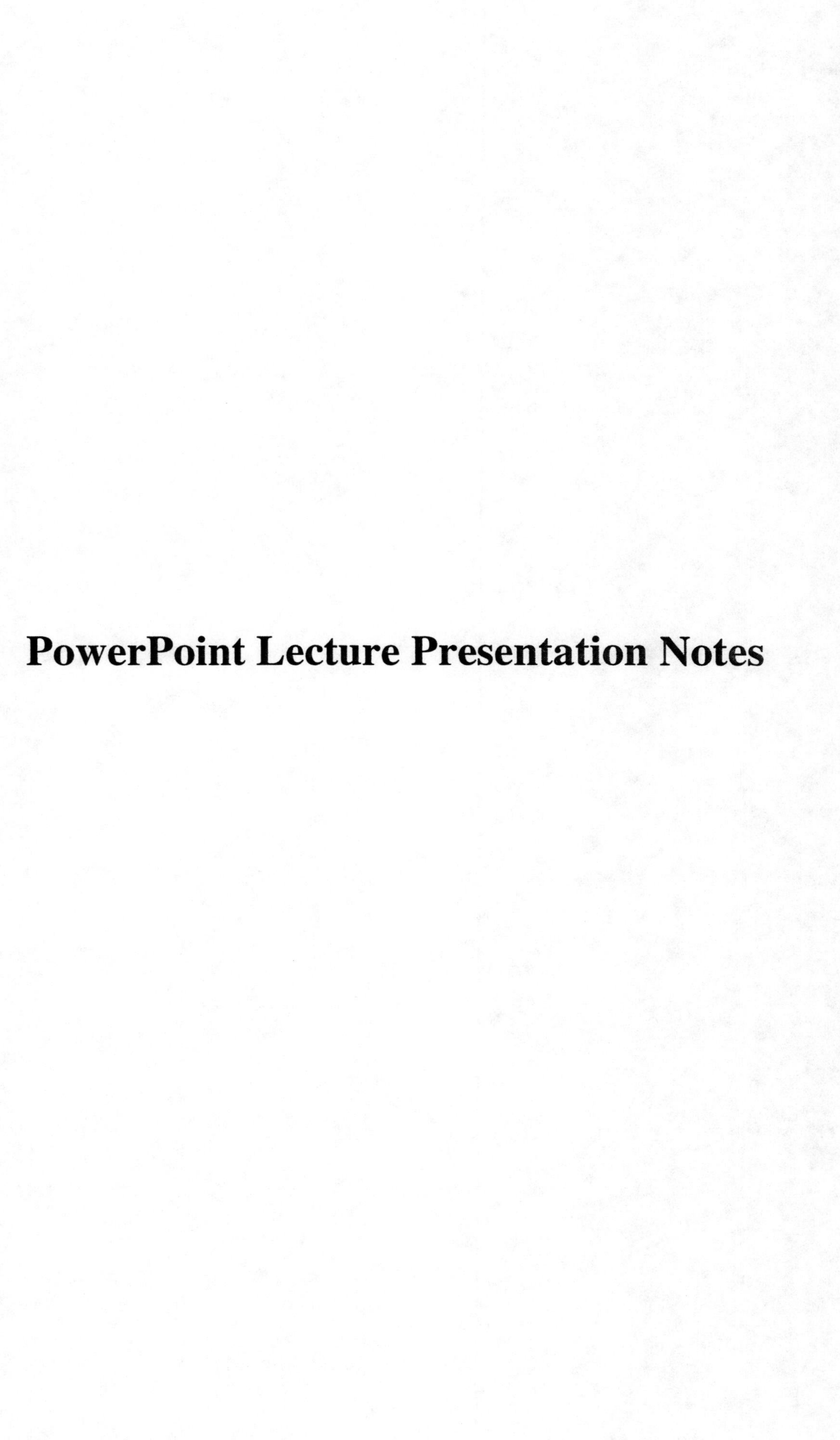

PowerPoint Lecture Presentation Notes

Chapter 1

Introduction to Finance

Lawrence J. Gitman
Jeff Madura

The Financial Environment: Firms, Investors, and Markets

Learning Goals

- Define finance and explain why it is relevant to students.
- Explain the components of the financial environment.
- Explain how investors monitor managers to ensure that managerial decisions are in the best interests of the owners.
- Describe how the financial environment has become internationalized.

What is Finance?

- Finance represents the processes that transfer money among businesses, individuals, and governments.

What is Finance?

- Financial decisions affecting firms:
  - Dell computer expands its product line.
  - Gap builds additional stores.
  - Nike closes a production plant in Asia.
  - Ford borrows $3 billion.
  - Perot Systems issues stock valued at $3 billion.

What is Finance?

- Financial events affecting investors:
  - Nike stock declines 5 percent after a financial crisis occurs in Asia.
  - Microsoft stock declines after the court rules against the company in an antitrust case.
  - Lotus stock rises by 50 percent on news it is being acquired by IBM.

What is Finance?

- Financial events resulting from government actions:
  - Yields on bonds decline in response to Federal Reserve decisions.
  - Interest rates rise in response to inflationary fears.
  - The dollar declines as U.S. investors invest more money abroad.

The Relevance of Finance

- This book discusses finance from two primary perspectives: the financial manager and the investor.
- It also discusses how financial institutions and financial markets affect both types of decision makers.
- Thus, this text will help to prepare students for careers in finance or in business in general.
- It also helps to prepare students for making personal financial decisions as investors.

Components of the Financial Environment

- Financial Managers
  - Financial managers are responsible for deciding how to raise and invest company funds.
  - Collectively, these decisions are referred to as financial management.
  - Financial managers are expected to make decisions that will maximize stock price and firm value and are frequently compensated in a manner that encourages the achievement of these activities.

Financial Managers

TABLE 1.1 Career Opportunities in Financial Management

Position	Description
Financial analyst	Primarily prepares the firm's financial plans and budgets. Other duties include financial forecasting, performing financial comparisons, and working closely with accounting.
Capital expenditures manager	Evaluates and recommends proposed asset investments. May be involved in the financial aspects of implementing approved investments.
Project finance manager	In large firms, arranges financing for approved asset investments. Coordinates consultants, investment bankers, and legal counsel.
Cash manager	Maintains and controls the firm's daily cash balances. Frequently manages the firm's cash collection and disbursement activities and short-term investments and coordinates short-term borrowing and banking relationships.
Credit analyst/manager	Administers the firm's credit policy by evaluating credit applications, extending credit, and monitoring and collecting accounts receivable.
Pension fund manager	In large companies, oversees or manages the assets and liabilities of the employees' pension fund.
Foreign exchange manager	Manages specific foreign operations and the firm's exposure to exchange rate fluctuations.

 Table 1.1

Financial Managers

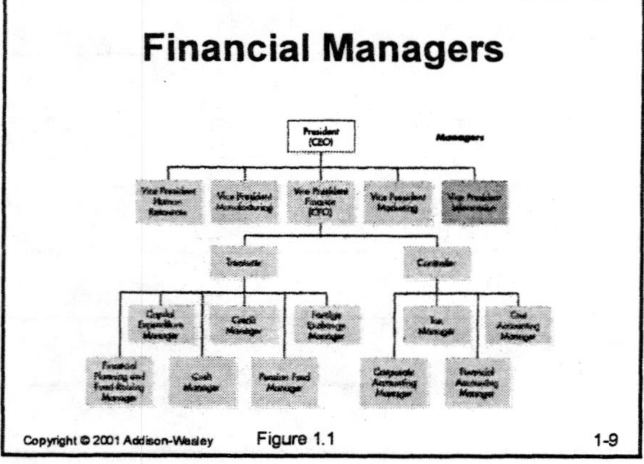

Figure 1.1

Financial Managers

- Interaction Between Financial Management and Other Business Functions

Financial Managers

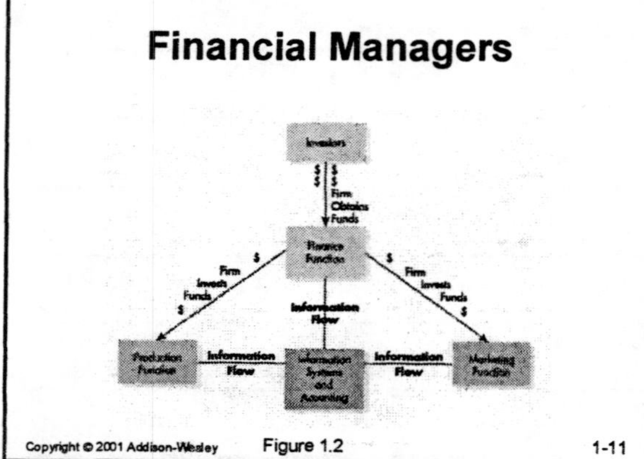

Figure 1.2

Investment Decisions by Financial Managers

- Financial managers are responsible for assessing the value of investment being considered by the firm.
- Good investment decisions have a profound effect on the activities and the success of any business.
- Both current and fixed asset decisions must be considered.
- Investments are evaluated in terms of both risk and return.

Financing Decisions by Financial Managers

- Financial managers are responsible for selecting the type of security and the amount of capital raised.
- The financial manager must also decide between long-term and short-term capital.
- For publicly traded firms, either equity or debt can be issued to obtain long term capital.
- The firm can also use internally generated capital (retained equity) to fund investments.

Components of the Financial Environment

- Investors
  - Investors represent individuals or financial institutions that provide funds to firms, government agencies, or individuals who need funds.
  - For publicly traded corporations, individuals provide funds to firms by purchasing their stocks and bonds.
  - Financial institutions that provide funds to firms are called institutional investors.
  - Some institutional investors provide loans, while others purchase securities issued by firms.

Debt Financing Provided by Investors

- Loans provided to firms by financial institutions in exchange for fixed, periodic interest, and end-of-the-period principal repayment.
- Debt securities (bonds) purchased by both individuals and institutions.
- Investors profit by either purchasing debt at a discount or by receiving periodic interest payments and most debt can typically be traded in the financial markets.

Equity Financing Provided by Investors

- When investors provide equity capital, they are purchasing ownership in a firm.
- Stocks of publicly traded firms can be bought and sold in the market to other investors.
- Investors can receive a return in the form of dividends and/or capital gains.

Return and Risk from Investing

- Dividends represent a distribution of profits to the owners, while capital gains (losses) result when the security is later sold for more (less) than its purchase price.
- Most investors are risk averse, meaning they prefer less risk to more.
- The riskier the firm (stock), the greater will be an investor's *expected* return.

Investors Use of Financial Services

- Financial services firms include:
  - Financial planning firms
  - Banks, S&Ls, and credit unions
  - Brokerage firms
  - Insurance companies
  - Online sources

Components of the Financial Environment

- Financial Markets
  - Financial markets represent forums that facilitate the flow of funds between investors, firms, and government units and agencies.
  - Examples of financial markets include the equity market and the debt market.
  - Each financial market is served by financial institutions that act as intermediaries between buyers and sellers.
  - Financial institutions acting as intermediaries include banks, brokerage firms, and insurance companies.

Careers of Participants in Financial Markets

TABLE 1.2 **Career Opportunities in Financial Markets**

Career	Career opportunities
Banking and related institutions	*Loan officers* evaluate and make recommendations on various types of loans. *Retail bank managers* run bank offices and supervise the programs offered by the bank. *Trust officers* administer trust funds for estates, foundations, and business firms.
Personal financial planning	*Financial planners* advise individuals on all aspects of their personal finances and help them develop comprehensive financial plans to meet their objectives.
Real estate	*Real estate agents/brokers* negotiate the sale or lease of residential and commercial property. *Appraisers* estimate the market values of all types of property. *Real estate lenders* analyze and make decisions with regard to loan applications. *Mortgage bankers* find and arrange financing for real estate projects. *Property managers* handle the day-to-day operations of properties to achieve maximum returns for their owners.
Insurance	*Insurance agents/brokers* sell insurance policies to meet clients' needs and assist in claims processing and settlement. *Underwriters* appraise and select the risks that their company will insure and set the associated premiums.
Investments	*Stockbrokers*, or account executives, assist clients in choosing, buying and selling securities. *Securities analysts* study stocks and bonds and advise securities firms and insurance companies with regard to them. *Portfolio managers* build and manage portfolios of securities for firms and individuals. *Investment bankers* provide advice to security issuers and act as intermediaries between issuers and purchasers of newly issued stocks and bonds.

Table 1.2

Integration of Components in Financial Markets

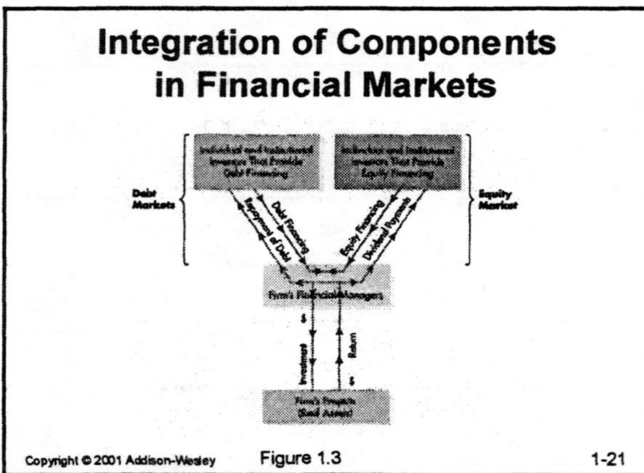

Figure 1.3

Investor Monitoring of Firms

- Using Information to Value the Firm
  - Stock prices change continuously in response to changes in the supply and demand for shares.
  - Supply and demand changes in response to new information that is expected to impact a firm's prospects.
  - Favorable information will impact share prices positively, while unfavorable information will have a negative impact on prices.

Investor Monitoring of Firms

- How Investors Influence Firm Value
  - Because actions by management have an influence on firm performance and hence stock value, investors attempt to ensure that managers' actions will maximize firm value.
  - Investors can influence management action through:
    - Trading
    - Shareholder activism
    - Threat of takeover

Investor Monitoring of Firms

- Effects of Asymmetric Information
  - Investors monitor firms by reviewing financial statements and relying on reports by third-party services such as Moody's, Standard & Poors, and Internet web sites.
  - However, the information provided by financial statements and information services is incomplete.
  - Asymmetric information results from the fact that more information is available to a firm's managers than to its investors, and this information can affect stock prices.

Investor Monitoring of Firms

- Effects of Asymmetric Information
  - Some institutional investors subscribe to proprietary information services not available to individual investors that reduce asymmetric information.
  - As a result, many individual investors choose to pay institutional investors (such as brokers) to make investment decisions for them.

The International Finance Environment

- Risks of International Business
  - Exchange rate risk
  - Political risk
  - Risks resulting from cultural differences

Using This Textbook

- Part 1: The Financial Marketplace
- Part 2: Financial Tools for Firms and Investors
- Part 3: Financial Management
- Part 4: Investment Management
- Part 5: How Investors Monitor and Control a Firm's Managers

Chapter 2

Introduction to Finance

Lawrence J. Gitman
Jeff Madura

Financial Institutions and Markets

Learning Goals

- Explain how financial institutions serve as intermediaries between investors and firms.
- Provide and overview of financial markets.
- Explain how firms and investors trade money market and capital market securities in the financial markets in order to satisfy their needs.
- Describe the major securities exchanges.
- Describe derivative securities and explain why they are used by firms and investors.
- Describe the foreign exchange market.

Effective Financial Systems

- An effective financial system must possess three characteristics:
  - Monetary systems that provide an efficient medium for exchanging goods and services
  - Facilitate capital formation whereby excess capital from savers is made available to borrowers (investors)
  - Efficient and complete financial markets which provide for the transfer of financial assets (such as stocks and bonds), and for the conversion of such assets into cash

Financial Institutions

- Financial institutions serve as intermediaries by channeling the savings of individuals, businesses, and governments into loans or investments.
- They are a primary source of funds for both individuals and businesses.
- In addition, they are the main store of deposits for individuals through checking accounts (demand deposits) and savings accounts (time deposits).

Key Customers of Financial Institutions

- The key customers of financial institutions are individuals, businesses, and governments.
- Savings of individuals provide the main supply of funds to both businesses and other individuals.
- As a group, individuals are net suppliers of funds.
- Firms, on the other hand, are net demanders of funds.
- Finally, like individuals, governments are net demanders of funds.
- The different types of financial institutions are described on the following slide.

Financial Intermediaries in the United States

Depository Institutions
- Commercial Banks
- S&Ls
- Savings Banks
- Credit

Contractual Savings Institutions
- Life Insurance Companies
- Private Pension Funds
- State and Local Government Retirement Funds

Investment Institutions
- Investment Companies and Mutual Funds
- Real Estate Investment Trusts
- Money Market Funds

Finance Companies
- Sales Finance Companies
- Consumer Finance Companies
- Commercial Finance Companies

Selected Securities Market Institutions
- Mortgage Banking Companies
- Investment Bankers and Brokerage Companies
- Organized Securities Markets
- Credit Reporting Organizations
- Government Credit-Related Agencies

Commercial Banks

- Commercial banks accumulate deposits from savers and use the proceeds to provide credit to firms, individuals, and government agencies.
- Banks provide personal loans to individuals and commercial loans to firms.
- Commercial banks earn much of their profit by earning a higher rate on loans than the rate they pay on deposits.
- In recent years, banks have expanded the range of services they provide for customers.

Sources and Uses of Funds at Commercial Banks

- Banks obtain most of their funds by accepting deposits, primarily from individuals but also from firms and governments.
- These deposits are insured by the FDIC to a maximum of $100,000 per depositor.
- Banks use most of their funds to provide loans to individuals or firms, or to purchase debt securities.
- Some popular means by which banks extend credit to firms include term loans and lines of credit.

Sources and Uses of Funds at Commercial Banks

- Term loans typically last from 4 to 8 years.
- Lines of credit allow firms to access a specified amount of funds over a specified period of time and are generally used to meet working capital requirements.
- Lines of credit must typically be renewed each year by the firm requesting them.
- Commercial banks also invest in debt securities that are issued by firms.

Role of Commercial Banks as Financial Intermediaries

- Commercial banks serve as financial intermediaries in several ways.
- First, they repackage deposits received from investors into loans that are provided to firms.
- Second, banks employ credit analysts who have the ability to assess the creditworthiness of firms that wish to borrow funds.

Role of Commercial Banks as Financial Intermediaries

- Third, banks can diversify loans across several borrowers thereby reducing the risk of default.
- Fourth, banks have recently served as intermediaries by placing (issuing) securities that are issued by firms.

Regulation of Commercial Banks

- Banks are regulated by the Federal Reserve System (the Fed), which serves as the central bank of the United States.
- Banks are also regulated by the Federal Deposit Insurance Corporation (FDIC) which insures depositors.
- The general philosophy of regulators who monitor the banking system is to promote competition while at the same time limiting risk to safeguard the system.

Mutual Funds

- Mutual funds are owned by investment companies.
- Mutual funds sell shares to individuals and pools the proceeds to invest in securities.
- Money market mutual funds invest in short-term money market securities issued by firms and other financial institutions.
- Bond mutual funds invest in bonds.
- Stock mutual funds pool the proceeds received from investors to invest in stocks.

Role of Mutual Funds as Intermediaries

- When mutual funds invest in newly issued debt or equity securities, they are helping to finance new investment by firms.
- When mutual funds purchase debt or equity securities already held by investors, they help to transfer ownership by investors.
- Mutual funds enable small investors to diversify their portfolios to a greater extent than possible themselves.

Role of Mutual Funds as Intermediaries

- Mutual funds also benefit investors by providing professional management expertise that most individual investors do not posses.
- Mutual funds managers are armed with substantial resources with which to make investment decisions.
- Finally, because mutual funds may own a substantial percentage of a given firm's stock, they are able to exert considerable influence on firm and stock performance through management.

Securities Firms

- Securities firms are a category of firms that include investment banks, investment companies, and brokerage firms.
- They serve an investment banking function by placing securities issued by firms and government agencies.
- They serve a brokerage role by helping investors purchase securities or sell securities that they previously purchased.

Insurance Companies

- Insurance companies provide various types of insurance including: life insurance, property and casualty insurance, and health insurance.
- They function as intermediaries by accepting customer premiums and paying claims.
- They pool premiums and invest in securities issued by firms and government agencies and employ portfolio managers to make investment decisions.

Pension Funds

- Pension funds invest payments (contributions) from employees and/or employers on behalf of employees.
- Pension funds employ portfolio managers to invest funds from pooling the contributions.
- Because of the large size of their investments in the stocks and bonds of firms, pension funds closely monitor the firms in which they invest.

Comparison of Financial Institutions

TABLE 2.1 Major Financial Institutions

Institutions	Description
Commercial Bank	Accepts both demand (checking) and time (savings) deposits. Offers interest-earning savings accounts (NOW accounts) against which checks can be written. Offers money market deposit accounts, which pay interest at rates competitive with other short-term investment vehicles. Makes loans directly to borrowers or through the financial markets.
Mutual Fund	Pools funds of savers and makes them available to business and government demanders. Obtains funds through sales of shares and uses proceeds to acquire bonds and stocks. Creates a diversified and professionally managed portfolio of securities to achieve a specified investment objective. Thousands of funds, with a variety of investment objectives, exist. Money market mutual funds provide competitive returns with very high liquidity.
Securities Firm	Provides investment banking services by helping firms to obtain funds. Provides brokerage services to facilitate the sales of existing securities.
Insurance Company	The largest type of financial intermediary handling individual savings. Receives premium payments and places these funds in loans or investments to cover future benefit payments. Lends funds to individuals, businesses, and governments or channels them through the financial markets.

Table 2.1 (Panel 1)

Comparison of Financial Institutions

TABLE 2.1 Major Financial Institutions

Institutions	Description
Pension Fund	Accumulates payments (contributions) from employees of firms or government units, and often from employers, in order to provide retirement income. Money is sometimes transferred directly to borrowers, but the majority is lent or invested via the financial markets.
Savings Institution	Similar to a commercial bank except that it may not hold demand (checking) deposits. Obtains funds from savings, NOW, and money market deposits. Also raises capital through the sale of securities in the financial markets. Lends funds primarily to individuals and businesses or real estate mortgage loans. Channels some funds into investments in the financial markets.
Savings Bank	Similar to a savings institution in that it holds savings, NOW, and money market deposit accounts. Makes residential real estate loans to individuals.
Finance Company	Obtains funds by issuing securities and lends funds to individuals and small businesses.
Credit Union	Deals primarily in transfer of funds between consumers. Membership is generally based on some common bond, such as working for a given employer. Accepts members' savings deposits, NOW account deposits, and money market accounts.

Table 2.1 (Panel 2)

Consolidation of Financial Institutions

- In recent years, financial conglomerates have been created that offer commercial banking services, investment banking services, brokerage services, mutual funds, and insurance services.
- In general, financial conglomeration is expected to increase the competition among financial intermediaries, lowering the prices paid by individuals and firms for these services.

Globalization of Financial Institutions

- Financial institutions have expanded internationally in recent years.
- This expansion was spurred by the expansion of multinational corporations, and because banks recognized they could capitalize on their global image by establishing branches in foreign cities.
- This global expansion is expected to continue in the future.

Overview of Financial Markets

- Public Offering versus Private Placement
  - A public offering is the nonexclusive sale of securities to the general public.
  - Public offerings are normally executed with the help of a securities firm that provides investment banking services.
  - The securities firm may underwrite the offering, which means that it guarantees the amount to be received by the issuing firm.

Overview of Financial Markets

- Public Offering versus Private Placement
  - A private placement is the sale of new securities directly to an investor or a group of investors.
  - In general, only institutional investors such as pension funds or insurance companies can afford to invest in private placements.

Overview of Financial Markets

- Primary Markets versus Secondary Markets
  - Marketable financial assets can be categorized according to whether they trade in the primary market or the secondary market.
  - Primary markets are where new securities (IPOs) are issued.
  - Secondary markets are where securities are bought and sold after initially issued in the primary markets.
  - In addition, financial assets may be money market instruments or capital market instruments.

Key Types of Securities

- Key Money Market Securities
  - U.S. Treasury Bills
  - Negotiable CDs
  - Banker's Acceptances
  - Federal Funds
  - Commercial Paper
  - Repurchase Agreements

Key Types of Securities

- Key Money Market Securities
  - U.S. Treasury Notes and Bonds
  - U.S. Government Agency Bonds
  - State and Local Government Bonds
  - Corporate Bonds
  - Corporate Stocks
  - Real Estate Mortgages

Major Securities Exchanges

- Organized Exchanges
  - Organized securities exchanges are *tangible* secondary markets where outstanding securities are bought and sold.
  - They account for over 60% of the dollar volume of domestic shares traded.
  - Only the largest and most profitable companies meet the requirements necessary to be *listed* on the New York Stock Exchange.

Major Securities Exchanges

- Organized Exchanges
  - Only those that own a *seat* on the exchange can make transactions on the floor (there are currently 1,366 seats).
  - Trading is conducted through an *auction process* where *specialists* "make a market" in selected securities.
  - As compensation for executing orders, specialists make money on the *spread* (the bid price minus the ask price).

Major Securities Exchanges

- Organized Exchanges

Requirements	NYSE	AMEX
Shares held by public	1,100,000	400,000
Stockholders with 100+ shares	2,000	1,200
Pretax income (latest year)	$2,500,000	$750,000
Pretax income (prior 2 years)	$2,000,000	N/A
MV of public shares held	$18,000,000	$300,000
Tangible assets	$16,000,000	$4,000,000

Major Securities Exchanges

- Over-the-Counter Exchange
  - The over-the-counter (OTC) market is an intangible market for securities transactions.
  - Unlike organized exchanges, the OTC is both a primary market and a secondary market.
  - The OTC is a computer-based market where dealers make a market in selected securities and are linked to buyers and sellers through the NASDAQ System.
  - Dealers also make money on the *spread*.

Derivative Securities Markets

- Derivative securities are financial contracts whose values are derived from the values of underlying financial assets.
- Derivatives allow investors to take (leveraged) positions based on their expectations of movements in the underlying assets.
- Investors can use derivatives to take speculative positions or can use them to (hedge) reduce exposure to risk on other investments or portfolios.

Chapter 2

Introduction to Finance

Lawrence J. Gitman
Jeff Madura

End of Chapter

Chapter 3

Introduction to Finance

Lawrence J. Gitman
Jeff Madura

Corporate Securities: Bonds and Stocks

Learning Goals

- Describe the legal aspects of bond financing and bond cost.
- Discuss the general features, ratings, popular types, and international issues of corporate bonds.
- Differentiate between debt and equity capital.
- Review the rights and features of common stock.
- Discuss the rights and features of preferred stock.
- Understand the role of the investment banker in securities offerings.

Corporate Bonds

- Corporate bonds are debt securities issued by the corporation itself.
- Investors lend money to the corporation in exchange for a specified promised amount of (coupon) interest income.
- Most bonds are issued with face values of $1,000 and maturities of 10 to 30 years.
- At the end of the bond term, investors receive the face value of the bond.

Corporate Bonds

- Legal Aspects
  - The bond indenture specifies the conditions under which it has been issued.
  - It outlines both the rights of bondholders and duties of the issuing corporation.
  - It also specifies the timing of interest and principal payments, any restrictive covenants, and sinking fund requirements.

Corporate Bonds

- Legal Aspects
  - Common standard debt provisions in the indenture typically include:
    - The maintenance of satisfactory accounting records
    - Periodically furnishing audited financial statements
    - The payment of taxes and other liabilities when due
    - The maintenance of all facilities in good working order
    - Identification of any collateral pledged against the bond

Corporate Bonds

- Legal Aspects
  - Common restrictive provisions (or covenants) in the indenture typically include:
    - The maintenance of a minimum level of liquidity
    - Prohibiting the sale of accounts receivable
    - The imposition of certain fixed asset investments
    - Constraints on subsequent borrowing
    - Limits on annual cash dividend payments

Corporate Bonds

- Legal Aspects
  - An additional restrictive provision often included in the indenture is a sinking fund requirement, which specifies the manner in which a bond is systematically retired prior to maturity.
  - Sinking funds typically dictate that the firm make semi-annual or annual payments to a trustee who then purchases the bonds in the market.

Corporate Bonds

- Cost of Bonds
  - In general, the *longer the bond's maturity*, the higher the interest rate (or cost) to the firm.
  - In addition, the *larger the size* of the offering, the lower will be the cost (in % terms) of the bond.
  - Finally, the *greater the risk* of the issuing firm, the higher the cost of the issue.

Corporate Bonds

- General Features
  - The conversion feature of convertible bonds allows bondholders to exchange their bonds for a specified number of shares of common stock.
  - Bondholders will exercise this option only when the market price of the stock is greater than the conversion price.
  - A call feature, which is included in most corporate issues, gives the issuer the opportunity to repurchase the bond prior to maturity at the call price.

Corporate Bonds

- General Features
  - In general, the call premium is equal to one year of coupon interest and compensates the holder for having it called prior to maturity.
  - Furthermore, issuers will exercise the call feature when interest rates fall and the issuer can refund the issue at a lower cost.
  - Issuers typically must pay a higher rate to investors for the call feature compared to issues without the feature.

Corporate Bonds

- General Features
  - Bonds also are occasionally issued with stock purchase warrants attached to them to make them more attractive to investors.
  - Warrants give the bondholder the right to purchase a certain number of shares of the same firm's common stock at a specified price during a specified period of time.
  - Including warrants typically allows the firm to raise debt capital at a lower cost than would be possible in their absence.

Bond Ratings

TABLE 3.1 Moody's and Standard & Poor's Bond Ratings*

Moody's	Interpretation	Standard & Poor's	Interpretation
Aaa	Prime quality	AAA	Bank investment quality
Aa	High grade	AA	
A	Upper medium grade	A	
Baa	Medium grade	BBB	
Ba	Lower medium grade or speculative	BB	Speculative
B	Speculative	B	
Caa	From very speculative to	CCC	
Ca	near or in default	CC	
C	Lowest grade	C	Income bond
		D	In default

*Some ratings may be modified to show relative standing within a major rating category; for example, Moody's uses numerical modifiers (1, 2, 3), whereas Standard & Poor's uses plus (+) and minus (−) signs.

Source: Moody's Investor Services Inc. and Standard & Poor's Corporation.

 Table 3.1

Forms of Debt

- Bearer Bonds
  - Bearer bonds are often referred to as coupon bonds because they are not registered to any particular person.
  - The coupons are submitted twice a year and the authorized bank pays the interest.

For instance, a twenty year $1,000 bond paying 8% interest would have 40 coupons for $40 each. Bearer bonds can be used like cash. They are highly negotiable. There are still many in circulation. However, the Tax Reform Act of 1982 ended the issuance of bearer bonds.

Forms of Debt

- Registered Bonds
  - Today, bonds are sold in a *fully registered* form. They come with your name already on them. Twice a year, you receive a check for the interest. At maturity, the registered owner receives a check for the principal.
  - A *partially registered* bond is a cross between a registered bond and a coupon bond. The bond comes registered to you; however, it has coupons attached which you send in for payment.

Popular Types of Bonds

TABLE 3.2 Characteristics and Priority of Lender's Claim of Traditional Types of Bonds

Bond type	Characteristics	Priority of lender's claim
Unsecured Bonds		
Debentures	[illegible]	[illegible]
Subordinated debentures	[illegible]	[illegible]
Income bonds	[illegible]	[illegible]
Secured Bonds		
Mortgage bonds	Secured real estate or buildings.	[illegible]
Collateral trust bonds	[illegible] 25 to 35% greater than bond value.	[illegible]
Equipment trust certificates	[illegible] A type of leasing.	[illegible]

 Table 3.2

Popular Types of Bonds

TABLE 3.3 Characteristics of Contemporary Types of Bonds

Bond type	Characteristics*
Zero- (or low-) coupon bonds	Issued with no (zero) or a very low coupon (stated interest) rate and sold at a large discount from par. A significant portion (or all) of the investor's return comes from gain in value (i.e., par value minus purchase price). Generally callable at par value. Because the issuer can annually deduct the current year's interest accrual without having to pay the interest until the bond matures (or is called), its cash flow each year is increased by the amount of the tax shield provided by the interest deduction.
Junk bonds	Debt rated Ba or lower by Moody's or BB or lower by Standard & Poor's. Commonly used during the 1980s by rapidly growing firms to obtain growth capital, most often as a way to finance mergers and takeovers. High-risk bonds with high yields—typically yielding 3% more than the best-quality corporate debt.
Floating-rate bonds	Stated interest rate is adjusted periodically within stated limits in response to changes in specified money market or capital market rates. Popular when future inflation and interest rates are uncertain. Tend to sell at close to par because of the automatic adjustment to changing market conditions. Some issues provide for annual redemption at par at the option of the bondholder.
Extendible notes	Short maturities, typically 1 to 5 years, that can be renewed for a similar period at the option of holders. Similar to a floating-rate bond. An issue might be a series of 3-year renewable notes over a period of 15 years; every 3 years, the notes could be extended for another 3 years, at a new rate competitive with market interest rates at the time of renewal.
Putable bonds	Bonds that can be redeemed at par (typically $1,000) at the option of their holder either at specific dates after the date of issue and every 1 to 5 years thereafter or when and if the firm takes specified actions such as being acquired, acquiring another company, or issuing a large amount of additional debt. In return for its conferring the right to "put the bond" at specified times or when the firm takes certain actions, the bond's yield is lower than that of a nonputable bond.

*The claims of lenders (i.e., bondholders) against issuers of each of these types of bonds vary, depending on their other features. Each of these bonds can be unsecured or secured.

 Table 3.3

International Bond Issues

- Companies and governments borrow internationally by issuing bonds in either the Eurobond market or the foreign bond market.
- A Eurobond is issued by an international borrower and sold to investors in countries with currencies other than the country in which the bond is denominated.
- In contrast, a foreign bond is issued in a host country's financial market, in the host country's currency, by a foreign borrower.

Contrasting Debt and Equity Capital

TABLE 3.4 Key Differences Between Debt and Equity Capital

	Type of capital	
Characteristic	Debt	Equity
Voice in management*	No	Yes
Claims on income and assets	Senior to equity	Subordinate to debt
Maturity	Stated	None
Tax treatment	Interest deduction	No deduction

*In the event that the issuer violates its stated contractual obligations to them, debtholders and preferred stockholders *may* receive a voice in management; otherwise, only common stockholders have voting rights.

 Table 3.4

Common Stock

- Common stockholders are the true owners of the business and are sometimes referred to as residual claimants or owners.
- Because they bear greater risk than other claimants, common stockholders expect to receive higher returns (from dividends and/or capital gains) than other claimants such as bondholders.

Common Stock

- Ownership
  - The common stock of a company can be privately owned, closely owned, or publicly owned.
  - Many small corporations are privately or closely owned where shares are traded very infrequently without the aid of an exchange market.
  - Large and/or publicly owned corporations have widely held shares which are actively traded on an exchange market.

Common Stock

- Par Value
  - Unlike the case for bonds and preferred stock, par value for common stock is a relatively useless value.
  - Firms often issue stock with no par value, in which case they will record it on the books at the sale price.
  - Low par values may have some advantages in states where some corporate taxes are based on par value.

Stockholder Rights

- Voting Rights
  - In general, voting rights are relatively meaningless since share ownership is very widely dispersed among a large number of individual shareholders. As a result, directors and top management are relatively well-insulated.
  - This has begun to diminish to some extent in recent years due to the rapid expansion of large institutional investors such as mutual funds and insurance companies.

Stockholder Rights

- Voting Rights
  - Traditional voting
    - Under traditional voting, each share owned gives the shareholder the right to vote for one individual for each set on the board of directors.
    - Under this system, if the majority of shareholders vote as a block, the minority could never elect a director.

Stockholder Rights

- Voting Rights
  - Traditional voting
  - Cumulative voting
    - This system empowers minority stockholders by permitting each stockholder to cast all of his or her votes for one candidate for the firm's board of directors.

Stockholder Rights

- Voting Rights
  - Traditional voting
  - Cumulative voting
  - Example
    - Under *traditional voting*, a shareholder with 100 shares can vote 100 shares for each of 5 members of the board of directors.
    - Under *cumulative voting*, a shareholder with 100 shares can vote 500 shares for just one member running for the board of directors.

Stockholder Rights

- Voting Rights
- Preemptive Rights
  - A preemptive right gives a shareholder the right to maintain his or her proportionate share of the company by requiring that all new shares issued must be done so through a "rights offering."
  - Under a *rights offering*, a shareholder who owns 10% of the shares outstanding has the right to purchase 10% of any additional shares issued.

Stockholder Rights

- Voting Rights
- Preemptive Rights
- Proxies
  - Proxies are frequently used in the voting process since many smaller stockholders do not attend the annual meeting. Shareholders must sign a proxy statement giving their votes to another party who will then vote their shares.

Common Stock

- Dividends
  - Payment of dividends is at the discretion of the Board of Directors.
  - Dividends may be made in cash, additional shares of stock, and even merchandise.
  - Stockholders are residual claimants— they receive dividend payments only after all claims have been settled with the government, creditors, and preferred stockholders.

Common Stock

- International Stock Issues
  - The international market for common stock is not as large as that for international debt.
  - However, cross-border trading and issuance of stock has increased dramatically during the past 20 years.
  - Much of this increase has been driven by the desire of investors to diversify their portfolios internationally.

Common Stock

- International Stock Issues
  - Stocks issued in foreign markets
    - A growing number of firms are beginning to list their stocks on foreign markets.
    - Issuing stock internationally both broadens the company's ownership base and helps it to integrate itself in the local business scene.

Common Stock

- International Stock Issues
  - Foreign stocks in United States markets
    - Only the largest foreign firms choose to list their stocks in the United States because of the rigid reporting requirements of the U.S. markets.
    - Most foreign firms instead choose to tap the U.S. markets using ADRs—claims issued by U.S. banks representing ownership shares of foreign stock trading in U.S. markets.

 3-30

Preferred Stock

- Preferred stock is an equity instrument that usually pays a fixed dividend and has a prior claim on the firm's earnings and assets in case of liquidation.
- The dividend is expressed as either a dollar amount or as a percentage of its par value.
- Therefore, unlike common stock a preferred stock's par value may have real significance.
- If a firm fails to pay a preferred stock dividend, the dividend is said to be in arrears.

 3-31

Preferred Stock

- In general, an arrearage must be paid before common stockholders receive a dividend.
- Preferred stocks which possess this characteristic are called cumulative preferred stocks.
- Preferred stocks are also often referred to as *hybrid* securities because they possess the characteristics of both common stocks and bonds.
- Preferred stocks are like common stocks because they are perpetual securities with no maturity date.

 3-32

Preferred Stock

- Preferred stocks are like bonds because they are fixed income securities. Dividends never change.
- Because preferred stocks are perpetual, many have *call features* which give the issuing firm the option to retire them should the need or advantage arise.
- In addition, some preferred stocks have *mandatory sinking funds* which allow the firm to retire the issue over time.
- Finally, *participating preferred stock* allows preferred stockholders to participate with common stockholders in the receipt of dividends beyond a specified amount.

Preferred Stocks and Bonds Contrasted

- Preferred stocks are riskier than bonds from the investor perspective because:
  - Bond terms are legal obligations.
  - The investor cannot expect the firm to redeem preferred stock for a preset face value. It must be sold in the market at an uncertain price.
- Preferred stock prices are therefore more variable and thus riskier than bond prices.

Disadvantages of Preferred Stock

- Preferred stock offers no protection from inflation.
- Preferred stock tends to be less marketable than either bonds or common stock resulting in a large bid-ask spread.
- Inferior position to bondholders.
- Yields are insufficient for most (non-corporate) investors to justify risk.

Investment Banking

- Corporations typically raise debt and equity capital using the services of investment bankers through public offerings.
- When underwriting a security issue, an investment banker guarantees that the issuer will receive a specified amount of money from the issue.
- The investment banker purchases the securities from the firm at a lower price than the planned resale price.

Investment Banking

- When underwriting an issue, the investment banker bears the risk of price changes between the time of purchase and the time of resale.
- With a private placement, the investment banker arranges for the direct sale of the issue to one or more individuals or firms and receives a commission for acting as the intermediary in the transaction.
- When a firm issues securities on a best-efforts basis, compensation is based on the number of securities sold.

Investment Banking

- Advising
  - Underwriters also act as advisors and consultants for corporations.
  - They can assist firms in planning both the timing of an issue and the amount and features of an issue.
  - They can also assist in evaluating mergers and acquisitions.

Investment Banking

- Selecting an Investment Banker
  - An investment banker may be selected through competitive bidding, where the banker or group of bankers that bids the highest price for an issue is chosen for the underwriting.
  - With a negotiated offering, the investment banker is merely hired rather than awarded the issue through a competitive bid.

Investment Banking

- Syndicating the Underwriting
  - Underwriting syndicates are typically formed when companies bring large issues to the market.
  - Each investment banker in the syndicate normally underwrites a portion of the issue in order to reduce the risk of loss for any single firm and insure wider distribution of shares.
  - The syndicate does so by creating a selling group which distributes the shares to the investing public.

Investment Banking

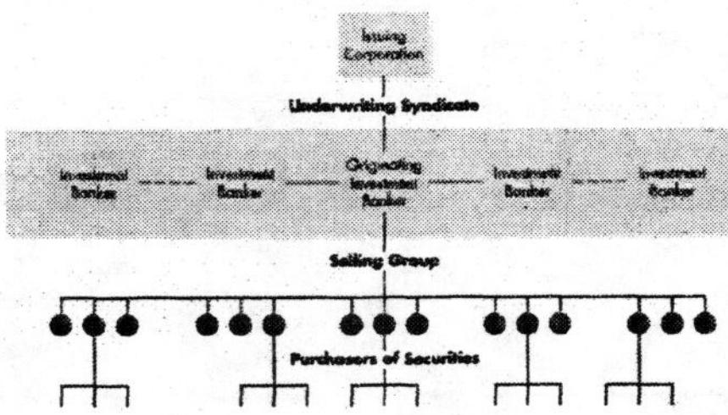

Figure 3.1

Investment Banking

- Fulfilling Legal Requirements
  - Before a new security can be issued, the firm must file a registration statement with the SEC at least 20 days before approval is granted.
  - One part of the registration statement called the prospectus details the firm's operating and financial position.
  - However, a prospectus may be distributed to potential investors during the approval period as long as a red herring is printed on the front cover.

Investment Banking

- Fulfilling Legal Requirements
  - As an alternative to filing cumbersome registration statements, firms with more than $150 million in outstanding stock can use a procedure called shelf registration.
  - This allows the firm to file a single document that covers all issues during the subsequent 2-year period.
  - As a result, the approved securities are kept "on the shelf" until the need for or market conditions are appropriate for an issue.

Investment Banking

- Pricing and Distributing an Issue
  - In general, underwriters wait until the end of the registration period to price securities to ensure marketability.
  - If the issue is fully sold, it is considered an *oversubscribed* issue; if not fully sold, it is considered *undersubscribed*.
  - In order to stabilize the issue at the initial offering price as it is being offered for sale, investment bankers often place orders to purchase the security themselves.

Investment Banking

- Cost of Investment Banking Services
  - Investment bankers earn their income by profiting on the spread.
  - The spread is difference between the price paid for the securities by the investment banker and the eventual selling price in the marketplace.
  - In general, costs for underwriting equity are highest, followed by preferred stock, and then bonds.
  - In percentage terms, costs can be as high as 17% for small stock offerings to as low as 1.6% for large bond issues.

Investment Banking

- Private Placements
  - Although diminishing in frequency, firms can also negotiate private placements rather than public offerings.
  - Private placements can reduce administrative and issuance costs for firms since registration with and approval from the SEC is not required.
  - However, they do pose problems for purchasers since the securities cannot not be resold via secondary markets.

Chapter 3

Introduction to Finance
Lawrence J. Gitman
Jeff Madura

End of Chapter

Chapter 4

Introduction to Finance

Lawrence J. Gitman
Jeff Madura

Interest Rate Fundamentals

Learning Goals

- Discuss the components that influence the risk-free interest rate at a given point in time.
- Explain why the risk-free interest rate changes over time.
- Explain why the risk-free interest rate varies among possible maturities (investment horizons).
- Explain the relationship between risk and nominal rate of interest.
- Explain why required returns of risky assets change over time.

Interest Rate Fundamentals

- The interest rate represents the cost of money to a borrower and the return on invested money to an investor (or lender).
- The real rate of interest (k^*) reflects the rate of interest that would exist if there was no expected inflation and no risk.
- The risk-free rate of interest (R_F) reflects only the real rate of interest (k^*) plus a premium (IP) to compensate investors for inflation (rising prices).

$$R_F = k^* + IP$$

Interest Rate Fundamentals

- The *nominal rate of interest* (k_N) is the rate of interest actually charged by the supplier of funds and paid by the demander of funds.
- All nominal (observed) rates contain an inflation premium (*IP*) to compensate investors for inflation and a risk premium (*RP*) to compensate investors for issuer risk characteristics such as the risk of default.

$$k_N = k^* + IP + RP$$

Interest Rate Fundamentals

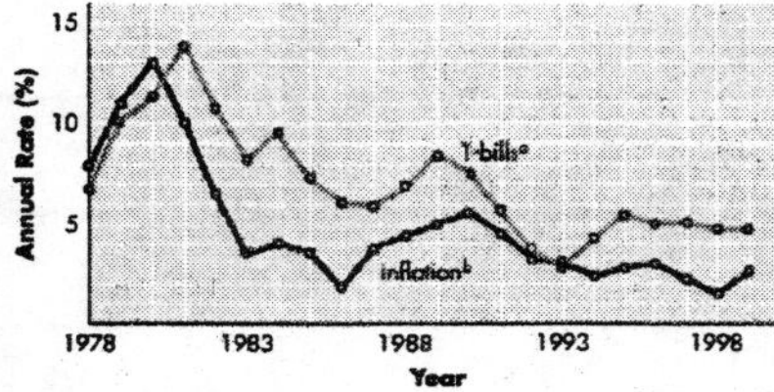

 Figure 4.1

Explaining Changes in the Risk-Free Rate

- In this text, we will use the rate of interest on U.S. Treasury Bills (T-Bills) as proxy for the risk-free rate of interest because the return on this investment compensates investors only for the real rate of return plus an inflation premium.
- Understanding changes in the risk-free rate is important because changes in this rate are reflected in all other interest rates.

How the Equilibrium Interest Rate Is Determined

- The interest rate on borrowed funds is determined by the total (aggregate) supply of funds by investors and the total (aggregate) demand for funds by borrowers.
- The aggregate supply of funds is dependent on the interest rate offered to investors.
- At low interest rates, aggregate supply should be low because of the low reward to investors.
- The opposite is true at high interest rates.

How the Equilibrium Interest Rate Is Determined

- Like aggregate supply, the aggregate demand for funds also depends on the prevailing interest rate.
- If the nominal interest rate is low, aggregate demand should be high because the cost of funds is relatively low.
- The opposite would be true at high interest rates.
- The combined effect of aggregate supply and demand is demonstrated in Figure 4.2 on the following slide.

How the Equilibrium Interest Rate Is Determined

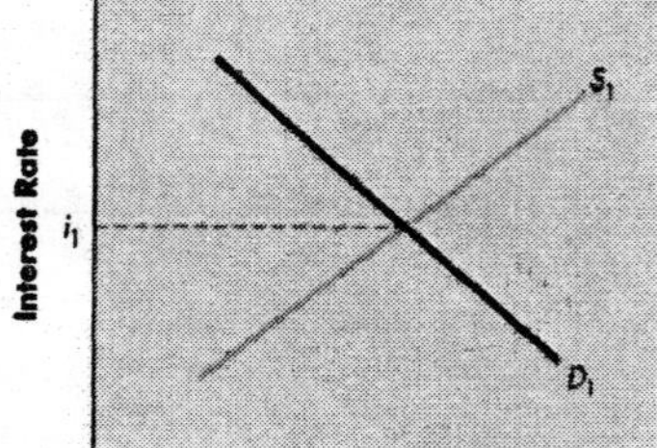

 Figure 4.2

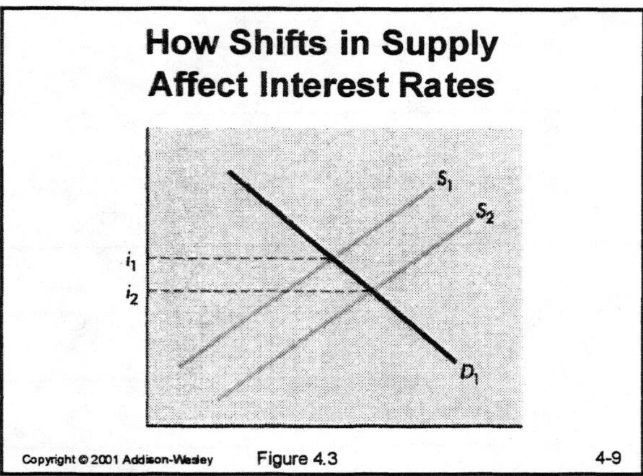

Factors that Affect Shifts in Supply

- Shift in savings by investors
- Shift in monetary policy
  - Open market operations
  - Discount rate
- How the Fed uses monetary policy to reduce interest rates
- How the Fed uses monetary policy to increase interest rates

Factors that Affect Shifts in Supply

S_2
S_1
i_2
i_1
D_1

Figure 4.4

How Shifts in the Demand for Funds Affect Interest Rates

- Shift in the government demand for funds
- Shift in the business demand for funds
- Shift in the household demand for funds
- Combining shifts in supply and demand

How Shifts in the Demand for Funds Affect Interest Rates

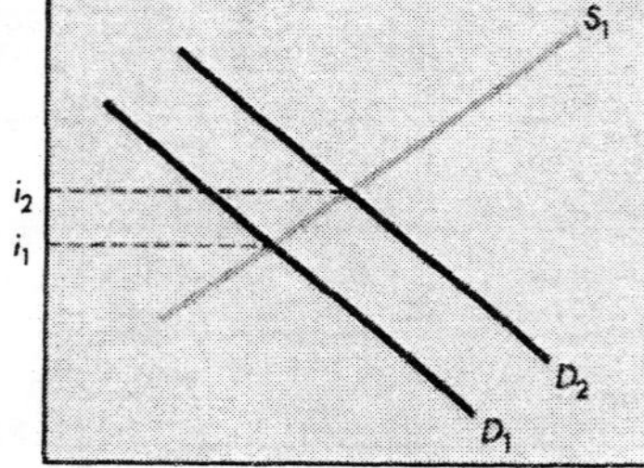

Figure 4.5

Term Structure of Interest Rates

- The term structure of interest rates relates the interest rate to the time to maturity for securities with a common default risk profile.
- Typically, treasury securities are used to construct yield curves since all have zero risk of default.
- However, yield curves could also be constructed with AAA or BBB corporate bonds or other types of similar risk securities.

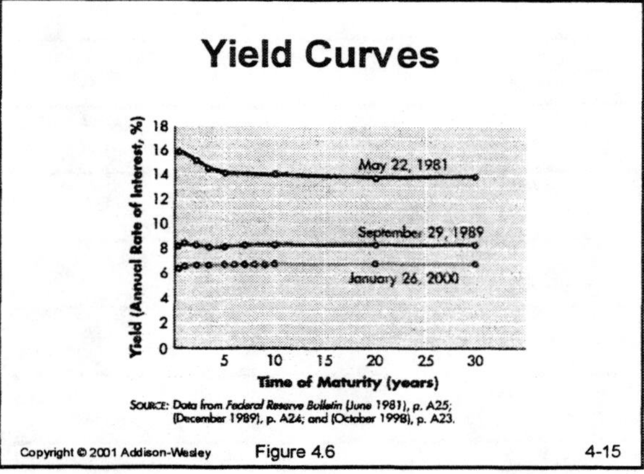

Theories of Term Structure

- Expectations Theory
  - This theory suggests that the shape of the yield curve reflects investors' expectations about the future direction of inflation and interest rates.
  - Therefore, an upward-sloping yield curve reflects expectations of higher future inflation and interest rates.
  - In general, the very strong relationship between inflation and interest rates supports this theory.

Theories of Term Structure

- Liquid Preference Theory
  - This theory contends that long-term interest rates tend to be higher than short-term rates for two reasons:
    - Long-term securities are perceived to be riskier than short-term securities.
    - Borrowers are generally willing to pay more for long-term funds because they can lock in at a rate for a longer period of time and avoid the need to roll over the debt.

Theories of Term Structure

- Market Segmentation Theory
  - This theory suggests that the market for debt at any point in time is segmented on the basis of maturity.
  - As a result, the shape of the yield curve will depend on the supply and demand for a given maturity at a given point in time.

Risk Premiums

- Risk Premiums on Debt Securities
  - The nominal rate of interest for a debt security with a specific maturity (k_1) is equal to the risk-free rate (R_F) for that same maturity, plus the risk premium (RP_1).

$$k_1 = R_F + RP_1$$

  - The risk premium represents the additional amount required by investors to compensate them for uncertainty surrounding the return on the security and varies with the risk of the borrower.

Risk Premiums

- Risk Premiums on Debt Securities
  - One of the most important reasons for the existence of a risk premium on some debt securities is default risk.
  - Default risk is the possibility that the issuer of the security will default on its payments to the investors holding the debt securities.
  - Other issue- and issuer-related risks include liquidity risk, contractual provisions, maturity risk, and tax provisions as summarized in Table 4.1.

Risk Premiums on Debt Securities

TABLE 4.1

Issuer- and Issue-Related Risk Components

Component	Description
Default Risk	The possibility that the issuer of debt will not pay the contractual interest or principal as scheduled. The greater the uncertainty as to the borrower's ability to meet these payments, the greater the risk premium. High bond ratings reflect the low default risk, and low bond ratings reflect high default risk.
Maturity Risk (also called *interest rate risk*)	The fact that the longer the maturity, the more the value of a debt security will change in response to a given change in interest rates. If interest rates on otherwise similar-risk securities suddenly rise because of a change in the money supply, the prices of long-term debt securities will decline by more than the prices of debt securities, and vice versa.[a]

[a]A detailed discussion of the effects of interest rates on the price or value of bonds and other fixed-income securities is presented in Chapter 7.

 Table 4.1 (Panel 1)

Risk Premiums on Debt Securities

TABLE 4.1

Issuer- and Issue-Related Risk Components

Component	Description
Liquidity Risk	The ease with which debt securities can be converted into cash without experiencing a loss in value. Generally, securities that are actively traded on major exchanges and over the counter have low liquidity risk. Less actively traded securities that have a "thin" market have high liquidity risk.
Contractual Provisions	Conditions that are often included in a debt agreement of a stock issue. Some of these reduce risk, whereas others may increase risk. For example, a provision allowing a bond issuer to retire its bonds prior to maturity would increase the bond's risk.
Tax Risk	The chance that Congress will make unfavorable changes in tax laws. The greater the potential impact of a change in tax law on the return of a given debt security, the greater its tax risk. Generally, long-term securities are subject to greater tax risk than those that are closer to their maturity dates.

 Table 4.1 (Panel 2)

Risk Premiums

- Risk Premiums on Equity Securities
  - The risk premiums on equity securities are not as easy to determine as they are on debt securities because equities do not have an observable interest rate that indicates the return to investors.
  - Investors will not necessarily agree on the exact risk premium that is required for every stock.
  - This explains why some investors will purchase a stock while others will not.

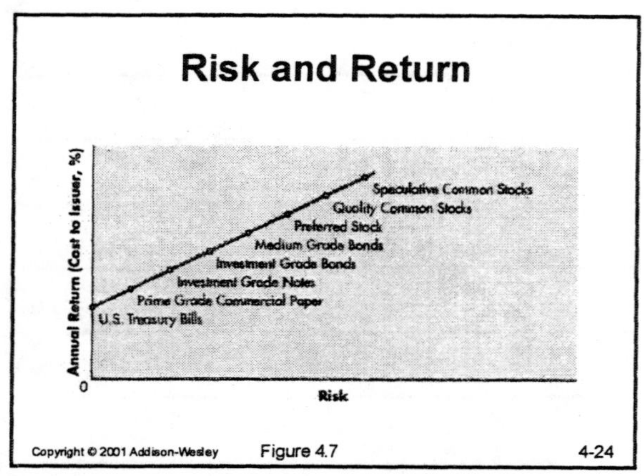
Risk and Return
Annual Return (Cost to Issuer, %)
Speculative Common Stocks
Quality Common Stocks
Preferred Stock
Medium Grade Bonds
Investment Grade Bonds
Investment Grade Notes
Prime Grade Commercial Paper
U.S. Treasury Bills
0
Risk
Copyright © 2001 Addison-Wesley
Figure 4.7
4-24

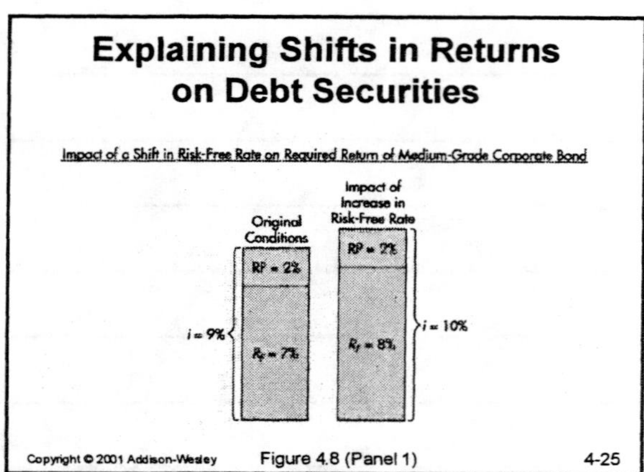
Explaining Shifts in Returns on Debt Securities
Impact of a Shift in Risk-Free Rate on Required Return of Medium-Grade Corporate Bond
Original Conditions
Impact of Increase in Risk-Free Rate
RP = 2%
RP = 2%
i = 9%
R_f = 7%
R_f = 8%
i = 10%
Copyright © 2001 Addison-Wesley
Figure 4.8 (Panel 1)
4-25

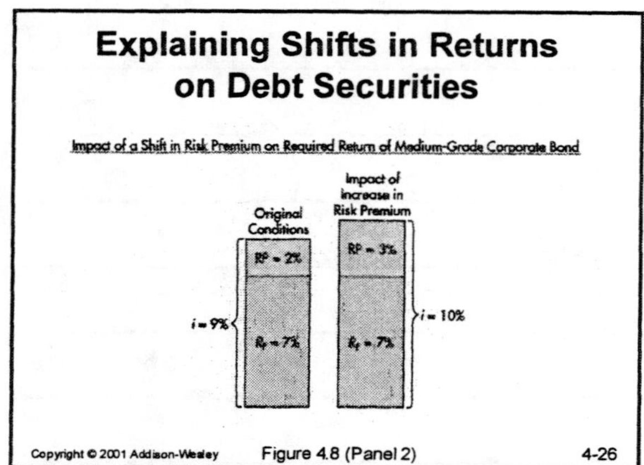
Explaining Shifts in Returns on Debt Securities
Impact of a Shift in Risk Premium on Required Return of Medium-Grade Corporate Bond
Original Conditions
Impact of Increase in Risk Premium
RP = 2%
RP = 3%
i = 9%
R_f = 7%
R_f = 7%
i = 10%
Copyright © 2001 Addison-Wesley
Figure 4.8 (Panel 2)
4-26

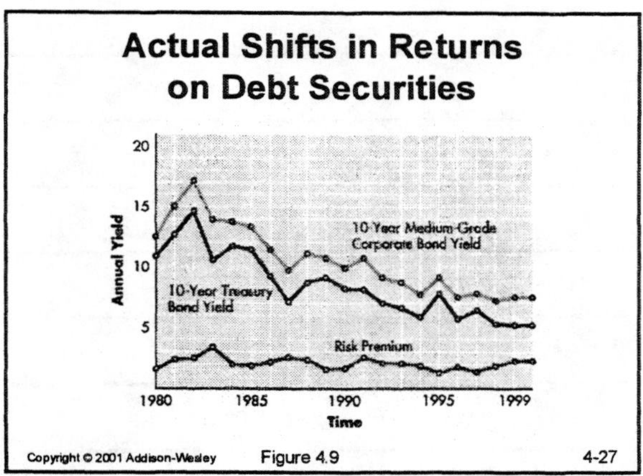

Explaining Shifts in Required Returns

- Actual Shifts in Returns on Equity Securities
  - Shifts in the risk-free rate
  - Shifts in the risk premium on equity securities

4-28

Chapter
4

Introduction to Finance
Lawrence J. Gitman
Jeff Madura

End of Chapter

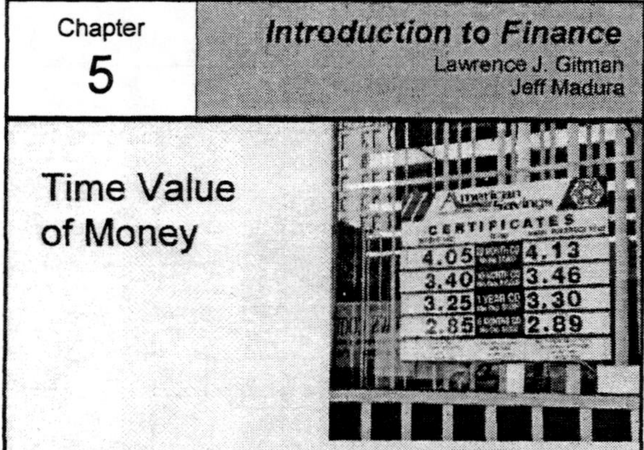

Learning Goals

- Discuss the role of time value in finance and the use of computational aids to simplify its application.
- Understand the concept of future value and its calculation for a single amount; understand the effects on future value and the true rate of interest of compounding more frequently than annually.
- Understand the concept of present value, its calculation for a single amount, and the relationship of present to future cash flow.

5-1

Learning Goals

- Find the future value and present value of an ordinary annuity, the future value of an annuity due, and the present value of a perpetuity.
- Calculate the present value of a mixed stream of cash flows, describe the procedures involved in:
  - Determining deposits to accumulate to a future sum
  - Loan amortization
  - Finding interest or growth rates

5-2

The Role of Time Value in Finance

- Most financial decisions involve costs and benefits that are spread out over time.
- Time value of money allows comparison of cash flows from different periods.
- Question
  - Would it be better for a company to invest $100,000 in a product that would return a total of $200,000 in one year, or one that would return $500,000 after two years?
- Answer
  - It depends on the interest rate!

Basic Concepts

- Future Value
  - Compounding or growth over time
- Present Value
  - Discounting to today's value
- Single cash flows and series of cash flows can be considered
- Time lines are used to illustrate these relationships

Computational Aids

- Use the equations
- Use the financial tables
- Use financial calculators
- Use spreadsheets

Computational Aids

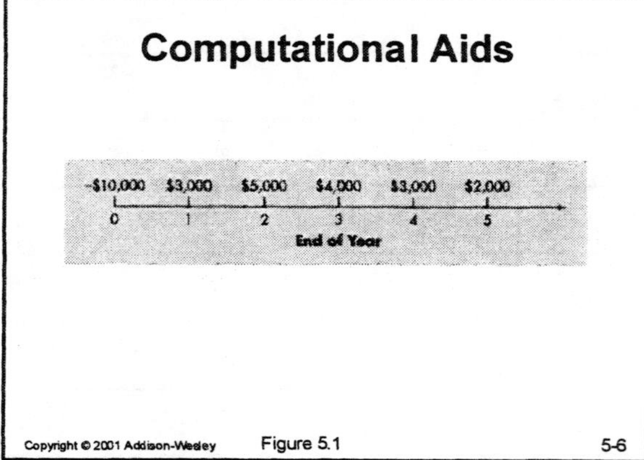

Figure 5.1

Computational Aids

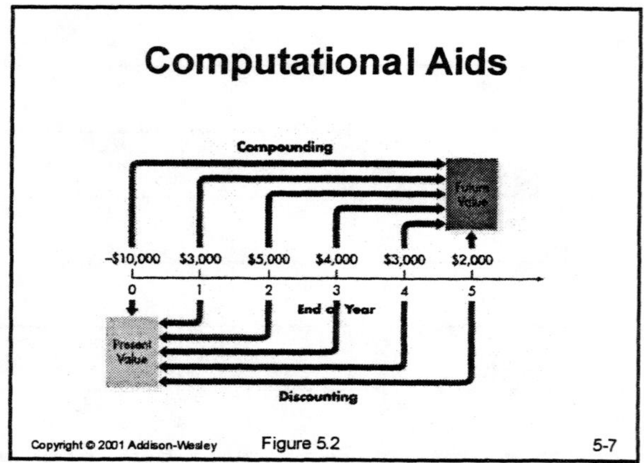

Figure 5.2

Computational Aids

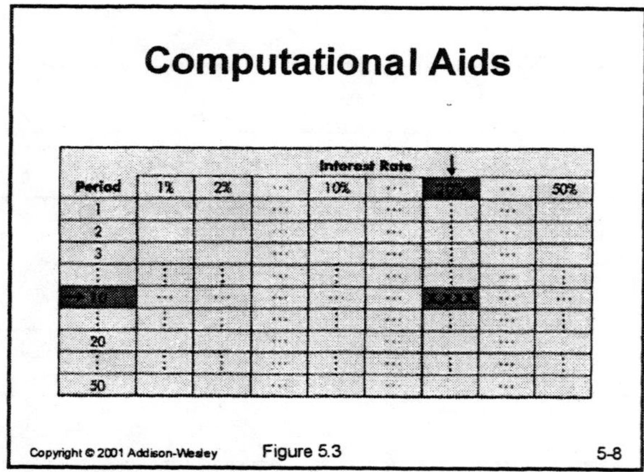

Figure 5.3

Computational Aids

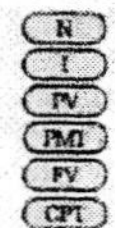

N — Number of Periods
I — Interest Rate per Period
PV — Present Value
PMT — Amount of Payment; Used Only for Annuities
FV — Future Value
CPT — Compute Key Used to Initiate Financial Calculation Once All Values Are Input

 Figure 5.4

Simple Interest

- With simple interest, you don't earn interest on interest.

Year 1: 5% of $100 = $5 + $100 = $105
Year 2: 5% of $100 = $5 + $105 = $110
Year 3: 5% of $100 = $5 + $110 = $115
Year 4: 5% of $100 = $5 + $115 = $120
Year 5: 5% of $100 = $5 + $120 = $125

Compound Interest

- With compound interest, a depositor earns interest on interest!

Year 1: 5% of $100.00 = $5.00 + $100.00 = $105.00
Year 2: 5% of $105.00 = $5.25 + $105.00 = $110.25
Year 3: 5% of $110.25 = $5 .51+ $110.25 = $115.76
Year 4: 5% of $115.76 = $5.79 + $115.76 = $121.55
Year 5: 5% of $121.55 = $6.08 + $121.55 = $127.63

Time Value Terms

PV_0 = present value or beginning amount

k = interest rate

FV_n = future value at end of "n" periods

n = number of compounding periods

A = an annuity (series of equal payments or receipts)

Four Basic Models

$$FV_n = PV_0(1+k)^n = PV(FVIF_{k,n})$$

$$PV_0 = FV_n[1/(1+k)^n] = FV(PVIF_{k,n})$$

$$FVA_n = A\frac{(1+k)^n - 1}{k} = A(FVIFA_{k,n})$$

$$PVA_0 = A\frac{1 - [1/(1+k)^n]}{k} = A(PVIFA_{k,n})$$

Future Value Example

- Algebraically and Using *FVIF* Tables
  - You deposit \$2,000 today at 6% interest. How much will you have in 5 years?

$$\$2{,}000 \times (1.06)^5 = \$2{,}000 \times FVIF_{6\%,5}$$

$$\$2{,}000 \times 1.3382 = \$2{,}676.40$$

Future Value Example

- Using Microsoft® Excel
  - You deposit $2,000 today at 6% interest. How much will you have in 5 years?

PV	$ 2,000
k	6.00%
n	5
FV?	$2,676

Microsoft® Excel Function
= FV(interest, periods, pmt, PV)
= FV(.06, 5, , 2000)

A Graphic View of Future Value

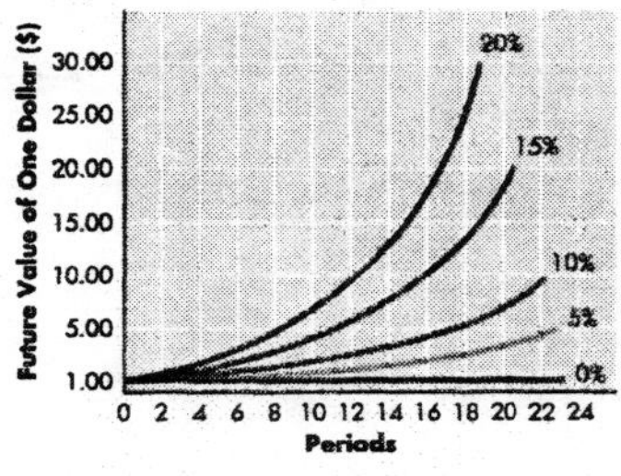

 Figure 5.5

Compounding More Frequently Than Annually

- Compounding more frequently than once a year results in a higher effective interest rate because you are earning on interest on interest more frequently.
- As a result, the effective interest rate is greater than the nominal (annual) interest rate.
- Furthermore, the effective rate of interest will increase the more frequently interest is compounded.

Compounding More Frequently Than Annually

- For example, what would be the difference in future value if I deposit $100 for 5 years and earn 12% annual interest compounded (a) annually, (b) semiannually, (c) quarterly, and (d) monthly?

Annually:	$100 \times (1 + .12)^5 = \$176.23$
Semiannually:	$100 \times (1 + .06)^{10} = \$179.09$
Quarterly:	$100 \times (1 + .03)^{20} = \$180.61$
Monthly:	$100 \times (1 + .01)^{60} = \$181.67$

Compounding More Frequently Than Annually

	On Microsoft® Excel			
	Annually	SemiAnnually	Quarterly	Monthly
PV	$ 100.00	$ 100.00	$ 100.00	$ 100.00
k	12.0%	0.06	0.03	0.01
n	5	10	20	60
FV	$176.23	$179.08	$180.61	$181.67

Continuous Compounding

- With continuous compounding the number of compounding periods per year approaches infinity.
- Through the use of calculus, the equation thus becomes:

FV_n (continuous compounding) = $PV \times (e^{k \times n})$

where "e" has a value of 2.7183

- Continuing with the previous example, find the future value of the $100 deposit after 5 years if interest is compounded continuously.

$FV_n = 100 \times (2.7183)^{.12 \times 5} = \$182.22$

Nominal and Effective Rates

- The nominal interest rate is the stated or contractual rate of interest charged by a lender or promised by a borrower.
- The effective interest rate is the rate actually paid or earned.
- In general, the effective rate is greater than the nominal rate whenever compounding occurs more than once per year.

$$EAR = (1 + k/m)^m - 1$$

Nominal and Effective Rates

- For example, what is the effective rate of interest on your credit card if the nominal rate is 18% per year, compounded monthly?

$$EAR = (1 + .18/12)^{12} - 1$$

$$EAR = 19.56\%$$

Present Value

- Present value is the current dollar value of a future amount of money.
- It is based on the idea that a dollar today is worth more than a dollar tomorrow.
- It is the amount today that must be invested at a given rate to reach a future amount.
- It is also known as discounting, the reverse of compounding.
- The discount rate is often also referred to as the opportunity cost, the discount rate, the required return, and the cost of capital.

Present Value Example

- Algebraically and Using *PVIF* Tables
  - How much must you deposit today in order to have $2,000 in 5 years if you can earn 6% interest on your deposit?

$\$2{,}000 \times [1/(1.06)^5] = \$2{,}000 \times PVIF_{6\%,5}$

$\$2{,}000 \times 0.74758 = \$1{,}494.52$

Present Value Example

- Using Microsoft® Excel
  - How much must you deposit today in order to have $2,000 in 5 years if you can earn 6% interest on your deposit?

FV	$ 2,000
k	6.00%
n	5
PV?	$1,495

Microsoft® Excel Function
=PV(interest, periods, pmt, FV)
=PV(.06, 5, , 2000)

A Graphic View of Present Value

Figure 5.6

Annuities

- Annuities are *equally-spaced* cash flows of equal size.
- Annuities can be either inflows or outflows.
- An ordinary (deferred) annuity has cash flows that occur at the end of each period.
- An annuity due has cash flows that occur at the beginning of each period.
- An annuity due will *always be greater* than an otherwise equivalent ordinary annuity because interest will compound for an additional period.

Annuities

TABLE 5.1 Comparison of Ordinary Annuity and Annuity Due Cash Flows ($1,000, 5 Years)

	Annual cash flows	
End of year*	Annuity A (*ordinary*)	Annuity B (*annuity due*)
0	$ 0	$1,000
1	1,000	1,000
2	1,000	1,000
3	1,000	1,000
4	1,000	1,000
5	1,000	0
Totals	$5,000	$5,000

*The ends of years 0, 1, 2, 3, 4, and 5 are equivalent to the beginnings of years 1, 2, 3, 4, 5, and 6, respectively.

Table 5.1

Future Value of an Ordinary Annuity

- Using the *FVIFA* Tables
  - An annuity is an equal annual series of cash flows.
  - Example
    - How much will your deposits grow to if you deposit $100 at the end of each year at 5% interest for three years?

FVA = 100(*FVIFA*,5%,3) = $315.25

Year 1	$100 deposited at end of year	= $100.00
Year 2	$100 x .05 = $5.00 + $100 + $100	= $205.00
Year 3	$205 x .05 = $10.25 + $205 + $100	= $315.25

Future Value of an Ordinary Annuity

- Using Microsoft® Excel
  - An annuity is an equal annual series of cash flows.
  - Example
    - How much will your deposits grow to if you deposit $100 at the end of each year at 5% interest for three years?

PMT	$ 100
k	5.0%
n	3
FV?	$ 315.25

Microsoft® Excel Function
=FV(interest, periods, pmt, PV)
=FV(.06,5,100,)

Future Value of an Annuity Due

- Using the *FVIFA* Tables
  - An annuity is an equal annual series of cash flows.
  - Example
    - How much will your deposits grow to if you deposit $100 at the beginning of each year at 5% interest for three years.

$FVA = 100(FVIFA,5\%,3)(1+k) = \$330.96$

FVA = 100(3.152)(1.05) = $330.96

Future Value of an Annuity Due

- Using Microsoft® Excel
  - An annuity is an equal annual series of cash flows.
  - Example
    - How much will your deposits grow to if you deposit $100 at the beginning of each year at 5% interest for three years.

PMT	$ 100.00
k	5.00%
n	3
FV	$315.25
FVA?	$ 331.01

Microsoft® Excel Function
=FV(interest, periods, pmt, PV)
=FV(.06, 5,100,)
=315.25*(1.05)

Present Value of an Ordinary Annuity

- Using *PVIFA* Tables
  - An annuity is an equal annual series of cash flows.
  - Example
    - How much could you borrow if you could afford annual payments of $2,000 (which includes both principal and interest) at the end of each year for three years at 10% interest?

PVA = 2,000(*PVIFA*,10%,3) = $4,973.70

Present Value of an Ordinary Annuity

- Using Microsoft® Excel
  - An annuity is an equal annual series of cash flows.
  - Example
    - How much could you borrow if you could afford annual payments of $2,000 (which includes both principal and interest) at the end of each year for three years at 10% interest?

PMT	$ 2,000
I	10.0%
n	3
PV?	$4,973.70

Microsoft® Excel Function
=PV(interest, periods, pmt, FV)
=PV(.10, 3, 2000,)

Present Value of a Mixed Stream

- Using Microsoft® Excel
  - A mixed stream of cash flows reflects no particular pattern
  - Find the present value of the following mixed stream assuming a required return of 9%.

Year	Cash Flow
1	400
2	800
3	500
4	400
5	300
NPV	$1,904.76

Microsoft® Excel Function
=NPV(interest, cells containing CFs)
=NPV(.09,B3:B7)

Present Value of a Perpetuity

- A perpetuity is a special kind of annuity.
- With a perpetuity, the periodic annuity or cash flow stream continues forever.

$$PV = \text{Annuity}/k$$

- For example, how much would I have to deposit today in order to withdraw $1,000 each year forever if I can earn 8% on my deposit?

$$PV = \$1{,}000/.08 = \$12{,}500$$

Loan Amortization

TABLE 5.7 **Loan Amortization Schedule ($6,000 Principal, 10% Interest, 4-Year Repayment Period)**

			Payments		
End of year	Beginning-of-year principal (1)	Loan payment (2)	Interest [0.10 × (2)] (3)	Principal [(1) − (3)] (4)	End-of-year principal [(2) − (4)] (5)
1	$6,000.00	$1,892.74	$600.00	$1,292.74	$4,707.26
2	4,707.26	1,892.74	470.73	1,422.01	3,285.25
3	3,285.25	1,892.74	328.53	1,564.21	1,721.04
4	1,721.04	1,892.74	172.10	1,720.64	—[a]

[a]Because of rounding, a slight difference ($.40) exists between the beginning-of-year-4 principal (in column 1) and the year-4 principal payment (in column 4).

 Table 5.7

Determining Interest or Growth Rates

- At times, it may be desirable to determine the compound interest rate or growth rate implied by a series of cash flows.
- For example, you invested $1,000 in a mutual fund in 1994 which grew as shown in the table below?

1994	$ 1,000
1995	1,127
1996	1,158
1997	2,345
1998	3,985
1999	4,677
2000	5,525

It is important to note that although there are 7 years shown, there are only 6 time periods between the initial deposit and the final value.

Determining Interest or Growth Rates

- At times, it may be desirable to determine the compound interest rate or growth rate implied by a series of cash flows.
- For example, you invested $1,000 in a mutual fund in 1994 which grew as shown in the table below?

1994	$ 1,000
1995	1,127
1996	1,158
1997	2,345
1998	3,985
1999	4,677
2000	5,525

Thus, $1,000 is the present value, $5,525 is the future value, and 6 is the number of periods.

Determining Interest or Growth Rates

- At times, it may be desirable to determine the compound interest rate or growth rate implied by a series of cash flows.
- For example, you invested $1,000 in a mutual fund in 1994 which grew as shown in the table below?

1994	$ 1,000
1995	1,127
1996	1,158
1997	2,345
1998	3,985
1999	4,677
2000	5,525

PV	$ 1,000
FV	$ 5,525
n	6
k?	33.0%

Determining Interest or Growth Rates

- At times, it may be desirable to determine the compound interest rate or growth rate implied by a series of cash flows.
- For example, you invested $1,000 in a mutual fund in 1994 which grew as shown in the table below?

1994	$ 1,000
1995	1,127
1996	1,158
1997	2,345
1998	3,985
1999	4,677
2000	5,525

Microsoft® Excel Function

=Rate(periods, pmt, PV, FV)

=Rate(6, ,1000, 5525)

Using Microsoft® Excel

- The Microsoft® Excel Spreadsheets used in the this presentation can be downloaded from the *Introduction to Finance* companion web site: http://www.awl.com/gitman_madura

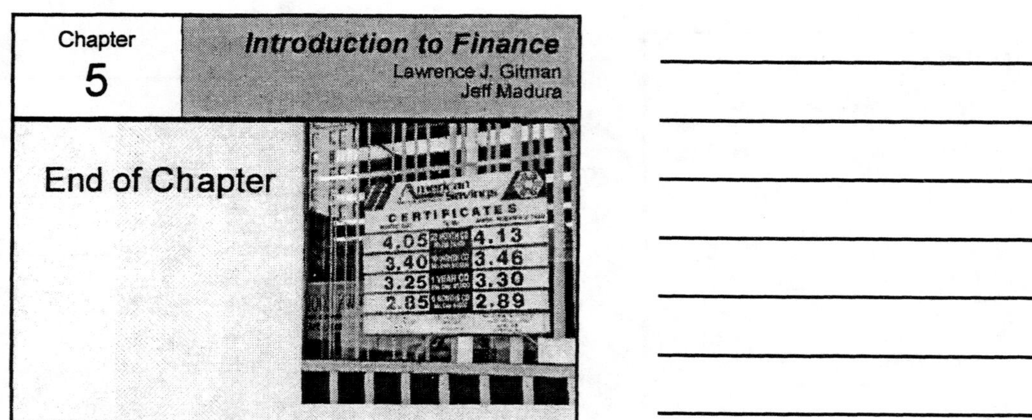

Chapter 6

Introduction to Finance

Lawrence J. Gitman
Jeff Madura

Return and Risk

Learning Goals

- Understand the meaning and fundamentals of risk, return, and risk aversion.
- Describe procedures for measuring the risk of a single asset.
- Discuss the risk measurement for a single asset using the standard deviation and coefficient of variation.
- Understand the risk and return characteristics of a portfolio in terms of correlation and diversification, and the impact of international assets on a portfolio.

Learning Goals

- Review the two types of risk and the derivation and role of beta in measuring the relevant risk of both an individual security and a portfolio.
- Explain the capital asset pricing model (CAPM) and its relationship to the security market line (SML).

Introduction

- If everyone knew ahead of time how much a stock would sell for some time in the future, investing would be a simple endeavor.
- Unfortunately, it is difficult—if not impossible—to make such predictions with any degree of certainty.
- As a result, investors often use history as a basis for predicting the future.
- We will begin this chapter by evaluating the risk and return characteristics of individual assets, and end by looking at portfolios of assets.

Fundamental Concepts about Return and Risk

- In the context of business and finance, risk is defined as the chance of suffering a financial loss.
- Assets (real or financial) which have a greater chance of loss are considered more risky than those with a lower chance of loss.
- Risk may be used interchangeably with the term uncertainty to refer to the variability of returns associated with a given asset.

Fundamental Concepts about Return and Risk

- Return represents the total gain or loss on an investment.
- The most basic way to calculate return is as follows:

$$k_t = \frac{P_t - P_{t-1} + C_t}{P_{t-1}}$$

Where:

k_t = actual required or expected return during period t

P_t = current price

P_{t-1} = price during the previous time period

C_t = any cash flow accruing from the investment

Fundamental Concepts about Return and Risk

- For example, compute the holding period return if you purchased a stock for \$100, received a \$5 dividend, and sold the stock for \$110.

$$k_t = \frac{P_t - P_{t-1} + C_t}{P_{t-1}}$$

$$k_t = \frac{110 - 100 + 5}{100} = \frac{15}{100} = 15\%$$

Chapter Example

Risk and Return

year	Return Stock A	 Stock B
1	6%	20%
2	12%	30%
3	8%	10%
4	-2%	-10%
5	18%	50%
6	6%	20%

Single Financial Assets

- Historical Return
  - Arithmetic average
    - The historical average (also called arithmetic average or mean) return is simple to calculate.
    - The accompanying text outlines how to calculate this and other measures of risk and return.
    - All of these calculations were discussed and taught in your introductory statistics course.
    - This slideshow will demonstrate the calculation of these statistics using Microsoft® Excel.

Historical Return

- Arithmetic Average

	Return	
year	Stock A	Stock B
1	0.06	0.2
2	0.12	0 3
3	0.08	0.1
4	-0.02	-0.1
5	0.18	0.5
6		2
Arithmetic		
Average	=AVERAGE(B6:B11)	=AVERAGE(C6:C11)

What you type

	Return	
year	Stock A	Stock B
1	6%	20%
2	12%	30%
3	8%	10%
4	-2%	-10%
5	18%	50%
6		20%
Arithmetic		
Average	8%	20%

What you see

Single Financial Assets

- Historical Risk
  - Variance
    - Historical risk can be measured by the variability of an asset's returns in relation to its average.
    - Variance is computed by summing squared deviations and dividing by the number of observations minus one (n - 1).
    - Squaring the differences ensures that both positive and negative deviations are given equal consideration.
    - The sum of the squared differences is then divided by the number of observations minus one (n - 1).

Historical Risk

- Variance

	Stock A			
year	Observed Return for	Observed - Mean	Difference Squared	Variance
1	6%	-2%	0.00040	
2	12%	4%	0.00160	
3	8%	0%	-	
4	-2%	-10%	0.01000	
5	18%	10%	0.01000	
6	6%	-2%	0.00040	
Average	8.00%	Sum of Dif	0.02240	0.00448

Historical Risk

- Variance

	Stock B			
	Observed	Observed	Difference	
year	Return for	- Mean	Squared	Variance
1	20%	0%	-	
2	30%	10%	0.01000	
3	10%	-10%	0.01000	
4	-10%	-30%	0.09000	
5	50%	30%	0.09000	
6	20%	0%	-	
Average	20.00%	Sum of Dif	0.20000	0.04000

Historical Risk

- Variance

year	Observed Return for Stock A	Observed Return for Stock B
1	0.06	0.2
2	0.12	0.3
3	0.08	0.1
4	-0.02	-0.1
5	0.18	0.5
6		0.2
Average	=AVER[illegible]B4:B9)	=AVERAGE(C4:C9)
Variance	=VARA(B4:B9)	=VARA(C4:C9)

What you type

year	Observed Return for Stock A	Observed Return for Stock B
1	6%	20%
2	12%	30%
3	8%	10%
4	-2%	-10%
5	18%	50%
6	[illegible]	20%
Average	[illegible]	20.00%
Variance	0.45%	4.00%

What you see

Single Financial Assets

- Historical Risk
  - Standard deviation
    - Squaring the deviations makes the variance difficult to interpret.
    - In other words, by squaring percentages, the resulting deviations are in percent squared terms.
    - The standard deviation simplifies interpretation by taking the square root of the squared percentages.
    - In other words, standard deviation is in the same units as the computed average.
    - If the average is 10%, the standard deviation might be 20%, whereas the variance would be 20% squared.

Historical Risk

- Standard deviation

year	Observed Return for Stock A	Observed Return for Stock B
1	0.06	0.2
2	0.12	0.3
3	0.08	0.1
4	-0.02	-0.1
5	0.18	0.5
6		
Average		VERAGE(C4:C9)
Standard Deviation	=STDEV(B4:B9)	=STDEV(C4:C9)

What you type

year	Observed Return for Stock A	Observed Return for Stock B
1	6%	20%
2	12%	30%
3	8%	10%
4	-2%	-10%
5	18%	50%
6		20%
Avera		20.00%
Standard Deviation	6.69%	20.00%

What you see

Historical Risk

- Normal Distribution

$R - 2\sigma$ $R - 1\sigma$ R $R + 1\sigma$ $R + 2\sigma$

68%

95%

Single Financial Assets

- Expected Return and Risk
  - Investors and analysts often look at historical returns as a starting point for predicting the future.
  - However, they are much more interested in what the returns on their investments will be in the future.
  - For this reason, we need a method for estimating future or "ex-ante" returns.
  - One way of doing this is to assign probabilities for future states of nature and the returns that would be realized if a particular state of nature does occur.

Expected Return and Risk

Expected Return

$E(R) = \Sigma p_i R_i$

Where:

p_i = probability of the *i*th scenario

R_i = forecasted return in the *i*th scenario

Also, the variance of $E(R)$ may be computed as:

$$\sigma^2 = \sum p_i[R_i - E(R)]^2$$

And the standard deviation as:

$$\sqrt{\sigma^2} = \sqrt{\sum p_i[R_i - E(R)]^2}$$

Expected Return and Risk

Expected Return			
State	Probability	Stock A	Stock B
Boom	30%	17%	29%
Normal	50%	12%	15%
Bust	20%	5%	-2%
Expected Return		12.1%	15.8%

Expected Return and Risk

Expected Return			
State	Probability	Stock A	Stock B
Boom	0.3	0.17	0.29
Normal	0.5	0.12	0.15
Bust	0.2	0.05	-0.02
Expected Return		=(B12*C12)+(B13*C13)+(B14*C14)	=(B12*D12)+(B13*D13)+(B14*D14)

Expected Return and Risk

Risk, Variance, & Standard Deviation			
State	Pi	Stock A	$pi[Ai - E(R)]^2$
Boom	0.30	17	7.203
Normal	0.50	12	0.005
Bust	0.20	5	10.082
Expected Return		12	
Variance = Sum of $pi[Ai - E(R)]^2$			17.290
Standard Deviation = $(Var)^{1/2}$			4.158

Expected Return and Risk

Risk, Variance, & Standard Deviation			
State	Pi	Stock A	$pi[Ai - E(R)]^2$
Boom	0.3	17	=B3*(C3-C6)^2
Normal	0.5	12	=B4*(C4-C6)^2
Bust	0.2	5	=B5*(C5-C6)^2
Expected Return		=(B3*C3)+(B4*C4)+(B5*C5)	
Variance = Sum of $pi[Ai - E(R)]^2$			=SUM(D3:D5)
Standard Deviation = $(Var)^{1/2}$			=(D7)^(1/2)

Single Financial Assets

- Coefficient of Variation (CV)
  - One problem with using standard deviation as a measure of risk is that we cannot easily make risk comparisons between two assets.
  - The coefficient of variation overcomes this problem by measuring the amount of risk per unit of return.
  - The higher the coefficient of variation, the more risk per return.
  - Therefore, if given a choice, an investor would select the asset with the lower coefficient of variation.

Coefficient of Variation

Coefficient of Variation			
State	Pi	Stock A	Stock B
Boom	0.3	17	30
Normal	0.5	12	15
Bust	0.2	5	-5
Expected Return		**12.1**	**15.5**
Standard Deviation		**4.16**	**10.517**
Coefficient of Variation		**0.344**	**0.679**

Portfolio of Assets

- An investment portfolio is any collection or combination of financial assets.
- If we assume all investors are rational and therefore risk averse, that investor will *ALWAYS* choose to invest in portfolios rather than in single assets.
- Investors will hold portfolios because he or she will *diversify* away a portion of the risk that is inherent in "putting all your eggs in one basket."
- If an investor holds a single asset, he or she will fully suffer the consequences of poor performance.
- This is not the case for an investor who owns a diversified portfolio of assets.

Portfolio of Assets

- Diversification is enhanced depending upon the extent to which the returns on assets "move" together.
- This movement is typically measured by a statistic known as correlation as shown in Figure 6.3 below.

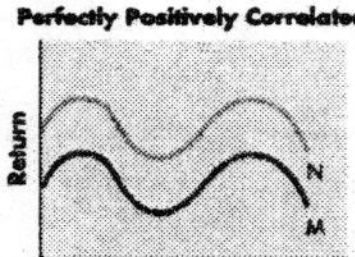

Figure 6.3

Portfolio of Assets

- Even if two assets are not perfectly negatively correlated, an investor can still realize diversification benefits from combining them in a portfolio as shown in Figure 6.4 below.

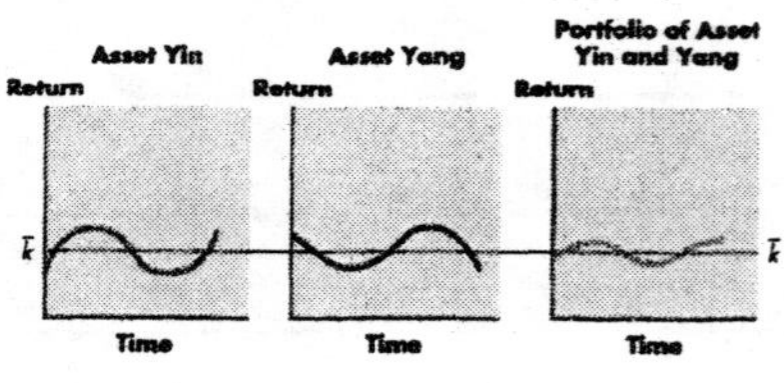

 Figure 6.4

Portfolio of Assets

- Recall Stocks A and B

Risk and Return		
	Return	
year	Stock A	Stock B
1	6%	20%
2	12%	30%
3	8%	10%
4	-2%	-10%
5	18%	50%
6	6%	20%

Portfolio AB

- 50% in A, 50% in B

	Stock A		Stock B		Portfolio AB
Year	Percent Weight	Percent Return	Percent Weight	Percent Return	Weighted Return
1	50%	6	50%	20	13
2	50%	12	50%	30	21
3	50%	8	50%	10	9
4	50%	-2	50%	-10	-6
5	50%	18	50%	50	34
6	50%	6	50%	20	13
Weight A	50%		Sum of Weighted Returns		84
Weight B	50%		Portfolio Average Return		14

Portfolio AB

- 50% in A, 50% in B

	Stock A		Stock B		Portfolio AB
	Percent	Percent	Percent	Percent	Weighted
Year	Weight	Return	Weight	Return	Return
1	=B$12			20	=(B6*C6)+(D6*E6)
2	=B$12			30	=(B7*C7)+(D7*E7)
3	=B$12			10	=(B8*C8)+(D8*E8)
4	=B$12	-2	=B$13	-10	=(B9*C9)+(D9*E9)
5	=B$12	18	=B$13	50	=(B10*C10)+(D10*E10)
6	=B$12	6	=B$13	20	=(B11*C11)+(D11*E11)
Weight A	0.5		Sum of Weighted Returns		=SUM(F6:F11)
Weight B	=(1-B12)		Portfolio Average Return		=F12/6

Where the contents of cell B12 and B13 = 50% in this case

Here are cells B12 and B13

Portfolio AB

- 50% in A, 50% in B

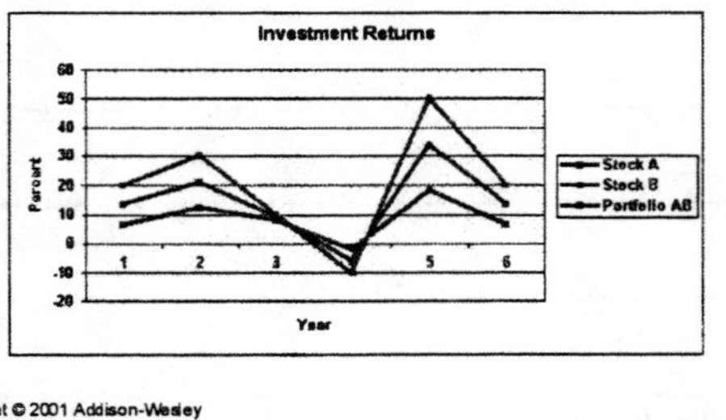

Portfolio AB

- 40% in A, 60% in B

	Stock A		Stock B		Portfolio AB
	Percent	Percent	Percent	Percent	Weighted
Year	Weight	Return	Weight	Return	Return
1	40%	6	60%	20	14.4
2	40%	12	60%	30	22.8
3	40%	8	60%	10	9.2
4			60%	-10	-6.8
5			60%	50	37.2
6	40%	6	60%	20	14.4
Weight A	40%		Sum of Weighted Returns		91.2
Weight B	60%		Portfolio Average Return		15.2

Changing the weights

Portfolio AB

- 20% in A, 80% in B

	Stock A		Stock B		Portfolio AB
Year	Percent Weight	Percent Return	Percent Weight	Percent Return	Weighted Return
1	20%	6	80%	20	17.2
2	20%	12	80%	30	26.4
3	20%	8	80%	10	9.6
4	[illegible]	[illegible]	80%	-10	-8.4
5	[illegible]	[illegible]	80%	50	43.6
6	20%	6	80%	20	17.2
Weight A	20%		Sum of Weighted Returns		105.6
Weight B	80%		Portfolio Average Return		17.6

Portfolio Return and Risk

- Summarizing Changes in Return and Risk as the Composition of the Portfolio Changes

Weight A	Return A (%)	Return B (%)	Return AB (%)	SD-A (%)	SD-B (%)	SD-AB (%)
100%	8.0	20.0	8.0	6.7	20.0	6.7
80%	8.0	20.0	10.4	6.7	20.0	9.3
60%	8.0	20.0	12.8	6.7	20.0	11.9
40%	8.0	20.0	15.2	6.7	20.0	14.6
20%	8.0	20.0	17.6	6.7	20.0	17.3
0%	8.0	20.0	20	6.7	20.0	20.0

Portfolio Return and Risk

- Perfect Negative Correlation

	Stock A		Stock B		Portfolio AB
Year	Percent Weight	Percent Return	Percent Weight	Percent Return	Weighted Return
1	50%	20	50%	0	10
2	50%	16	50%	4	10
3	50%	12	50%	8	10
4	50%	8	50%	12	10
5	50%	4	50%	16	10
6	50%	0	50%	20	10
Weight A	50%		Sum of Weighted Returns		60
Weight B	50%		Portfolio Average Return		10

Portfolio Return and Risk

- Perfect Negative Correlation

Weight A	Return A (%)	Return B (%)	Return AB (%)	SD-A (%)	SD-B (%)	SD-AB (%)
100%	10.0	10.0	10.0	7.5	7.5	7.5
80%	10.0	10.0	10.0	7.5	7.5	4.5
60%	10.0	10.0	10.0	7.5	7.5	1.5
50%	10.0	10.0	10.0	7.5	7.5	0.0
40%	10.0	10.0	10.0	7.5	7.5	1.5
20%	10.0	10.0	10.0	7.5	7.5	4.5
0%	10.0	10.0	10.0	7.5	7.5	7.5

Notice that if we weight the portfolio just right (50/50 in this case), we can completely eliminate risk.

Adding Assets to a Portfolio

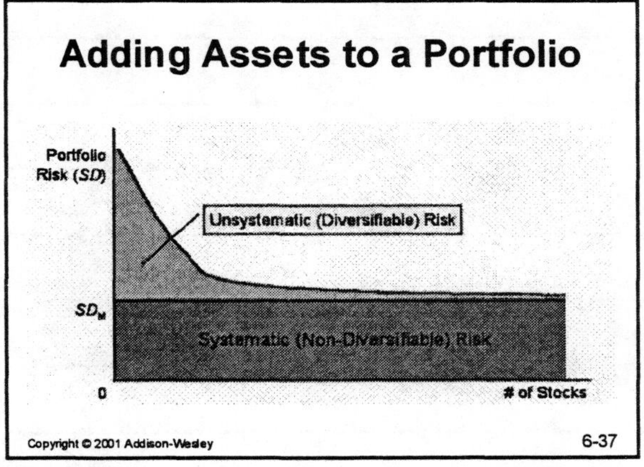

Adding Assets to a Portfolio

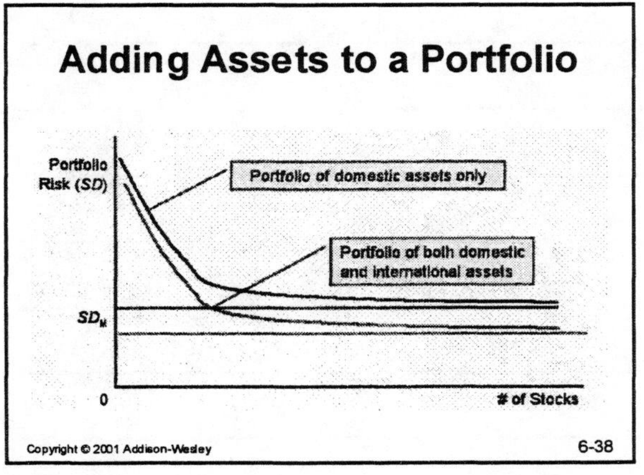

Portfolios of Assets

- Capital Asset Pricing Model (CAPM)
  - If you notice in the last slide, a good part of a portfolio's risk (the standard deviation of returns) can be eliminated simply by holding a lot of stocks.
  - The risk you can't get rid of by adding stocks (systematic) cannot be eliminated through diversification because that variability is caused by events that affect most stocks similarly.
  - Examples would include changes in macroeconomic factors such interest rates, inflation, and the business cycle.

Portfolios of Assets

- Capital Asset Pricing Model (CAPM)
  - In the early 1960s, researchers (Sharpe, Treynor, and Lintner) developed an asset pricing model that measures only the amount of systematic risk a particular asset has.
  - In other words, they noticed that most stocks go down when interest rates go up, but some go down a whole lot more.
  - They reasoned that if they could measure this variability—the systematic risk—then they could develop a model to price assets using only this risk.
  - The unsystematic (company-related) risk is irrelevant because it could easily be eliminated simply by diversifying.

Portfolios of Assets

- Capital Asset Pricing Model (CAPM)
  - To measure the amount of systematic risk an asset has, they simply regressed the returns for the "market portfolio"—the portfolio of ALL assets—against the returns for an individual asset.
  - The slope of the regression line—beta—measures an asset's systematic (non-diversifiable) risk.
  - In general, cyclical companies like auto companies have high betas while relatively stable companies, like public utilities, have low betas.
  - Let's look at an example to see how this works.

Portfolios of Assets

- Capital Asset Pricing Model (CAPM)

Year	Market Return	Stock B Return
1	10	20
2	16	30
3	9	10
4	-4	-10
5	28	50
6	13	20

- We will demonstrate the calculation using the regression analysis feature in Microsoft® Excel.

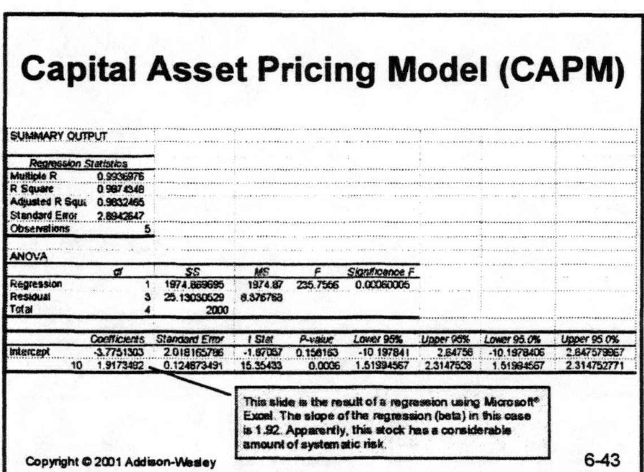

Capital Asset Pricing Model (CAPM)

SUMMARY OUTPUT

Regression Statistics	
Multiple R	0.9936976
R Square	0.9874348
Adjusted R Squ:	0.9832465
Standard Error	2.8942647
Observations	5

ANOVA

	df	SS	MS	F	Significance F
Regression	1	1974.869695	1974.87	235.7566	0.00060005
Residual	3	25.13030529	8.376768		
Total	4	2000			

	Coefficients	Standard Error	t Stat	P-value	Lower 95%	Upper 95%	Lower 95.0%	Upper 95.0%
Intercept	-3.7751303	2.0181657786	-1.87067	0.158163	-10.197841	2.64756	-10.1978406	2.847579967
10	1.9173492	0.124873491	15.35433	0.0006	1.51994567	2.3147528	1.51984567	2.314752771

This slide is the result of a regression using Microsoft® Excel. The slope of the regression (beta) in this case is 1.92. Apparently, this stock has a considerable amount of systematic risk.

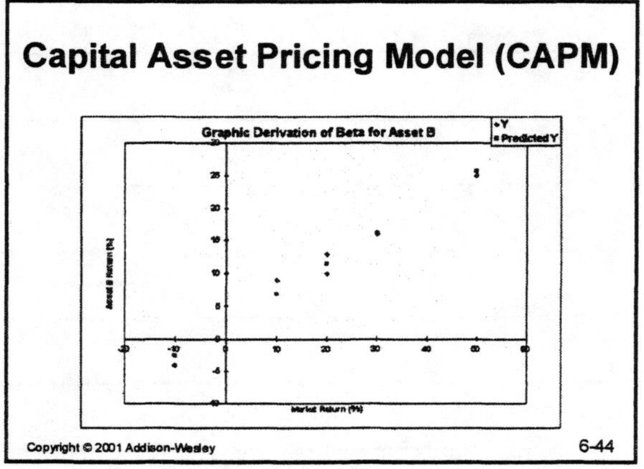

Capital Asset Pricing Model (CAPM)

TABLE 6.6 Selected Beta Coefficients and Their Interpretations

Beta	Comment	Interpretation
2.0	Move in same direction as market	Twice as responsive as the market
1.0		Same response as the market
.5		Only half as responsive as the market
0		Unaffected by market movement
− .5	Move in opposite direction to market	Only half as responsive as the market
−1.0		Same response as the market
−2.0		Twice as responsive as the market

 Table 6.6

Capital Asset Pricing Model (CAPM)

TABLE 6.7 Beta Coefficients for Selected Stocks (April 7, 2000)

Stock	Beta	Stock	Beta
Amazon.com	1.55	McDonalds Corp.	.85
Anheuser-Busch	.70	Merrill Lynch & Company	1.90
Cisco Systems	1.45	Microsoft Corp.	1.05
Coca-Cola	1.10	NIKE Inc.	.95
Exxon Mobil Corp.	.80	Procter & Gamble	.90
Gap (The) Inc.	1.45	Quicksilver Inc.	1.15
General Motors	1.05	Sempra Energy	.55
Harley-Davidson	1.15	Sony Corporation	.90
Intel Corp.	1.05	Southwest Airlines	1.25
IBM	1.00	Yahoo! Inc.	1.65

Source: Value Line Investment Survey (New York: Value Line Publishing, April 7, 2000).

 Table 6.7

Portfolios of Assets

- Capital Asset Pricing Model (CAPM)
  - The required return for *all* assets is composed of two parts: the risk-free rate and a risk premium.
  - The risk premium is a function of both market conditions and the asset itself.
  - The risk-free rate (r_f) is usually estimated from the return on U.S. T-Bills.

Portfolios of Assets

- Capital Asset Pricing Model (CAPM)
  - The risk premium for a stock is composed of two parts:
    - The market risk premium, which is the return required for investing in any risky asset rather than the risk-free rate.
    - Beta, a risk coefficient which measures the sensitivity of the particular stock's return to changes in market conditions.

Portfolios of Assets

- Capital Asset Pricing Model (CAPM)
  - After estimating beta, which measures a specific asset's systematic risk, relatively easy to estimate variables may be obtained to calculate an asset's required return.

$$E(R_i) = RFR + b[E(R_m) - RFR]$$

Where:

$E(R_i)$ = asset's expected or required return

RFR = risk-free rate of return

b = an asset or portfolio's beta

$E(R_m)$ = expected return on the market portfolio

Portfolios of Assets

- Capital Asset Pricing Model (CAPM)
  - Example
    - Calculate the required return for Federal Express assuming it has a beta of 1.25, the rate on U.S. T-Bills is 5.07%, and the expected return for the S&P 500 is 15%.

$$E(R_i) = 5.07 + 1.25\ [15\% - 5.07\%]$$

$$E(R_i) = 17.48\%$$

Capital Asset Pricing Model (CAPM)

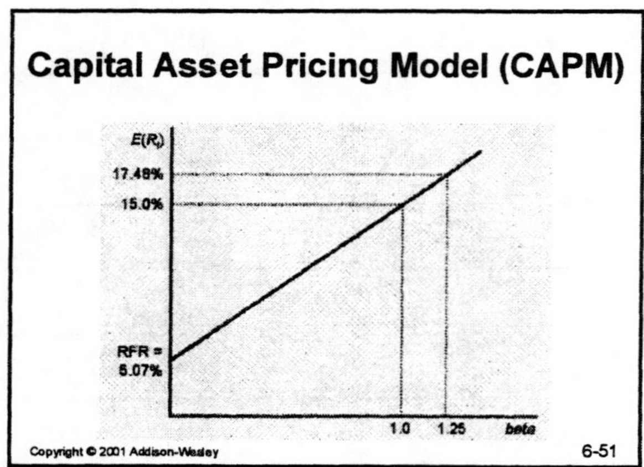

Capital Asset Pricing Model (CAPM)

Required Return

$k = r_f + (r_m - R_f)B$

Example: If the rate of return on U.S. T-bills is 5%, and the expected return for the S&P 500 is 15%, what would be the required return for Microsoft with a beta 1.5, and Florida Power and Light with a beta of 0.8?

		MSFT	FPL
	r_f	5.0%	5.0%
	r_m	15.0%	15.0%
	B	1.5	0.8
Answer	k?	20.0%	13.0%

Capital Asset Pricing Model (CAPM)

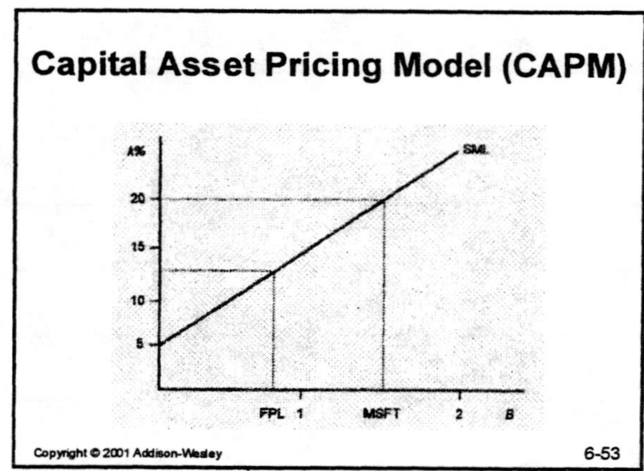

Capital Asset Pricing Model (CAPM)

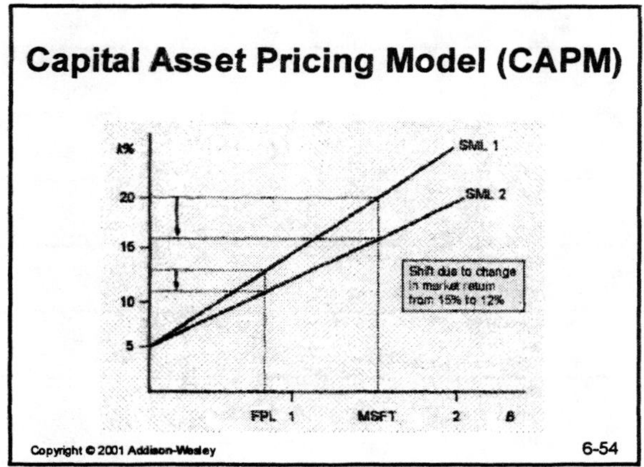

Capital Asset Pricing Model (CAPM)

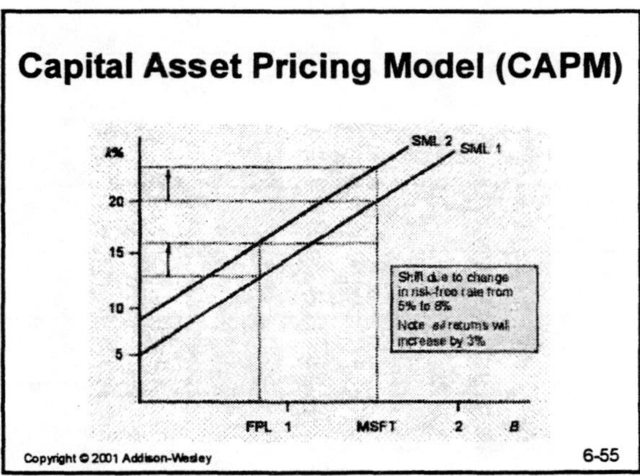

Portfolios of Assets

- Some Comments on the CAPM
  - The CAPM is based on an assumed efficient market with the following characteristics:
    - Many small investors each having the same information and expectations with respect to securities
    - Rational investors who are risk averse
    - No restrictions on investment
    - No taxes
    - No transactions costs

Portfolios of Assets

- Some Comments on the CAPM
  - Because these assumptions do not strictly hold, the CAPM should only be viewed as a useful conceptual framework for understanding the risk and return on an investment.
  - In addition, the data used to approximate the beta and other components of the CAPM are historical.
  - Because the CAPM is an expectational model, these variables may or may not reflect the future variability of returns.

Using Microsoft® Excel

- The Microsoft® Excel Spreadsheets used in the this presentation can be downloaded from the *Introduction to Finance* companion web site: http://www.awl.com/gitman_madura

Chapter 6

Introduction to Finance

Lawrence J. Gitman
Jeff Madura

End of Chapter

Chapter
7

Introduction to Finance
Lawrence J. Gitman
Jeff Madura

Valuation

Learning Goals

- Describe the key inputs and basic model used in the valuation process.
- Review the basic bond valuation model.
- Discuss bond value behavior, particularly the impact that required return and time to maturity have on bond value.
- Explain yield to maturity and the procedure used to value bonds that pay interest annually.

Learning Goals

- Perform basic common stock valuation using each of three models: zero-growth, constant-growth, and variable-growth.
- Understand the relationships among financial decisions, return, risk, and stock value.

Valuation Fundamentals

- The (market) value of *any* investment asset is simply the *present value* of expected cash flows.
- The interest rate that these cash flows are discounted at is called the asset's *required return.*
- The required return is a function of the expected rate of *inflation* and the perceived *risk* of the asset.
- Higher perceived risk results in a higher required return and lower asset market values.

Basic Valuation Model

$$V_0 = \frac{CF_1}{(1+k)^1} + \frac{CF_2}{(1+k)^2} + \ldots + \frac{CF_n}{(1+k)^n}$$

Where:

V_0 = value of the asset at time zero

CF_t = cash flow expected at the end of year t

k = appropriate required return (discount rate)

n = relevant time period

Basic Valuation Model

- Using present value interest factor notation, $PVIF_{k,n}$ from Chapter 5, the previous equation can be rewritten as:

$$V_0 = [(CF_1 \times PVIF_{k,1})] + [CF_2 \times (PVIF_{k,2})] + \ldots + [CF_n \times (PVIF_{k,n})]$$

- Example
  - Nina Diaz, a financial analyst for King industries, a diversified holding company, wishes to estimate the value of three of its assets—common stock in Unitech, an interest in an oil well, and an original painting by a well-known artist. Forecasted cash flows, required returns, and the resulting present values are shown in Table 7.1 on the following two slides.

Basic Valuation Model

TABLE 7.1 Valuation of King Industries' Assets

Asset	Cash flow, CF		Appropriate required return	Valuation[a]
Unilock stock[b]	$300/year indefinitely		12%	$V_0 = \$300 \times (PVIFA_{12\%,\infty})$
				$= \$300 \times \frac{1}{.12} = \underline{\underline{\$2,500}}$
Oil well[c]	Year (t)	CF_t	20%	$V_0 = [\$2,000 \times (PVIF_{20\%,1})]$
	1	$ 2,000		$+ [\$4,000 \times (PVIF_{20\%,2})]$
	2	4,000		$+ [\$0 \times (PVIF_{20\%,3})]$
	3	0		$+ [\$10,000 \times (PVIF_{20\%,4})]$
	4	10,000		$= [\$2,000 \times (.833)]$
				$+ [\$4,000 \times (.694)]$
				$+ [\$0 \times (.579)]$
				$+ [\$10,000 \times (.482)]$
				$= \$1,666 + \$2,776$
				$+ \$0 + \$4,820$
				$= \underline{\underline{\$9,262}}$

[a] Based on PVIF interest factors from Table A-2. Using a calculator, the values of the oil well and original painting would have been $9,266.98 and $42,260.03, respectively.

[b] This is a perpetuity (infinite-lived annuity), and therefore the present value interest factor given in Equation [illegible] is applied.

[c] This is a mixed stream of cash flows and therefore requires a number of PVIFs, as noted.

Table 7.1 (Panel 1)

Basic Valuation Model

TABLE 7.1 Valuation of King Industries' Assets

Asset	Cash flow, CF	Appropriate required return	Valuation
Original painting[d]	$85,000 at end of year 5	15%	$V_0 = \$85,000 \times (PVIF_{15\%,5})$
			$= \$85,000 \times (.497)$
			$= \underline{\underline{\$42,245}}$

[d] This is a lump-sum cash flow and therefore requires a single PVIF.

Table 7.1 (Panel 2)

Bond Fundamentals

- A bond is a long-term debt instrument that pays the bondholder a specified amount of periodic interest over a specified period of time.
- Note: a bond is equal to *debt*.

Bond Fundamentals

- The bond's *principal* is the amount borrowed by the company and the amount owed to the bondholder on the maturity date.
- The bond's *maturity date* is the time at which a bond becomes due and the principal must be repaid.
- The bond's *coupon rate* is the specified interest rate (or dollar amount) that must be periodically paid.
- The bond's *current yield* is the annual interest (income) divided by the current price of the security.

Bond Fundamentals

- The bond's yield to maturity is the yield (expressed as a compound rate of return) earned on a bond from the time it is acquired until the maturity date of the bond.
- A *yield curve* graphically shows the relationship between the time to maturity and yields for debt in a given risk class.

Bonds with Maturity Dates

- Annual Compounding

$$B_0 = \frac{I_1}{(1+i)^1} + \frac{I_2}{(1+i)^2} + \ldots + \frac{(I_n + P_n)}{(1+i)^n}$$

- For example, find the price of a 10% coupon bond with three years to maturity if market interest rates are currently 10%.

$$B_0 = \frac{100}{(1+.10)^1} + \frac{100}{(1+i)^2} + \frac{(100+1{,}000)}{(1+.10)^3}$$

Bonds with Maturity Dates

- Annual Compounding
  - Using Microsoft® Excel
    - For example, find the price of a 10% coupon bond with three years to maturity if market interest rates are currently 10%.

Finding the Value of a Bond	
Coupon Interest ($)	$ 100
Maturity (periods)	3
Face Value ($)	$ 1,000
Market Interest Rate (%)	10%
Market Price ($)	($1,000.00)

Note: the equation for calculating price is =PV(rate,nper,pmt,fv)

Bonds with Maturity Dates

- Annual Compounding
  - Using Microsoft® Excel
    - For example, find the price of a 10% coupon bond with three years to maturity if market interest rates are currently 10%.

Finding the Value of a Bond	
Coupon Interest ($)	$ 100
Maturity (periods)	3
Face Value ($)	$ 1,000
Market Interest Rate (%)	10%
Market Price ($)	($1,000.00)

When the coupon rate matches the discount rate, the bond always sells for its par value.

Bonds with Maturity Dates

- Annual Compounding
  - Using Microsoft® Excel
    - What would happen to the bond's price if interest rates increased from 10% to 15%?

Finding the Value of a Bond	
Coupon Interest ($)	$ 100
Maturity (periods)	3
Face Value ($)	$ 1,000
Market Interest Rate (%)	15%
Market Price ($)	($885.84)

When the interest rate goes up, the bond price will always go down.

Bonds with Maturity Dates

- Annual Compounding
  - Using Microsoft® Excel
    - What would happen to the bond's price it had a 15-year maturity rather than a 3-year maturity?

Finding the Value of a Bond	
Coupon Interest ($)	$ 100
Maturity (periods)	15
Face Value ($)	$ 1,000
Market Interest Rate (%)	15%
Market Price ($)	($707.63)

And the longer the maturity, the greater the price decline.

Bonds with Maturity Dates

- Annual Compounding
  - Using Microsoft® Excel
    - What would happen to the original 3-year bond's price if interest rates dropped from 10% to 5%?

Finding the Value of a Bond	
Coupon Interest ($)	$ 100
Maturity (periods)	3
Face Value ($)	$ 1,000
Market Interest Rate (%)	5%
Market Price ($)	($1,136.16)

When interest rates go down, bond prices will always go up.

Bonds with Maturity Dates

- Annual Compounding
  - Using Microsoft® Excel
    - What if we considered a similar bond, but with a 15-year maturity rather than a 3-year maturity?

Finding the Value of a Bond	
Coupon Interest ($)	$ 100
Maturity (periods)	15
Face Value ($)	$ 1,000
Market Interest Rate (%)	5%
Market Price ($)	($1,518.98)

And the longer the maturity, the greater the price increase will be.

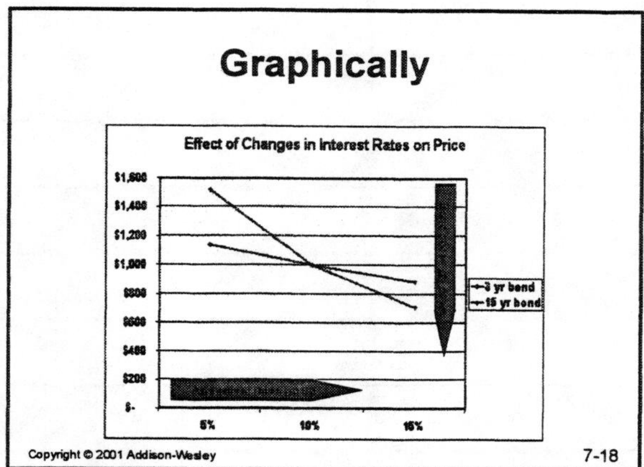

Bonds with Maturity Dates

- Semi-Annual Compounding
  - Using Microsoft® Excel
    - If we had the same bond, but with semi-annual coupon payments, we would have to divide the 10% coupon rate by two, divided the discount rate by two, and multiply n by two.

Finding the Value of a Bond	
Coupon Interest ($)	$ 50
Maturity (periods)	6
Face Value ($)	$ 1,000
Market Interest Rate (%)	3%
Market Price ($)	($1,137.70)

For the original example, divide the 10% coupon by 2, divide the 15% discount rate by 2, and multiply 3 years by 2.

Bonds with Maturity Dates

- Semi-Annual Compounding
  - Using Microsoft® Excel
    - If we had the same bond, but with semi-annual coupon payments, we would have to divide the 10% coupon rate by two, divided the discount rate by two, and multiply n by two.

Finding the Value of a Bond	
Coupon Interest ($)	$ 50
Maturity (periods)	6
Face Value ($)	$ 1,000
Market Interest Rate (%)	3%
Market Price ($)	($1,137.70)

Thus, the value is slightly larger than the price of the annual coupon bond (1,136.16) because the investor receives payments sooner.

Coupon Effects on Price Volatility

- The amount of bond price volatility depends on three basic factors:
  - Length of time to maturity
  - Risk
  - Amount of coupon interest paid by the bond
- First, we already have seen that the longer the term to maturity, the greater is a bond's volatility.
- Second, the riskier a bond, the more variable the required return will be, resulting in greater price volatility.
- Finally, the amount of coupon interest also impacts a bond's price volatility.
- Specifically, the lower the coupon rate, the greater will be the bond's volatility, because it will be longer before the investor receives a significant portion (the par value) of the cash flow from his or her investment.

Coupon Effects on Price Volatility

10 Year Bond		
Interest	Price	Price
Rate	5% Coupon	15% Coupon
0%	$ 1,500	$ 2,500
10%	$ 693	$ 1,307
20%	$ 371	$ 790

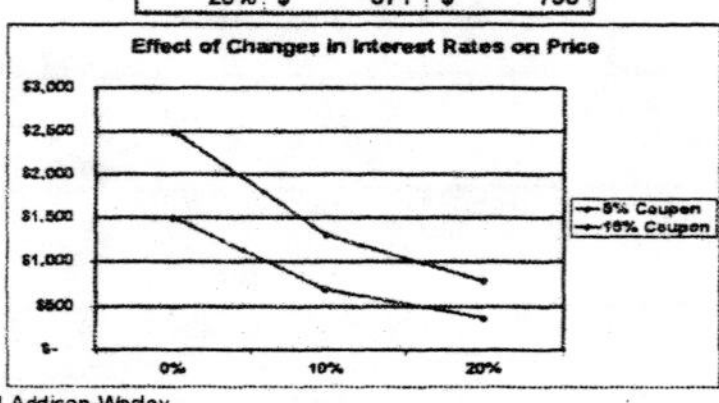

Price Converges on Par at Maturity

- It is also important to note that a bond's price will approach par value as it approaches the maturity date, *regardless* of the interest rate and *regardless* of the coupon rate.

10% Coupon Bond		
Interest	Price	Price
Rate	20 Years	1 Year
0%	$ 3,000	$ 1,100
10%	$ 1,000	$ 1,000
20%	$ 513	$ 917

Price Converges on Par at Maturity

- It is also important to note that a bond's price will approach par value as it approaches the maturity date, *regardless* of the interest rate and *regardless* of the coupon rate.

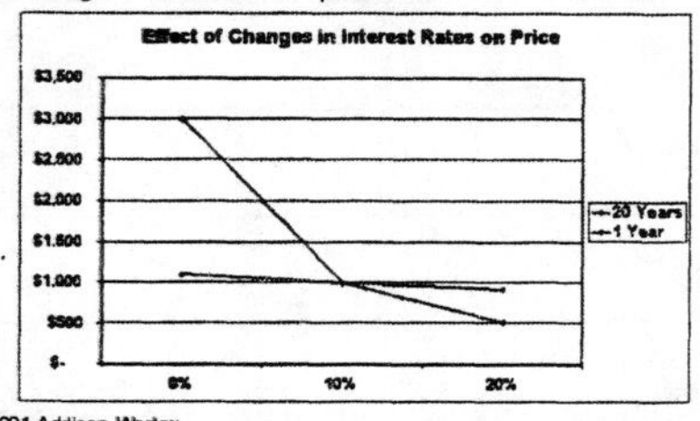

Yields

- The current yield measures the annual return to an investor based on the current price.

$$\text{Current yield} = \frac{\text{Annual coupon interest}}{\text{Current market price}}$$

- For example, a 10% coupon bond which is currently selling at $1,150 would have a current yield of:

$$\text{Current yield} = \frac{\$100}{\$1{,}150} = 8.7\%$$

Yields

- The yield to maturity measures the compound annual return to an investor and considers all bond cash flows. It is essentially the bond's IRR based on the current price.

$$PV = \frac{I_1}{(1+i)^1} + \frac{I_2}{(1+i)^2} + \ldots + \frac{(I_n + P_n)}{(1+i)^n}$$

- Notice that this is the same equation we saw earlier when we solved for price. The only difference then was that we were solving for a different unknown. In this case, we *know* the market price but are solving for return.

Yields

- The yield to maturity measures the compound annual return to an investor and considers all bond cash flows. It is essentially the bond's IRR based on the current price.
- Using Microsoft® Excel
  - For example, suppose we wished to determine the YTM on the following bond.

Finding Yield to Maturity	
Market Price ($)	($1,000.00)
Coupon Interest ($)	$ 100
Maturity (periods)	10
Face Value ($)	$ 1,000
Market Interest Rate (%)	?

Yields

- The yield to maturity measures the compound annual return to an investor and considers all bond cash flows. It is essentially the bond's IRR based on the current price.
- Using Microsoft® Excel
  - For example, suppose we wished to determine the YTM on the following bond.

Finding Yield to Maturity		Period	Cash Flow
		0	($1,000.00)
Market Price ($)	($1,000.00)	1	$ 100
Coupon Interest ($)	$ 100	2	$ 100
Maturity (periods)	10	3	$ 100
Face Value ($)	$ 1,000	4	$ 100
Market Interest Rate (%)	10%	5	$ 100
		6	$ 100
		7	$ 100
		8	$ 100
		9	$ 100
		10	$ 1,100

=IRR(d10:d20)

To compute the yield on this bond we simply listed all of the bond cash flows in a column and computed the IRR

Yields

- The yield to maturity measures the compound annual return to an investor and considers all bond cash flows. It is essentially the bond's IRR based on the current price.
  - Note that the yield to maturity will only be equal to the current yield if the bond is selling for its face value ($1,000).
  - And that rate will also be the same as the bond's coupon rate.
  - For premium bonds, the current yield > YTM.
  - For discount bonds, the current yield < YTM.

Common Stock Valuation

- Stock returns are derived from both dividends and capital gains, where the capital gain results from the appreciation of the stock's market price due to the growth in the firm's earnings. Mathematically, the expected return may be expressed as follows:

$$E(r) = D/P + g$$

- For example, if the firm's \$1 dividend on a \$25 stock is expected to grow at 7%, the expected return is:

$$E(r) = 1/25 + .07 = 11\%$$

Stock Valuation Models

- The Basic Stock Valuation Equation

$$P_0 = \frac{D_1}{(1+k)^1} + \frac{D_2}{(1+k)^2} + \ldots + \frac{D_n}{(1+k)^n}$$

Stock Valuation Models

- The Zero Growth Model
  - The zero dividend growth model assumes that the stock will pay the same dividend each year, year after year.
  - For assistance and illustration purposes, I have developed a spreadsheet tutorial using Microsoft® Excel.
  - A non-functional excerpt from the spreadsheet appears on the following slide.

Stock Valuation Models

- The Zero Growth Model
  - Using Microsoft® Excel

1. Zero Growth (Constant Dividend) Model		
A. Solving for Price:	V = D/k, where D = dividend and k = required return	
	What would an investor be willing to pay for a stock if she expected to receive a dividend of $2.50 each year indefinitely and her required return is 15%?	
	D	$ 2.50
	k	15.00%
	V?	$ 16.67

Stock Valuation Models

- The Zero Growth Model
  - Using Microsoft® Excel

B. Solving for Return:	k = D/V	
	What rate of return would an investor expect if the current price of a stock is $119 and she expected the firm to pay a constant dividend of $4/year?	
	V	$ 119.00
	D	$ 4.00
	k?	3.4%

Stock Valuation Models

- The Constant Growth Model
  - The constant dividend growth model assumes that the stock will pay dividends that grow at a constant rate each year, year after year.
  - For assistance and illustration purposes, I have developed a spreadsheet tutorial using Microsoft® Excel.
  - A non-functional excerpt from the spreadsheet appears on the following slide.

Stock Valuation Models

- The Constant Growth Model
  - Using Microsoft® Excel

Valuation		
(Note: [illegible])		
1. Constant Growth Model		
A. Solving for Price:	$V = D_0(1+g)/(k-g) = D_1/(k-g)$, where D_0 = current dividend, k = required return, and g = growth rate	
	What would an investor be willing to pay for a stock if she just received a dividend of $2.50, her required return is 15%, and she expected dividends to grow at a rate of 5% per year	
	D_0	$ 2.50
	k	15.00%
	g	5.00%
	[illegible]	$ 26.25

Stock Valuation Models

- The Constant Growth Model
  - Using Microsoft® Excel

B. Solving for Return:	$k = D_0(1+g)/V + g = D_1/V + g$	
	What is my expected return on a stock that costs $26.50, just paid a dividend of $2.50, and has an expected growth rate of 5%?	
	D_0	$ 2.50
	V	$ 26.25
	g	5.00%
	k?	15.00%

Stock Valuation Models

- Variable Growth Model
  - The non-constant (variable) dividend growth model assumes that the stock will pay dividends that grow at one rate during one period, and at another rate in another year or thereafter.
  - A non-functional excerpt from the spreadsheet appears on the following slide.

Stock Valuation Models

- The Variable Growth Model
  - Using Microsoft® Excel

Valuation

(Note: The tables below have been written using formulas which allow you to alter the information or assumptions.)

1. Non-Constant Growth Model

A. Solving for Price:	**This model involves the computation of year-to-year dividends which are then dicounted at the investors required rate of return.**
	What would an investor be willing to pay for a stock if she just received a dividend of $2.50, her required return is 15%, and she expected dividneds to grow at a rate of 10% per year for the first two years, and then at a rate of 5% thereafter

Stock Valuation Models

- The Variable Growth Model
  - Using Microsoft® Excel

What would an investor be willing to pay for a stock if she just received a dividend of $2.50, her required return is 15%, and she expected dividneds to grow at a rate of 10% per year for the first two years, and then at a rate of 5% thereafter.

Step 1:	Compute the expected dividends during the first growth period.	
	g	10.0%
	D_0	$ 2.50
	D_1	$ 2.75
	D_2	$ 3.03

Stock Valuation Models

- The Variable Growth Model
  - Using Microsoft® Excel

What would an investor be willing to pay for a stock if she just received a dividend of $2.50, her required return is 15%, and she expected dividneds to grow at a rate of 10% per year for the first two years, and then at a rate of 5% thereafter.

Step 2:	Compute the Estimated Value of the stock at the end of year 2 using the Constant Growth Model	
	D_2	$ 3.03
	k	15.00%
	g	5.00%
	V_2?	$ 31.76

Stock Valuation Models

- The Variable Growth Model
  - Using Microsoft® Excel

What would an investor be willing to pay for a stock if she just received a dividend of \$2.50, her required return is 15%, and she expected dividneds to grow at a rate of 10% per year for the first two years, and then at a rate of 5% thereafter.

Step 3: Compute the Present Value of all expected cash flows to find the price of the stock today.

		Cash Flow	PV at 15%
1	D_1	\$ 2.75	\$ 2.39
2	D_2	\$ 3 03	\$ 2.29
3	V_2?	\$ 31.76	\$ 20 88
	V_0	?	\$ 25 56

Decision Making and Common Stock Value

- Changes in Dividends or Dividend Growth
  - Valuation equations measure the stock value at a point in time based on expected return and risk.
  - Changes in expected dividends or dividend growth can have a profound impact on the value of a stock.

Price Sensitivity to Changes in Dividends and Dividend Growth (Using the Constant Growth Model)

D_0	\$ 2.00	\$ 2.50	\$ 3.00	\$ 2.00	\$ 2.00	\$ 2.00
g	3.0%	3.0%	3.0%	3.0%	6.0%	9.0%
D_1	\$ 2.06	\$ 2.58	\$ 3.09	\$ 2.06	\$ 2.12	\$ 2.18
k_s	10.0%	10.0%	10.0%	10.0%	10.0%	10.0%
P	\$ 29.43	\$ 36.79	\$ 44.14	\$ 29.43	\$ 53.00	\$ 218.00

Decision Making and Common Stock Value

- Changes in Dividends or Dividend Growth
  - Changes in risk and required return can also have significant effects on price.

Price Sensitivity to Changes Risk (Required Return) (Using the Constant Growth Model)

D_0	\$ 2.00	\$ 2.00	\$ 2.00	\$ 2.00	\$ 2.00	\$ 2.00
g	3.0%	3.0%	3.0%	3.0%	3.0%	3.0%
D_1	\$ 2.06	\$ 2.06	\$ 2.06	\$ 2.06	\$ 2.06	\$ 2.06
k_s	5.0%	7.5%	10.0%	12.5%	15.0%	17.5%
P	\$ 103.00	\$ 45.78	\$ 29.43	\$ 21.68	\$ 17.17	\$ 14.21

Decision Making and Common Stock Value

- Changes in Dividends or Dividend Growth
  - Changes in expected dividends or dividend growth can have a profound impact on the value of a stock

Price Sensitivity to Changes in Both Dividends and Required Return (Using the Constant Growth Model)						
D_0	\$ 2.00	\$ 2.50	\$ 3.00	\$ 2.00	\$ 2.50	\$ 3.00
g	3.0%	6.0%	9.0%	3.0%	6.0%	9.0%
D_1	\$ 2.06	\$ 2.65	\$ 3.27	\$ 2.06	\$ 2.65	\$ 3.27
k_S	5.0%	7.5%	10.0%	12.5%	15.0%	17.5%
P	**\$ 103.00**	**\$ 176.67**	**\$ 327.00**	**\$ 21.68**	**\$ 29.44**	**\$ 38.47**

Using Microsoft® Excel

- The Microsoft® Excel Spreadsheets used in the this presentation can be downloaded from the *Introduction to Finance* companion web site: http://www.awl.com/gitman_madura

Chapter 7

Introduction to Finance

Lawrence J. Gitman
Jeff Madura

End of Chapter

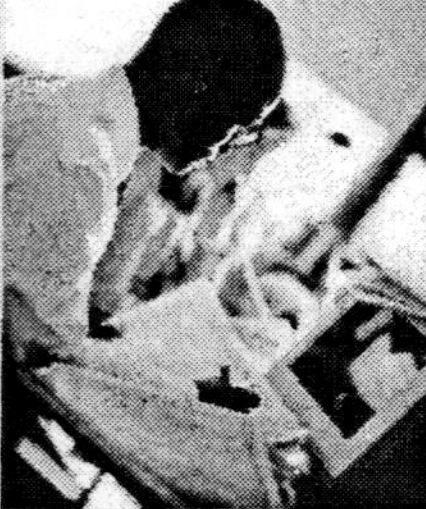

Chapter 8

Introduction to Finance

Lawrence J. Gitman
Jeff Madura

Financial Statements and Analysis

Learning Goals

- Review the contents of the stockholder's report, and the procedures for consolidating financial statements.
- Understand who uses financial ratios and how.
- Use ratios to analyze a firm's liquidity and activity.
- Discuss the relationship between debt and financial leverage and the ratios used to analyze a firm's debt.
- Use ratios to analyze a firm's profitability and its market value.
- Use the DuPont system of analysis to perform a complete ratio analysis.

The Stockholders' Report

- The guidelines used to prepare and maintain financial records and reports are known as generally accepted accounting principles (GAAP).
- GAAP is authorized by the Financial Accounting Standards Board (FASB).
- Public corporations with more than $5 million in assets and more than 500 stockholders are required by the SEC to provide their stockholders with an annual stockholders' report.

Financial Statements

- The Income Statement
  - The income statement provides a financial summary of a company's operating results during a specified period.
  - Although they are prepared annually for reporting purposes, they are generally computed monthly by management and quarterly for tax purposes.

Financial Statements

TABLE 8.1 Daton Company Income Statements ($000)

	For the years ended December 31	
	2001	2000
Sales revenue	$3,074	$2,567
Less: Cost of goods sold	2,088	1,711
Gross profits	$ 986	$ 856
Less: Operating expenses		
Selling expense	$ 100	$ 108
General and administrative expenses	194	187
Lease expense[a]	35	35
Depreciation expense	239	223
Total operating expense	$ 568	$ 553

[a]Lease expense is shown here as a separate item rather than being included as interest expense and amortization, as specified by the FASB for financial-reporting purposes. The approach used here is consistent with tax-reporting rather than financial-reporting procedures.

 Table 8.1 (Panel 1)

Financial Statements

TABLE 8.1 Daton Company Income Statements ($000)

	For the years ended December 31	
	2001	2000
Operating profits	$ 418	$ 303
Less: Interest expense	93	91
Net profits before taxes	$ 325	$ 212
Less: Taxes (rate = 29%)[b]	94	64
Net profits after taxes	$ 231	148
Less: Preferred stock dividends	10	10
Earnings available for common stockholders	$ 221	$ 138
Earnings per share (EPS)[c]	$ 2.90	$ 1.81
Dividend per share (DPS)[d]	$ 1.29	$ .75

[b]The 29% tax rate for 2001 results because the firm has certain special tax write-offs that do not show up directly on its income statement.

[c]Calculated by dividing the earnings available for common stockholders by the number of shares of common stock outstanding—76,262 in 2001 and 76,244 in 2000. Earnings per share in 2001: $221,000 ÷ 76,262 = $2.90; in 2000: $138,000 ÷ 76,244 = $1.81.

[d]Calculated by dividing the dollar amount of dividends paid to common stockholders by the number of shares of common stock outstanding. Dividends per share in 2001: $98,000 ÷ 76,262 = $1.29; in 2000: $57,183 ÷ 76,244 = $.75.

 Table 8.1 (Panel 2)

Financial Statements

- The Balance Sheet
  - The balance sheet presents a summary of a firm's financial position at a given point in time.
  - Assets indicate what the firm owns, equity represents the owners' investment, and liabilities indicate what the firm has borrowed.

Financial Statements

TABLE 8.2 Daton Company Balance Sheets ($000)

	December 31	
Assets	2001	2000
Current assets		
Cash	$ 363	$ 288
Marketable securities	68	51
Accounts receivable	503	365
Inventories	289	300
Total current assets	$1,223	$1,004
Gross fixed assets (at cost)[a]		
Land and buildings	$2,072	$1,903
Machinery and equipment	1,866	1,693
Furniture and fixtures	358	316
Vehicles	275	314
Other (includes financial leases)	98	96
Total gross fixed assets (at cost)	$4,669	$4,322
Less: Accumulated depreciation	2,295	2,056
Net fixed assets	$2,374	$2,266
Total assets	$3,597	$3,270

[a] In 2001, the firm has a 6-year financial lease requiring annual beginning-of-year payments of $35,000. Four years of the lease have yet to run.

Table 8.2 (Panel 1)

Financial Statements

TABLE 8.2 Daton Company Balance Sheets ($000)

	December 31	
Liabilities and stockholders' equity	2001	2000
Current liabilities		
Accounts payable	$ 382	$ 270
Notes payable	79	99
Accruals	159	114
Total current liabilities	$ 620	$ 483
Long-term debt (includes financial leases)[b]	$1,023	$ 967
Total liabilities	$1,643	$1,450
Stockholders' equity		
Preferred stock—cumulative 5%, $100 par, 2,000 shares authorized and issued[c]	$ 200	$ 200
Common stock—$2.50 par, 100,000 shares authorized, shares issued and outstanding in 2001: 76,262; in 2000: 76,244	191	190
Paid-in capital in excess of par on common stock	428	418
Retained earnings	1,135	1,012
Total stockholders' equity	$1,954	$1,820
Total liabilities and stockholders' equity	$3,597	$3,270

[b] Annual principal repayments on a portion of the firm's total outstanding debt amount to $71,000.
[c] The annual preferred stock dividend would be $5 per share (5% × $100 par), or a total of $10,000 annually ($5 per share × 2,000 shares).

Table 8.2 (Panel 2)

Financial Statements

- Statement of Retained Earnings
  - The statement of retained earnings reconciles the net income earned and dividends paid during the year with the change in retained earnings.

Financial Statements

TABLE 8.3 Daton Company Statement of Retained Earnings ($000) for the Year Ended December 31, 2001

Retained earnings balance (January 1, 2001)		$1,012
Plus: Net profits after taxes (for 2001)		231
Less: Cash dividends (paid during 2001)		
Preferred stock	($10)	
Common stock	(98)	
Total dividends paid		(108)
Retained earnings balance (December 31, 2001)		$1,135

 Table 8.3

Financial Statements

- Statement of Cash Flows
  - The statement of cash flows provides a summary of the cash flows over the period of concern, typically the year just ended.
  - This statement not only provides insight into a company's investment and financing and operating activities, but also ties together the income statement and previous and current balance sheets.

Financial Statements

TABLE 8.4 Dalton Company Statement of Cash Flows ($000) for the Year Ended December 31, 2001

Cash Flow from Operating Activities		
Net profits after taxes	$ 231	
Depreciation	239	
Increase in accounts receivable	(138)[a]	
Decrease in inventories	11	
Increase in accounts payable	112	
Increase in accruals	45	
Cash provided by operating activities		$ 500
Cash Flow from Investment Activities		
Increase in gross fixed assets	($347)	
Change in business interests	0	
Cash provided by investment activities		(347)
Cash Flow from Financing Activities		
Decrease in notes payable	($20)	
Increase in long-term debts	56	
Changes in stockholders' equity[b]	11	
Dividends paid	($108)	
Cash provided by financing activities		(61)
Net increase in cash and marketable securities		$ 92

[a]As is customary, parentheses are used to denote a negative number, which in this case is a cash outflow.

[b]Retained earnings are excluded here, because their change is actually reflected in the combination of the "net profits after taxes" and "dividends paid" entries.

 Table 8.4

Consolidating International Financial Statements

- FASB 52 mandated that companies based in the United States translate their foreign-currency denominated assets and liabilities into dollars using the current rate (translation) method.
- Under the translation method, companies translate foreign-currency-denominated assets and liabilities into dollars for consolidation with the parent company's financial statements.
- Income statement items are usually treated similarly, although they can also be translated at the average exchange rate during the period (year).

Consolidating International Financial Statements

- Equity accounts, on the other hand, are translated into dollars by using the exchange rate that prevailed when the parent's equity investment was made (the historical rate).
- Retained earnings are adjusted to reflect each year's operating profits (or losses), but do not consider any profits or losses resulting from currency changes.
- Instead, translation gains and losses are accumulated in an equity reserve account called the cumulative translation adjustment.

Consolidating International Financial Statements

- Translation gains (losses) increase (decrease) this account balance.
- However, the gains and losses are not "realized" until the parent company sells or shuts down the subsidiary.

Using Financial Ratios

- Interested Parties
  - Ratio analysis involves methods of calculating and interpreting financial ratios to assess a firm's financial condition and performance.
  - It is of interest to shareholders, creditors, and the firm's own management.

Types of Ratio Comparisons

- Trend or Time-Series Analysis
  - Used to evaluate a firm's performance over time.
- Cross-Sectional Analysis
  - Used to compare different firms at the same point in time.
  - Industry comparative analysis
    - One specific type of cross sectional analysis. Used to compare one firm's financial performance to the industry's average performance.
- Combined Analysis
  - Combined analysis simply uses a combination of both time-series analysis and cross-sectional analysis.

Types of Ratio Comparisons

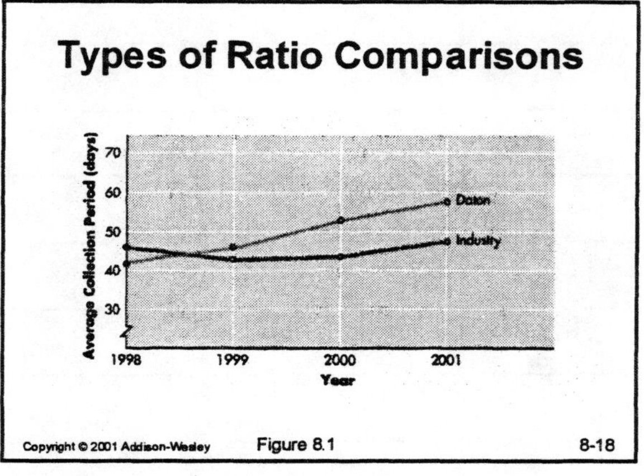

Figure 8.1

Cautions for Doing Ratio Analysis

- Ratios must be considered together; a single ratio by itself means relatively little.
- Financial statements that are being compared should be dated at the same point in time.
- Use audited financial statements when possible.
- The financial data being compared should have been developed in the same way.
- Be wary of inflation distortions.

Ratio Analysis Example

- Using Daton Company Financial Statements
  - Liquidity ratios
  - Activity ratios
  - Financial leverage ratio
  - Leverage ratios
  - Profitability ratios

Ratio Analysis

- Liquidity Ratios
  - Current Ratio

$$\text{Current ratio} = \frac{\text{Total current assets}}{\text{Total current liabilities}}$$

$$\text{Current ratio} = \frac{\$1,233,000}{\$620,000} = 1.97$$

Ratio Analysis

- Liquidity Ratios
  - Quick ratio

$$\text{Quick ratio} = \frac{\text{Total current assets - Inventory}}{\text{Total current liabilities}}$$

$$\text{Quick ratio} = \frac{\$1,233,000 - \$289,000}{\$620,000} = 1.51$$

Ratio Analysis

- Activity Ratios
  - Inventory Turnover

$$\text{Inventory turnover} = \frac{\text{Cost of goods sold}}{\text{Inventory}}$$

$$\text{Inventory turnover} = \frac{\$2,088,000}{\$289,000} = 7.2$$

Ratio Analysis

- Activity Ratios
  - Average collection period

$$ACP = \frac{\text{Accounts receivable}}{\text{Net sales/360}}$$

$$ACP = \frac{\$503,000}{\$3,074,000/360} = 58.9 \text{ days}$$

Ratio Analysis

- Activity Ratios
  - Average payment period

$$APP = \frac{\text{Accounts payable}}{\text{Annual purchases/360}}$$

$$ACP = \frac{\$382,000}{(.70 \times \$2,088,000)/360} = 94.1 \text{ days}$$

Ratio Analysis

- Activity Ratios
  - Total asset turnover

$$\text{Total asset turnover} = \frac{\text{Net sales}}{\text{Total assets}}$$

$$\text{Total asset turnover} = \frac{\$3,074,000}{\$3,579,000} = .85$$

Ratio Analysis

- Financial Leverage Ratio
  - Debt ratio

$$\text{Debt ratio} = \frac{\text{Total liabilities}}{\text{Total assets}}$$

$$\text{Debt ratio} = \frac{\$1,643,000}{\$3,579,000} = 45.7\%$$

Ratio Analysis

- Leverage Ratios
  - Times interest earned ratio

$$\text{Times interest earned} = \frac{\text{EBIT}}{\text{Interest}}$$

$$\text{Times interest earned} = \frac{\$418,000}{\$93,000} = 4.5$$

Ratio Analysis

- Leverage Ratios
  - Fixed-payment coverage ratio (FPCR)

$$\text{FPCR} = \frac{\text{EBIT + Lease pymts}}{\text{Interest + Lease pymts} + \{(\text{Princ pymts + PSD}) \times [1/(1 - t)]\}}$$

$$\text{FPCR} = \frac{\$418,000 + \$35,000}{\$93,000 + \$35,000 + \{(\$71,000 + \$10,000) \times [1/(1 - .29)]\}} = 1.9$$

Ratio Analysis

- Profitability Ratios
  - Common-size income statements

TABLE 8.6 Dolan Company Common-Size Income Statements

	For the years ended December 31		Evaluation[a]
	2001	2000	2000–2001
Sales revenue	100.0%	100.0%	same
Less: Cost of goods sold	67.9	66.7	worse
(1) Gross profit margin	32.1%	33.3%	worse
Less: Operating expenses			
Selling expense	3.3%	4.2%	better
General and administrative expenses	6.8	6.7	better
Lease expense	1.1	1.3	better
Depreciation expense	7.3	9.3	better
Total operating expense	18.5%	21.5%	better
(2) Operating profit margin	13.6%	11.8%	better
Less: Interest expense	3.0	3.5	better
Net profits before taxes	10.6%	8.3%	better
Less: Taxes	3.1	2.5	worse[b]
Net profits after taxes	7.5%	5.8%	better
Less: Preferred stock dividends	.3	.4	better
(3) Net profit margin	7.2%	5.4%	better

[a] Subjective assessments based on data provided.
[b] Taxes as a percent of sales increased noticeably between 2000 and 2001 due to differing costs and expenses, whereas the average tax rates (taxes ÷ net profits before taxes) for 2000 and 2001 remained about the same—30% and 29%, respectively.

Table 8.6

Ratio Analysis

- Profitability Ratios
  - Gross profit margin

$$GPM = \frac{\text{Gross profit}}{\text{Net sales}}$$

$$GPM = \frac{\$986,000}{\$3,074,000} = 32.1\%$$

Ratio Analysis

- Profitability Ratios
  - Operating profit margin

$$OPM = \frac{\text{EBIT}}{\text{Net sales}}$$

$$OPM = \frac{\$418,000}{\$3,074,000} = 13.6\%$$

Ratio Analysis

- Profitability Ratios
  - Net profit margin

$$NPM = \frac{\text{Net profits after taxes}}{\text{Net sales}}$$

$$NPM = \frac{\$231{,}000}{\$3{,}074{,}000} = 7.5\%$$

Ratio Analysis

- Profitability Ratios
  - Return on total assets (ROA)

$$ROA = \frac{\text{Net profits after taxes}}{\text{Total assets}}$$

$$ROA = \frac{\$231{,}000}{\$3{,}597{,}000} = 6.4\%$$

Ratio Analysis

- Profitability Ratios
  - Return on equity (ROE)

$$ROE = \frac{\text{Net profits after taxes}}{\text{Stockholders' equity}}$$

$$ROE = \frac{\$231{,}000}{\$1{,}954{,}000} = 11.8\%$$

Ratio Analysis

- Profitability Ratios
  - Earnings per share (EPS)

$$EPS = \frac{\text{Earnings available to common stockholder}}{\text{Number of shares outstanding}}$$

$$EPS = \frac{\$221,000}{76,262} = \$2.90$$

Ratio Analysis

- Profitability Ratios
  - Price earnings (P/E) ratio

$$P/E = \frac{\text{Market price per share of common stock}}{\text{Earnings per share}}$$

$$P/E = \frac{\$32.25}{\$2.90} = 11.1$$

Ratio Analysis

- Profitability Ratios
  - Market/book (M/B) ratio

$$M/B = \frac{\text{Market price per share of common stock}}{\text{Book value per share of common stock}}$$

$$M/B = \frac{\$32.25}{\$23.00} = 1.40$$

Summarizing All Ratios

TABLE 8.7 Summary of Bartley Company Ratios (1999–2001, Including 2001 Industry Averages)

Ratio	Formula	Year 1999[a]	Year 2000[b]	Year 2001[b]	Industry average 2001[c]	Evaluation[d]: Cross-sectional 2001	Evaluation[d]: Time-series 1999–2001	Evaluation[d]: Overall
Liquidity								
Current ratio	Current assets / Current liabilities	2.04	2.08	1.97	2.05	OK	OK	OK
Quick (acid-test) ratio	(Current assets − Inventory) / Current liabilities	1.32	1.46	1.51	1.43	OK	good	good
Activity								
Inventory turnover	Cost of goods sold / Inventory	5.1	5.7	7.2	6.6	good	good	good
Average collection period	Accounts receivable / Average sales per day	43.9 days	51.2 days	58.9 days	44.3 days	poor	poor	poor
Average payment period	Accounts payable / Average purchases per day	75.8 days	81.2 days	94.1 days	66.5 days	poor	poor	poor
Total asset turnover	Sales / Total assets	0.94	0.79	0.85	0.75	OK	OK	OK
Debt								
Debt ratio	Total liabilities / Total assets	36.8%	44.3%	45.7%	40.0%	OK	OK	OK
Times interest earned ratio	Earnings before interest and taxes / Interest	5.6	3.3	4.5	4.3	good	OK	OK
Fixed-payment coverage ratio	[illegible]	2.4	1.4	1.9	1.5	good	OK	good

 Table 8.7 (Panel 1)

Summarizing All Ratios

Ratio	Formula	Year 1999[a]	Year 2000[b]	Year 2001[b]	Industry average 2001[c]	Evaluation[d]: Cross-sectional 2001	Evaluation[d]: Time-series 1999–2001	Evaluation[d]: Overall
Profitability								
Gross profit margin	Gross profits / Sales	31.4%	33.3%	32.1%	30.0%	OK	OK	OK
Operating profit margin	Operating profits / Sales	14.6%	11.8%	13.6%	11.0%	good	OK	good
Net profit margin	Earnings available for common stockholders / Sales	8.2%	5.4%	7.2%	6.2%	good	OK	good
Earnings per share (EPS)	Earnings available for common stockholders / Number of shares of common stock outstanding	$3.26	$1.81	$2.90	$2.26	good	OK	good
Return on total assets (ROA)	Earnings available for common stockholders / Total assets	7.8%	4.2%	6.1%	4.6%	good	OK	good
Return on common equity (ROE)	Earnings available for common stockholders / Common stock equity	13.7%	8.5%	12.6%	8.5%	good	OK	good
Market								
Price/earnings (P/E) ratio	Market price per share of common stock / Earnings per share	10.5	10.0[e]	11.1	12.5	OK	OK	OK
Market/book (M/B) ratio	Market price per share of common stock / Book value per share of common stock	1.25	0.85[e]	1.40	1.30	OK	OK	OK

[a] Calculated from data not included in this chapter.
[b] Calculated by using the financial statements presented in Tables 8.1 and 8.2.
[c] Obtained from sources not included in this chapter.
[d] Subjective assessments based on data provided.
[e] The market price per share at the end of 2000 was [illegible].

 Table 8.7 (Panel 2)

DuPont System of Analysis

- The DuPont system is used to dissect the firm's financial statements and to assess its financial condition.
- It merges the income statement and balance sheet into two summary measures of profitability: ROA and ROE as shown in Figure 8.2 on the following slide.
- The top portion focuses on the income statement, and the bottom focuses on the balance sheet.
- The advantage of the DuPont system is that it allows you to break ROE into a profit-on-sales component, an efficiency-of-asset-use component, and a use-of-leverage component.

DuPont System of Analysis

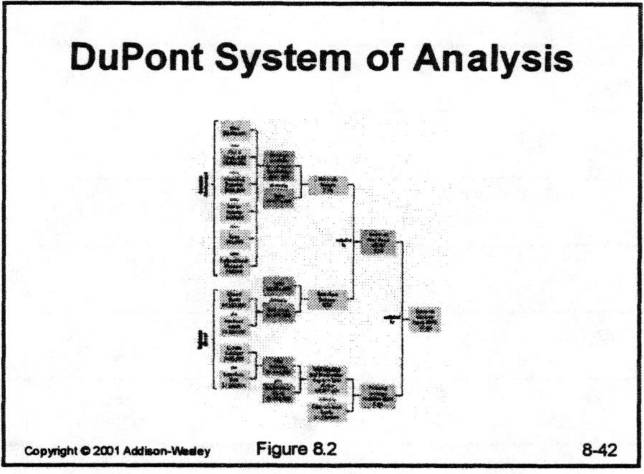

Figure 8.2

DuPont System of Analysis

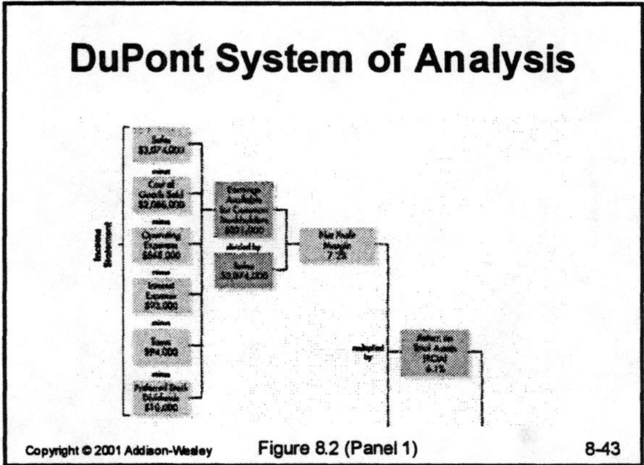

Figure 8.2 (Panel 1)

DuPont System of Analysis

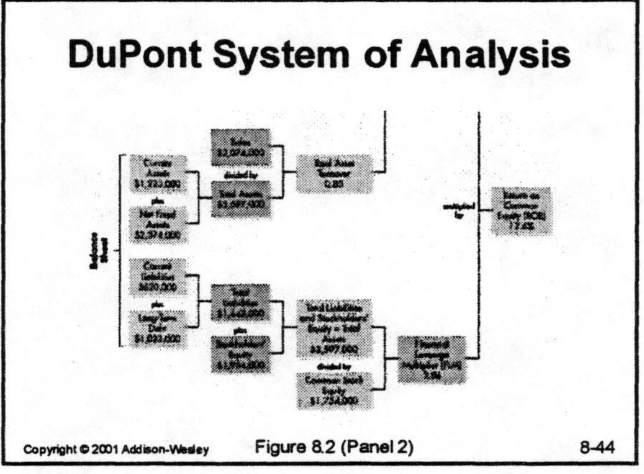

Figure 8.2 (Panel 2)

Chapter
8

Introduction to Finance
Lawrence J. Gitman
Jeff Madura

End of Chapter

Chapter 9

Introduction to Finance

Lawrence J. Gitman
Jeff Madura

The Firm and Its Financial Environment

Learning Goals

- Review the common forms of business organization.
- Describe the financial management function, its relationship to economics and accounting, and the financial managers primary activities.
- Explain the wealth maximization goal of the firm and the role of ethics in the firm.
- Discuss the agency issue.

Learning Goals

- Review the fundamentals of business taxation of ordinary income and capital gains.
- Understand the effect of depreciation on the firm's cash flows, the depreciable value of an asset, its depreciable life, and tax depreciation methods.
- Discuss the firm's cash flows, particularly the statement of cash flows.

Basic Forms of Business Organization

- Sole Proprietorships
- Partnerships
- Corporations

Sole Proprietorships

- Account for majority of small businesses.
- Most businesses start out as sole proprietorships.
- 75 percent of all businesses in the United States are sole proprietorships.

Partnerships

- Two or more owners.
- Account for 10 percent of all businesses.
- Finance, insurance, and real estate firms are the most common types of partnerships.

Corporations

- Separate legal entity.
- Although only 15 percent of all businesses are incorporated, corporations account for nearly 90 percent of receipts and 80 percent of net profits.
- Most growing small businesses eventually become corporations.

Strengths and Weaknesses of Organization Forms

TABLE 9.1 Strengths and Weaknesses of the Basic Legal Forms of Business Organization

	Legal form		
	Sole proprietorship	Partnership	Corporation
Strengths	• Owner receives all profits • Low organizational costs • Income included and taxed on proprietor's personal tax return • Independence • Secrecy • Ease of dissolution	• Can raise more funds than sole proprietorships • Borrowing power enhanced by more owners • More available brain power and managerial skill • Income included and taxed on partners' personal tax returns	• Owners have *limited liability*, which guarantees that they cannot lose more than they invest • Can achieve large size via sale of stock • Ownership (stock) is readily transferable • Long life of firm • Can hire professional managers • Has better access to financing • Receives certain tax advantages

 Table 9.1 (Panel 1)

Strengths and Weaknesses of Organization Forms

TABLE 9.1 Strengths and Weaknesses of the Basic Legal Forms of Business Organization

	Legal form		
	Sole proprietorship	Partnership	Corporation
Weaknesses	• Owner has *unlimited liability*—total wealth can be taken to satisfy debts • Limited fund-raising power tends to inhibit growth • Proprietor must be "jack of all trades" • Difficult to give employees long-run career opportunities • Lacks continuity when proprietor dies	• Owners have *unlimited liability* and may have to cover debts of other partners • Partnership is dissolved when a partner dies • Difficult to liquidate or transfer partnership	• Taxes generally higher, because corporate income is taxed and dividends paid to owners are also taxed • More expensive to organize than other business forms • Subject to greater government regulation • Lacks secrecy, because stockholders must receive financial reports

 Table 9.1 (Panel 2)

Corporate Organization

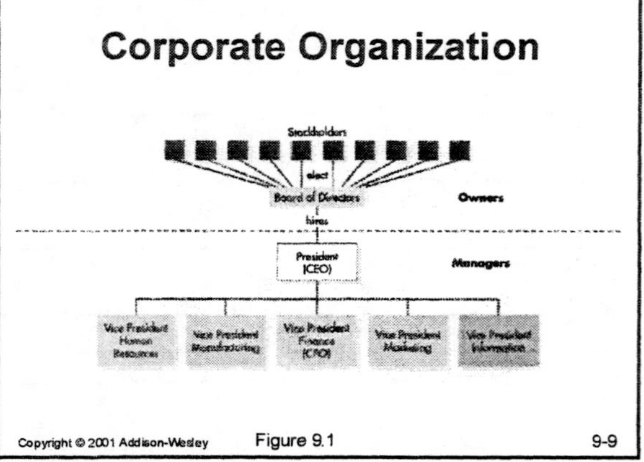

 Figure 9.1

The Managerial Finance Function

- The size and importance of the managerial finance function depends on the size of the firm.
- In small companies, the finance function may be performed by the company president or accounting department.
- As the business expands, finance typically evolves into a separate department linked to the president.

The Managerial Finance Function

- Relationship to Economics
  - The field of finance is actually an outgrowth of economics.
  - In fact, finance is sometimes referred to as financial economics.
  - Financial managers must understand the economic framework within which they operate in order to react or anticipate to changes in conditions.

The Managerial Finance Function

- Relationship to Economics
  - The primary economic principal used by financial managers is marginal analysis which says that financial decisions should be implemented only when benefits exceed costs.

The Managerial Finance Function

- Relationship to Accounting
  - The firm's finance (treasurer) and accounting (controller) functions are closely-related and overlapping.
  - In smaller firms, the financial manager generally performs both functions.

The Managerial Finance Function

- Relationship to Accounting
  - One major difference in perspective and emphasis between finance and accounting is that accountants generally use the accrual method, while in finance the focus is on cash flows.
  - The significance of this difference can be illustrated using the following simple example.

The Managerial Finance Function

- Relationship to Accounting
  - The Ferris Corporation experienced the following activity last year:

Sales:	$100,000 (50% still uncollected)
Cost of Goods:	$60,000 (all paid in full under supplier terms)
Expenses:	$30,000 (all paid in full)

  - Now contrast the differences in performance under the accounting method versus the cash method.

The Managerial Finance Function

- Relationship to Accounting

INCOME STATEMENT SUMMARY

	ACCRUAL	CASH
Sales	$100,000	$50,000
– COGS	($60,000)	($60,000)
Gross Margin	$40,000	($10,000)
– Expenses	($30,000)	($30,000)
Net Profit/(Loss)	$10,000	($40,000)

The Managerial Finance Function

- Relationship to Accounting
  - Finance and accounting also differ with respect to decision-making.
  - While accounting is primarily concerned with the presentation of financial data, the financial manager is primarily concerned with analyzing and interpreting this information for decision-making purposes.
  - The financial manager uses this data as a vital tool for making decisions about the financial aspects of the firm.

Key Activities of the Financial Manager

Making Investment Decisions	Balance Sheet		Making Financing Decisions
	Current Assets	Current Liabilities	
	Fixed Assets	Long-Term Funds	

 Figure 9.2

Goal of the Firm

- Maximize Profit???

Which Investment is Preferred?

	EPS ($)			
Investment	**Year 1**	**Year 2**	**Year 3**	**Total**
A	$ 2.90	$ -	$ -	$ 2.80
B	$ -	$ -	$ 3.00	$ 3.00

Profit maximization fails to account for differences in the level of cash flows (as opposed to profits), the timing of these cash flows, and the risk of these cash flows.

Goal of the Firm

- Maximize Shareholder Wealth!!!
  - Why?
    - Because maximizing shareholder wealth properly considers cash flows, the timing of these cash flows, and the risk of these cash flows.
    - This can be illustrated using the following simple valuation equation:

$$\text{Share price} = \frac{\text{Future dividends}}{\text{Required return}}$$

level and timing of cash flows

risk of cash flows

Goal of the Financial Manager

- Maximize Shareholder Wealth!!!
  - It can also be described using the following flow chart:

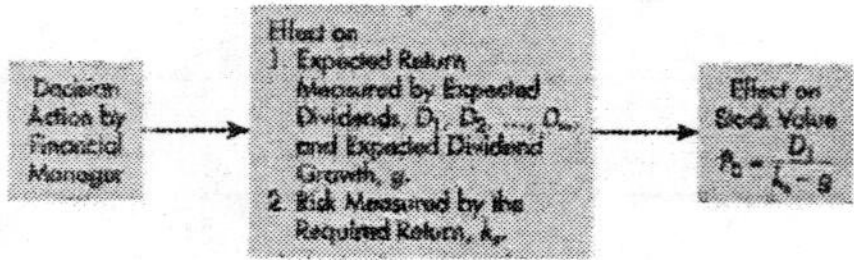

 Figure 7.3

Goal of the Financial Manager

- Economic Value Added (EVA)
  - Economic value added (EVA) is a popular measure used by many firms to determine whether an investment—proposed or existing—positively contributes to the owners' wealth.
  - EVA is calculated by subtracting the cost of funds used to finance an investment from its after-tax operating profits.
  - Investments with positive EVAs increase shareholder wealth and those with negative EVAs reduce shareholder value.

Goal of the Financial Manager

- What about other stakeholders?
  - Stakeholders include all groups of individuals who have a direct economic link to the firm including:
    - Employees
    - Customers
    - Suppliers
    - Creditors
    - Owners
  - The "stakeholder view" prescribes that the firm make a conscious effort to avoid actions that could be detrimental to the wealth position of its stakeholders.
  - Such a view is considered to be "socially responsible."

The Role of Ethics

- Ethics Defined
  - Ethics: the standards of conduct or moral judgment—have become an overriding issue in both our society and the financial community.
  - Ethical violations attract widespread publicity.
  - Negative publicity often leads to negative impacts on a firm.

The Role of Ethics

- Opinions
  - A wide majority (94%) of business school deans, business leaders, and members of Congress responding to a recent survey felt that the business community is troubled by ethical issues.
  - A majority (63%) of the respondents perceived that a firm strengthens its competitive position by maintaining high ethical standards.

The Role of Ethics

- Considering Ethics
  - To assess the ethical viability of a proposed action, ask:
    - Does the action unfairly single out an individual or group?
    - Does the action affect the morals, or legal rights of any individual or group?
    - Does the action conform to accepted moral standards?
    - Are there alternative courses of action that are less likely to cause actual or potential harm?

The Role of Ethics

- Ethics and Share Price
  - Ethics programs seek to:
    - Reduce litigation and judgment costs
    - Maintain a positive corporate image
    - Build shareholder confidence
    - Gain the loyalty and respect of all stakeholders
  - The expected result of such programs is to positively affect the firm's share price.

The Agency Issue

- The Problem
  - Whenever a manager owns less than 100% of the firm's equity, a potential agency problem exists.
  - In theory, managers would agree with shareholder wealth maximization.
  - However, managers are also concerned with their personal wealth, job security, fringe benefits, and lifestyle.
  - This would cause managers to act in ways that do not always benefit the firm shareholders.

The Agency Issue

- Resolving the Problem
  - Market forces such as major shareholders and the threat of a hostile takeover act to keep managers in check.
  - Agency costs may be incurred to ensure management acts in shareholders' interests.

The Agency Issue

- Resolving the Problem
  - Examples would include bonding or monitoring management behavior, and structuring management compensation to make shareholders' interests their own.
  - However, recent studies have failed to find a strong relationship between CEO compensation and share price.

Business Taxation

- Both individuals and businesses must pay taxes on income.
- The income of sole proprietorships and partnerships is taxed as the income of the individual owners, whereas corporate income is subject to corporate taxes.
- Both individuals and businesses can earn two types of income: ordinary and capital gains.
- Under current law, tax treatment of ordinary income and capital gains changes frequently due frequently changing tax laws.

Business Taxation

- Ordinary Income
  - Ordinary income is earned through the sale of a firm's goods or services and is taxed at the rates depicted in Table 9.2 on the following slide.

Calculate federal income taxes due if taxable income is $80,000.

Tax = [.15 × ($50,000)] + [.25 × ($25,000)] + [.34 × ($80,000 - $75,000)]

Tax = $15,450

Business Taxation

- Ordinary Income

TABLE 9.2 Corporate Tax Rate Schedule

Range of taxable income	Tax calculation: Base tax	+	(Marginal rate × Amount over base bracket)
$ 0 to $ 50,000	$ 0	+	(15% × amount over $ 0)
50,000 to 75,000	7,500	+	(25 × amount over 50,000)
75,000 to 100,000	13,750	+	(34 × amount over 75,000)
100,000 to 335,000	22,250	+	(39 × amount over 100,000)
335,000 to 10,000,000	113,900	+	(34 × amount over 335,000)
Over $10,000,000	3,400,000	+	(35 × amount over 10,000,000)

Table 9.2

Business Taxation

- Average and Marginal Tax Rates
  - A firm's marginal tax rate represents the rate at which additional income is taxed.
  - The average tax rate is the firm's taxes divided by taxable income.
  - This is illustrated using the simple example below.

What is the marginal and average tax rate for the previous example?

Marginal Tax Rate = 34%

Average Tax Rate = $15,450/$80,000 = 19.31%

Business Taxation

- Tax on Interest and Dividend Income
  - For corporations only, 70 percent of all dividend income received from an investment in the stock of another corporation in which the firm has less than 20 percent ownership is excluded from taxation.
  - This exclusion is provided to avoid triple taxation for corporations.
  - Unlike dividend income, all interest income received is fully taxed.

Business Taxation

- Debt versus Equity Financing
  - In calculating taxes, corporations may deduct operating expenses and interest expense but not dividends paid.
  - This creates a built-in tax advantage for using debt financing, as the following example will demonstrate.

A firm with 100,000 shares outstanding needs to raise an additional $500,000 in capital. They can do so by selling bonds that pay 6% interest or by issuing 10,000 additional shares at $50/share. The firm pays $3.00 in dividends for each share outstanding.

Business Taxation

- Debt versus Equity Financing

The Impact of Debt versus Equity Financing

	Debt Financing	Equity Financing
Operating Profit (EBIT)	$ 700,000	$ 700,000
Less: Interest Expense	30,000	-
Earnings Before Taxes	$ 670,000	$ 700,000
Less: Taxes (40%)	268,000	280,000
Earnings After Taxes	$ 402,000	$ 420,000
Shares Outstanding	100,000	110,000
Dividends Paid	$ 300,000	$ 330,000
Earnings Available to Common	$ 102,000	$ 90,000
Earnings Per Share (EPS)	$ 1.02	$ 0.82

Business Taxation

- Debt versus Equity Financing
  - As the example shows, the use of debt financing can increase cash flow and EPS, and decrease taxes paid.
  - The tax deductibility of interest and other certain expenses reduces the actual (after-tax) cost to the profitable firm.
  - It is the non-deductibility of dividends paid that results in double taxation under the corporate form of organization.

Business Taxation

- Capital Gains
  - A capital gain results when a firm sells an asset such as a stock held as an investment for more than its initial purchase price.
  - The difference between the sale price and the purchase price is called a capital gain.
  - For corporations, capital gains are added to ordinary income and taxed like ordinary income at the firm's marginal tax rate.

Depreciation

- Depreciation is the systematic charging of a portion of the costs of fixed assets against annual revenues over time.
- Depreciation for tax purposes is determined by using the modified accelerated cost recovery system (MACRS).
- On the other hand, a variety of other depreciation methods are often used for reporting purposes.

Depreciation

- Depreciation and Cash Flows
  - Financial managers are much more concerned with cash flows rather than profits.
  - To adjust the income statement to show cash flows from operations, all non-cash charges should be added back to net profit after taxes.
  - By lowering taxable income, depreciation and other non-cash expenses create a tax shield and enhance cash flow as shown in Table 9.3.

Depreciation

- Depreciation and Cash Flows

TABLE 9.3 Nolte Corporation Income Statement Calculated on Both Accrual and Cash Bases ($000) for the Year Ended December 31, 2001

		Accrual Basis		Cash Flow Basis
Sales revenue		$1,700		$1,700
Less: Cost of goods sold		1,000		1,000
Gross profits		$ 700		$ 700
Less: Operating expenses				
Selling expense	$ 80		$ 80	
General and administrative expense	150		150	
Depreciation expense (noncash charge)	100		0	
Total operating expense		330		230
Operating profits		$ 370		$ 470
Less: Interest expense		70		70
Net profits before taxes		$ 300		$ 400
Less: Taxes		120		120
Net profits after taxes		$ 180		
Cash flow from operations				$ 280

 Table 9.3

Depreciation

- Depreciable Value and Depreciable Life
  - Under the basic MACRS procedures, the depreciable value of an asset is its full cost, including outlays for installation.
  - No adjustment is required for expected salvage value.
  - For tax purposes, the depreciable life of an asset is determined by its MACRS recovery predetermined period.
  - MACRS property classes and rates are shown in Tables 9.4 and Table 9.5 on the following slides.

Depreciation

TABLE 9.4 First Four Property Classes Under MACRS

Property class (recovery period)	Definition
3 years	Research equipment and certain special tools.
5 years	Computers, typewriters, copiers, duplicating equipment, cars, light-duty trucks, qualified technological equipment, and similar assets.
7 years	Office furniture, fixtures, most manufacturing equipment, railroad track, and single-purpose agricultural and horticultural structures.
10 years	Equipment used in petroleum refining or in the manufacture of tobacco products and certain food products.

 Table 9.4

Depreciation

TABLE 9.5 Rounded Depreciation Percentages by Recovery Year Using MACRS for First Four Property Classes

Recovery year	Percentage by recovery year[a]			
	3 years	5 years	7 years	10 years
1	33%	20%	14%	10%
2	45	32	25	18
3	15	19	18	14
4	7	12	12	12
5		12	9	9
6		5	9	8
7			9	7
8			4	6
9				6
10				6
11				4
Totals	100%	100%	100%	100%

[a]These percentages have been rounded to the nearest whole percent to simplify calculations while retaining realism. To calculate the actual depreciation for tax purposes, be sure to apply the actual unrounded percentages or directly apply double-declining balance (200%) depreciation using the half-year convention.

 Table 9.5

Depreciation

For an installed cost of $40,000, Nolte Corporation acquired a machine having a recovery period of 5 years. Using the applicable MACRS rates, the depreciation expense each year is as follows:

Year	Cost	MACRS Rates	Depreciation
1	$ 40,000	20%	$ 8,000
2	$ 40,000	32%	$ 12,800
3	$ 40,000	19%	$ 7,600
4	$ 40,000	12%	$ 4,800
5	$ 40,000	12%	$ 4,800
6	$ 40,000	5%	$ 2,000
Totals		100%	$ 40,000

Cash Flow

- The statement of cash flows summarizes the firm's cash flow over a given period of time.
- The statement of cash flows is divided into three sections:
  - Operating flows
  - Investment flows
  - Financing flows
- The nature of these flows is shown in Figure 9.3 on the following slide.

Cash Flow

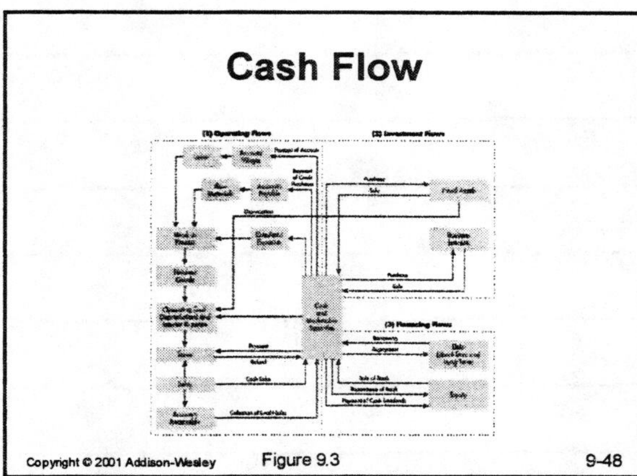

 Figure 9.3

Classifying Sources and Uses of Cash

TABLE 9.6 The Sources and Uses of Cash

Sources	Uses
Decrease in any asset	Increase in any asset
Increase in any liability	Decrease in any liability
Net profits after taxes	Net loss
Depreciation and other noncash charges	Dividends paid
Sale of stock	Repurchase or retirement of stock

 Table 9.6

Cash Flow

TABLE 9.7 Nolte Corporation Statement of Cash Flows ($000) for the Year Ended December 31, 2001

Cash Flow from Operating Activities		
Net profits after taxes	$180	
Depreciation	100	
Decrease in accounts receivable	100	
Decrease in inventories	300	
Increase in accounts payable	200	
Decrease in accruals	(100)[a]	
Cash provided by operating activities		$780

[a]As is customary, parentheses are used to denote a negative number, which in this case is a cash outflow.

 Table 9.7 (Panel 1)

Cash Flow

TABLE 9.7 **Nolte Corporation Statement of Cash Flows ($000) for the Year Ended December 31, 2001**

Cash Flow from Investment Activities		
Increase in gross fixed assets	($300)	
Changes in business interests	0	
Cash provided by investment activities		(300)
Cash Flow from Financing Activities		
Decrease in notes payable	($100)	
Increase in long-term debts	200	
Changes in stockholders' equity[b]	0	
Dividends paid	(80)	
Cash provided by financing activities		20
Net increase in cash and marketable securities		$500

[b]Retained earnings are excluded here, because their change is actually reflected in the combination of the "Net profits after taxes" and "Dividends paid" entries.

 Table 9.7 (Panel 2)

Cash Flow

- Interpreting the Statement of Cash Flows
  - The statement of cash flows ties the balance sheet at the beginning of the period with the balance sheet at the end of the period after considering the performance of the firm during the period through the income statement.
  - "Net increase" (decrease) in cash and marketable securities should be equivalent to the difference between the cash and marketable securities on the balance sheet at the beginning of the year and the end of the year.

Using Microsoft® Excel

- The Microsoft® Excel Spreadsheets used in the this presentation can be downloaded from the *Introduction to Finance* companion web site: http://www.awl.com/gitman_madura

Chapter
9

Introduction to Finance
Lawrence J. Gitman
Jeff Madura

End of Chapter

Chapter 10

Introduction to Finance

Lawrence J. Gitman
Jeff Madura

Capital Budgeting: Cash Flow Principles

Learning Goals

- Understand the key capital expenditure motives and the steps in the capital budgeting process.
- Define basic capital budgeting terminology.
- Discuss the major components of relevant cash flows, expansion versus replacement cash flows, and international capital budgeting and long-term investments.

Learning Goals

- Calculate the initial investment associated with a proposed capital expenditure.
- Determine the relevant operating cash inflows using the income statement format.
- Find the terminal cash flow.

Introduction

- Capital budgeting is the process of identifying, evaluating, and implementing a firm's investment opportunities.
- It seeks to identify investments that will enhance a firm's competitive advantage and increase shareholder wealth.
- The typical capital budgeting decision involves a large up-front investment followed by a series of smaller cash inflows.
- Poor capital budgeting decisions can ultimately result in company bankruptcy.

Key Motives for Capital Expenditures

- Capital expenditures are made for many reasons.
- The basic motives for capital expenditures are to expand, replace, or renew fixed assets or to obtain some other less tangible benefit over a long period.
- Specific examples of key motives are shown on the following slide.
- Details with regard to these motives can be found on the book's web site:
  - http://www.awl.com/ gitman_madura.

Key Motives for Capital Expenditures

- Examples
  - Replacing worn out or obsolete assets
  - Improving business efficiency
  - Acquiring assets for expansion into new products or markets
  - Acquiring another business
  - Complying with legal requirements
  - Satisfying work-force demands
  - Environmental requirements

Steps in the Process

- Step 1: Proposal Generation
  - How are projects initiated?
  - How much is available to spend?
- Step 2: Review and Analysis
  - Preliminary project review
  - Technically feasible?
  - Compatible with corporate strategy?
- Step 3: Decision Making
  - What are the costs and benefits?
  - What is the project's return?
  - What are the risks involved?

Our Focus

Steps in the Process

- Step 4: Implementation
  - When to implement?
  - How to implement?
- Step 5: Follow-Up
  - Is the project within budget?
  - What lessons can be drawn?

Independent versus Mutually Exclusive Projects

- Mutually exclusive projects are investments that compete in some way for a company's resources. A firm can select one or another but not both.
- Independent projects, on the other hand, do not compete with the firm's resources. A company can select one, or the other, or both—so long as they meet minimum profitability thresholds.

Unlimited Funds versus Capital Rationing

- If the firm has unlimited funds for making investments, then all independent projects that provide returns greater than some specified level can be accepted and implemented.
- However, in most cases firms face capital rationing restrictions since they only have a given amount of funds to invest in potential investment projects at any given time.

Accept-Reject versus Ranking Approaches

- Two basic approaches to capital budgeting decisions are available.
  - The accept-reject approach involves evaluating capital expenditure proposals to determine whether they meet the firm's minimum acceptance criterion.
  - The ranking approach involves ranking projects on the basis of some predetermined measure, such as the rate of return.

Conventional versus Nonconventional Cash Flow Patterns

- A conventional cash flow pattern consists of an initial outflow followed only by a series of inflows as shown in Figure 10.1.
- A nonconventional cash flow pattern is one in which an initial outflow is followed by a series of inflows and outflows as shown in Figure 10.2.
- Difficulties often arise in evaluating projects with nonconventional cash flow patterns; we will limit our discussion in this book to conventional projects.

Conventional versus Nonconventional Cash Flow Patterns

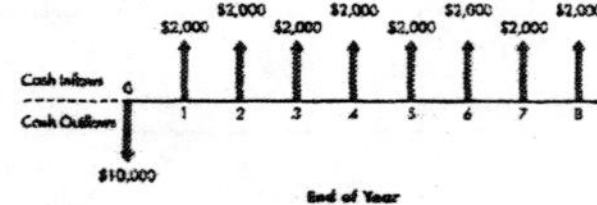

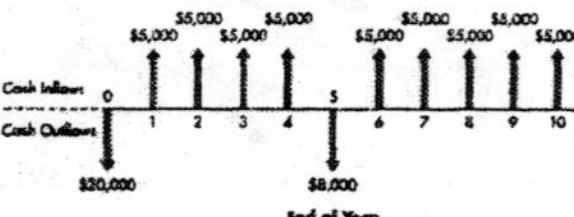

 Figures 10.1 and 10.2

The Relevant Cash Flows

- Incremental Cash Flows
  - Only cash flows associated with the investment.
  - Effects on the firm's other investments (both positive and negative) must also be considered.
- For example, if a day-care center decides to open another facility, the impact of customers who decide to move from one facility to the new facility must be considered.

The Relevant Cash Flows

- Incremental Cash Flows
  - Only cash flows associated with the investment.
  - Effects on the firms other investments (both positive and negative) must also be considered.
- Note that cash outlays already made (sunk costs) are *irrelevant* to the decision process.
- However, opportunity costs, which are cash flows that could be realized from the best alternative use of the asset, are *relevant*.

The Relevant Cash Flows

- Incremental Cash Flows
  - Only cash flows associated with the investment.
  - Effects on the firms other investments (both positive and negative) must also be considered.
- Estimating incremental cash flows is relatively straightforward in the case of expansion projects, but not so in the case of replacement projects.
- With replacement projects, incremental cash flows must be computed by subtracting existing project cash flows from those expected from the new project.

The Relevant Cash Flows

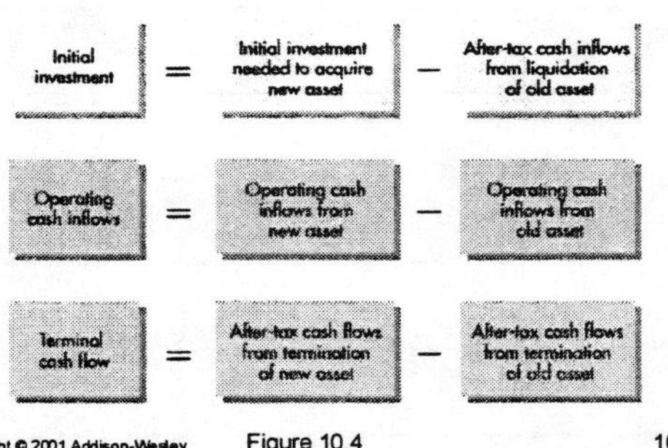

Figure 10.4

The Relevant Cash Flows

- Examples of relevant cash flows:
  - Cash inflows, outflows, and opportunity costs
  - Changes in working capital
  - Installation, removal and training costs
  - Terminal values
  - Depreciation
  - Existing asset effects

The Relevant Cash Flows

- Major Cash Flow Components:
  - Initial cash flows are cash flows resulting initially from the project. These are typically net negative outflows.
  - Operating cash flows are the cash flows generated by the project during its operation. These cash flows typically are net positive cash flows.
  - Terminal cash flows result from the disposition of the project. These are typically positive net cash flows.

The Relevant Cash Flows

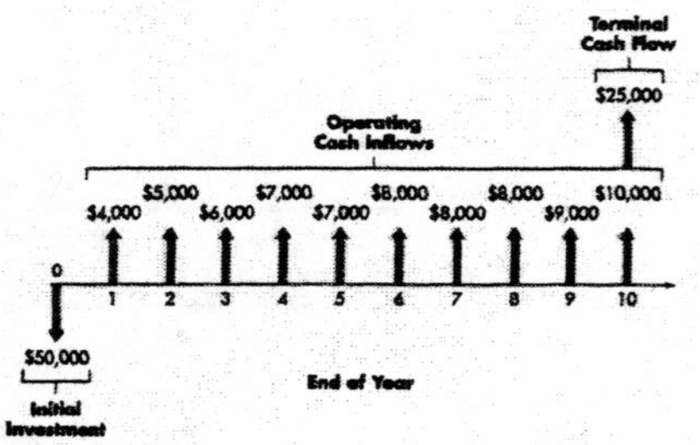

Figure 10.3

International Capital Budgeting

- International capital budgeting analysis differs from purely domestic analysis because:
  - Cash inflows and outflows occur in a foreign currency.
  - Foreign investments potentially face significant political risks.
- Despite these risks, the pace of foreign direct investment has accelerated significantly since the end of World War II.

Chapter Example

- Morton Company, a large diversified manufacturer of electronics components, is trying to determine the initial investment required to replace an old machine with a new, more sophisticated model. The machine's purchase price is $380,000 and an additional $20,000 will be needed to install it.
- It will be depreciated under the MACRS 5-year recovery period. The old machine was purchased 3 years ago at a cost of $240,000 and was also depreciated under the MACRS 5-year class rates.
- Morton has found a buyer willing to pay $280,000 for the present machine. Morton expects that a $35,000 increase in current assets and an $18,000 increase in current liabilities will be required to support the new machine. Morton is in the 40% tax bracket for both ordinary income and capital gains.

Finding the Initial Investment

TABLE 10.1 The Basic Format for Determining Initial Investment

Installed cost of new asset =
  Cost of new asset
  + Installation costs
− After-tax proceeds from sale of old asset =
  Proceeds from sale of old asset
  ∓Tax on sale of old asset
± Change in net working capital
Initial investment

Table 10.1

Finding the Initial Investment

TABLE 10.2 Tax Treatment on Sales of Assets

Form of taxable income	Definition	Tax treatment	Assumed tax rate
Capital gain	Portion of the sale price that is in excess of the initial purchase price.	Regardless of how long the asset has been held, the total capital gain is taxed as ordinary income.	40%
Recaptured depreciation	Portion of the sale price that is in excess of book value and represents a recovery of previously taken depreciation.	All recaptured depreciation is taxed as ordinary income.	40%
Loss on sale of asset	Amount by which sale price is less than book value.	If asset is depreciable and used in business, loss is deducted from ordinary income.	40% of loss is a tax savings
		If asset is not depreciable or is not used in business, loss is deductible only against capital gains.	40% of loss is a tax savings

Table 10.2

Finding the Initial Investment

Installed cost of proposed machine		
Cost of proposed machine	$380,000	
+ Installation costs	20,000	
Total installed cost—proposed (depreciable value)		$400,000
− After-tax proceeds from sale of present machine		
Proceeds from sale of present machine	$280,000	
− Tax on sale of present machine	84,160	
Total after-tax proceeds—present		195,840
+ Change in net working capital		17,000
Initial investment		$221,160

Finding Operating Cash Inflows

- Morton Company's estimates of its revenues and expenses (excluding depreciation), with and without the proposed new machine described in the preceding example, are given in Table 10.4. Note that both the expected life of the proposed machine and the remaining useful life of the present machine are 5 years.

TABLE 10.4 Morton Company's Revenue and Expenses (Excluding Depreciation) for Proposed and Present Machines

With proposed machine			With present machine		
Year	Revenue (1)	Expenses (excl. depr.) (2)	Year	Revenue (1)	Expenses (excl. depr.) (2)
1	$2,520,000	$2,300,000	1	$2,200,000	$1,990,000
2	2,520,000	2,300,000	2	2,300,000	2,110,000
3	2,520,000	2,300,000	3	2,400,000	2,230,000
4	2,520,000	2,300,000	4	2,400,000	2,250,000
5	2,520,000	2,300,000	5	2,250,000	2,120,000

Table 10.4

Finding Operating Cash Inflows

- The amount to be depreciated with the proposed machine is calculated by summing the price of $380,000 and the installation costs of $20,000. The proposed machine is to be depreciated under MACRS using a 5-year recovery period. The resulting depreciation on this machine for each of the 6 years, as well as the remaining 3 years of depreciation (years 4, 5, 6) on the present machine, are calculated in Table 10.5 on the following two slides.

Finding Operating Cash Inflows

TABLE 10.5 Depreciation Expense for Proposed and Present Machines for Morton Company

Year	Cost (1)	Applicable MACRS depreciation percentages (from Table 9.5) (2)	Depreciation [(1) × (2)] (3)
With proposed machine			
1	$400,000	20%	$ 80,000
2	400,000	32	128,000
3	400,000	19	76,000
4	400,000	12	48,000
5	400,000	12	48,000
6	400,000	5	20,000
Totals		100%	$400,000

Table 10.5 (Panel 1)

Finding Operating Cash Inflows

TABLE 10.5 Depreciation Expense for Proposed and Present Machines for Morton Company

Year	Cost (1)	Applicable MACRS depreciation percentages (from Table 9.5) (2)	Depreciation [(1) × (2)] (3)
With present machine			
1	$240,000	12% (year-4 depreciation)	$28,800
2	240,000	12 (year-5 depreciation)	28,800
3	240,000	5 (year-6 depreciation)	12,000
4	Because the present machine is at the end of the third year of its cost recovery at the time the analysis is performed, it has only the final 3 years of depreciation (as noted above) yet applicable.		0
5			0
6			0
Total			$69,600[a]

[a]The total $69,600 represents the book value of the present machine at the end of the third year, as calculated in the preceding example.

Table 10.5 (Panel 2)

Finding Operating Cash Inflows

- The operating cash inflows in each year can be calculated using the income statement format as shown in Table 10.6 below. The results as applied to the Morton Company are depicted in Table 10.7 on the following two slides.

TABLE 10.6 Calculation of Operating Cash Inflows Using the Income Statement Format

Revenue
− Expenses (excluding depreciation)
Profits before depreciation and taxes
− Depreciation
Net profits before taxes
− Taxes
Net profits after taxes
+ Depreciation
Operating cash inflows

Table 10.6

Finding Operating Cash Inflows

TABLE 10.7 Calculation of Operating Cash Inflows for Morton Company's Proposed and Present Machines

	Year 1	2	3	4	5	6
With proposed machine						
Revenue[a]	$2,520,000	$2,520,000	$2,520,000	$2,520,000	$2,520,000	$ 0
− Expenses (excl. depr.)[b]	2,300,000	2,300,000	2,300,000	2,300,000	2,300,000	0
Profits before depr. and taxes	$ 220,000	$ 220,000	$ 220,000	$ 220,000	$ 220,000	$ 0
− Depreciation[c]	80,000	128,000	76,000	48,000	48,000	20,000
Net profits before taxes	$ 140,000	$ 92,000	$ 144,000	$ 172,000	$ 172,000	−$20,000
− Taxes (rate = 40%)	56,000	36,800	57,600	68,800	68,800	− 8,000
Net profits after taxes	$ 84,000	$ 55,200	$ 86,400	$ 103,200	$ 103,200	−$12,000
+ Depreciation[c]	80,000	128,000	76,000	48,000	48,000	20,000
Operating cash inflows	$ 164,000	$ 183,200	$ 162,400	$ 151,200	$ 151,200	$ 8,000

[a]From column 1 of Table 10.4.
[b]From column 2 of Table 10.4.
[c]From column 3 of Table 10.5.

 Table 10.7 (Panel 1)

Finding Operating Cash Inflows

TABLE 10.7 Calculation of Operating Cash Inflows for Morton Company's Proposed and Present Machines

	Year 1	2	3	4	5	6
With present machine						
Revenue[a]	$2,200,000	$2,300,000	$2,400,000	$2,400,000	$2,250,000	$ 0
− Expenses (excl. depr.)[b]	1,990,000	2,110,000	2,230,000	2,250,000	2,120,000	0
Profits before depr. and taxes	$ 210,000	$ 190,000	$ 170,000	$ 150,000	$ 130,000	$ 0
− Depreciation[c]	28,800	28,800	12,000	0	0	0
Net profits before taxes	$ 181,200	$ 161,200	$ 158,000	$ 150,000	$ 130,000	$ 0
− Taxes (rate = 40%)	72,480	64,480	63,200	60,000	52,000	0
Net profits after taxes	$ 108,720	$ 96,720	$ 94,800	$ 90,000	$ 78,000	$ 0
+ Depreciation[c]	28,800	28,800	12,000	0	0	0
Operating cash inflows	$ 137,520	$ 125,520	$ 106,800	$ 90,000	$ 78,000	$ 0

[a]From column 1 of Table 10.4.
[b]From column 2 of Table 10.4.
[c]From column 3 of Table 10.5.

 Table 10.7 (Panel 2)

Finding Operating Cash Inflows

- Table 10.8 demonstrates the calculation of Morton Company's incremental (relevant) operating cash inflows for each year.

TABLE 10.8 Incremental (Relevant) Operating Cash Inflows for Morton Company

Year	Operating cash inflows: Proposed machine[a] (1)	Present machine[a] (2)	Incremental (relevant) [(1) − (2)] (3)
1	$164,000	$137,520	$26,480
2	183,200	125,520	57,680
3	162,400	106,800	55,600
4	151,200	90,000	61,200
5	151,200	78,000	73,200
6	8,000	0	8,000

[a]From final row for respective machine in Table 10.7.

 Table 10.8

Finding the Terminal Cash Flows

- Terminal cash flow is the cash flow resulting from termination and liquidation of a project at the end of its economic life. The general format for calculating terminal cash flow is shown in Table 10.9 below.

TABLE 10.9 The Basic Format for Determining Terminal Cash Flow

After-tax proceeds from sale of new asset =
Proceeds from sale of new asset
∓ Tax on sale of new asset
− After-tax proceeds from sale of old asset =
Proceeds from sale of old asset
∓ Tax on sale of old asset
± Change in net working capital
Terminal cash flow

 Table 10.9

Finding the Terminal Cash Flows

- Continuing with the Morton Company example, assume that the firm expects to be able to liquidate the new machine at the end of its 5-year usable life to net $50,000 after paying removal and cleanup costs. The old machine can be liquidated at the end of the 5 years to net $0 because it will then be completely obsolete. The firm expects to recover its $17,000 net working capital investment upon termination of the project. Both ordinary income and capital gains are taxed at 40%.

Finding the Terminal Cash Flows

- The proposed (new) machine will have a book value of $20,000 (equal to the year 6 depreciation at the end of 5 years). The present (old) machine will be fully depreciated and therefore have a book value of zero at the end of 5 years. Because the sale price of $50,000 for the new machine is greater than its $20,000 book value, it will have to pay tax of $30,000 on recaptured depreciation. Applying the ordinary tax rate of 40% results in a tax of $12,000. Because the present machine would net $0 at termination and its book value would also be $0, its after-tax proceeds would also be $0. Substituting these values in the format in Table 10.9 results in a terminal cash flow of $55,000 as shown on the following slide.

Finding the Terminal Cash Flows

After-tax proceeds from sale of proposed machine		
Proceeds from sale of proposed machine	$50,000	
− Tax on sale of proposed machine	12,000	
Total after-tax proceeds—proposed		$38,000
− After-tax proceeds from sale of present machine		
Proceeds from sale of present machine	$ 0	
∓ Tax on sale of present machine	0	
Total after-tax proceeds—present		0
+ Change in net working capital		17,000
Terminal cash flow		$55,000

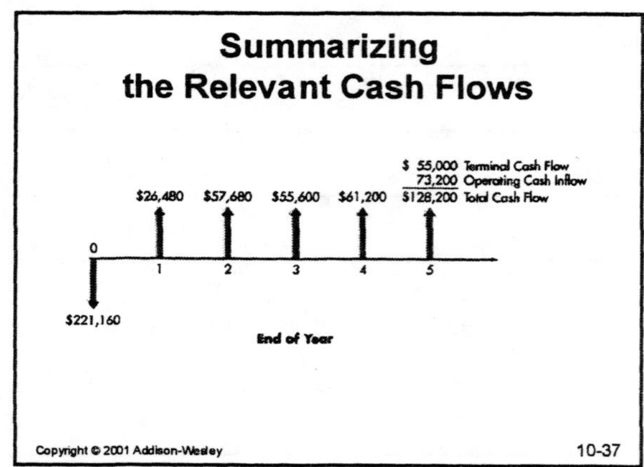

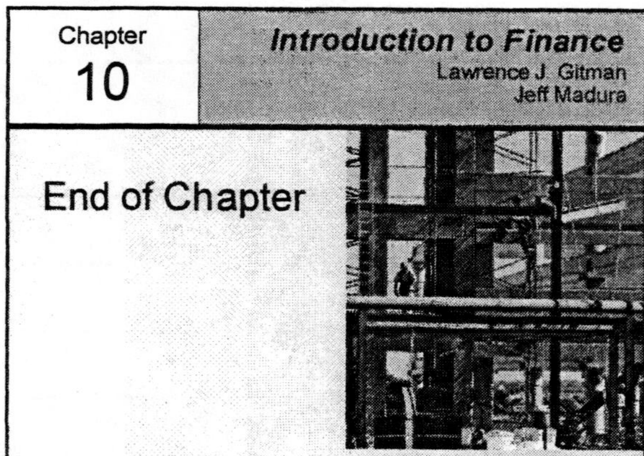

Chapter 11

Introduction to Finance

Lawrence J. Gitman
Jeff Madura

Capital Budgeting Techniques: Certainty and Risk

Learning Goals

- Calculate, interpret and evaluate the payback period.
- Apply net present value (NPV) and internal rate of return (IRR) to relevant cash flows to choose acceptable capital expenditures.
- Use net present value profiles to compare NPV and IRR techniques in light of conflicting rankings.

Learning Goals

- Recognize sensitivity and scenario analysis and simulation as behavioral approaches for dealing with project risk.
- Discuss the unique risks that multinational companies face.
- Understand how to determine and use risk-adjusted discount rates (RADRs).

Capital Budgeting Techniques

- We will use one basic problem to illustrate all the techniques described in this chapter.
  - Onlab Company, a medium-sized metal fabricator is currently contemplating two projects: Project A requires an initial investment of $42,000, Project B an initial investment of $45,000. The projected relevant cash flows are presented in Table 11.1 and depicted on a time line in Figure 11.1 on the following slides.

Capital Budgeting Techniques

TABLE 11.1 Capital Expenditure Data for Onlab Company

	Project A	Project B
Initial investment	$42,000	$45,000
Year	**Operating cash inflows**	
1	$14,000	$28,000
2	14,000	12,000
3	14,000	10,000
4	14,000	10,000
5	14,000	10,000
Average	$14,000	$14,000

Table 11.1

Capital Budgeting Techniques

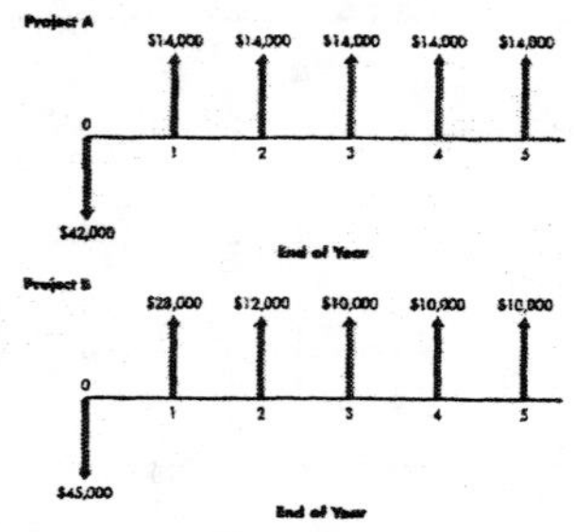

Figure 11.1

Payback Period

- The payback period simply measures how long (in years and/or months) it takes for a firm to recover its initial investment in a project.
- Decision Critera:
  - If the payback period is less than the maximum acceptable payback period, accept the project.
  - If the payback period is greater than the maximum acceptable payback period, reject the project.

Payback Period

- Assume the maximum payback for Onlab's Projects is 2.75 years.
- Based on this criteria, we would make the following decision with regard to Projects A and B.

Project A: Payback = 3.0 years > 2.75 years: Reject

Project B: Payback = 2.5 years < 2.75 years: Accept

Payback Period

- Pros and Cons of Payback
  - The payback period is widely used by large firms to evaluate small projects and by small firms to evaluate most projects.
  - Its popularity results from its simplicity and intuitive appeal.
  - It is also appealing that it considers cash flows rather than accounting profits.

Payback Period

- Pros and Cons of Payback
  - The major weakness of the payback period is that the appropriate payback requirement is merely a subjectively determined number.
  - A second weakness is that this approach fails to fully account for the time value of money.
  - A third weakness is the failure to recognize cash flows that occur after the required payback period as illustrated in Table 11.2.

Payback Period

- Pros and Cons of Payback

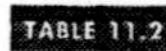
Calculation of the Payback Period for Rincon Company's Two Alternative Investment Projects

	Project X	Project Y
Initial investment	$10,000	$10,000
Year	**Cash inflows**	
1	$5,000	$3,000
2	5,000	4,000
3	1,000	3,000
4	100	4,000
5	100	3,000
Payback period	2 years	3 years

 Table 11.2

Net Present Value (NPV)

- Net present value is found by subtracting the present value of the after-tax outflows from the present value of the after-tax inflows.

The net **present value (NPV)** is found by subtracting a project's initial investment (CF_0) from the present value of its cash inflows (CF_t) discounted at a rate equal to the firm's cost of capital (k).

NPV = Present value of cash inflows − Initial investment

$$NPV = \sum_{t=1}^{n} \frac{CF_t}{(1+k)^t} - CF_0$$

Decision Criteria

If NPV > 0, accept the project
If NPV < 0, reject the project
If NPV = 0, indifferent

Net Present Value (NPV)

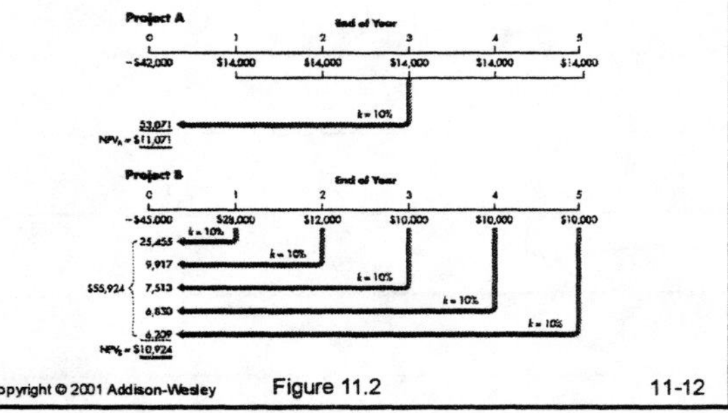

 Figure 11.2

Internal Rate of Return (IRR)

- The internal rate of return (IRR) is probably the most widely used and sophisticated capital budgeting technique.
- The internal rate of return (IRR) is the discount rate that will equate the present value of the outflows with the present value of the inflows.
- It is the compound annual rate of return the firm will earn if it invests in the project and receives the given cash inflows.
- The IRR is the project's intrinsic rate of return.

Internal Rate of Return (IRR)

$$\$0 = \sum_{t=1}^{n} \frac{CF_t}{(1+IRR)^t} - CF_0$$

$$\sum_{t=1}^{n} \frac{CF_t}{(1+IRR)^t} = CF_0$$

Decision Criteria

- If IRR > k, accept the project
- If IRR < k, reject the project
- If IRR = k, indifferent

Internal Rate of Return (IRR)

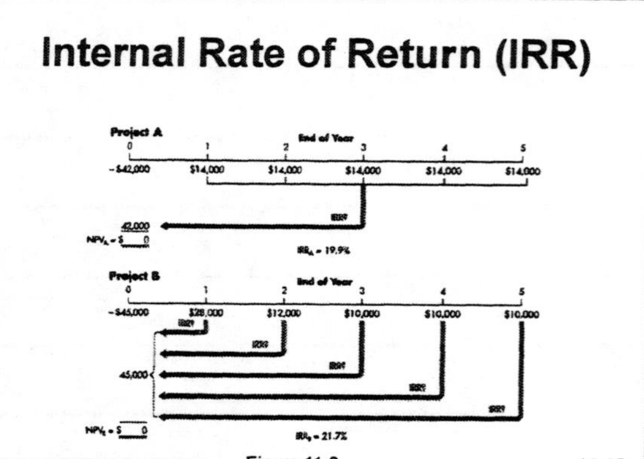

 Figure 11.3

Comparing NPV and IRR

- Net Present Value Profile
  - Projects can be compared by graphically constructing net present value profiles that depict project NPVs for various discount rates.
  - To prepare net present value profiles for Onlab Company's two projects, A and B, the first step is to develop a number of "discount rate-net present value" coordinates. Using the data in Table 11.1 and Figure 11.1 we can obtain three such coordinates for each project as shown in Table 11.3 and shown graphically as in Figure 11.4.

Comparing NPV and IRR

- Net Present Value Profile

TABLE 11.3 Discount-Rate–NPV Coordinates for Projects A and B

Discount rate	Net present value: Project A	Project B
0%	$28,000	$25,000
10	11,071	10,924
19.9	0	—
21.7	—	0

 Table 11.3

Comparing NPV and IRR

- Conflicting Rankings
  - Ranking is important when projects are mutually exclusive or when capital rationing is necessary.
  - When projects are mutually exclusive, ranking enables a firm to determine which project is best from a financial viewpoint.
  - When capital rationing is necessary, ranking projects will provide a logical starting point for determining what group of projects to accept.

Comparing NPV and IRR

- Conflicting Rankings
  - Conflicting rankings using NPV and IRR result from *differences* in the magnitude and timing of cash flows.
  - The underlying cause of conflicting rankings is the implicit assumption concerning the reinvestment of intermediate cash inflows.
  - NPV assumes that intermediate cash flows are reinvested at the cost of capital, whereas IRR assumes they are reinvested at the less conservative IRR.

Comparing NPV and IRR

- Conflicting Rankings
  - This can be illustrated by graphically depicting the NPV profile as shown in Figure 11.4 below.

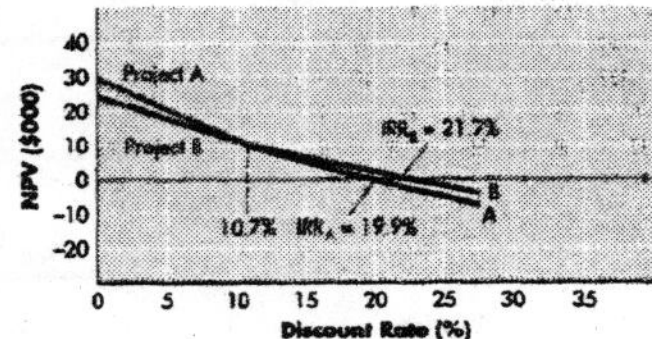

Figure 11.4

Comparing NPV and IRR

- Which Approach is Better?
  - On a purely theoretical basis, NPV is better because it implicitly assumes intermediate cash flows are reinvested at the more conservative cost of capital.
  - In addition, certain mathematical properties may cause a project with a non-conventional cash flow pattern to have zero or more than one real IRR.
  - From a practical perspective, financial managers prefer IRR due to their general preference for working with more intuitively appealing rates of return.

Behavioral Approaches for Dealing with Risk

- Sensitivity Analysis
  - Bigpaw Tire Company has a 10% cost of capital and is considering investing in one of two mutually exclusive projects A or B. Each project has a $10,000 initial cost and a useful life of 15 years.
  - As financial manager, you have provided pessimistic, most-likely, and optimistic estimates of the equal annual cash inflows for each project as shown in Table 11.5.

Behavioral Approaches for Dealing with Risk

- Sensitivity Analysis

TABLE 11.5 Sensitivity Analysis of Bigpaw's Projects A and B

	Project A	Project B
Initial investment	$10,000	$10,000
	Annual cash inflows	
Outcome		
Pessimistic	$ 1,500	$ 0
Most likely	2,000	2,000
Optimistic	2,500	4,000
Range	$ 1,000	$ 4,000
	Net present values[a]	
Outcome		
Pessimistic	$ 1,409	−$10,000
Most likely	5,212	5,212
Optimistic	9,015	20,424
Range	$ 7,606	$30,424

[a]These values were calculated by using the corresponding annual cash inflows. A 10% cost of capital and a 15-year life for the annual cash inflows were used.

Table 11.5

Behavioral Approaches for Dealing with Risk

- Simulation
  - Simulation is a statistically based behavioral approach that applies predetermined probability distributions and random numbers to estimate risky outcomes.
  - By tying the various cash flow components together in a mathematical model and repeating the process, the financial manager can develop a probability distribution of projected returns as shown in Figure 11.5.

Behavioral Approaches for Dealing with Risk

- Simulation

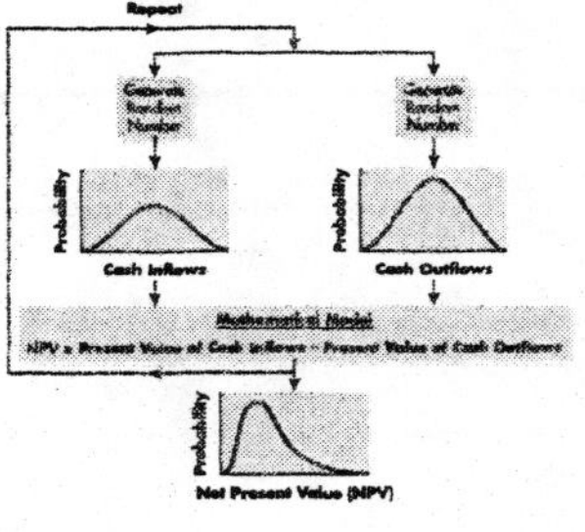

Figure 11.5

Behavioral Approaches for Dealing with Risk

- International Risk Considerations
  - Exchange rate risk refers to the danger that an unexpected change in the exchange rate between the dollar and the currency in which a project's cash flows are denominated can reduce the value of the project.
  - Short-term exchange rate risk can be managed by hedging using instruments such as currency futures and options.
  - Long-term exchange rate risk can be minimized by financing the project in the local currency.

Behavioral Approaches for Dealing with Risk

- International Risk Considerations
  - Political risk is much more difficult to protect against.
  - Therefore, it is important for managers to account for this risk before making an investment by adjusting project cash inflows or using risk-adjusted discount rates.
  - Other considerations in international capital budgeting include taxes and transfer pricing.
  - Finally, it is important that firms view international investments from a strategic view, rather than from a strictly financial perspective.

Risk-Adjusted Discount Rates (RADR)

- The risk-adjusted discount rate (RADR) is the rate of return that must be earned on a given project to compensate the firm's owners adequately.
- The higher the risk of a project, the higher the RADR, and therefore the lower the NPV for a given project.

$$\text{NPV} = \sum_{t=1}^{n} \frac{CF_t}{(1+\text{RADR})^t} - CF_0$$

Risk-Adjusted Discount Rates (RADR)

- Onlab Company wishes to use the risk-adjusted discount rate approach to determine, according to NPV, whether to implement project A or B.
- Onlab's management after much analysis has assigned a "risk index" of 1.6 to project A and 1.0 to project B. The associated RADR for Onlab's various risk index measures is given on the following slide. Calculation and results are depicted in Figure 11.6.

Risk-Adjusted Discount Rates (RADR)

	Risk index	Required return (RADR)
	0.0	6% (risk-free rate, R_F)
	0.2	7
	0.4	8
	0.6	9
	0.8	10
Project B →	1.0	11
	1.2	12
	1.4	13
Project A →	1.6	14
	1.8	16
	2.0	18

Risk-Adjusted Discount Rates (RADR)

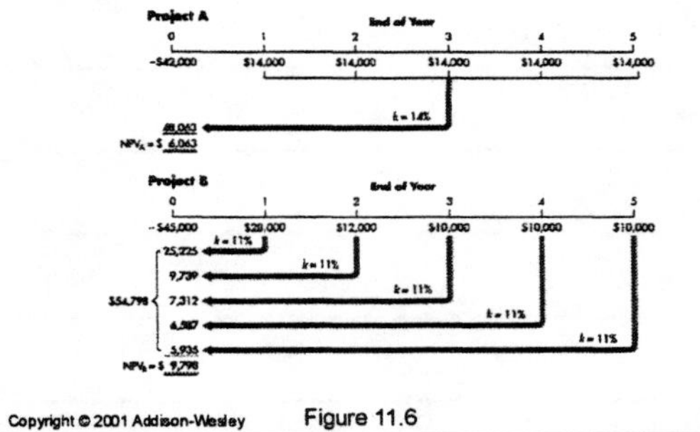

Figure 11.6

Risk-Adjusted Discount Rates (RADR)

- The popularity of RADRs stems from two facts:
  - They are consistent with the general disposition of financial decision makers toward rates of return.
  - They are easily estimated and applied.
- In practice, firms often establish a number of risk classes with RADRs assigned to each class as illustrated in Table 11.6.

Risk-Adjusted Discount Rates (RADR)

TABLE 11.6 Onlab Company's Risk Classes and RADRs

Risk class	Description	Risk-adjusted discount rate, RADR
I	*Below-average risk:* Projects with low risk. Typically involve routine replacement without renewal of existing activities.	8%
II	*Average risk:* Projects similar to those currently implemented. Typically involve replacement or renewal of existing activities.	10%[a]
III	*Above-average risk:* Projects with higher than normal, but not excessive, risk. Typically involve expansion of existing or similar activities.	14%
IV	*Highest risk:* Projects with very high risk. Typically involve expansion into new or unfamiliar activities.	20%

[a]This RADR is actually the firm's cost of capital, which is discussed in detail in Chapter 12. It represents the firm's required return on its existing portfolio of projects, which is assumed unchanged with acceptance of the "average-risk" project.

 Table 11.6

Chapter 11

Introduction to Finance

Lawrence J. Gitman
Jeff Madura

End of Chapter

Chapter 12

Introduction to Finance

Lawrence J. Gitman
Jeff Madura

Cost of Capital

Learning Goals

- Understand the basic cost of capital concept and the specific sources of capital it includes.
- Determine the cost of long-term debt and the cost of preferred stock.
- Calculate the cost of common stock equity and convert it into the cost of retained earnings and the cost of new issues of common stock.

Learning Goals

- Find the weighted average cost of capital (WACC).
- Describe the procedures used to determine break points and the weighted marginal cost of capital (WMCC).
- Explain how the weighted marginal cost of capital can be used with the investment opportunities schedule to make the firm's financing/investment decisions.

An Overview of the Cost of Capital

- The cost of capital is an important financial concept that links the firm's long-term investment decisions with the wealth of the owners.
- It is a "magic number" that is used to decide whether a proposed corporate investment will increase or decrease the firm's stock price.
- The cost of capital is the rate of return that a firm must earn on its project investments to maintain the market value of its stock.

The Firm's Capital Structure

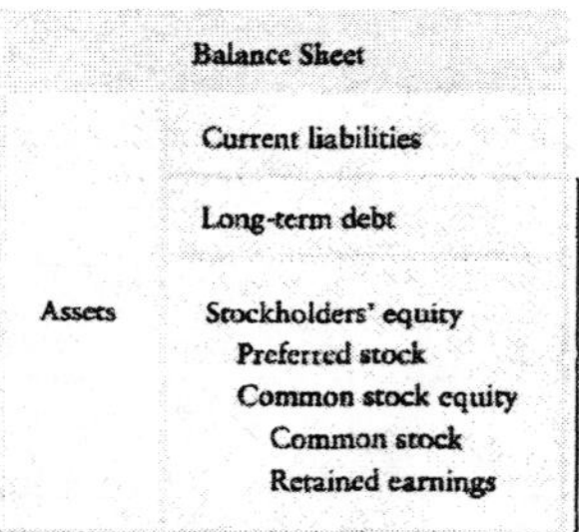

The Basic Concept

- Why do we need to determine a company's overall "weighted average cost of capital"?
  - Assume that ABC company has the following investment opportunity:
    - Initial Investment = $100,000
    - Useful Life = 20 years
    - IRR = 7%
    - Least cost source of financing, Debt = 6%
  - Given the above information, a firm's financial manger would be inclined to accept and undertake the investment.

The Basic Concept

- Why do we need to determine a company's overall "weighted average cost of capital?"
  - Imagine now that only one week later, the firm has another available investment opportunity
    - Initial investment = $100,000
    - Useful life = 20 years
    - IRR = 12%
    - Least cost source of financing, Equity = 14%
  - Given the above information, the firm would reject this second, yet clearly more desirable investment opportunity.

The Basic Concept

- As the above simple example clearly illustrates, using this piecemeal approach to evaluate investment opportunities is clearly not in the best interest of the firm's shareholders.
- Over the long haul, the firm must undertake investments that maximize firm value.
- This can only be achieved if it undertakes projects that provide returns in excess of the firm's overall weighted average cost of financing (or WACC).

Some Basic Assumptions

- Business risk—the risk to the firm of being unable to cover operating costs—is assumed to be unchanged. This means that the acceptance of a given project does not affect the firm's ability to meet operating costs.
- Financial risk—the risk to the firm of being unable to cover required financial obligations—is assumed to be unchanged. This means that the projects are financed in such a way that the firm's ability to meet financing costs is unchanged.
- After-tax costs are considered relevant—the cost of capital is measured on an after-tax basis.

The Cost of Specific Sources of Capital

- The After-Tax Cost of Debt (k_i)
  - The pre-tax cost of debt is equal to the the yield-to-maturity on the firm's debt adjusted for flotation costs.
  - Recall from Chapter 7 that a bond's yield-to-maturity depends upon a number of factors including the bond's coupon rate, maturity date, par value, current market conditions, and selling price.
  - After obtaining the bond's yield, a simple adjustment must be made to account for the fact that interest is a tax-deductible expense to the issuing firm.

The Cost of Specific Sources of Capital

- The After-Tax Cost of Debt (k_i)
  - You will recall from Chapter 7 that the YTM on a bond can be calculated in three ways:
    - Trial and error
    - Using a financial calculator
    - Using Microsoft® Excel
  - We will demonstrate the calculation of the cost of debt using Microsoft® Excel.
  - Your instructor will review trial and error and/or using a financial calculator as needed.

The Cost of Specific Sources of Capital

- The After-Tax Cost of Debt (k_i)
  - Suppose a company could issue 9% coupon, 20 year debt with a face value of $1,000 for $980. Suppose further that flotation costs will amount to 2% of par value. Find the pre-tax cost of debt.

Finding the Cost of Debt

Par Value	$	(1,000.00)
Flotation Costs (% of Par)		2.00%
Flotation Costs ($)	$	(20.00)
Issue Price	$	980.00
Net Proceeds Price	$	960.00
Coupon Interest (%)		9.00%
Coupon Interest ($)	$	(90.00)
Time to maturity		20
Before-tax cost of debt		9.45%

Microsoft® Excel formula
for computing the cost of debt (k_d)
=RATE(B10,B9,B7,B3)

The Cost of Specific Sources of Capital

- The After-Tax Cost of Debt (k_i)

$$k_i = k_d (1 - t)$$

Find the after-tax cost of debt assuming the company in the previous example is in the 40% tax bracket:

k_i = 9.45% (1-.40) = 5.67%

This suggests that the after-tax cost of raising debt capital is 5.67%.

The Cost of Specific Sources of Capital

- The Cost of Preferred Stock (k_p)

$$k_p = D_p (P_p - F)$$

In the above equation, F represents flotation costs (in $). As was the case for debt, the cost of raising new preferred stock will be more than the yield on the firm's existing preferred stock since the firm must pay investment bankers to sell (or float) the issue.

The Cost of Specific Sources of Capital

- The Cost of Preferred Stock (k_p)

$$k_p = D_p/(P_p - F)$$

$$k_p = D_p/N_p$$

For example, if a company could issue preferred stock that pays a $5 annual dividend, sell it for $55 per share, and have to pay $3 per share to sell it, the cost of preferred stock would be:

k_p = $5/($55 - $3) = $5/$52 = 9.62%

The Cost of Specific Sources of Capital

- The Cost of Common Equity
  - There are two forms of common stock financing: retained earnings and new issues of common stock.
  - In addition, there are two different ways to estimate the cost of common equity: any form of the dividend valuation model and the capital asset pricing model (CAPM).
  - The dividend valuation models are based on the premise that the value of a share of stock is based on the present value of all future dividends.

The Cost of Specific Sources of Capital

- The Cost of Common Equity
  - Using the constant growth model, we have:

$$k_s = (D_1/P_0) + g$$

  - We can also estimate the cost of common equity using the CAPM:

$$k_s = r_f + b(k_m - r_f)$$

  - The CAPM differs from dividend valuation models in that it explicitly considers the firm's risk as reflected in beta.

The Cost of Specific Sources of Capital

- The Cost of Common Equity
  - On the other hand, dividend valuation models do not explicitly consider risk.
  - These models use the market price (P_0) as a reflection of the expected risk-return preference of investors in the marketplace.
  - Although both are theoretically equivalent, dividend valuation models are often preferred because the data required are more readily available.

The Cost of Specific Sources of Capital

- The Cost of Common Equity
  - The two methods also differ in that the dividend valuation model (unlike the CAPM) can easily be adjusted for flotation costs when estimating the cost of new equity.
  - This will be demonstrated in the examples that follow.

The Cost of Specific Sources of Capital

- The Cost of Common Equity
  - Cost of retained earnings (k_s)
    - Security market line approach

$$k_s = r_f + b(k_m - r_f)$$

    - For example, if the 3-month T-bill rate is currently 5.0%, the market risk premium is 9%, and the firm's beta is 1.20, the firm's cost of retained earnings will be:

$$k_s = 5.0 + 1.2(9) = 15.8\%$$

The Cost of Specific Sources of Capital

- The Cost of Common Equity
  - Cost of retained earnings (k_s)
    - Constant dividend growth model

$$k_s = (D_1/P_0) + g$$

    - For example, assume a firm has just paid a dividend of $2.50 per share, expects dividends to grow at 10% indefinitely, and is currently selling for $50 per share.

First, $D_1 = 2.50(1 + .10) = 2.75$, and

$$k_s = (2.75/50) + .10 = 15.5\%$$

The Cost of Specific Sources of Capital

- The Cost of Common Equity
  - Cost of retained earnings (k_s)
    - The previous example indicates that our estimate of the cost of retained earnings is somewhere between 15.5% and 15.8%. At this point, we could either choose one or the other estimate or average the two.
    - Using some managerial judgement and preferring to err on the high side, we will use 15.8% as our final estimate of the cost of retained earnings.

The Cost of Specific Sources of Capital

- The Cost of Common Equity
  - Cost of new equity (k_n)
    - Constant dividend growth model

$$k_n = [D_1/(P_0 - F)] + g$$

    - Continuing with the previous example, how much would it cost the firm to raise new equity if flotation costs amount to $4.00 per share?

$$k_n = [2.75/(50 - 4)] + .10 = 15.97\% \text{ or } 16\%$$

The Weighted Average Cost of Capital

- The weighted average cost of capital (WACC), k_a, reflects the expected average future cost of funds over the long run.
- It is found by weighting the cost of each specific type of capital by its proportion in the firm's capital structure.
- The calculation of the WACC is straight-forward and is shown on the following slide.

The Weighted Average Cost of Capital

$$\text{WACC } (k_a) = w_i k_i + w_p k_p + w_s k_s$$

- Capital Structure Weights
  - The weights in the above equation are intended to represent a specific financing mix (where w_i = % of debt, w_p = % of preferred, and w_s = % of common).
  - Specifically, these weights are the target percentages of debt and equity that will minimize the firm's overall cost of raising funds.

The Weighted Average Cost of Capital

$$\text{WACC } (k_a) = w_i k_i + w_p k_p + w_s k_s$$

- Capital Structure Weights
  - For example, assume the market value of the firm's debt is $40 million, the market value of the firm's preferred stock is $10 million, and the market value of the firm's equity is $50 million.
  - Dividing each component by the total of $100 million gives us market value weights of 40% debt, 10% preferred, and 50% common.

The Weighted Average Cost of Capital

$$\text{WACC } (k_a) = w_i k_i + w_p k_p + w_s k_s$$

- Capital Structure Weights
  - Using the costs previously calculated along with the market value weights, we may calculate the weighted average cost of capital as follows:
    - WACC = .4(5.67%) + .1(9.62%) + .5 (15.8%) = 11.13%
  - This assumes the firm has sufficient retained earnings to fund any anticipated investment projects.

The WMCC and Investment Decisions

- The Weighted Marginal Cost of Capital (WMCC)
  - The WACC typically increases as the volume of new capital raised within a given period increases.
  - This is true because companies need to raise the return to investors in order to entice them to invest to compensate them for the increased risk introduced by larger volumes of capital raised.
  - In addition, the cost will eventually increase when the firm runs out of cheaper retained equity and is forced to raise new, more expensive equity capital.

The WMCC and Investment Decisions

- The Weighted Marginal Cost of Capital (WMCC)
  - Finding breaking points
    - Finding the break points in the WMCC schedule will allow us to determine at what level of new financing the WACC will increase due to the factors listed above.

$$BP_j = AF_j/w_j$$

Where:
BP_j = breaking point form financing source j
AF_j = amount of funds available at a given cost
w_j = target capital structure weight for source j

The WMCC and Investment Decisions

- The Weighted Marginal Cost of Capital (WMCC)
  - Finding breaking points
    - Assume that in the example we have been using that the firm has $2 million of retained earnings available. When it is exhausted, the firm must issue new (more expensive) equity. Furthermore, the company believes it can raise $1 million of cheap debt after which it will cost 7% (after-tax) to raise additional debt.
    - Given this information, the firm can determine its break points as follows:

The WMCC and Investment Decisions

- The Weighted Marginal Cost of Capital (WMCC)
  - Finding breaking points
    - This implies that the firm can fund up to $4 million of new investment before it is forced to issue new equity and $2.5 million of new investment before it is forced to raise more expensive debt.
    - Given this information, we may calculate the WMCC as follows:

$$BP_{equity} = \$2,000,000/.5 = \$4,000,000$$

$$BP_{debt} = \$1,000,000/.4 = \$2,500,000$$

The WMCC and Investment Decisions

WACC for Ranges of Total New Financing

Range of total New Financing	Source of Capital	Weight	Cost	Weighted Cost
$0 to $2.5 million	Debt	40%	5.67%	2.268%
	Preferred	10%	9.62%	0.962%
	Common	50%	15.80%	7.900%
			WACC	11.130%
$2.5 to $4.0 million	Debt	40%	7.00%	2.800%
	Preferred	10%	9.62%	0.962%
	Common	50%	15.80%	7.900%
			WACC	11.662%
over $4.0 million	Debt	40%	7.00%	2.800%
	Preferred	10%	9.62%	0.962%
	Common	50%	16.00%	8.000%
			WACC	11.762%

The WMCC and Investment Decisions

WMCC
11.76%
11.75%
11.66%
11.50%
11.25%
11.13%
$2.5
$4.0
Total Financing (millions)

The WMCC and Investment Decisions

- Investment Opportunities Schedule (IOS)
  - Now assume the firm has the following investment opportunities available:

Project	IRR	Initial Ivestment	Cumulative Investment
A	13.0%	$ 1,000,000	$ 1,000,000
B	12.0%	$ 1,000,000	$ 2,000,000
C	11.5%	$ 1,000,000	$ 3,000,000
D	11.0%	$ 1,000,000	$ 4,000,000
E	10.0%	$ 1,000,000	$ 5,000,000

  - Combining the WMCC with the IOS yields the following:

The WMCC and Investment Decisions

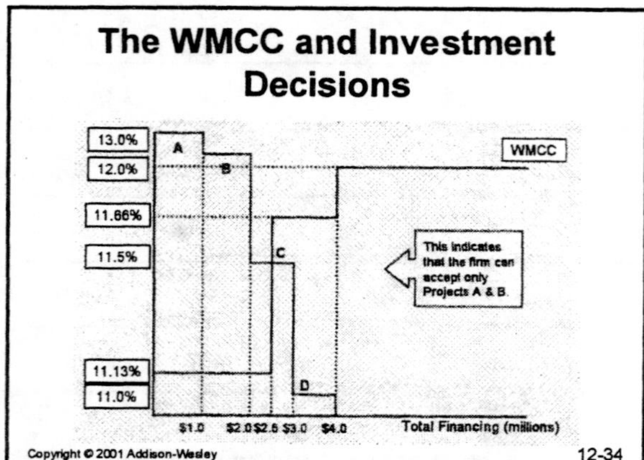

Using Microsoft® Excel

- The Microsoft® Excel Spreadsheets used in the this presentation can be downloaded from the *Introduction to Finance* companion web site: http://www.awl.com/gitman_madura

Chapter
12

Introduction to Finance
Lawrence J. Gitman
Jeff Madura

End of Chapter

Chapter 13

Introduction to Finance

Lawrence J. Gitman
Jeff Madura

Capital Structure and Dividends

Learning Goals

- Describe the basic types of capital, external assessment of capital structure, the capital structure of non-United States firms, and the optimal capital structure.
- Discuss the EBIT-EPS approach to capital structure.
- Review the return and risk of alternative capital structures and their linkage to market value, and other important capital structure considerations.

Learning Goals

- Explain cash dividend payment procedures, dividend reinvestment plans, the residual theory of dividends, and the key arguments with regard to dividend relevance or irrelevance.
- Understand the key factors involved in formulating a dividend policy and the three basic types of dividend policies.
- Evaluate the key aspects of stock dividends, stock splits, and stock repurchases.

The Firm's Capital Structure

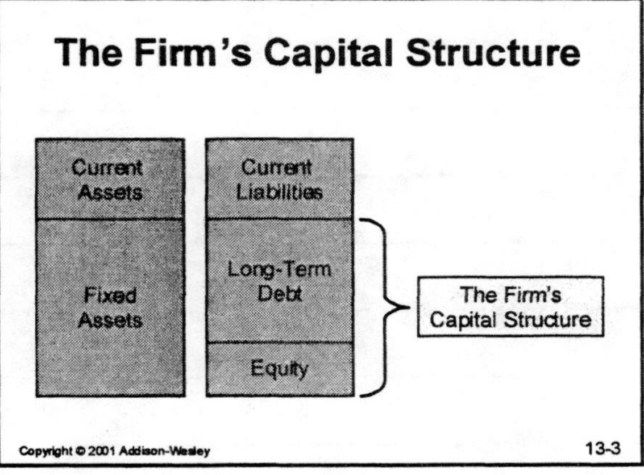

The Firm's Capital Structure

- According to finance theory, firms possess a target capital structure that will minimize their cost of capital.
- Unfortunately, theory can not yet provide financial managers with a specific methodology to help them determine what their firm's optimal capital structure might be.
- Theoretically, however, a firm's optimal capital structure will just balance the benefits of debt financing against its costs.

The Firm's Capital Structure

- The major benefit of debt financing is the tax shield provided by the federal government regarding interest payments.
- The costs of debt financing result from:
  - The increased probability of bankruptcy caused by debt obligations.
  - The agency costs resulting from lenders monitoring the firm's actions.
  - The costs associated with the firm's managers having more information about the firm's prospects than do investors (asymmetric information).

The Firm's Capital Structure

- Capital Structures of United States and Non-United States Firms
  - In general, non-United States companies have much higher debt levels than United States companies primarily because United States capital markets are relatively more developed.
  - In addition, in most European countries and Japan, banks are more involved because they are permitted to make equity investments in non-financial corporations—a practice prohibited in the United States.

The Firm's Capital Structure

- Similarities between United States and foreign corporations include:
  - Similarity of industry capital structure patterns.
  - Similarity of large corporation capital structures.
- In addition, it is expected that differences in capital structures will further diminish as countries rely less on banks and more on security issuance.

The Optimal Capital Structure

- In general, it is believed that the market value of a company is maximized when the cost of capital (the firm's discount rate) is minimized.
- The value of the firm can be defined algebraically as follows:

$$V = \frac{EBIT \times (1 - t)}{k_a}$$

- It can be described graphically as shown on the following two slides.

The Optimal Capital Structure

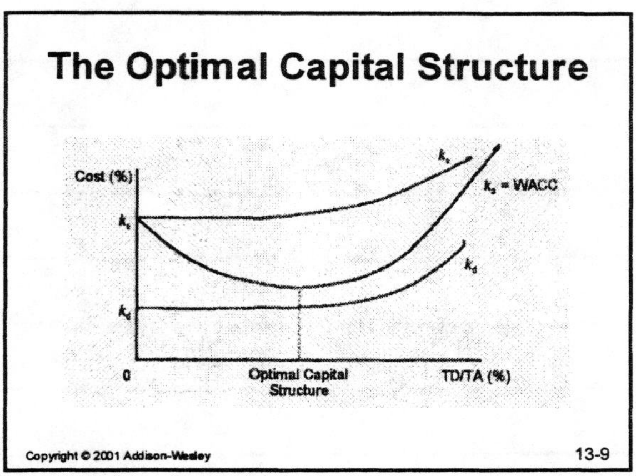

The Optimal Capital Structure

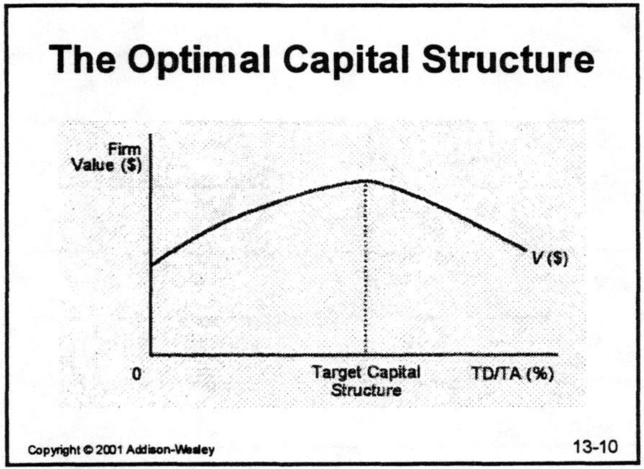

Debt Ratios for Selected Industries

TABLE 13.1 Debt Ratios for Selected Industries and Lines of Business (1998–1999)

Industry or line business	Debt ratio	Times interest earned ratio
Manufacturing industries		
Books	61.0%	3.2
Dairy products	85.1	4.1
Electronic computers	65.8	4.3
Iron and steel foundries	56.8	4.0
Machine tools and metalworking equipment	63.6	4.1
Wines, distilled liquors, liqueurs	67.7	3.2
Women's dresses	55.8	2.4
Wholesaling industries		
Furniture	68.1	3.6
General groceries	73.2	2.6
Men's and boys' clothing	63.1	2.4

Table 13.1 (Panel 1)

Debt Ratios for Selected Industries

TABLE 13.1 Debt Ratios for Selected Industries and Lines of Business (1998–1999)

Industry or line business	Debt ratio	Times interest earned ratio
Retailing industries		
Autos, new and used	72.5	2.8
Department stores	60.0	3.3
Restaurants	89.7	2.6
Service industries		
Accounting, auditing, bookkeeping	73.5	5.0
Advertising agencies	79.3	5.0
Auto repair—general	61.1	4.0
Insurance agents and brokers	99.4	3.5

(Source: *RMA Annual Statement Studies*, 1999–2000 (fiscal years ended 4/1/98 through 3/31/99) (Philadelphia: Robert Morris Associates, 1999). Copyright © 1999 by Robert Morris Associates.)

Note: Robert Morris Associates recommends that these ratios be regarded only as general guidelines and not as absolute industry norms. No claim is made as to the representativeness of these figures.

Table 13.1 (Panel 2)

EPS-EBIT Approach to Capital Structure

- The EPS-EBIT approach to capital structure involves selecting the capital structure that maximizes EPS over the expected range of EBIT.
- Using this approach, the emphasis is on maximizing the owners' returns (EPS).
- A major shortcoming of this approach is the fact that earnings are only one of the determinants of shareholder wealth maximization.
- This method does not explicitly consider the impact of risk.

EPS-EBIT Approach to Capital Structure

- Example
  - The capital structure of Buzz Company, a soft drink manufacturer is shown in the table below. Currently, Buzz Company uses only equity in its capital structure. Thus the current debt ratio is 0.00%. Assume Buzz Company is in the 40% tax bracket.

Buzz Company Current Capital Structure	
Long-term debt	$ -
Common stock (25,000 shares @ $20)	$ 500,000
Total Capital (assets)	$ 500,000

EPS-EBIT Approach to Capital Structure

- EPS-EBIT coordinates for Buzz Company's current capital structure can be found by assuming two EBIT values and calculating the associated EPS in the table below.

EBIT	$ 100,000	$ 200,000
Interest	$ -	$ -
EBT	$ 100,000	$ 200,000
T	$ 40,000	$ 80,000
NI	$ 60,000	$ 120,000
EPS	$ 2.40	$ 4.80

- This can be plotted on an EPS-EBIT plane shown on the following slide.

EPS-EBIT Approach to Capital Structure

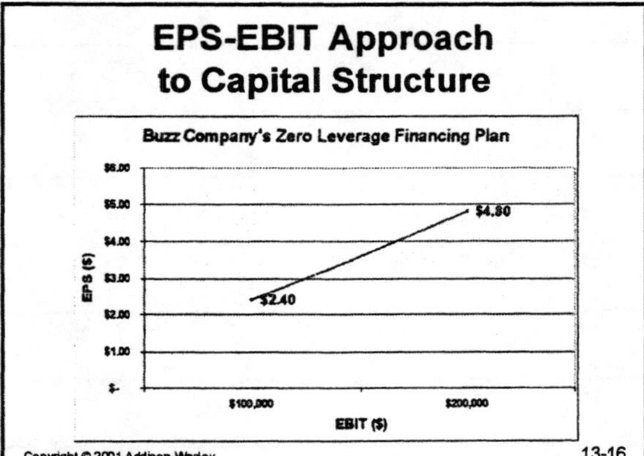

EPS-EBIT Approach to Capital Structure

- Buzz Company is considering altering its capital structure while maintaining its original $500,000 capital base as shown in the table below.

Buzz Company's Current and Alternative Capital Structures

Debt Ratio	Total Assets	Debt	Equity	Int. Rate (%)	Annual Int. ($)	No. of Shares
0%	$ 500,000	$ -	$ 500,000	0.0%	$ -	25,000
30%	$ 500,000	$ 150,000	$ 350,000	10.0%	$ 15,000	17,500
60%	$ 500,000	$ 300,000	$ 200,000	16.5%	$ 49,500	10,000

- We can use this information to calculate the EPS-EBIT coordinates as shown on the following slide.

EPS-EBIT Approach to Capital Structure

	Capital Structure			
	30% Debt Ratio		60% Debt Ratio	
EBIT	$ 100,000	$ 200,000	$ 100,000	$ 200,000
Interest	$ 15,000	$ 15,000	$ 49,500	$ 49,500
EBT	$ 85,000	$ 185,000	$ 50,500	$ 150,500
T	$ 34,000	$ 74,000	$ 20,200	$ 60,200
NI	$ 51,000	$ 111,000	$ 30,300	$ 90,300
EPS	$ 2.91	$ 6.34	$ 3.03	$ 9.03

- This may be shown graphically as shown on the following slide.

EPS-EBIT Approach to Capital Structure

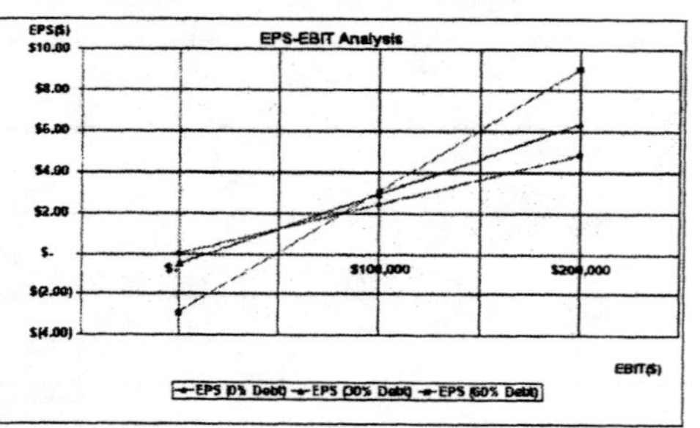

Basic Shortcoming of EPS-EBIT Analysis

- Although EPS maximization is generally good for the firm's shareholders, the basic shortcoming of this method is that it does not necessary maximize shareholder wealth because it fails to consider risk.
- If shareholders did not require risk premiums (additional return) as the firm increased its use of debt, a strategy focusing on EPS maximization would work.
- Unfortunately, this is not the case.

Choosing the Optimal Capital Structure

- The following discussion will attempt to create a framework for making capital budgeting decisions that maximizes shareholder wealth (i.e., considers both risk and return).
- Perhaps the best way to demonstrate this is through the following example.
  - Assume that Buzz Company is attempting to choose the best of several alternative capital structures—specifically, debt ratios of 0, 10, 20, 30, 40, 50, and 60 percent. Furthermore, for each of these capital structures, the firm has estimated EPS, the CV of EPS, and required return.

Choosing the Optimal Capital Structure

- If we assume that all earnings are paid out as dividends, we can use the zero growth valuation model [$P_0 = EPS/k_s$] to estimate share value as shown in the table below.

TABLE 13.3 Calculation of Share Value Estimates Associated with Alternative Capital Structures for Buzz Company

Capital structure debt ratio	Estimated expected EPS (1)	Estimated coefficient of variation of EPS (2)	Estimated required return, k_s (3)	Estimated share value [(1) ÷ (3)] (4)
0%	$2.40	0.71	0.115	$20.87
10	2.55	0.74	0.117	21.79
20	2.72	0.78	0.121	22.48
30	2.91	0.83	0.125	23.28
40	3.12	0.91	0.140	22.29
50	3.18	1.07	0.165	19.27
60	3.03	1.40	0.190	15.95

 Table 13.3

Choosing the Optimal Capital Structure

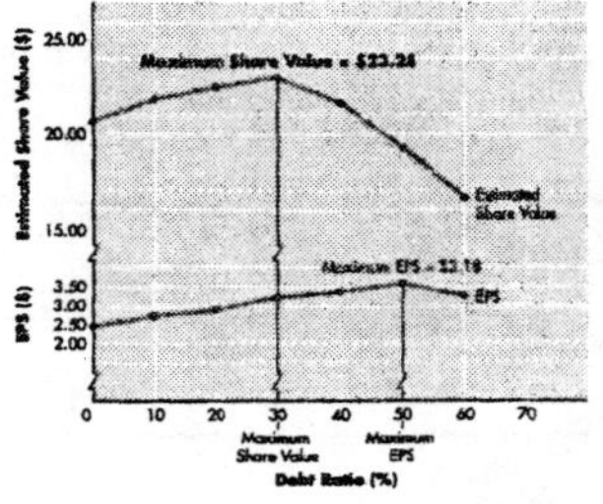

 Figure 13.4

Other Important Considerations

TABLE 13.4 Important Factors to Consider in Making Capital Structure Decisions

Factor	Description
Revenue stability	Firms that have stable and predictable revenues can more safely undertake highly leveraged capital structures than can firms with volatile patterns of sales revenue. Firms with growing sales tend to benefit from added debt because they can reap the positive benefits of financial leverage, which magnifies the effect of these increases.
Cash flow	When considering a new capital structure, the firm must focus on its ability to generate the cash flows necessary to meet obligations. Cash forecasts reflecting an ability to service debts (and preferred stock) must support any shift in capital structure.
Contractual obligations	A firm may be contractually constrained with respect to the type of funds that it can raise. For example, a firm might be prohibited from selling additional debt except when the claims of holders of such debt are made subordinate to the existing debt. Contractual constraints on the sale of additional stock, as well as on the ability to distribute dividends on stock, might also exist.

Table 13.4 (Panel 1)

Other Important Considerations

TABLE 13.4 Important Factors to Consider in Making Capital Structure Decisions

Factor	Description
Management preferences	Occasionally, a firm will impose an internal constraint on the use of debt to limit its risk exposure to a level deemed acceptable to management. In other words, because of risk aversion, the firm's management constrains the firm's capital structure at a level that may or may not be the true optimum.
Control	A management concerned about control may prefer to issue debt rather than (voting) common stock. Under favorable market conditions, a firm that wanted to sell equity could make a *preemptive offering* or issue *nonvoting shares* (see Chapter 3), allowing each shareholder to maintain proportionate ownership. Generally, only in closely held firms or firms threatened by takeover does control become a major concern in the capital structure decision.
External risk assessment	The firm's ability to raise funds quickly and at favorable rates depends on the external risk assessments of lenders and bond raters. The firm must therefore consider the impact of capital structure decisions both on share value and on published financial statements from which lenders and raters assess the firm's risk.
Timing	At times when the general level of interest rates is low, debt financing might be more attractive; when interest rates are high, the sale of stock may be more appealing. Sometimes both debt and equity capital become unavailable at what would be viewed as reasonable terms. General economic conditions—especially those of the capital market—can thus significantly affect capital structure decisions.

Table 13.4 (Panel 2)

Dividend Fundamentals

- Cash Dividend Payment Procedures
  - A dividend is a redistribution from earnings.
  - Most companies maintain a dividend policy whereby they pay a regular dividend on a quarterly basis.
  - Some companies pay an extra dividend to reward shareholders if they've had a particularly good year. Many companies pay dividends according to a preset payout ratio, which measures the proportion of dividends to earnings.
  - Many companies have paid regular dividends for over a hundred years.

Dividend Fundamentals

- Cash Dividend Payment Procedures
  - Dividend growth tends to lag behind earnings growth for most corporations (see example next slide).
  - Since dividend policy is one of the factors that drives an investor's decision to purchase a stock, most companies announce their dividend policy and telegraph any expected changes in policy to the public.
  - Therefore, it can be seen that many companies use their dividend policy to provide information not otherwise available to investors.

Dividend Fundamentals

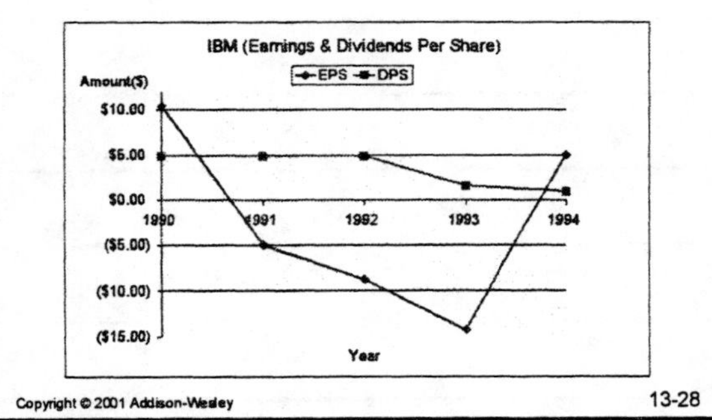

Dividend Fundamentals

- Cash Dividend Payment Procedures
  - Date of record: The date on which investors must own shares in order to receive the dividend payment.
  - ex dividend date: Four days prior to the date of record. The day on which a stock trades ex dividend (exclusive of dividends).
  - In the financial press: Transactions in the stock on the ex dividend date are indicated by an "x" next to the volume of transactions.
  - In general, stock prices fall by an amount equal to the quarterly dividend on the ex dividend date.
  - Distribution date: The day on which a dividend is paid (payment date) to stockholders. It is usually two or more weeks before stockholders who owned shares on the date of record receive their dividends.

Cash Dividend Payment Procedures

- Example
  - At the quarterly dividend meeting on June 10th, the Jillian Company board of directors declared an \$.80 cash dividend for holders of record on Monday, July 1st. The firm had 100,000 shares of stock outstanding. The payment (distribution) date was set at August 1st. Before the meeting, the relevant accounts showed the following.

Cash	\$200,000	Dividends Payable	\$0
		Retained Earnings	\$1,000,000

Cash Dividend Payment Procedures

- When the dividend was announced by the directors, \$80,000 of the retained earnings (\$.80/share × 100,000 shares) was transferred to the dividends payable account. As a result, the key accounts changed as follows:

Cash	\$200,000	Dividends Payable	\$80,000
		Retained Earnings	\$920,000

Cash Dividend Payment Procedures

- Jillian Company's stock began selling ex dividend on June 25th, 4 days prior to the date of record (July 1st). This date was found by subtracting 6 days (because of the weekend) from July 1st.
- Stockholders of record on June 24th or earlier received the rights to the dividends, while those purchasing on June 25th or later did not. Assuming a stable market, the price of the stock was expected to drop by \$.80/share on June 25th. When the August 1st payment date arrived, the firm mailed payments to holders of record and recorded the following:

Cash Dividend Payment Procedures

Cash	$120,000	Dividends Payable	$0
		Retained Earnings	$920,000

- Thus, the net effect of the dividend payment is a reduction of the firm's assets (through a reduction in cash) and equity (through a reduction in retained earnings) by a total of $80,000 (the dividend payment).

Dividend Reinvestment Plans

- Dividend reinvestment plans (DRIPS) permit stockholders to reinvest their dividends to purchase additional shares rather than to be paid out in cash.
- With *bank-directed* DRIPS, banks purchase additional shares on the open market in huge blocks which substantially reduces per share commissions.
- With *company-directed* DRIPS, the company itself issues new shares in exchange for the cash dividend completely eliminating commissions.
- With *brokerage-directed* DRIPS, brokerage firms such as Charles Schwab will reinvest dividends for shareholders who hold stocks in *street name* at no charge.

Advantages of DRIPS

- For Stockholders
  - Substantial reduction in commission costs.
  - They provide investors with an *automatic* savings mechanism.
- For Companies
  - Goodwill
  - Reduction in cost of delivering dividend checks.
  - An inexpensive means of raising equity capital for firms company-directed plans.

Dividend Policy Theory

- The Residual Theory of Dividends
  - The residual theory of dividends suggests that dividend payments should be viewed as residual—the amount left over after all acceptable investment opportunities have been undertaken.
  - Using this approach, the firm would treat the dividend decision in three steps as shown on the following slide.

Dividend Policy Theory

Step 1
Determine the optimal level of capital expenditures which is given by the point of intersection of the investment opportunities schedule (IOS) and weighted marginal cost of capital schedule (WMCC).

Step 2
Using the optimal capital structure proportions, estimate the total amount of equity financing needed to support the expenditures estimated in Step 1.

Step 3
Because the cost of retained earnings is less than new equity, use retained earnings to meet the equity requirement in Step 2. If inadequate, sell new stock. If there is an excess of retained earnings, distribute the surplus amount—the residual—as dividends.

Dividend Policy Theory

- The Residual Theory of Dividends
  - In sum, this theory suggests that no cash dividend is paid as long as the firm's equity need is in excess of the amount of retained earnings.
  - Furthermore, it suggests that the required return demanded by stockholders is not influenced by the firm's dividend policy—a premise that in turn suggests that dividend policy is irrelevant.

Dividend Policy Theory

- Dividend Irrelevance Arguments
  - Merton Miller and Franco Modigliani (MM) developed a theory that shows that in perfect financial markets (certainty, no taxes, no transactions costs or other market imperfections), the value of a firm is unaffected by the distribution of dividends.
  - They argue that value is driven only by the future earnings and risk of its investments.
  - Retaining earnings or paying them in dividends does not affect this value.

Dividend Policy Theory

- Dividend Irrelevance Arguments
  - Some studies suggested that large dividend changes affect stock price behavior.
  - MM argued, however, that these effects are the result of the information conveyed by these dividend changes, not to the dividend itself.
  - Furthermore, MM argue for the existence of a "clientele effect."
  - Investors preferring dividends will purchase high dividend stocks, while those preferring capital gains will purchase low dividend paying stocks.

Dividend Policy Theory

- Dividend Irrelevance Arguments
  - In summary, MM and other dividend irrelevance proponents argue that—all else being equal—an investor's required return, and therefore the value of the firm, is unaffected by dividend policy because:
    - The firm's value is determined solely by the earning power and risk of its assets.
    - If dividends do affect value, they do so because of the information content, which signals management's future expectations.
    - A clientele effect exists that causes shareholders to receive the level of dividends they expect.

Dividend Policy Theory

- Dividend Relevance Arguments
  - Contrary to dividend irrelevance proponents, Gordon and Lintner suggested stockholders prefer current dividends and that a positive relationship exists between dividends and market value.
  - Fundamental to this theory is the "bird-in-the-hand" argument which suggests that investors are generally risk-averse and attach less risk to current as opposed to future dividends or capital gains.
  - Because current dividends are less risky, investors will lower their required return—thus boosting stock prices.

Factors that Affect Dividend Policy

- Legal Constraints
  - Most state securities regulations prevent firms from paying out dividends from any portion of the company's "legal capital" which is measured by the par value of common stock—or par value plus paid-in-capital.
  - Dividends are also sometimes limited to the sum of the firm's most recent and past retained earnings—although payments in excess of current earnings is usually permitted.
  - Most states also prohibit dividends when firms have overdue liabilities or are legally insolvent or bankrupt.

Factors that Affect Dividend Policy

- Legal Constraints
  - Even the IRS has ruled in the area of dividend policy.
  - Specifically, the IRS prohibits firms from acquiring earnings to reduce stockholders' taxes.
  - The IRS can determine that a firm has accumulated an excess of earnings to allow owners to delay paying ordinary income taxes (on dividends), it may levy an excess earnings accumulation tax on any retained earnings above $250,000.
  - It should be noted, however, that this ruling is seldom applied.

Factors that Affect Dividend Policy

- Contractual Constraints
  - In many cases, companies are constrained in the extent to which they can pay dividends by restrictive provisions in loan agreements and bond indentures.
  - Generally, these constraints prohibit the payment of cash dividends until a certain level of earnings are achieved or to a certain dollar amount or percentage of earnings.
  - Any violation of these constraints generally triggers the demand for immediate payment.

Factors that Affect Dividend Policy

- Internal Constraints
  - A company's ability to pay dividends is usually constrained by the amount of available cash rather than the level of retained earnings against which to charge them.
  - Although it is possible to borrow to pay dividends, lenders are usually reluctant to grant them because using the funds for this purpose produces no operating benefits that help to repay them.

Factors that Affect Dividend Policy

- Growth Prospects
  - Newer, rapidly-growing firms generally pay little or no dividends.
  - Because these firms are growing so quickly, they must use most of their internally generated funds to support operations or finance expansion.
  - On the other hand, large, mature firms generally pay cash dividends since they have access to adequate capital and may have limited investment opportunities.

Factors that Affect Dividend Policy

- Owner Considerations
  - As mentioned earlier, empirical evidence supports the notion that investors tend to belong to "clienteles"— where some prefer high dividends, while others prefer capital gains.
  - They tend to sort themselves in this way for a variety of reasons, including:
    - Tax status
    - Investment opportunities
    - Potential dilution of ownership

Factors that Affect Dividend Policy

- Market Considerations
  - Perhaps the most important aspect of dividend policy is that the firm maintain a level of predictability.
  - Stockholders that prefer dividend-paying stocks prefer a continuous stream of fixed or increasing dividends.
  - Shareholders also view the firm's dividend payment as a "signal" of the firm's future prospects.
  - Fixed or increasing dividends are often considered a "positive" signal, while erratic dividend payments are viewed as "negative" signals.

Types of Dividend Policies

- Constant-Payout-Ratio Policy
  - With a constant-payout-ratio dividend policy, the firm establishes that a specific percentage of earnings is paid to shareholders each period.
  - A major shortcoming of this approach is that if the firm's earnings drop or are volatile, so too will the dividend payments.
  - As mentioned earlier, investors view volatile dividends as negative and risky—which can lead to lower share prices.

Types of Dividend Policies

- Regular Dividend Policy
  - A regular dividend policy is based on the payment of a fixed-dollar dividend each period.
  - It provides stockholders with positive information indicating that the firm is doing well and it minimizes uncertainty.
  - Generally, firms using this policy will increase the regular dividend once earnings are proven to be reliable.

Types of Dividend Policies

- Low-Regular-and-Extra Dividend Policy
  - Using this policy, firms pay a low regular dividend, supplemented by additional dividends when earnings can support it.
  - When earnings are higher than normal, the firm will pay this additional dividend, often called an extra dividend, without the obligation to maintain it during subsequent periods.
  - This type of policy is often used by firms whose sales and earnings are susceptible to swings in the business cycle.

Other Forms of Dividends

- Stock Dividends
  - A stock dividend is paid in stock rather than in cash.
  - Many investors believe that stock dividends increase the value of their holdings.
  - In fact, from a market value standpoint, stock dividends function much like stock splits. The investor ends up owning more shares, but the value of their shares is less.
  - From a book value standpoint, funds are transferred from retained earnings to common stock and additional paid-in-capital.

Other Forms of Dividends

- Stock Dividends

The current stockholder's equity on the balance sheet of Trimline Corporation, a distributor of prefabricated cabinets, is shown in the following accounts.

Preferred stock	$	300,000
Common stock (100,000 shares at $4 par)		400,000
Paid-in-capital in excess of par		600,000
Retained earnings		700,000
Total stockholders equity	$	2,000,000

Other Forms of Dividends

- Stock Dividends
  - If Trimline declares a 10% stock dividend and the current market price of the stock is $15/share, $150,000 of retained earnings (10% x 100,000 shares x $15/share) will be capitalized.
  - The $150,000 will be distributed between the common stock (par) account and paid-in-capital in excess of par account based on the par value of the common stock. The resulting balances are as follows.

Other Forms of Dividends

- Stock Dividends

Preferred stock	$	300,000
Common stock **(110,000 shares** at $4 par)		440,000
Paid-in-capital in excess of par		710,000
Retained earnings		550,000
Total stockholders equity	$	2,000,000

Because 10,000 new shares (10% x 100,000) have been issued at the current price of $15/share, $150,000 ($15/share x 10,000 shares) is shifted from retained earnings to the common stock and paid-in-capital accounts.

Other Forms of Dividends

- Stock Dividends

Preferred stock	$	300,000
Common stock **(110,000 shares** at $4 par)		440,000
Paid-in-capital in excess of par		710,000
Retained earnings		550,000
Total stockholders equity	$	2,000,000

A total of $40,000 ($4 par x 10,000 shares) is added to common stock. The remaining $110,000 [($15 - $4) x 10,000 shares] is added to the paid-in-capital in excess of par account. Total stockholders equity has not changed.

Other Forms of Dividends

- Stock Dividends
  - From a shareholder's perspective, stock dividends result in a dilution of shares owned.
  - For example, assume a stockholder owned 100 shares at $20/share ($2,000 total) before a stock dividend.
  - If the firm declares a 10% stock dividend, the shareholder will have 110 shares of stock. However, the total value of her shares will still be $2,000.
  - Therefore, the value of her share must have fallen to $18.18/share ($2,000/110).

Other Forms of Dividends

- Disadvantages of stock dividends include:
  - The cost of issuing the new shares.
  - Taxes and listing fees on the new shares.
  - Other recording costs.
- Advantages of stock dividends include:
  - The company conserves needed cash.
  - Signaling effect to the shareholders that the firm is retaining cash because of lucrative investment opportunities.

Other Forms of Dividends

- Stock Split
  - A stock split is a recapitalization that affects the number of shares outstanding, par value, earnings per share, and market price.
  - The rationale for a stock split is that it lowers the price of the stock and makes it more attractive to individual investors.
  - For example, assume a share of stock is currently selling for $135 and splits 3 for 2.
  - The new share price will be equal to 2/3 x $135, or $90.

Other Forms of Dividends

- Stock Split
  - Continuing with the example, assume that the investor held 100 shares before the split with a total value of $13,500.
  - After the split, the shareholder will hold:
    $13,500/$90 = 150 shares worth $90 each

Other Forms of Dividends

- Stock Split
  - A reverse stock split reduces the number of shares outstanding and raises stock price—the opposite of a stock split.
  - The rationale for a reverse stock split is to add respectability to the stock and convey the meaning that it isn't a junk stock.

> Research on both stock splits and stock dividends generally supports the theory that they do not affect the value of shares.
>
> They are often used, however, to send a signal to investors that good things are going to happen.

Other Forms of Dividends

- Not only do stock splits leave the market value of shareholders unaffected, but they also have little affect from an accounting standpoint as this 2-for-1 split demonstrates.

Before 2-for-1 Split		
Common stock **(200,000 shares at $2 par**		400,000
Paid-in-capital in excess of par		4,000,000
Retained earnings		2,000,000
Total stockholders equity	$	6,400,000
After 2-for-1 Split		
Common stock **(400,000 shares at $1 par)**		400,000
Paid-in-capital in excess of par		4,000,000
Retained earnings		2,000,000
Total stockholders equity	$	6,400,000

Other Forms of Dividends

- Stock Repurchases
  - Stock repurchase: The purchasing and retiring of stock by the issuing corporation.
  - A repurchase is a partial liquidation since it decreases the number of shares outstanding.
  - It may also be thought of as an alternative to cash dividends.

Other Forms of Dividends

- Alternative Reasons for Stock Repurchases
  - To use the shares for another purpose
  - To alter the firm's capital structure
  - To increase EPS and ROE resulting in a higher market price
  - To reduce the chance of a hostile takeover

Chapter 13

Introduction to Finance

Lawrence J. Gitman
Jeff Madura

End of Chapter

Chapter 14

Introduction to Finance

Lawrence J. Gitman
Jeff Madura

Financial Planning

Learning Goals

- Understand the financial planning process, including long-term (strategic) financial plans and short-term (operating) plans.
- Discuss cash planning, sales forecasts, and the procedures for preparing the cash budget.
- Describe how the cash budget is evaluated and the procedures for coping with uncertainty in the cash budget.

Learning Goals

- Prepare a pro forma income statement using both the percent-of-sales method and a breakdown of costs and expenses into their fixed and variable components.
- Explain the procedures used to develop a pro forma balance sheet using the judgmental approach and an external financing required figure.
- Cite the weaknesses of the simplified approaches to pro forma preparation and the common uses of pro forma financial statements.

The Financial Planning Process

- Long-Term (Strategic) Financial Plans
  - Long-term (strategic) financial plans lay out a company's planned financial actions and the anticipated impact of those actions over periods ranging from 2 to 10 years.
  - Firms that are exposed to a high degree of operating uncertainty tend to use shorter plans.
  - These plans are one component of a company's integrated strategic plan (along with production and marketing plans) that guide a company toward achievement of its goals.

The Financial Planning Process

- Long-Term (Strategic) Financial Plans
  - Long-term financial plans consider a number of financial activities including:
    - Proposed fixed asset investments
    - Research and development activities
    - Marketing and product development
    - Capital structure
    - Sources of financing
  - These plans are generally supported by a series of annual budgets and profit plans.

The Financial Planning Process

- Short-Term (Operating) Financial Plans
  - Short-term (operating) financial plans specify short-term financial actions and the anticipated impact of those actions and typically cover a 1- to 2-year operating period.
  - Key inputs include the sales forecast and other operating and financial data.
  - Key outputs include operating budgets, the cash budget, and pro forma financial statements.
  - This process is described graphically on the following slide.

The Financial Planning Process

- Short-Term (Operating) Financial Plans

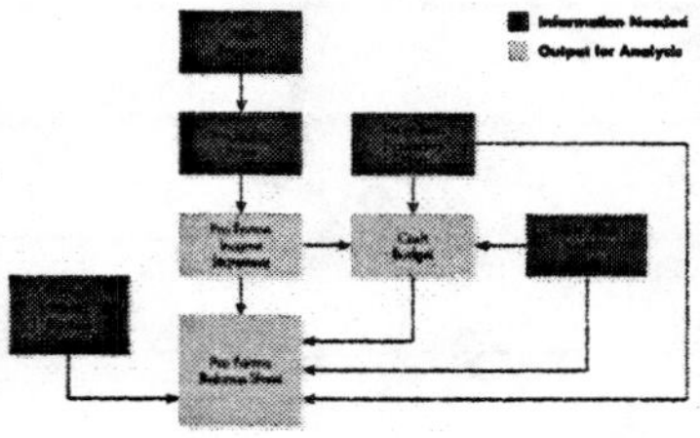

Figure 14.1

The Financial Planning Process

- Short-Term (Operating) Financial Plans
  - As indicated in the previous exhibit, short-term financial planning begins with a sales forecast.
  - From this sales forecast, production plans are developed that consider lead times and raw material requirements.
  - From the production plans, direct labor, factory overhead, and operating expense estimates are developed.
  - From this information, the pro forma income statement and cash budget are prepared—ultimately leading to the development of the pro forma balance sheet.

Cash Planning: Cash Budgets

- The cash budget is a statement of the firm's planned inflows and outflows of cash.
- It is used to estimate short-term cash requirements with particular attention to anticipated cash surpluses and shortfalls.
- Surpluses must be invested and shortfalls must be funded.
- The cash budget is a useful tool for determining the timing of cash inflows and outflows during a given period.
- Typically, monthly budgets are developed covering a 1-year time period.

Cash Planning: Cash Budgets

- The cash budget begins with a sales forecast, which is simply a prediction of the sales activity during a given period.
- A prerequisite to the sales forecast is a forecast for the economy, the industry, the company, and other external and internal factors that might influence company sales.
- The sales forecast is then used as a basis for estimating the monthly cash inflows that will result from projected sales—and outflows related to production, overhead and other expenses.

Cash Planning: Cash Budgets

TABLE 14.1 The General Format of the Cash Budget

	Jan.	Feb.	...	Nov.	Dec.
Cash receipts	$XXX	$XXG		$XXM	$XXT
Less: Cash disbursements	XXA	XXH	...	XXN	XXU
Net cash flow	$XXB	$XXI		$XXO	$XXV
Add: Beginning cash	XXC	XXD	XXJ	XXP	XXQ
Ending cash	$XXD	$XXJ		$XXQ	$XXW
Less: Minimum cash balance	XXE	XXK	...	XXR	XXY
Required total financing		$XXL		$XXS	
Excess cash balance	$XXF				$XXZ

 Table 14.1

Cash Planning: Cash Budgets

- An Example: The Intercom Company
  - Intercom Company, a defense contractor, is developing a cash budget for October, November, and December. Intercom's sales in August and September were $100,000 and $200,000 respectively. Sales of $400,000, $300,000 and $200,000 have been forecast for October, November, and December. Historically, 20% of the firm's sales have been for cash, 50% have been collected after 1 month, and the remaining 30% after 2 months. In December, Intercom will receive a $30,000 dividend from stock in a subsidiary.

Cash Planning: Cash Budgets

- An Example: The Intercom Company
  - Based on this information, we are able to develop the following schedule of cash receipts for Intercom Company

TABLE 14.2 A Schedule of Projected Cash Receipts for Intercom Company ($000)

Forecast sales	Aug. $100	Sept. $200	Oct. $400	Nov. $300	Dec. $200
Cash sales (0.20)	$ 20	$ 40	$ 80	$ 60	$ 40
Collections of A/R:					
Lagged 1 month (0.50)		50	100	200	150
Lagged 2 months (0.30)			30	60	120
Other cash receipts					30
Total cash receipts			$210	$320	$340

 Table 14.2

Cash Planning: Cash Budgets

- An Example: The Intercom Company
  - Intercom Company has also gathered the relevant information for the development of a cash disbursement schedule. Purchases will represent 70% of sales—10% will be paid immediately in cash, 70% is paid the month following the purchase, and the remaining 20% is paid two months following the purchase. The firm will also expend cash on rent, wages and salaries, taxes, capital assets, interest, dividends, and a portion of the principal on its loans. The resulting disbursement schedule thus follows.

Cash Planning: Cash Budgets

- An Example: The Intercom Company

TABLE 14.3 A Schedule of Projected Cash Disbursements for Intercon Company ($000)

Purchases (0.70 × sales)	Aug. $70	Sept. $140	Oct. $280	Nov. $210	Dec. $140
Cash purchases (0.10)	$ 7	$ 14	$ 28	$ 21	$ 14
Payments of A/P:					
Lagged 1 month (0.70)		49	98	196	147
Lagged 2 months (0.20)			14	28	56
Rent payments			5	5	5
Wages and salaries			48	38	28
Tax payments					25
Fixed asset outlays				130	
Interest payments					10
Cash dividend payments			20		
Principal payments					20
Total cash disbursements			$213	$418	$305

 Table 14.3

Cash Planning: Cash Budgets

- An Example: The Intercom Company
  - The Cash Budget for Intercom can be derived by combining the receipts budget with the disbursements budget. At the end of September, Intercom's cash balance was $50,000, notes payable was $0, and marketable securities balance was $0. Intercom also wishes to maintain a minimum cash balance of $25,000. As a result, it will have excess cash in October, and a deficit of cash in November and December. The resulting cash budget follows.

Cash Planning: Cash Budgets

- An Example: The Intercom Company

TABLE 14.4 A Cash Budget for Intercom Company ($000)

	Oct.	Nov.	Dec.
Total cash receipts[a]	$210	$320	$340
Less: Total cash disbursements[b]	213	418	305
Net cash flow	$ (3)	$ (98)	$ 35
Add: Beginning cash	50	47	(51)
Ending cash	$ 47	$ (51)	$ (16)
Less: Minimum cash balance	25	25	25
Required total financing (notes payable)[c]	—	$ 76	$ 41
Excess cash balance (marketable securities)[d]	$ 22	—	—

[a]From Table 14.2.
[b]From Table 14.3.
[c]Values are placed in this line when the ending cash is less than the desired minimum cash balance. These amounts are typically financed short-term and therefore are represented by notes payable.
[d]Values are placed in this line when the ending cash is greater than the desired minimum cash balance. These amounts are typically assumed to be invested short-term and therefore are represented by marketable securities.

 Table 14.4

Evaluating Cash Budgets

- Cash budgets indicate the extent to which cash shortages or surpluses are expected in the months covered by the forecast.

Intercom Company Key Account Balances ($000)			
Account	Oct	Nov	Dec
Cash	25	25	25
Marketable Securities	22	-	-
Notes Payable	-	76	41

- The excess cash of $22,000 in October should be invested in marketable securities. The deficits in November and December need to be financed.

Coping with Uncertainty in the Cash Budget

- One way to cope with cash budgeting uncertainty is to prepare several cash budgets based on several forecasted scenarios (i.e., pessimistic, most likely, optimistic).
- From this range of cash flows, the financial manager can determine the amount of financing necessary to cover the most adverse situation.
- This method will also provide a sense of the riskiness of alternatives.
- An example of this sort of "sensitivity analysis" for the Intercom Company for the month of October is shown on the following slide.

Coping with Uncertainty in the Cash Budget

TABLE 14.5 A Sensitivity Analysis of Intercon Company's Cash Budget ($000)

	October			November			December		
	Pessimistic	Most likely	Optimistic	Pessimistic	Most likely	Optimistic	Pessimistic	Most likely	Optimistic
Total cash receipts	$160	$210	$285	$ 210	$320	$ 410	$ 275	$340	$422
Less: Total cash disbursements	200	213	248	380	418	467	280	305	320
Net cash flow	$(40)	$ (3)	$ 37	$(170)	$ (98)	$ (57)	$ (5)	$ 35	$102
Add: Beginning cash	50	50	50	10	47	87	(160)	(51)	30
Ending cash	$ 10	$ 47	$ 87	$(160)	$ (51)	$ 30	$(165)	$(16)	$132
Less: Minimum cash balance	25	25	25	25	25	25	25	25	25
Required total financing	$ 15	—	—	$ 185	$ 76—	$ 190	$ 41	—	
Excess cash balance	—	$ 22	$ 62	—	—	$ 5	—	—	$107

 Table 14.5

Profit Planning: Pro Forma Financial Statements

- Pro forma financial statements are projected, or forecast, financial statements—income statements and balance sheets.
- The inputs required to develop pro forma statements using the most common approaches include:
  - Financial statements from the preceding year
  - The sales forecast for the coming year
  - Key assumptions about a number of factors
- The development of pro forma financial statements will be demonstrated using the financial statements for Carson Manufacturing.

Profit Planning: Pro Forma Financial Statements

TABLE 14.6 An Income Statement for Carson Manufacturing Company for the Year Ended December 31, 2001

Sales revenue		
Model X (1,000 units at $20/unit)	$20,000	
Model Y (2,000 units at $40/unit)	80,000	
Total sales		$100,000
Less: Cost of goods sold		
Labor	$28,500	
Material A	8,000	
Material B	5,500	
Overhead	38,000	
Total cost of goods sold		80,000
Gross profits		$ 20,000
Less: Operating expenses		10,000
Operating profits		$ 10,000
Less: Interest expense		1,000
Net profits before taxes		$ 9,000
Less: Taxes (0.15 × $9,000)		1,350
Net profits after taxes		$ 7,650
Less: Common stock dividends		4,000
To retained earnings		$ 3,650

 Table 14.6

Profit Planning: Pro Forma Financial Statements

TABLE 14.7 A Balance Sheet for Carson Manufacturing Company (December 31, 2001)

Assets		Liabilities and equities	
Cash	$ 6,000	Accounts payable	$ 7,000
Marketable securities	4,000	Taxes payable	300
Accounts receivable	13,000	Notes payable	8,300
Inventories	16,000	Other current liabilities	3,400
Total current assets	$39,000	Total current liabilities	$19,000
Net fixed assets	$51,000	Long-term debt	$18,000
Total assets	$39,000	Stockholders' equity	
		Common stock	$30,000
		Retained earnings	$23,000
		Total liabilities and stockholders' equity	$90,000

 Table 14.7

Profit Planning: Pro Forma Financial Statements

- Step 1: Start with a Sales Forecast
  - The first and key input for developing pro forma financial statements is the sales forecast for Carson Manufacturing.

TABLE 14.8 2002 Sales Forecast for Carson Manufacturing Company

Unit sales	
Model X	1,500
Model Y	1,950
Dollar sales	
Model X ($25/unit)	$ 37,500
Model Y ($50/unit)	97,500
Total	$135,000

 Table 14.8

Profit Planning: Pro Forma Financial Statements

- Step 1: Start with a Sales Forecast

TABLE 14.8 2002 Sales Forecast for Carson Manufacturing Company

Unit sales	
Model X	1,500
Model Y	1,950
Dollar sales	
Model X ($25/unit)	$ 37,500
Model Y ($50/unit)	97,500
Total	$135,000

  - This forecast is based on an increase from $20 to $25 per unit for Model X and $40 to $50 per unit for Model Y.
  - These increases are required to cover anticipated increases in various costs, including labor, materials, and overhead.

 Table 14.8

Profit Planning: Pro Forma Financial Statements

- Step 2: Develop the Pro Forma Income Statement
  - One method for developing a pro forma income statement is the percent-of-sales method.
  - This method starts with the sales forecast and then expresses the cost of goods sold, operating expenses, and other accounts as a percentage of projected sales.
  - By using the dollar values taken from Carson's 2001 income statement (Table 14.6), we find that these percentages are as follows:

Profit Planning: Pro Forma Financial Statements

- Step 2: Develop the Pro Forma Income Statement

$$\frac{\text{Cost of goods sold}}{\text{Sales}} = \frac{\$80{,}000}{\$100{,}000} = 80.0\%$$

$$\frac{\text{Operating expenses}}{\text{Sales}} = \frac{\$10{,}000}{\$100{,}000} = 10.0\%$$

$$\frac{\text{Interest expense}}{\text{Sales}} = \frac{\$1{,}000}{\$100{,}000} = 1.0\%$$

Profit Planning: Pro Forma Financial Statements

- Step 2: Develop the Pro Forma Income Statement
  - Using these percentages and the 20021 sales forecast we developed, the entire income statement can be projected.
  - The results are shown on the following slide.
  - It is important to note that this method implicitly assumes that all costs are variable and that all increase or decrease in proportion to sales.
  - This will understate profits when sales are increasing and overstate them when sales are decreasing.

Profit Planning: Pro Forma Financial Statements

- Step 2: Develop the Pro Forma Income Statement

TABLE 14.9 A Pro Forma Income Statement, Using the Percent-of-Sales Method, for Carson Manufacturing Company for the Year Ended December 31, 2002

Sales revenue	$135,000
Less: Cost of goods sold (0.80)	108,000
Gross profits	$ 27,000
Less: Operating expenses (0.10)	13,500
Operating profits	$ 13,500
Less: Interest expense (0.01)	1,350
Net profits before taxes	$ 12,150
Less: Taxes (0.15 × $12,150)	1,823
Net profits after taxes	$ 10,327
Less: Common stock dividends	4,000
To retained earnings	$ 6,327

Table 14.9

Profit Planning: Pro Forma Financial Statements

- Step 2: Develop the Pro Forma Income Statement
  - Clearly, some of the firm's expenses will increase with the level of sales while others will not.
  - As a result, the strict application of the percent-of-sales method is a bit naïve.
  - The best way to generate a more realistic pro forma income statement is to segment the firm's expenses into fixed and variable components.
  - This may be demonstrated as follows.

Profit Planning: Pro Forma Financial Statements

- Step 2: Develop the Pro Forma Income Statement

Income Statements
Carson Manufacturing Company

	2001 Actual	2002 Pro forma
Sales revenue	$100,000	$135,000
Less: Cost of good sold		
Fixed cost	40,000	40,000
Variable cost (0.40 × sales)	40,000	54,000
Gross profits	$ 20,000	$ 41,000
Less: Operating expenses		
Fixed expense	5,000	5,000
Variable expense (0.05 × sales)	5,000	6,750
Operating profits	$ 10,000	$ 29,250
Less: Interest expense (all fixed)	1,000	1,000
Net profits before taxes	$ 9,000	$ 28,250
Less: Taxes (0.15 × net profits before taxes)	1,350	4,238
Net profits after taxes	$ 7,650	$ 24,012

Profit Planning: Pro Forma Financial Statements

- Step 3: Develop the Pro Forma Balance Sheet
  - Probably the best approach to use in developing the pro forma balance sheet is the judgmental approach.
  - Using this approach, the values of some balance sheet accounts are estimated while others are calculated.
  - The company's external financing (required) is used as the balancing account.
  - To apply this method to Carson Manufacturing, a number of simplifying assumptions must be made.

Profit Planning: Pro Forma Financial Statements

- Step 3: Develop the Pro Forma Balance Sheet
  - A minimum cash balance of $6,000 is desired.
  - Marketable securities will remain at their current level of $4,000.
  - Accounts receivable will be approximately $16,875 which represents 45 days of sales on average [(45/365) × $135,000].
  - Ending inventory will remain at about $16,000. 25% ($4,000) represents raw materials and 75% ($12,000) is finished goods.
  - A new machine costing $20,000 will be purchased. Total depreciation will be $8,000. Adding $20,000 to existing net fixed assets of $51,000 and subtracting the $8,000 depreciation yields a net fixed assets figure of $63,000.

Profit Planning: Pro Forma Financial Statements

- Step 3: Develop the Pro Forma Balance Sheet
  - Purchases will be $40,500 which represents 30% of annual sales (30% × $135,000). Carson takes about 72 days to pay on its accounts payable. As a result, accounts payable will equal $8,100 [(72/360) × $40,500].
  - Taxes payable will be $455 which represents one-fourth of the 1998 tax liability.
  - Notes payable will remain unchanged at $8,300.
  - There will be no change in other current liabilities, long-term debt, and common stock.
  - Retained earnings will change in accordance with the pro forma income statement.

Profit Planning: Pro Forma Financial Statements

- Step 3: Develop the Pro Forma Balance Sheet

TABLE 14.10 A Pro Forma Balance Sheet, Using the Judgmental Approach, for Carson Manufacturing Company (December 31, 2002)

Assets			Liabilities and equities	
Cash		$ 6,000	Accounts payable	$ 8,100
Marketable securities		4,000	Taxes payable	455
Accounts receivable		16,875	Notes payable	8,300
Inventories			Other current liabilities	3,400
Raw materials	$ 4,000		Total current liabilities	$ 20,255
Finished goods	12,000		Long-term debt	$ 18,000
Total inventory		16,000	Stockholders' equity	
Total current assets		$ 42,875	Common stock	$ 30,000
Net fixed assets		$ 63,000	Retained earnings	$ 29,327
Total assets		$ 105,875	Total	$ 97,582
			External financing required[a]	$ 8,293
			Total liabilities and stockholders' equity	$105,875

[a]The amount of external financing needed to force the firm's balance sheet to balance. Because of the nature of the judgmental approach, the balance sheet is not expected to balance without some type of adjustment.

 Table 14.10

Evaluation of Pro Forma Statements

- Weaknesses of Simplified Approaches
  - The major weaknesses of the approaches to pro forma statement development outlined above lie in two assumptions:
    - That the firm's past financial performance will be replicated in the future.
    - That certain accounts can be forced to take on desired values.
  - For these reasons, it is imperative to first develop a forecast of the overall economy and make adjustments to accommodate other facts or events.

Using Microsoft® Excel

- The Microsoft® Excel Spreadsheets used in the Chapter 14 presentation can be downloaded from the *Introduction to Finance* companion web site: http://www.awl.com/gitman_madura

Chapter 14

Introduction to Finance
Lawrence J. Gitman
Jeff Madura

End of Chapter

Chapter

15

Introduction to Finance

Lawrence J. Gitman
Jeff Madura

Short-Term Financial Management

Learning Goals

- Describe the scope of short-term financial management and the cash conversion cycle.
- Explain the funding requirements of the cash conversion cycle and strategies for minimizing negotiated liabilities.
- Understand inventory management: differing views, common techniques, and international concerns.

Learning Goals

- Explain the key aspects of accounts receivable management including credit selection and standards, credit terms, and credit monitoring.
- Review the management of receipts and disbursements, including float, speeding collections, slowing payments, cash concentration and zero-balance accounts.
- Discuss current liability management, including spontaneous liabilities, unsecured short-term financing, and secured short-term financing.

Managing the Cash Conversion Cycle

- Short-term financial management—managing current assets and current liabilities—is one of the financial manager's most important and time-consuming activities.
- The goal of short-term financial management is to manage each of the firms' current assets and liabilities to achieve a balance between profitability and risk that contributes positively to overall firm value.
- Central to short-term financial management is an understanding of the firm's cash conversion cycle.

Managing the Cash Conversion Cycle

- The operating cycle (OC) is the time between ordering materials and collecting cash from receivables.
- The cash conversion cycle (CCC) is the time between when a firm pays its suppliers (payables) for inventory and collecting cash from the sale of the finished product.

Managing the Cash Conversion Cycle

- Both the OC and CCC may be computed mathematically as shown below.

$$OC = AAI + ACP$$

$$CCC = OC - APP$$

$$CCC = AAI + ACP - APP$$

Managing the Cash Conversion Cycle

- Justin Industries has annual sales of $10 million, cost of goods sold of 75% of sales, and purchases that are 65% of cost of goods sold. Justin has an average age of inventory (AAI) of 60 days, an average collection period (ACP) of 40 days, and an average payment period (APP) of 35 days.
- Using the values for these variables, the cash conversion cycle for Justin is 65 days (60 + 40 - 35 = 65) and is shown on a time line in Figure 15.1.

Managing the Cash Conversion Cycle

Time = 0
Operating Cycle (OC)
100 days
Purchase Raw Materials on Account
Sell Finished Goods on Account
Collect Accounts Receivable
Average Age of Inventory (AAI)
60 days
Average Collection Period (ACP)
40 days
Average Payment Period (APP)
35 days
Pay Accounts Payable
Cash Conversion Cycle (CCC)
65 days
Time →

Figure 15.1

Managing the Cash Conversion Cycle

- The resources Justin has invested in the cash conversion cycle assuming a 360-day year are:

	Inventory = ($10,000,000 × 0.75) × (60/360)	= $1,250,000
+	Accounts receivable = (10,000,000) × (40/360)	= 1,111,111
−	Accounts payable = (10,000,000 × 0.75 × 0.65) × (35/360)	= 473,958
=	Resources invested	= $1,887,153

- Obviously, reducing AAI or ACP or lengthening APP will reduce the cash conversion cycle, thus reducing the amount of resources the firm must commit to support operations.

Funding Requirements of the CCC

- Permanent versus Seasonal Funding Needs
  - If a firm's sales are constant, then its investment in operating assets should also be constant, and the firm will have only a permanent funding requirement.
  - If sales are cyclical, then investment in operating assets will vary over time, leading to the need for seasonal funding requirements in addition to the permanent funding requirements for its minimum investment in operating assets.

Funding Requirements of the CCC

- Permanent versus Seasonal Funding Needs
  - Crone Paper has seasonal funding needs. Crone has seasonal sales, with its peak sales driven by back-to-school purchases. Crone holds a minimum of $25,000 in cash and marketable securities, $100,000 in inventory, and $60,000 in account receivable. At peak times, inventory increases to $750,000 and accounts receivable increase to $400,000. To capture production efficiencies, Crone produces paper at a constant rate throughout the year. Thus accounts payable remain at $50,000 throughout the year.

Funding Requirements of the CCC

- Permanent versus Seasonal Funding Needs
  - Based on this data, Crone has a permanent funding requirement for its minimum level of operating assets of $135,000 ($25,000 + $100,000 + $60,000 - $50,000 = $135,000) and peak seasonal funding requirements in excess of its permanent need of $990,000 [($25,000 + $750,000 + $400,000 - $50,000) - $135,000 = $990,000].
  - Crone's total funding requirements for operating assets vary from a minimum of $135,000 (permanent) to a seasonal peak of $1,125,000 ($135,000 + 990,000) as shown in Figure 15.2 on the following slide.

Funding Requirements of the CCC

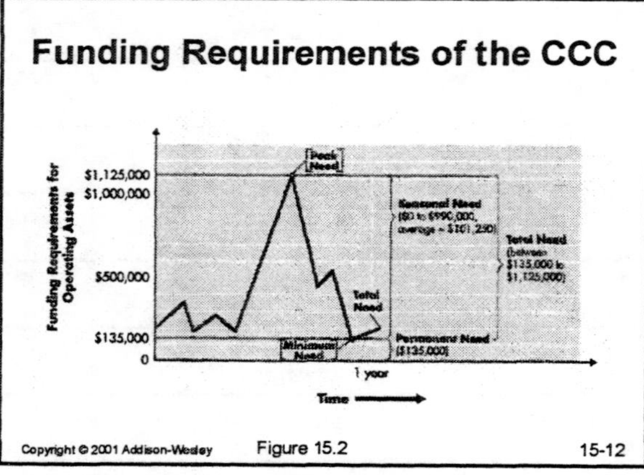

Figure 15.2

Funding Requirements of the CCC

- Aggressive versus Conservative Funding Strategies
  - Crone Paper has a permanent funding requirement of $135,000 and seasonal requirements that vary between $0 and $990,000 and average $101,250. If Crone can borrow short-term funds at 6.25% and long term funds at 8%, and can earn 5% on any invested surplus, then the annual cost of the aggressive strategy would be:

Cost of short-term financing	= 0.0625 × $101,250	=	$ 6,328.13
+ Cost of long-term financing	= 0.0800 × $135,000	=	10,800.00
− Earnings on surplus balances[1]	= 0.0500 × 0	=	0
Total cost of aggressive strategy			$17,128.13

[1]Because under this strategy the amount of financing exactly equals the estimated funding need, no surplus balances exist.

Funding Requirements of the CCC

- Aggressive versus Conservative Funding Strategies
  - Alternatively, Crone can choose a conservative strategy under which surplus cash balances are fully invested. In Figure 15.2, this surplus would be the difference between the peak need of $1,125,000 and the total need, which varies between $135,000 and $1,125,000 during the year.

Cost of short-term financing	= 0.0625 × $ 0	=	$ 0
+ Cost of long-term financing	= 0.0800 × $1,125,000	=	90,000.00
− Earnings on surplus balances[2]	= 0.0500 × 888,750	=	44,437.50
Total cost of conservative strategy			$45,562.50

[2]The average surplus balance would be calculated by subtracting the sum of the permanent need ($135,000) and the average seasonal need ($101,250) from the seasonal peak need ($1,125,000) to get $888,750 ($1,125,000 − $135,000 − $101,250). This represents the surplus amount of financing that on average could be invested in short-term vehicles that earn a 5% annual return.

Funding Requirements of the CCC

- Aggressive versus Conservative Funding Strategies
  - Clearly, the aggressive funding strategy's heavy reliance on short-term financing makes it riskier than the conservative strategy because of interest rate swings and possible difficulties in obtaining needed funds quickly when the seasonal peaks occur.
  - The conservative funding strategy avoids these risks through the locked-in interest rate and long-term financing, but is more costly. Thus the final decision is left to management.

Inventory Management

- Differing Views about Inventory
  - The different departments within a firm (finance, production, marketing, etc.) often have differing views about what is an "appropriate" level of inventory.
  - *Financial managers* would like to keep inventory levels low to ensure that funds are wisely invested.
  - *Marketing managers* would like to keep inventory levels high to ensure orders could be quickly filled.
  - *Manufacturing managers* would like to keep raw materials levels high to avoid production delays and to make larger, more economical production runs.

Techniques for Managing Inventory

- The ABC System
  - The ABC system of inventory management divides inventory into three groups of descending order of importance based on the dollar amount invested in each.
  - A typical system would contain, group A would consist of 20% of the items worth 80% of the total dollar value; group B would consist of the next largest investment, and so on.
  - Control of the A items would be intensive because of the high dollar investment involved.
  - The EOQ model would be most appropriate for managing both A and B items.

Techniques for Managing Inventory

- The Economic Order Quantity (EOQ) Model
  - EOQ assumes that relevant costs of inventory can be divided into order costs and carrying costs
  - Order costs decrease as the size of the order increases; carrying costs increase with increases in the order size
  - The EOQ model analyzes the tradeoff between order costs and carrying costs to determine the order quantity that minimizes the total inventory cost

Techniques for Managing Inventory

- The Economic Order Quantity (EOQ) Model

$$EOQ = \sqrt{\frac{2 \times S \times O}{C}}$$

Where:
S = usage in units per period (year)
O = order cost per order
C = carrying costs per unit per period (year)

Techniques for Managing Inventory

- The Economic Order Quantity (EOQ) Model
  - Assume that RLB, Inc., a manufacturer of electronic test equipment, uses 1,600 units of an item annually. Its order cost is $50 per order, and the carrying cost is $1 per unit per year. Substituting into the equation on the previous slide we get:

$$EOQ = \sqrt{\frac{2 \times 1{,}600 \times \$50}{\$1}} \approx 400 \text{ units}$$

  - The EOQ can be used to evaluate the total cost of inventory as shown on the following slides.

Techniques for Managing Inventory

- The Economic Order Quantity (EOQ) Model

$$\text{Ordering costs} = \frac{\text{Cost}}{\text{Order}} \times \frac{\text{\# of Orders}}{\text{Year}}$$

$$\text{Carrying costs} = \frac{\text{Carry costs/Year} \times \text{Order size}}{2}$$

Total costs = Ordering costs + Carrying costs

Techniques for Managing Inventory

- The Economic Order Quantity (EOQ) Model

RIB, Inc. Inventory Data		
Variable		**Value**
Annual Usage		1,600
Order Cost/order	$	50.00
Carrying Costs/year	$	1.00

Techniques for Managing Inventory

- The Economic Order Quantity (EOQ) Model

RIB, Inc.
Evaluation of Economic Order Quantity (EOQ)

Order Quantity	Annual Orders	Annual Order Order Cost	Annual Carrying Cost	Total Cost
100	16.0	$ 800	$ 50	$ 850
200	8.0	$ 400	$ 100	$ 500
300	5.3	$ 267	$ 150	$ 417
400	4.0	$ 200	$ 200	$ 400
500	3.2	$ 160	$ 250	$ 410
600	2.7	$ 133	$ 300	$ 433
700	2.3	$ 114	$ 350	$ 464
800	2.0	$ 100	$ 400	$ 500

Techniques for Managing Inventory

- The Economic Order Quantity (EOQ) Model

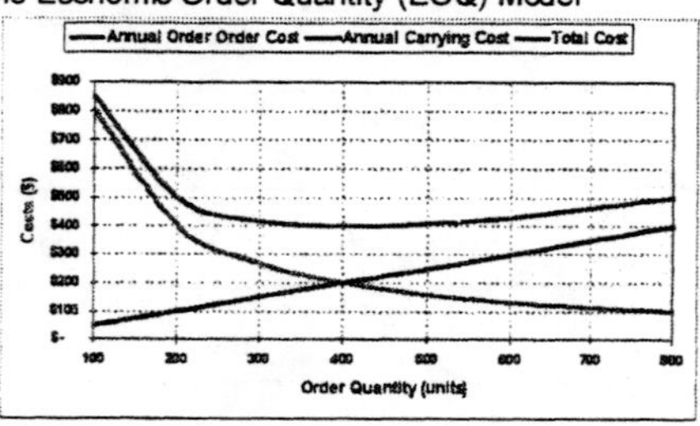

Techniques for Managing Inventory

- The Reorder Point
  - Once a company has calculated its EOQ, it must determine *when* it should place its orders.
  - More specifically, the reorder point must consider the lead time needed to place and receive orders.
  - If we assume that inventory is used at a constant rate throughout the year (no seasonality), the reorder point can be determined by using the following equation:

Reorder point = Lead time in days x Daily usage

Daily usage = Annual usage/360

Techniques for Managing Inventory

- The Reorder Point
  - Using the RIB example above, if they know that it requires 10 days to place and receive an order, and the annual usage is 1,600 units per year, the reorder point can be determined as follows:

Daily usage = 1,600/360 = 4.44 units/day

Reorder point = 10 x 4.44 = 44.44 or 45 units

  - Thus, when RIB's inventory level reaches 45 units, it should place an order for 400 units. However, if RIB wishes to maintain safety stock to protect against stock outs, they would order before inventory reached 45 units.

Techniques for Managing Inventory

- Materials Requirement Planning (MRP)
  - MRP systems are used to determine what to order, when to order, and what priorities to assign to ordering materials.
  - MRP uses EOQ concepts to determine how much to order using computer software.
  - It simulates each product's bill of materials structure (all of the product's parts), inventory status, and manufacturing process.
  - Like the simple EOQ, the objective of MRP systems is to minimize a company's overall investment in inventory without impairing production.

Techniques for Managing Inventory

- Just-In-Time System (JIT)
  - The JIT inventory management system minimizes the inventory investment by having material inputs arrive exactly at the time they are needed for production.
  - For a JIT system to work, extensive coordination must exist between the firm, its suppliers, and shipping companies to ensure that material inputs arrive on time.
  - In addition, the inputs must be of near perfect quality and consistency given the absence of safety stock.

Inventory Management

- International Inventory Management
  - International inventory management is typically much more complicated for exporters and MNCs.
  - The production and manufacturing economies of scale that might be expected from selling globally may prove elusive if products must be tailored for local markets.
  - Transporting products over long distances often results in delays, confusion, damage, theft, and other difficulties.

The Five C's of Credit

- Capital
- Character
- Collateral
- Capacity
- Conditions

Credit Scoring

- Credit scoring is a procedure resulting in a score that measures an applicant's overall credit strength, derived as a weighted-average of scores of various credit characteristics.
  - Paula's Stores, a major department store chain, uses a credit scoring model to make credit decisions. Paula's uses a system measuring six separate financial and credit characteristics. Scores can range from 0 (lowest) to 100 (highest). The minimum acceptable score necessary for granting credit is 75. The results of such a score for Herb Conseca are illustrated in the following slide.

Credit Scoring

Credit Standards for Oaula's Stores

Credit Score	Action
Greater than 75	Extend standard credit terms
65 to 75	Extend limited credit
Less than 65	Reject application

Credit Scoring of Herb Conseca by Paula's Stores

Financial and credit characteristic	Score (0 to 100)	Predetermined weight	Weighted score
Credit references	80	15%	12.00
Home ownership	100	15%	15.00
Income range	70	25%	17.50
Payment history	75	25%	18.75
Years at address	90	10%	9.00
Years on job	80	10%	8.00
		Credit Score	80.25

Changing Credit Standards

- Key Variables

Changes in Key Variables Resulting from A Relaxation of Credit Standards		
Variable	Direction of Change	Effect on Profits
Sales Volume	Increase	Positive
Investment in Accounts Receivable	Increase	Negative
Bad Debt Expense	Increase	Negative

Changes in Key Variables Resulting from A Tightening of Credit Standards		
Variable	Direction of Change	Effect on Profits
Sales Volume	Decrease	Negative
Investment in Accounts Receivable	Decrease	Positive
Bad Debt Expense	Decrease	Positive

Orbit Tool Example

- Orbit Tool, a manufacturer of lathe tools, is currently selling a product for $10/unit. Sales (all on credit) for last year were 60,000 units. The variable cost per unit is $6.
- The firm's total fixed costs are $120,000. Orbit is currently contemplating a relaxation of credit standards that is anticipated to increase sales 5% to 63,000 units. It is also anticipated that the ACP will increase from 30 to 45 days, and that bad debt expenses will increase from 1% of sales to 2% of sales. The opportunity cost of tying funds up in receivables is 15%
- Given this information, should Orbit relax its credit standards?

Orbit Tool Example

Orbit Tool Company Analysis of Relaxing Credit Standards	
Relevant Data	
Old Sales (units)	60,000
New Sales (units)	63,000
Price/unit ($)	$ 10
Variable Cost/unit ($)	$ 6
Contributin Margin/unit ($)	$ 4
Old Receivables Level (days)	30
New Receivables Level (days)	45
Old A/R Turnover (360/AR)	12
New A/R Turnover (360/AR)	8
Old Bad Debt Level (% of sales)	1%
New Bad Debt Level (% of sales)	2%
Opportunity Cost (%)	15%

Orbit Tool Example

- Additional Profit Contribution from Sales

Orbit Tool Company				
Analysis of Rexaxing Credit Standards				
Additional Profit Contribution from Sales:				
Old Sales Level	60,000	Price/Unit	$	10
New Sales Level	63,000	Variable Cost/Unit	$	6
Increase in Sales	3,000	Contribution Margin/Unit	$	4
Additional Profit Contribution from Sales		(sales incr x cont margin)	$	12,000

Orbit Tool Example

- Cost of Marginal Investment in A/R

Orbit Tool Company			
Analysis of Rexaxing Credit Standards			
Cost of Marginal Investment in A/R:			
Cost of Marginal Investment in A/R =	(Variable Vost/unit x # of units)		
	Receivables Turnover		
Average Investment Under Proposed Plan			$ 47,250
Average Investment Under Present Plan			$ 30,000
Marginal Investment in Accounts Receivable			$ 17,250
Opportunity Cost			15%
Cost of Marginal Investment in Accounts Receivable			$ (2,588)

Orbit Tool Example

- Cost of Marginal Bad Debts

Orbit Tool Company		
Analysis of Relaxing Credit Standards		
Cost of Marginal Bad Debts:		
Cost of Marginal Bad Debts = (% Bad Debt x Price/unit x # of Units)		
Cost of Marginal Bad Debts under Proposed Plan	$	12,600
Cost of Marginal Bad Debts under Present Plan	$	6,000
Cost of Marginal Bad Debts	$	(6,600)

Orbit Tool Example

- Net Profit from Implementation of Proposed Plan

Orbit Tool Company	
Analysis of Relaxing Credit Standards	
Additional Profit Contribution from Sales	$ 12,000
Cost of Marginal Investment in Accounts Receivable	(2,588)
Cost of Marginal Bad Debts	(6,600)
Net Profit From Implementation of Proposed Plan	$ 2,813

Changing Credit Terms

- A firm's credit terms specify the repayment terms required of all of its credit customers.
- Credit terms are composed of three parts:
  - The cash discount
  - The cash discount period
  - The credit period
- For example, with credit terms of 2/10 net 30, the discount is 2%, the discount period is 10 days, and the credit period is 30 days.

Changing Credit Terms

- Cash Discount

Variable	Direction of Change	Effect on Profits
Sales volume	increase	positive
Investment in A/R due to nondiscount takers paying earlier	decrease	positive
Investment in A/R due to new customers	increase	negative
Bad debt expense	decrease	positive
Profit per unit	decrease	negative

Changing Credit Terms

- Cash Discount
  - Orbit Tool is considering a initiating a cash discount of 2% for payment within 10 days of a purchase. The firm's current average collection period (ACP) is 30 days (A/R turnover = 360/30 = 12). Credit sales of 60,000 units at $10/unit and the variable cost/unit is $6.
  - Orbit expects that if the cash discount is initiated, 60% will take the discount and pay early. In addition, sales are expected to increase 5% to 63,000 units. The ACP is expected to drop to 15 days (A/R turnover = 360/15 = 24). Bad debts will drop from 1% to 0.5% of sales. The opportunity cost to the firm of tying up funds in receivables is 15%.

Changing Credit Terms

- Cash Discount

Orbit Tool Company The Effect of Initiating a Cash Discount			
Additional Profit Contribution from Sales:			
Old Sales Level	60,000	Price/Unit	$ 10
New Sales Level	63,000	Variable Cost/Unit	$ 6
Increase in Sales	3,000	Contribution Margin/Unit	$ 4
Additional Profit Contribution from Sales		(sales incr x cont margin)	$ 12,000

Changing Credit Terms

- Cash Discount

Orbit Tool Company The Effect of Initiating a Cash Discount		
Cost of Marginal Investment in A/R:		
Cost of Marginal Investment in A/R =	(Variable Yost/unit x # of units)	
	Receivables Turnover	
Average Investment Under Proposed Plan		$ 15,750
Average Investment Under Present Plan		$ 30,000
Marginal Investment in Accounts Receivable		$ 14,250
Opportunity Cost		15%
Cost of Marginal Investment in Accounts Receivable		$ 2,138

Changing Credit Terms

- Cash Discount

Orbit Tool Company	
The Effects of Initiating a Cash Discount	
Cost of Marginal Bad Debts:	
Cost of Marginal Bad Debts = (% Bad Debt x Price/unit x # of Units)	
Cost of Marginal Bad Debts under Proposed Plan	$ 3,150
Cost of Marginal Bad Debts under Present Plan	$ 6,000
Cost of Marginal Bad Debts	$ 2,850

Changing Credit Terms

- Cash Discount

Orbit Tool Company		
The Effects of Initiating a Cash Discount		
Cost of Cash Discount:		
Cost = (% discount x %credit sales x price/unit x units sold)		
Cost	$	(7,560)

Changing Credit Terms

- Cash Discount

Orbit Tool Company	
The Effects of Initiating a Cash Discount	
Additional Profit Contribution from Sales	$ 12,000
Cost of Marginal Investment in Accounts Receivable	2,138
Cost of Marginal Bad Debts	2,850
Cost of Initiating a Cash Discount	$ (7,560)
Net Profit From Implementation of Proposed Plan	$ 9,428

Collection Policy

- The firm's collection policy is its procedures for collecting a firm's accounts receivable when they are due.
- The effectiveness of this policy can be partly evaluated by evaluating the level of bad expenses.
- As seen in the previous examples, this level depends not only on collection policy but also on the firm's credit policy.
- In general, funds should be expended to collect bad debts up to the point where the marginal cost exceeds the marginal benefit (Point A on the following slide).

Collection Policy

TABLE 15.2 Analysis of a Cash Discount for Justin Industries

Additional profits from increased sales [50 units × ($3,000 − $2,300)]	$ 35,000
Current investment in accounts receivable ($2,300 × 1,100 units) × (40/360)[a]	$281,111
New investment in accounts receivable ($2,300 × 1,150 units) × (25/360)[b]	183,681
Reduction in accounts receivable investment	$ 97,430
Cost savings from reduced investments in accounts receivable (.14 × $97,430)[c]	$ 13,640
Cost of cash discount (0.80 × 0.02 × $3,000 × 1,150)	($55,200)
Net profit from proposed cash discount	($6,560)

[a]In analyzing the investment in accounts receivable, we use the cost of the product sold ($1,500 raw materials cost + $800 production cost = $2,300 unit cost) instead of the sale price, because the cost is a better indicator of the firm's investment.

[b]The new investment in accounts receivable is tied up for an average of 25 days instead of the 40 days under the original terms. The 25 days is calculated as [(0.7 × 10 days) + (0.3 × 32 days) + 8 days] = 24.6 days, which is rounded to 25 days.

[c]Justin's opportunity cost of funds is 14%.

 Table 15.2

Collection Policy

- Aging Accounts Receivable
  - Assume that Orbit Tool extends 30-day EOM credit terms to its customers. The firm's December 31, 1998 balance sheet shows $200,000 of accounts receivable. An evaluation of the $200,000 of accounts receivable results in the following breakdown:

Days	Current	0-30	31-60	61-90	Over 90	
Month	December	November	October	September	August	Total
Accounts Receivable	$ 60,000	$ 40,000	$ 66,000	$ 26,000	$ 8,000	$ 200,000
Percentage of Total	30%	20%	33%	13%	4%	100%

  - Given the firm's credit policy, any December receivables still on the books are considered current. November receivables are between 0 and 31 days overdue, and so on. The percentage breakdown is given in the bottom row indicating the firm may have had a particular problem in October which should be investigated.

Management of Receipts and Disbursements

- Float
  - Collection float is the delay between the time when a payer deducts a payment from its checking account ledger and the time when the payee actually receives the funds in spendable form.
  - Disbursement float is the delay between the time when a payer deducts a payment from its checking account ledger and the time when the funds are actually withdrawn from the account.
  - Both the collection and disbursement float have three separate components.

Management of Receipts and Disbursements

- Float
  - Mail float is the delay between the time when a payer places payment in the mail and the time when it is received by the payee.
  - Processing float is the delay between the receipt of a check by the payee and the deposit of it in the firm's account.
  - Clearing float is the delay between the deposit of a check by the payee and the actual availability of the funds which results from the time required for a check to clear the banking system.

Management of Receipts and Disbursements

- Speeding Collections
  - Concentration Banking
    - Concentration banking is a collection procedure in which payments are made to regionally dispersed collection centers.
    - Checks are collected at these centers several times a day and deposited in local banks for quick clearing.
    - It reduces the collection float by shortening both the mail and clearing float components.

Management of Receipts and Disbursements

- Speeding Collections
  - Lockboxes
    - A lockbox system is a collection procedure in which payers send their payments to a nearby post office box that is emptied by the firm's bank several times a day.
    - It is different from and superior to concentration banking in that the firm's bank actually services the lockbox which reduces the processing float.
    - A lockbox system reduces the collection float by shortening the processing float as well as the mail and clearing float.

Management of Receipts and Disbursements

- Speeding Collections
  - Direct Sends and Other Techniques
    - A direct send is a collection procedure in which the payee presents checks for payment directly to the banks on which they are drawn, thus reducing the clearing float.
    - Pre-authorized checks (PAC) are checks written against a customer's account for a previously agreed upon amount avoiding the need for the customer's signature.
    - Depository transfer checks (DTC) are unsigned checks drawn on one of the firm's accounts and deposited at a concentration bank to speed up transfers.

Management of Receipts and Disbursements

- Speeding Collections
  - Direct Sends and Other Techniques
    - A wire transfer is a telecommunications bookkeeping device that removes funds from the payer's bank and deposits them into the payee's bank—thereby reducing collections float.
    - Automated clearinghouse (ACH) debits are pre-authorized electronic withdrawals from the payer's account that are transferred to the payee's account via a settlement among banks by the automated clearinghouse.
    - ACHs clear in one day, thereby reducing mail, processing, and clearing float.

Management of Receipts and Disbursements

- Slowing Disbursements
  - Controlled disbursing involves the strategic use of mailing points and bank accounts to lengthen mail float and clearing float.
  - Playing the float is a method of consciously anticipating the resulting float or delay associated with the payment process and using it to keep funds in an account as long as possible.
  - Staggered funding is a method of playing the float by depositing a certain portion of a payroll into an account on several successive days following the issuance of checks.

Management of Receipts and Disbursements

- Slowing Disbursements
  - With an overdraft system, if the firm's checking account balance is insufficient to cover all checks presented, the bank will automatically lend money to cover the account.
  - A zero-balance account is an account in which a zero balance is maintained and the firm is required to deposit funds to cover checks drawn on the account only as they are presented for payment.

Current Liabilities Management

- Accounts Payable and Accruals
  - The final component of the cash conversion cycle is the average payment period.
  - The firm's goal is to pay as slowly as possible without damaging its credit rating.
  - This means that accounts payable should be paid on the last day possible given the supplier's stated credit terms.

Current Liabilities Management

- Accounts Payable and Accruals
  - Recall that Justin Company had an average payment period of 35 days (30 days until payment is mailed plus 5 days of payment float), which results in average accounts payable of $473,958. Thus the daily accounts payable generated is $13,542 ($473,958/35).
  - If Justin were to pay its accounts in 35 days instead of 30, its accounts payable would increase by $67,710 ($13,542 x 5). As a result, Justin would reduce its investment in operations by $67,710. Justin should therefore delay payment if it would not damage its credit rating.

Current Liabilities Management

- Cash Discounts
  - When a firm is offered credit terms that include a cash discount, it has two options:
    - Pay the full amount of the invoice at the end of the credit period, or pay the invoice amount less the cash discount at the end of the cash discount period.
  - The formula for calculating the interest rate associated with not taking the discount but paying at the end of the credit period when cash discount terms are offered is shown on the following slide.

Current Liabilities Management

- Cash Discounts

$$k_{discount} = \frac{d}{(1-d)} \times \frac{360}{(CP-DP)}$$

where

$k_{discount}$ = annual interest cost of not taking a cash discount
d = percent discount (in decimal form)
CP = credit period
DP = cash discount period

  - Assume a supplier of Justin Industries has changed its terms from net 30 to 2/10 net 30. Justin has a bank line of credit with a current interest rate of 10%. Should Justin take the cash discount or continue to use 30 days of credit from its supplier?

Current Liabilities Management

- Cash Discounts

$$k_{\text{discount}} = \frac{0.02}{(1-0.02)} \times \frac{360}{(30-10)} = 0.367 = \underline{\underline{36.7\%}}$$

  - The annualized rate charged by the supplier for not taking the cash discount is 36.7%, whereas the bank charges 10%. Justin should take the cash discount and obtain needed short-term financing by drawing on its bank line of credit.

Unsecured Sources of Short-Term Loans

- Bank Loans
  - The major type of loan made by banks to businesses is the short-term, self-liquidating loan which is intended to carry a firm through seasonal peaks in financing needs.
  - These loans are generally obtained as companies build up inventory and experience growth in accounts receivable.
  - As receivables and inventories are converted into cash, the loans are then retired.
  - These loans come in three basic forms: single-payment notes, lines of credit, and revolving credit agreements.

Unsecured Sources of Short-Term Loans

- Bank Loans
  - Loan Interest Rates
    - Most banks loans are based on the prime rate of interest which is the lowest rate of interest charged by the nation's leading banks on loans to their most reliable business borrowers.
    - Banks generally determine the rate to be charged to various borrowers by adding a premium to the prime rate to adjust it for the borrowers "riskiness."

Unsecured Sources of Short-Term Loans

- Bank Loans
  - Fixed- and Floating-Rate Loans
    - On a fixed-rate loan, the rate of interest is determined at a set increment above the prime rate and remains at that rate until maturity.
    - On a floating-rate loan, the increment above the prime rate is initially established and is then allowed to float with prime until maturity.
    - Like ARMs, the increment above prime is generally lower on floating rate loans than on fixed-rate loans.

 15-66

Unsecured Sources of Short-Term Loans

- Bank Loans
  - Line of Credit (LOC)
    - A line of credit is an agreement between a commercial bank and a business specifying the amount of unsecured short-term borrowing the bank will make available to the firm over a given period of time.
    - It is usually made for a period of 1 year and often places various constraints on borrowers.
    - Although not guaranteed, the amount of a LOC is the maximum amount the firm can owe the bank at any point in time.

 15-67

Unsecured Sources of Short-Term Loans

- Bank Loans
  - Line of Credit (LOC)
    - In order to obtain the LOC, the borrower may be required to submit a number of documents including a cash budget, and recent (and pro forma) financial statements.
    - The interest rate on a LOC is normally floating and pegged to prime.
    - In addition, banks may impose operating change restrictions giving it the right to revoke the LOC if the firm's financial condition changes.

 15-68

Unsecured Sources of Short-Term Loans

- Bank Loans
  - Line of Credit (LOC)
    - Both LOCs and revolving credit agreements often require the borrower to maintain compensating balances.
    - A compensating balance is simply a certain checking account balance equal to a certain percentage of the amount borrowed (typically 10 to 20 percent).
    - This requirement effectively increases the cost of the loan to the borrower.

Unsecured Sources of Short-Term Loans

- Bank Loans
  - Revolving Credit Agreements (RCA)
    - A RCA is nothing more than a *guaranteed* line of credit.
    - Because the bank guarantees the funds will be available, they typically charge a commitment fee which applies to the unused portion of of the borrowers credit line.
    - A typical fee is around 0.5% of the average unused portion of the funds.
    - Although *more expensive* than the LOC, the RCA is *less risky* from the borrower's perspective.

Unsecured Sources of Short-Term Loans

- Commercial Paper
  - Commercial paper is a short-term, unsecured promissory note issued by a firm with a high credit standing.
  - Generally only large firms in excellent financial condition can issue commercial paper.
  - Most commercial paper has maturities ranging from 3 to 270 days, is issued in multiples of $100,000 or more, and is sold at a discount form par value.
  - Commercial paper is traded in the money market and is commonly held as a marketable security investment.

Unsecured Sources of Short-Term Loans

- International Loans
  - The main difference between international and domestic transactions is that payments are often made or received in a foreign currency
  - A U.S.-based company that generates receivables in a foreign currency faces the risk that the U.S. dollar will appreciate relative to the foreign currency.
  - Likewise, the risk to a U.S. importer with foreign currency accounts payables is that the U.S. dollar will depreciate relative to the foreign currency.

Secured Sources of Short-Term Loans

- Characteristics
  - Although it may reduce the loss in the case of default, from the viewpoint of lenders, collateral does not reduce the riskiness of default on a loan.
  - When collateral is used, lenders prefer to match the maturity of the collateral with the life of the loan.
  - As a result, for short-term loans, lenders prefer to use accounts receivable and inventory as a source of collateral.

Secured Sources of Short-Term Loans

- Characteristics
  - Depending on the liquidity of the collateral, the loan itself is normally between 30 and 100 percent of the book value of the collateral.
  - Perhaps more surprisingly, the rate of interest on secured loans is typically higher than that on a comparable unsecured debt.
  - In addition, lenders normally add a service charge or charge a higher rate of interest for secured loans.

Secured Sources of Short-Term Loans

- Accounts Receivable as Collateral
  - Pledging accounts receivable occurs when accounts receivable are used as collateral for a loan.
  - After investigating the desirability and liquidity of the receivables, banks will normally lend between 50 and 90 percent of the face value of acceptable receivables.
  - In addition, to protect its interests, the lender files a lien on the collateral and is made on a *non-notification* basis (the customer is not notified).

Secured Sources of Short-Term Loans

- Accounts Receivable as Collateral
  - Factoring accounts receivable involves the outright sale of receivables at a discount to a factor.
  - Factors are financial institutions that specialize in purchasing accounts receivable and may be either departments in banks or companies that specialize in this activity.
  - Factoring is normally done on a notification basis where the factor receives payment directly from the customer.

Secured Sources of Short-Term Loans

- Inventory as Collateral
  - The most important characteristic of inventory as collateral is its marketability.
  - Perishable items such as fruits or vegetables may be marketable, but since the cost of handling and storage is relatively high, they are generally not considered to be a good form of collateral.
  - Specialized items with limited sources of buyers are also generally considered not to be desirable collateral.

Secured Sources of Short-Term Loans

- Inventory as Collateral
  - A floating inventory lien is a lenders claim on the borrower's general inventory as collateral.
  - This is most desirable when the level of inventory is stable and it consists of a diversified group of relatively inexpensive items.
  - Because it is difficult to verify the presence of the inventory, lenders generally advance less than 50% of the book value of the average inventory and charge 3 to 5 percent above prime for such loans.

Secured Sources of Short-Term Loans

- Inventory as Collateral
  - A trust receipt inventory loan is an agreement under which the lender advances 80 to 100 percent of the cost of a borrower's relatively expensive inventory in exchange for a promise to repay the loan on the sale of each item.
  - The interest charged on such loans is normally 2% or more above prime and are often made by a manufacturer's wholly-owned subsidiary (captive finance company).
  - Good examples would include GE Capital and GMAC.

Secured Sources of Short-Term Loans

- Inventory as Collateral
  - A warehouse receipt loan is an arrangement in which the lender receives control of the pledged inventory which is stored by a designated agent on the lender's behalf.
  - The inventory may stored at a central warehouse (terminal warehouse) or on the borrower's property (field warehouse).
  - Regardless of the arrangement, the lender places a guard over the inventory and written approval is required for the inventory to be released.
  - Costs run from about 3 to 5 percent above prime.

Using Microsoft® Excel

- The Microsoft® Excel Spreadsheets used in the this presentation can be downloaded from the *Introduction to Finance* companion web site: http://www.awl.com/gitman_madura

Chapter 15

Introduction to Finance
Lawrence J. Gitman
Jeff Madura

End of Chapter

Chapter 16

Introduction to Finance
Lawrence J. Gitman
Jeff Madura

Investment Information and Transactions

Learning Goals

- Review background material on investing.
- Describe the economic, industry, global, and market information sources used to make investment decisions.
- Describe the firm-specific information services used to make investment decisions.
- Identify the main United States and foreign securities exchanges in the United States that facilitate the investment process.
- Describe the types of securities transactions requested by investors and explain how these transactions are accommodated by brokerage firms.

Background on Investing

- Individual Investors
  - Long-term capital gains
  - Short-term capital gains
  - Day traders

Background on Investing

- Institutional Investors
  - Employed by institutions
  - Invest on behalf of others
  - Also called portfolio managers
  - Types of institutional investors include mutual fund portfolio managers and pension fund portfolio managers.

Background on Investing

- Impact of Investment Decisions on Wealth

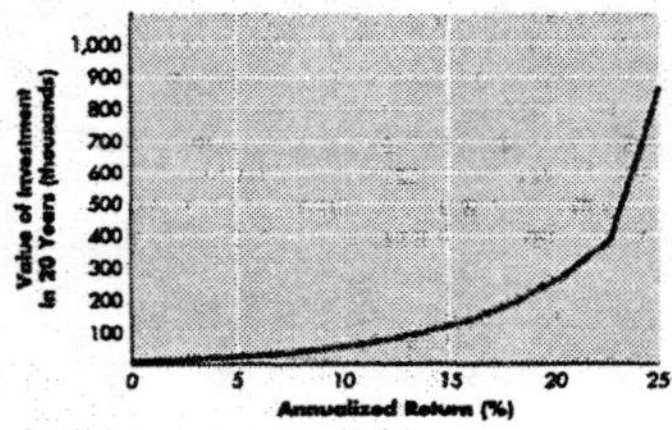

 Figure 16.1

General Information Used to Make Investment Decisions

TABLE 16.1 Sources of Economic Information

Published Sources	
Federal Reserve Bulletin	Provides data on economic conditions, including interest rates, unemployment rates, inflation rates, and money supply. Also provides information about activity in the stock market, bond market, and money markets. Published monthly.
Survey of Current Business	Issued monthly by the Department of Commerce. Provides data on national income and production levels, and employment levels. It also discloses various economic indicators.
Economic Report of the President	Reports the economic conditions over the last year, and provides an economic outlook. Published each January.
Quarterly Financial Report (QFR)	Issued by the Federal Trade Commission. Provides financial statement data for manufacturing companies, including income statements, balance sheets, and various financial ratios.
Federal Reserve Bank publications	Reports on national and regional economic conditions, economic statistics, research reports on specific banking issues, and reports on other economic issues.
Reports by securities firms	Provide economic summaries and outlooks as a service to existing and potential clients.

 Table 16.1 (Panel 1)

General Information Used to Make Investment Decisions

TABLE 16.1 Sources of Economic Information

Online Sources	
Bloomberg	(www.bloomberg.com) Provides economic reports.
Yahoo!	(www.yahoo.com) Provides information about U.S. economic conditions.
Moody's	(www.moodys.com) Provides an economic commentary.
Federal Reserve System	(www.bog.frb.fed.us/) Provides press releases related to the economy and offers economic research.
Investorlinks	(www.investorlinks.com/charts/index.html) Provides an outlook for U.S. gross domestic product, unemployment, inflation, payrolls, and the federal budget deficit.
U.S. Census Bureau	(www.census.gov/econ/www/toc.html) Provides an overview of the U.S. economy.

 Table 16.1 (Panel 2)

General Information Used to Make Investment Decisions

TABLE 16.2 Sources of Industry Information

Published Sources	
Value Line Survey	Provides background on the performance of various industries and offers an industry outlook. Also provides detailed information about various industries, including mean financial statistics among firms in each industry over time. Provides a table with comparative data that corresponds to its analysis of individual firms to facilitate comparison analysis to industry norms.
Standard and Poor's Industry Survey	Provides a detailed summary of several different industries. The summary includes a historical assessment of each industry, as well as statistics, and an outlook for investors who consider investing in that industry.
Standard and Poor's Analysts Handbook	Provides detailed information about various industries, including mean financial statistics (such as some financial ratios) among the firms in each industry over time. This provides investors with an industry norm to which any individual firm's statistics can be compared.
Reports by securities firms	Provide information on the outlook for specific industries to existing and potential clients.
Industry-specific periodicals	Focused on a single industry for those investors or analysts who concentrate their efforts in one industry.

 Table 16.2 (Panel 1)

General Information Used to Make Investment Decisions

TABLE 16.2 Sources of Industry Information

Online Sources	
Investorlinks	(www.investorlinks.com) Contains news articles related to specific industries.
The U.S. Census Bureau	(www.census.gov/econ/www/toc.html) Provides an overview of several broad industry sectors, including construction, mining, retail, and wholesale sectors.
Yahoo!	(www.yahoo.com) Provides stock indexes for various industry sectors.
CNBC	(www.cnbc.com/tickerguide/indices.html) Provides stock indexes for various industry sectors.
Bloomberg	(www.bloomberg.com) Identifies industry movers that, as measured by industry stock indexes, experienced substantial change recently.

 Table 16.2 (Panel 2)

General Information Used to Make Investment Decisions

TABLE 16.3 Sources of Global Information

Published Sources	
International Financial Statistics	Published by the International Monetary Fund. Provides data on exchange rates, interest rates, national income levels, and employment levels for each country.
Financial Times	Provides information about global economic conditions around the world. Published on weekdays in London.
Asian Wall Street Journal	Provides information about economic conditions in Asia. Published weekly.
European Wall Street Journal	Provides information about economic conditions in Europe. Published weekly.
Survey of Current Business	Issued monthly by the Department of Commerce. Provides data on direct foreign investment in the United States and by U.S. firms in foreign countries.
Reports by securities firms	Provide summaries of economic conditions in foreign countries and offers global outlooks to clients.

 Table 16.3 (Panel 1)

General Information Used to Make Investment Decisions

TABLE 16.3 Sources of Global Information

Online Sources	
The Federal Reserve	(www.bog.frb.fed.us/) Provides information on international economic conditions.
Investorlinks	(investorlinks.com/global.html) Provides economic statistics and economic indicators for various countries.
Bloomberg	(www.bloomberg.com) Provides information about international interest rates, exchange rates, and financial markets.
Yahoo!	(www.yahoo.com) Contains news about exchange rate movements and international economic conditions.

 Table 16.3 (Panel 2)

General Information Used to Make Investment Decisions

TABLE 16.4 Sources of Market Information

Published Sources	
The Wall Street Journal	Provides stock market quotations, bond market quotations, money market quotations, and quotations for various derivative securities markets. Includes information about securities markets around the world. Also provides articles that explain recent market conditions. Published on weekdays.
Investor's Business Daily	Provides price quotations on securities and also offers much information about market activity. Published on weekdays.
Barron's	Provides stock market quotations, bond market quotations, money market quotations, and quotations for various derivative security markets. Includes information about securities markets around the world. Also provides articles that explain recent market conditions. Barron's has more information about the markets than the *Wall Street Journal* and is less focused on general news about corporations. Published weekly.
Financial Times	Offers corporate news and investing news from around the world. Provides quotations for various securities markets and derivative securities markets. Published on weekdays in London.
Asian Wall Street Journal	Provides information about economic conditions and securities markets in Asia. Published weekly.
European Wall Street Journal	Provides information about economic conditions and securities markets in Europe. Published weekly.
Reports by securities firms	Provide clients with summaries of existing market conditions and forecasts of future market conditions.

 Table 16.4 (Panel 1)

General Information Used to Make Investment Decisions

TABLE 16.4 Sources of Market Information

Online Services	
Investorlinks	(www.investorlinks.com) Provides a summary of U.S. market conditions and important related news and highlights. A particular Investorlinks web site link (www.investorlinks.com/commentary/index.html) provides market commentary articles related to stock and bond markets.
Bloomberg	(www.bloomberg.com) Provides quotations and commentaries on various markets.
Yahoo!	(www.yahoo.com) Provides quotations for numerous market indexes.

 Table 16.4 (Panel 2)

Firm-Specific Information Used to Make Investment Decisions

- Annual Report
  - Income statement
  - Balance sheet
  - Statement of cash flows

Firm-Specific Information Used to Make Investment Decisions

TABLE 16.5 How Investors Use Balance Sheet and Income Statement Information

Assessment of liquidity	Investors assess a firm's liquidity by estimating various liquidity measures, such as *net working capital*, the *current ratio*, and the *quick ratio*. These measures attempt to measure a firm's ability to cover short-term obligations as they come due. If a firm has difficulty covering its short-term obligations, it may need either to borrow more funds or to sell some of its existing assets to obtain cash. Higher values relative to an industry norm reflect higher degrees of liquidity.
Assessment of efficiency	Investors assess a firm's efficiency by considering various activity ratios that measure the speed at which assets can generate cash. The *inventory turnover* measures the activity of a firm's inventory—how many times a year the inventory "turns over" (is sold). The *average collection period* measures the average age of accounts receivable. The *total asset turnover* measures the efficiency with which a firm uses its assets to generate revenues. Higher values relative to an industry norm reflect higher degrees of efficiency.

 Table 16.5 (Panel 1)

Firm-Specific Information Used to Make Investment Decisions

TABLE 16.5 How Investors Use Balance Sheet and Income Statement Information

Assessment of financial leverage	Investors assess a firm's ability to repay debt by considering its degree of financial leverage. A common measure of financial leverage is the *debt ratio*, which measures the proportion of total assets financed by creditors. A high debt ratio relative to an industry norm reflects a high degree of financial leverage and a high risk of default on future debt payments. An alternative measure of a firm's ability to repay its debt is the *times-interest-earned ratio*, which is the ratio of the firm's earnings before interest and taxes to its interest payments. A higher times-interest-earned ratio relative to an industry norm reflects a greater ability to cover future interest payments.
Profitability	Investors assess a firm's profitability by considering profitability ratios. Some profitability margins are measured as a percentage of sales over a specific period. The *gross profit margin* measures gross profits as a percentage of sales; the *operating profit margin* measures the operating profit as a percentage of sales; and the *net profit margin* measures net profit as a percentage of sales. Other profitability margins are measured as a percentage of balance sheet items. The *return on assets* measures net profit as a percentage of total assets, and the *return on equity* measures net profit as a percentage of the owners' investment in the firm (stockholders' equity). A higher value for all of the profitability measures identified here, relative to an industry norm, reflect high profitability.

Table 16.5 (Panel 2)

Other Financial Reports Used to Make Investment Decisions

- Other Financial Reports
  - 8-K, 9-K, 10-K
  - Security prospectus
  - External publications

Firm-Specific Information Provided by Publications

TABLE 16.6 Sources of Firm-Specific Information

Published Sources	
Standard & Poor's Corporation Records	Provides detailed financial information about each corporation, including selected income statement and balance sheet items, capital structure information, and the history of securities issuances by the corporation.
Standard & Poor's Stock Reports	Provide historical stock price information, balance sheet and income statement information, financial ratios, and an outlook for the future. The summaries of all firms are categorized according to the stock exchange on which their stock is traded.
Standard & Poor's Stock Guide	Provides financial information focused on the stock of a firm, including the proportion of the firm's stock that is held by institutional investors and the range of the stock price.
Standard & Poor's Bond Guide	A monthly publication offering financial information related to bonds that have been issued.
The Outlook	Provides information about existing market and future market conditions. Provides stock index quotations for numerous industries, so that investors can monitor the stock performance of any particular industry or compare an individual firm to a specific industry index. Published weekly by Standard & Poor's Corporation.
Moody's Industrial Manual	Provides detailed financial information about each corporation, including selected income statement and balance sheet items and capital structure information for each firm.
Moody's OTC Manual	Provides detailed financial information for each firm that is traded on the over-the-counter market.
Moody's Bank and Finance Manual	Provides information on firms in financial industries such as banking and insurance.
Value Line Investment Survey	Provides detailed information pulled from financial statements, along with projections of earnings for the future. It also discloses growth rates and measures of the firm's risk.
Reports by securities firms	Provide clients with reports on individual companies that the securities firms monitor.

Table 16.6 (Panel 1)

Firm-Specific Information Provided by Publications

TABLE 16.6 Sources of Firm-Specific Information

Online Sources	
Many firms provide their annual reports on their web sites.	
Report Gallery	(www.reportgallery.com) Provides annual reports for many firms.
Yahoo!	(www.yahoo.com) Provides a stock screener that allows investors to identify stocks that have particular financial characteristics.

Table 16.6 (Panel 2)

Firm-Specific Information Provided by Publications

Figure 16.2 (Panel 1)

Firm-Specific Information Provided by Publications

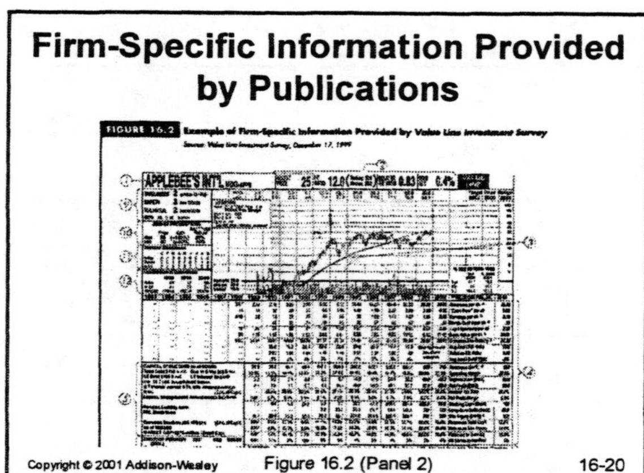

Figure 16.2 (Panel 2)

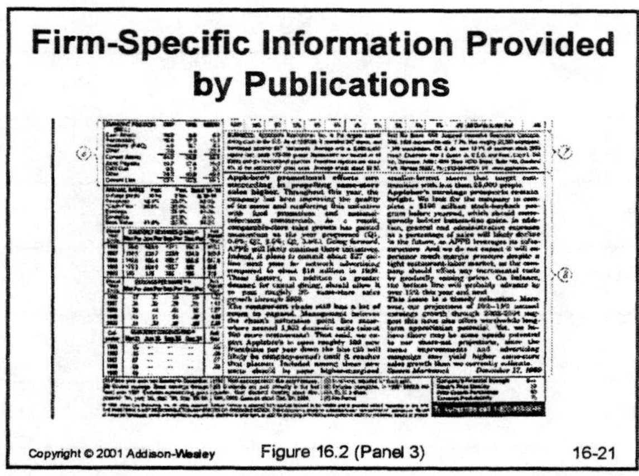

Firm-Specific Information Provided by Publications
Copyright © 2001 Addison-Wesley
Figure 16.2 (Panel 3)
16-21

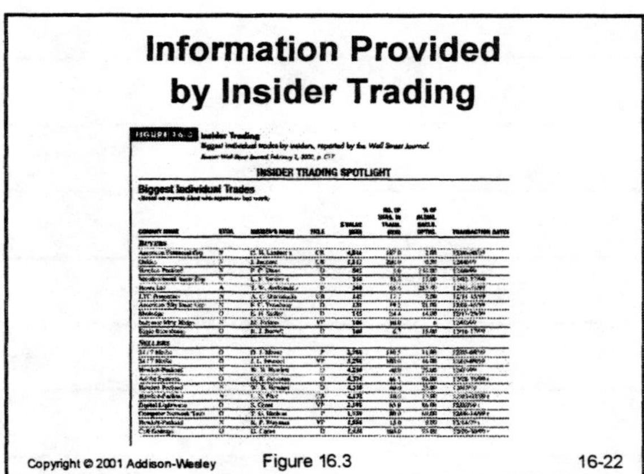

Information Provided by Insider Trading
INSIDER TRADING SPOTLIGHT
Biggest Individual Trades
Copyright © 2001 Addison-Wesley
Figure 16.3
16-22

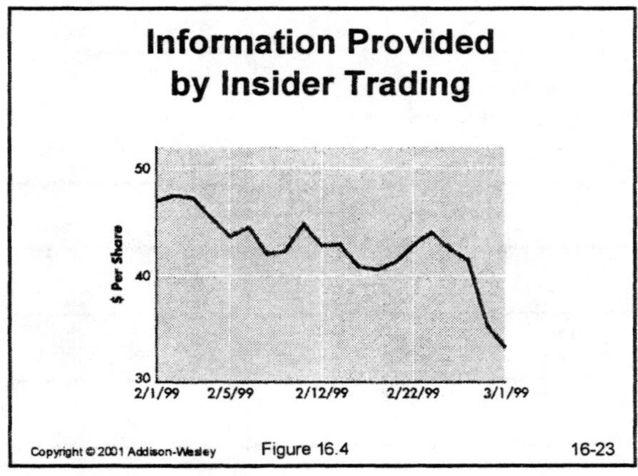

Information Provided by Insider Trading
$ Per Share
50
40
30
2/1/99
2/5/99
2/12/99
2/22/99
3/1/99
Copyright © 2001 Addison-Wesley
Figure 16.4
16-23

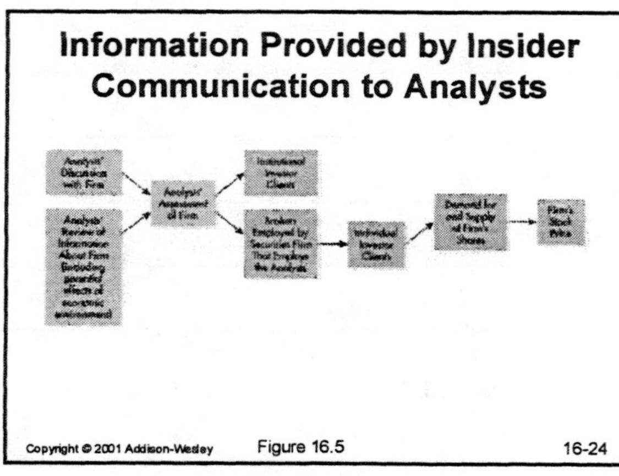

Information Signaled Through a Firm's Financial Decisions

- Dividend Policy
- Earnings Surprises
- Acquisitions
- Secondary Stock Offerings
- Stock Repurchases

Information Provided by Insider Communication to Analysts

$ Per Share
250
200
100
3/25/99
3/29/99
3/31/99
4/5/99

Figure 16.6

Securities Exchanges

- Securities exchanges facilitate the exchange of securities among investors.
- The main organized exchanges are the New York Stock Exchange (NYSE) and American Stock Exchange (AMEX).
- Both facilitate only secondary market transactions.
- The over-the-counter (OTC) market is an intangible securities market that facilitates both primary and secondary market transactions.

Securities Exchanges

- In 1998 the NASDAQ and AMEX merged and is expected to lead to an increase in the use of electronic orders.
- United States investors can invest in foreign stocks by purchasing those listed on foreign stock exchanges.
- United States investors can also invest in foreign stock by purchasing American depository receipts (ADRs) or through mutual funds which specialize in the purchase of foreign stocks.

Investor Transactions

- Market and Limit Orders
  - A market order is an order to buy or sell a stock at the prevailing market price.
  - A limit order is an order to buy a stock at or below a specified price, or to sell a stock at or above a specified price.
  - Limit orders can be for the day, good until canceled, or open (in effect for 6 months).

Investor Transactions

- Use of Technology
  - Technology has increased the speed at which orders are placed and executed.
  - There are now more than 5 million online brokerage accounts at services such as Ameritrade and E*Trade.
  - The typical trading commission on like is between $8 and $20 which is substantially less that what brokerage firms have traditionally charged.
  - The popularity of electronic orders and electronic execution of trades is continuing to grow.

Investor Transactions

- Stop Orders
  - Stop orders are orders to execute a transaction when the stock reaches a specified level.
  - A buy stop order represents an order to buy a stock if the price reaches a specified level (above the prevailing price) to take advantage of subsequent expected increases in price.
  - A sell stop order, on the other hand, is an order to sell a stock if the price reaches a specified level (below the prevailing price) to prevent further losses when prices are falling.

Investor Transactions

- Buying Stock on Margin
  - Buying on margin means that investors use borrowed funds to finance the purchase of securities.
  - Buying on margin allows investors to used financial leverage to magnify their gains (and losses).
  - Margin requirements are regulations imposed by the Federal Reserve on the proportion of invested funds that must be paid in cash.
  - The present margin requirement is that at least 50 percent of the invested funds must be in cash.

Investor Transactions

- Buying Stock on Margin
  - Margin requirements are intended to ensure that investors can cover their position if the value of their investment declines over time.
  - If investors purchase a stock on margin and the value of the stock declines, investors may receive a margin call from their broker, requesting that they put additional funds (maintenance margin) in the margined account.

Investor Transactions

- How Investing on Margin Affects Returns

$$R = \frac{(SP - II + D - LP)}{II}$$

where

R = the return from investing in a stock

SP = the proceeds from selling the stock at the end of the investment period

II = the initial investment of equity funds made by the investor at the beginning of the investment period

D = the dividends received over the investment period

LP = the loan payoff made to the broker after the stock is sold at the end of the investment period.

Investor Transactions

- How Investing on Margin Affects Returns
  - Stan Adams determined that a new Internet stock called Rocket.com is undervalued at its prevailing price of $10 per share. The stock is not expected to pay a dividend. Stan is trying to decide if he should purchase 100 shares with cash, or buy the 100 shares by borrowing half the funds needed. The loan would have a 10% annual interest rate. Stan plans to sell the stock in one year.

Investor Transactions

- How Investing on Margin Affects Returns
  - Stan wants to determine his expected return when paying for his entire investment using (1) 100% of his own funds, (2) borrowing 30% ($300 out of $1000), and (3) borrowing 50% ($500).
  - Stan wants to estimate his return based on two possible outcomes: (1) the stock rises to $14 in one year, and (2) the stock declines to $6 in one year. The results are shown on the following slide.

 16-36

Investor Transactions

- How Investing on Margin Affects Returns

Results If Share Price = $14 at the End of 1 Year:

	Using 100% of Own Funds (Margin = 100%)	Using 30% Borrowed Funds (Margin = 70%)	Using 50% Borrowed Funds (Margin = 50%)
SP	100 shares × $14 = $1,400	100 shares × $14 = $1,400	$100 shares × $14 = $1,400
II	$1,000	$700	$500
LP	$0	$300 + ($300 × 0.10) = $330	$500 + ($500 × 0.10) = $550
R	($1,400 − $1,000)/$1,000 = 40.00%	($1,400 − $700 − $330)/$700 = 52.86%	($1,400 − $500 − $55/$500 = 70%

Results If Share Price = $6 at the End of 1 Year:

	Using 100% of Own Funds (Margin = 100%)	Using 30% Borrowed Funds (Margin = 70%)	Using 50% Borrowed Funds (Margin = 50%)
SP	100 shares × 6 = $600	100 shares × $6 = $600	100 shares × $6 = $600
II	$1,000	$700	$500
LP	$0	$300 + ($300 × 0.10) = $330	$500 + ($500 × 0.10) = $550
R	($600 − $1,000)/$1,000 = −40.00%	($600 − $700 − $330)/$700 = −61.42%	$($600 − $500 − $550)/$500 = −90.00%

 16-37

Investor Transactions

- Short Sales
  - A short sale is the sale of a stock by an investor who does not own the stock.
  - Investors will typically "short a stock" when they believe the stock is overvalued and is likely to decline—hoping to sell high and buy low.
  - To short a stock, an investor must borrow a stock from another investor who owns it, and sell it in the market at the prevailing price.

 16-38

Investor Transactions

- Short Sales
  - The investor has an obligation to later repurchase the stock in the market so that it can be returned to the investor from whom it was borrowed.
  - An investor in a short sale will make a profit from the difference between the original sale price and the subsequent purchase price, less any dividends received.
  - If a stock price rises, the investor in a short sale will have to pay more to repurchase resulting in a loss.

Largest Short Positions

FIGURE 16.7
Largest Short Positions
Data on the largest short positions, reported by the *Wall Street Journal*.
Source: Wall Street Journal, January 24, 2000, p. C21.

Largest Short Positions

Rank	Jan. 14	Dec. 15	Change
NYSE			
1 AT&T	74,321,531	79,641,975	−5,320,444
2 Vodafone (Adr)	66,296,385	71,809,300	−5,512,915
3 America Online	64,305,968	60,848,701	3,457,267
4 Walt Disney-Hldg	61,897,330	61,068,546	828,784
5 Qwest Comm Intl	52,059,751	0	52,059,751
6 Sprint (Pcs)	43,591,236	36,301,743	7,289,493
7 Xerox	38,078,059	36,690,178	1,387,881
8 Lucent Technologies	38,026,314	38,858,872	−832,558
9 Wal Mart Stores	36,955,964	40,812,911	−3,856,947
10 Time Warner (Hldg)	36,631,438	38,997,033	−2,365,595
11 Nortel Networks	32,418,727	29,083,486	3,335,241
12 Columbia/HCA	31,602,801	31,990,328	−387,527
13 EMC	31,474,660	33,079,296	−1,604,636
14 BP Amoco P.L.C.	25,743,088	37,332,356	−11,589,268
15 Kroger	24,878,572	24,210,701	667,871
16 Citigroup	23,792,357	25,614,424	−1,822,067
17 Compaq Computer	23,631,238	22,769,674	861,564
18 Clear Channel Cm.	23,560,660	21,790,898	1,769,762
19 AT&T Liberty (CIA)	23,507,627	25,817,744	−2,310,117
20 Bell Atlantic	21,911,215	20,801,439	1,109,776
AMEX			
1 Nasdaq-100 Trust	23,047,808	27,458,603	−4,410,795
2 StandardandPoors Dp	15,357,657	19,187,459	−3,829,802
3 Trans World Cms	13,071,545	14,839,305	−1,767,760
4 Organogenesis	5,620,804	5,977,627	−356,823
5 Echo Bay Mines Ltd.	5,208,390	4,774,197	434,193

Figure 16.7

Chapter 16

Introduction to Finance
Lawrence J. Gitman
Jeff Madura

End of Chapter

Chapter
17

Introduction to Finance

Lawrence J. Gitman
Jeff Madura

How External Forces Affect a Firm's Value

Learning Goals

- Identify economic conditions that affect a firm's value and explain how those conditions can do so.
- Identify government policies that affect a firm's value and explain how those policies can do so.
- Identify industry conditions that affect a firm's value and explain how those conditions can do so.
- Identify global conditions that affect a firm's value and explain how those conditions can do so.

Economic Factors and a Firm's Value

- Economic Growth
  - Economic growth in the United States is commonly measured as the percentage change in the gross domestic product (GDP).
  - Firms in some industries are more exposed to changes in economic growth (autos, housing).
  - Financial managers must try to anticipate changes in economic growth and estimate the extent to which these changes will affect the firm's cash flows.

Economic Factors and a Firm's Value

- Economic Growth
  - When growth is expected to decline, financial managers reduce production, inventory, new projects, and new capital.
  - The reduction in cash flows from existing and planned new business can cause a firm's value to decline.
  - Investors tend to shift their investments to those firms that are more insulated from changes in economic conditions.

Economic Factors and a Firm's Value

- Interest Rates
  - Changes in interest rates can affect a firm's value in several ways.
  - First, increases in interest rates will raise the cost of borrowing for consumers, thus reducing the demand for a firm's products.
  - Second, increases in interest rates will raise the cost of financing for the firm which adversely affects firm value.
  - Increases in interest rates will also raise investor required rates of return which reduces firm value.

Economic Factors and a Firm's Value

- Interest Rates
  - Firms whose cash flows are most sensitive to interest rate movements are those that commonly sell products on credit.
  - Examples would include auto manufacturers, home builders, boat manufacturers, and appliance manufacturers.

Economic Factors and a Firm's Value

- Inflation
  - Inflation can force the firm to have higher cash outflows as the cost of purchasing supplies and hiring labor rises during periods of high inflation.
  - Some of these higher costs may be offset in whole or in part by rising prices for the firm's products.
  - Inflation can also affect the firm through its impact on interest rates.
  - Higher rates of inflation are normally accompanied by higher interest rates.

Economic Factors and a Firm's Value

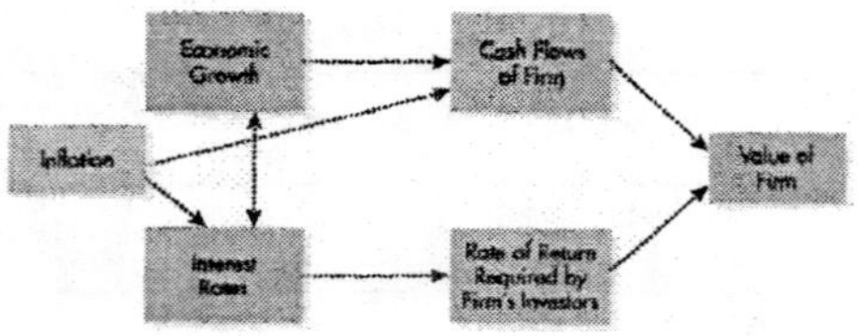

Economic Growth
Cash Flows of Firm
Inflation
Value of Firm
Interest Rates
Rate of Return Required by Firm's Investors

Figure 17.1

Government Effects on Firm Value

- Monetary Policy
  - Monetary policy describes the Federal Reserve's programs for controlling the United States money supply, which influences interest rates.
  - The Fed controls the money supply through (a) open market operations, (b) changes in the discount rate, or (c) changes in reserve requirements.
  - In general, reducing or slowing the growth in money supply increases interest rates which has a negative impact on firm value.

Government Effects on Firm Value

- Fiscal Policy
  - Fiscal policy describes the federal government's programs of taxation and public spending.
  - Expansionary fiscal policy would result from a reduction in the overall level of taxation and/or increase in federal spending.
  - On the other hand, contractionary fiscal policy would result from an increase in taxes or reduction in spending.

 17-9

Government Effects on Firm Value

- Fiscal Policy
  - An increase in personal tax rates will reduce disposable income, thereby reducing the demand for a firm's products; this has a negative affect on firm value.
  - An increase in corporate tax rates reduces firm cash flows directly; this has a negative affect on firm value.
  - Not only can the level of government spending affect firm value, but also the allocation of that spending.

 17-10

Government Effects on Firm Value

- Fiscal Policy
  - For example, fiscal policy that increases military equipment spending will benefit those firms that produce that equipment.
  - Finally, the aggregate level of government debt may also affect firm value.
  - If the level of debt increases, the government demand for funds will put upward pressure on interest rates, increasing the cost of financing for firms.

 17-11

Government Effects on Firm Value

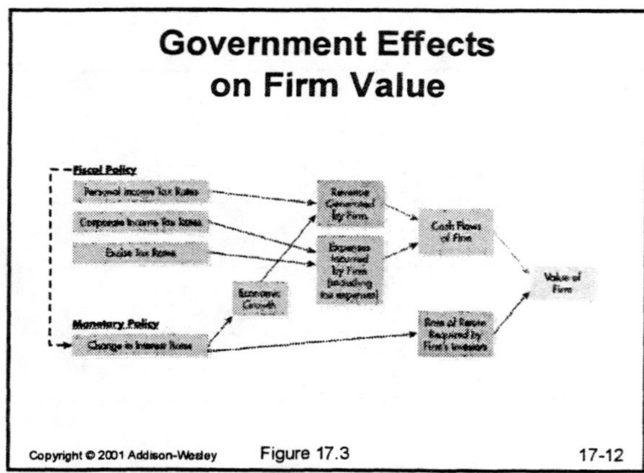

Figure 17.3

How Industry Conditions Affect Firm Value

- Industry Demand
  - Demand for products or services can change in response to changes in consumer preferences.
  - For example, as consumers became more health conscious, the demand for health industry related products (like exercise equipment) grew, while the demand for those that harm health (like cigarettes) declined.

How Industry Conditions Affect Firm Value

- Industry Competition
  - As competition within an industry increases, firms may be adversely affected for two reasons.
  - First, firms may have to reduce prices or face losing customers to competitors.
  - Second, increased competition will reduce revenues as market share declines.
  - In addition, in recent years, technology has intensified the competition in many industries.

How Industry Conditions Affect Firm Value

- Industry Labor and Regulatory Conditions
  - Labor conditions within industries change over time.
  - When an industry becomes unionized, firms within this industry are likely to experience substantially higher cash outflows as wages and benefits increase.
  - Some industries, such as public utilities, are more heavily regulated than others; this has the affect of preventing firm value from reaching its full potential.

How Industry Conditions Affect Firm Value

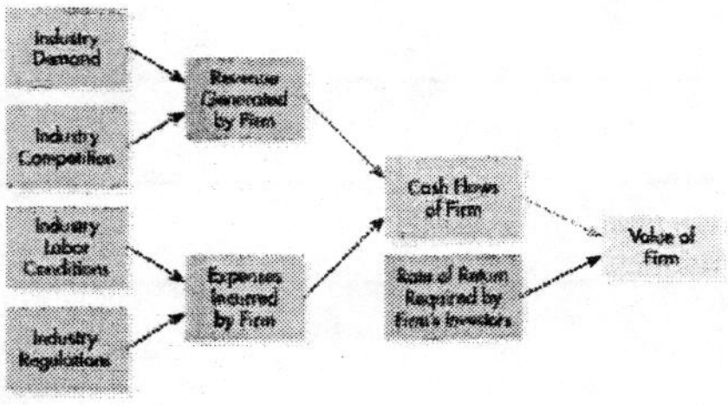

Industry Demand
Industry Competition
Industry Labor Conditions
Industry Regulations
Revenue Generated by Firm
Expenses Incurred by Firm
Cash Flows of Firm
Rate of Return Required by Firm's Investors
Value of Firm

 Figure 17.4

How Global Conditions Affect Firm Value

- Impact of Foreign Economic Growth
  - Firms that operate in more than one country are subject to the economic conditions within the countries that they operate.
  - This can benefit the firm if conditions in the foreign country are strong while the United States economy is weak.
  - Of course, it is also possible that the foreign economy is relatively weaker than the United States economy.
  - Diversifying across countries should generally have a net affect of reducing firm cash flow variability.

How Global Conditions Affect Firm Value

- Impact of Foreign Interest Rates
  - A change in foreign interest rates can affect the cash flows and the cost of financing of a United States firm.
  - If interest rates in foreign countries increases, United States firms that sell in those countries will be adversely affected as consumer demand declines.
  - Finally, if foreign interest rates rise, United States firms that obtain financing in those countries will experience an increase in financing costs.

How Global Conditions Affect Firm Value

- Impact of Exchange Rate Fluctuations
  - One of the main concerns of a firm when it considers engaging in international business is the effect that fluctuations in exchange rates can have on cash flows.
  - Exchange rate risk can affect both exporting and importing firms, firms that engage in direct foreign investment, and even purely domestic firms.

How Global Conditions Affect Firm Value

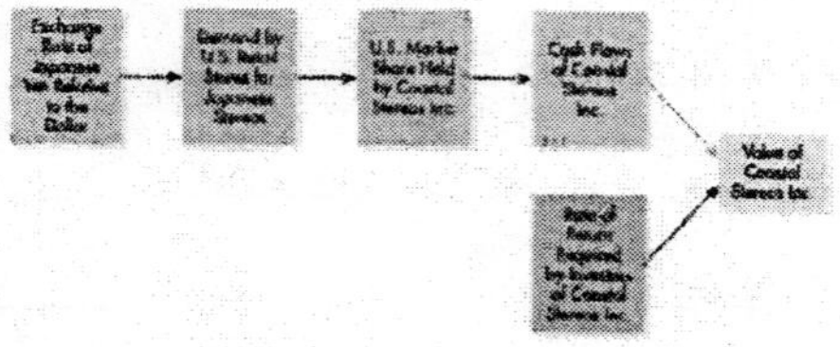

Figure 17.5

How Global Conditions Affect Firm Value

- Impact of Political Risk
  - Firms that are engaged in international business are typically exposed to political risk, or the risk that the host country's political actions will adversely affect the firm's performance.
  - Common examples of political risk include taxes imposed by the host government, government restrictions on fund transfers, consumer attitudes, and, at the extreme, expropriation.

How Global Conditions Affect Firm Value

Figure 17.6

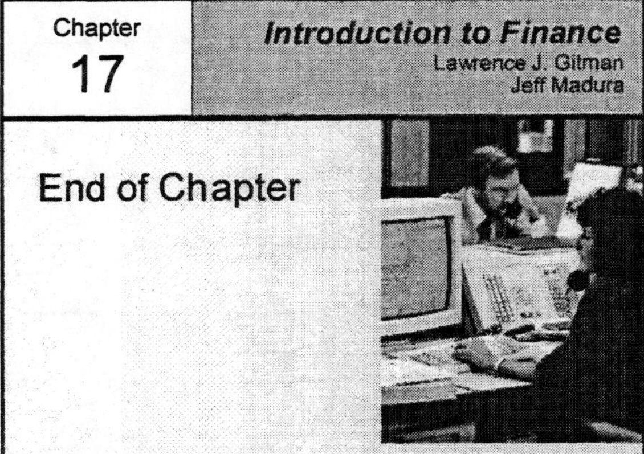

Chapter 18

Introduction to Finance

Lawrence J. Gitman
Jeff Madura

Investing in Stocks

Learning Goals

- Explain how stocks can be valued using valuation models that are alternatives to the dividend discount model.
- Explain the valuation of the stock market.
- Describe the valuation and performance of initial public offering (IPO) stocks.
- Identify benchmarks commonly used for assessing investment performance.
- Describe the forms of stock market efficiency.
- Describe the valuation, performance, measurement, and efficiency of foreign stocks.

Alternative Stock Valuation Models

- The Basic Stock Valuation Equation
  - Recall from Chapter 7, the basic stock valuation method (also referred to as the dividend discount model) can be expressed as:

$$V_0 = \frac{CF_1}{(1+k)^1} + \frac{CF_2}{(1+k)^2} + \cdots + \frac{CF_n}{(1+k)^n}$$

where

V_0 = value of the asset at time zero
CF_t = cash flow *expected* at the end of year t
k = appropriate required return (discount rate)
n = relevant time period

  - Unfortunately, this model is not directly applicable to valuing firms that have low or zero dividends—so alternative methods must be used.

Alternative Stock Valuation Models

- P/E Multiples
  - This approach is popular because many investors believe earnings are a good proxy for a firm's cash flows.
  - A firm's stock can be valued using the P/E method by multiplying the industry average P/E ratio by the firm's expected earnings.

Firm's stock price per share = (Expected earnings of firm per share) × (Mean industry P/E ratio)
= $4 × 12
= $48

Alternative Stock Valuation Models

- P/E Multiples
  - Critical to this approach is the determination of a firm's forecasted earnings.
  - Unfortunately, it is not uncommon for these forecasts to be off by as much as 20 to 40 percent.
  - Earnings can be forecast using outside sources (Value Line), or can be forecast directly using pro forma income statements.
  - This is demonstrated on the following slide.

Alternative Stock Valuation Models

- P/E Multiples

TABLE 18.1 Income Statement for Stream Inc. Example (in thousands)

	This Year	Next Year	Explanation
Sales revenue	$6,000	$6,600	10% growth
Less: Cost of goods sold	3,000	3,300	50% of sales revenue
Gross profits	3,000	3,300	
Less: Operating expenses	2,000	2,080	4% increase
Operating profits	1,000	1,220	
Less: Interest expense	300	300	no change
Net profits before taxes	700	920	
Less: Taxes	210	276	30% tax rate
Net profits after taxes	490	644	

 Table 18.1

Alternative Stock Valuation Models

- P/E Multiples

$$\text{Forecasted EPS} = \frac{\text{Forecasted earnings}}{\text{Number of shares outstanding}}$$

$$= \frac{656{,}000{,}000}{280{,}000{,}000}$$

$$= \$2.34$$

$$\text{Value of Stream's stock} = \text{Forecasted EPS} \times \text{Industry P/E ratio}$$

$$= \$2.34 \times 20$$

$$= \$46.80$$

Alternative Stock Valuation Models

- P/E Multiples
  - Limitations of applying P/E multiples include the following:
    - Uncertainty surrounding the proper earnings forecast.
    - Uncertainty surrounding the proper P/E multiple (see Table 18.2 on the following slide).
    - P/E multiple is not applicable to firms with negative earnings.

Alternative Stock Valuation Models

- P/E Multiples

TABLE 18.2 P/E Ratios and Other Information About Large Firms in the Computer Industry (as of March 2000)

Firm	Price Per Share	Reported EPS	P/E Ratio	Dividend Yield (Annual Dividend 4 Stock Price)
Apple Computer	$122.38	$3.69	33.16	0%
Compaq Computer	28.12	.32	88	.36%
Dell Computer	46.00	.61	75	0
Hewlett-Packard	146.44	3.19	45.90	.64
Sun Microsystems	96.44	.77	125.25	0
Unisys	26.94	1.63	16.53	0

Table 18.2

Alternative Stock Valuation Models

- Book Value Multiples
  - A book value multiple is the market value of the firm's common stock in relation to (as a multiple of) the book value of the firm's common stock as shown in the financial statements.
  - The market/book (M/B) ratio is the market value per share dividend by the book value per share and can be used for valuation purposes as shown below:

Firm's stock price per share
= (Book value of firm per share) × (Mean industry M/B ratio)
= ($10) × (5.0)
= $50

Alternative Stock Valuation Models

- Book Value Multiples
  - The M/B ratio is subject to error if an improper M/B is applied.
  - A second problem with this approach is that the book value of a firm does not reflect relevant information such as the firm's potential for growth.
  - Investors may adjust the industry M/B ratio for firms differences.
  - However, these adjustments are also subject to error.

Alternative Stock Valuation Models

- Revenue Multiples
  - A common revenue multiple used for valuing a firm's stock is the price/revenue (P/R) ratio, which is the ratio of the share price to a stock's revenue per share.

Firm's stock price per share
= (Expected revenues of firm per share) × (Mean industry P/R ratio)
= ($40) × (2.0)
= $80

  - Unfortunately, the P/R ratio generally suffers from the same shortcomings as the M/B ratio.

Alternative Stock Valuation Models

- Revenue Multiples

TABLE 18.3 Comparison of Multiples Used to Value Stocks

Method	Information Needed for Firm Being Valued	Information Needed for Comparable Firms
Price/earnings multiple	Forecast of annual earnings per share	Mean ratio of the stock price relative to annual earnings per share
Book value multiple	Book value	Mean ratio of the stock price relative to book value per share
Revenue multiple	Revenue	Mean ratio of the stock price relative to the annual revenue

 Table 18.3

Alternative Stock Valuation Models

- Valuation During the Recent Market Run-Up
  - Explanations based on the dividend discount model
  - Explanations based on the speculative-bubble theory

Valuation and Performance of IPO Stocks

- Valuation
- Performance

Stock Performance Benchmarks for Investors

- Market Indexes
  - Dow Jones Industrial Average
  - Standard & Poor's 500
  - New York Stock Exchange Index
  - Nasdaq Composite
- Sector Indexes
- Stock Price Quotations

Stock Quotations

Figure 18.2 (Panel 1)

Stock Quotations

FIGURE 18.2
Stock Quotations
Selected stock quotations, reported by the *Wall Street Journal*.

Figure 18.2 (Panel 2)

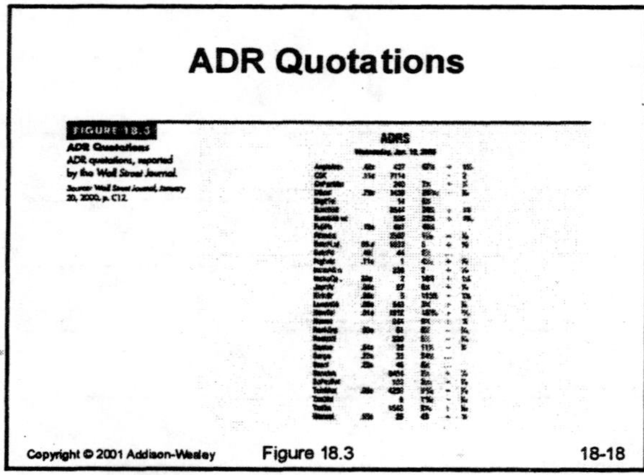

Stock Market Data Bank

FIGURE 18.4
Stock Market Data Bank
Data on the stock market, reported by the *Wall Street Journal*.
Source: *Wall Street Journal*, January 21, 2000, p. C2.

STOCK MARKET DATA BANK 1/20/00

Figure 18.4 (Panel 1)

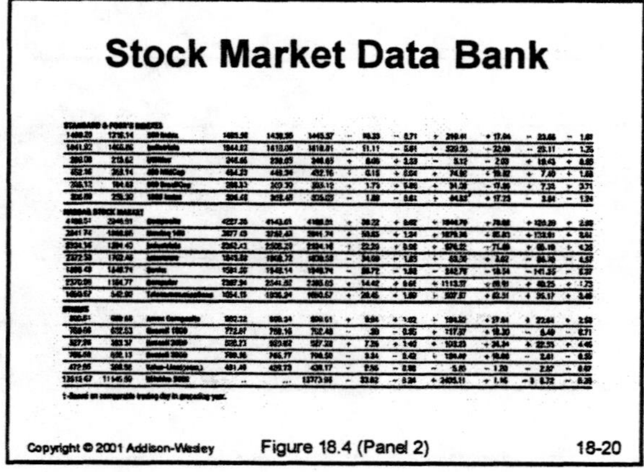

Stock Market Efficiency

- Forms of Efficiency

TABLE 18.4 Comparison of Forms of Efficiency

Form of Efficiency	Description	Type of Information Used to Test Whether Efficiency Exists
Weak-form	Stock prices reflect all market-related information.	Historical stock-price movements, and trading volume.
Semistrong-form	Stock prices reflect all publicly available information.	Analyst recommendations.
Strong-form	Stock prices reflect all information.	Inside information.

 Table 18.4

Stock Market Efficiency

- Evidence of Inefficiency
  - January effect
  - Monday and weekend effects
  - Size effect
  - Price/earnings effect

Stock Market Efficiency

- Limitations on Capitalizing on Price Discrepancies
  - Trading commissions
  - Tax effects
  - Relationships are not applicable to all firms

Foreign Stocks

- Valuing Foreign Stocks
  - Dividend discount model
  - Price/earnings (P/E) method
- Foreign Stock Performance Benchmarks
- Foreign Stock Market Efficiency

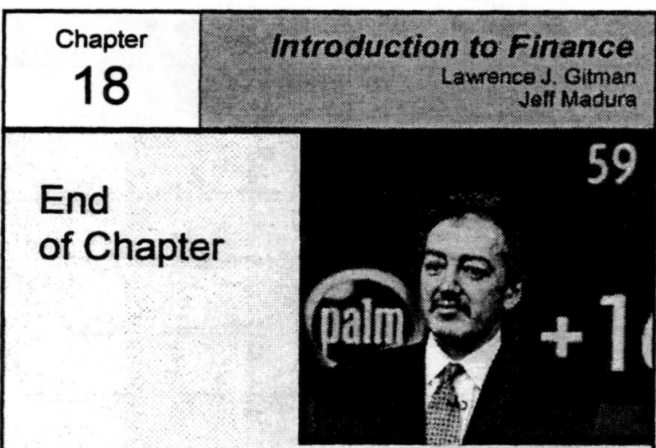

Chapter
18
Introduction to Finance
Lawrence J. Gitman
Jeff Madura
End
of Chapter
59
palm

Chapter 19

Introduction to Finance

Lawrence J. Gitman
Jeff Madura

Investing in Bonds

Learning Goals

- List the different types of bonds.
- Explain how investors use bond quotations.
- Describe how yields and returns are measured for bonds.
- Describe the risks of investing in bonds.
- Identify the factors that affect bond prices over time.
- Describe the strategies commonly used for investing in bonds.

Forms of Debt

- Bearer Bonds
  - Bearer bonds are often referred to as coupon bonds because they are not registered to any particular person.
  - The coupons are submitted twice a year and the authorized bank pays the interest.
  - For instance, a twenty year $1,000 bond paying 8% interest would have 40 coupons for $40 each. Bearer bonds can be used like cash. They are highly negotiable. There are still many in circulation. However, the Tax Reform Act of 1982 ended the issuance of bearer bonds.

Forms of Debt

- Registered Bonds
  - Today, bonds are sold in a fully registered form. They come with your name already on them. Twice a year, you receive a check for the interest. At maturity, the registered owner receives a check for the principal.
  - A partially registered bond is a cross between a registered bond and a coupon bond. The bond comes registered to you; however, it has coupons attached which you send in for payment.

Treasury Bonds

- Treasury bonds are issued by the federal government and are perceived to be free from default risk.
- Some Treasury bonds are stripped, splitting the bonds into a coupon security and a principal security.
- An inflation indexed Treasury bond is a bond whose coupon rate is lower than that of traditional bonds but whose principal value changes semiannually in response to changes in the inflation rate.

Municipal Bonds

- Municipal bonds are issued by state and local government agencies.
- Municipal bonds are particularly attractive because the income earned on "munis" is exempt from federal taxes.
- Municipal bonds with lower quality ratings generally have higher expected returns.

Federal Agency Bonds

- Federal agency bonds are bonds issued by federal agencies.
- Agency bonds are unlike Treasury bonds in that they are not guaranteed by the United States Treasury.
- Examples of agency issues include Ginnie Mae bonds, Freddie Mac bonds, and Fannie Mae bonds.

Corporate Bonds

- Corporate bonds are debt securities issued by large firms.
- Investors lend money to the corporation in exchange for a specified promised amount of (coupon) interest income.
- Most bonds are issued with face values of $1,000 and maturities of 10 to 30 years.
- At the end of the bond term, investors receive the face value of the bond.

Corporate Bonds

- Investors who are willing to tolerate more risk have the opportunity to purchase bonds with much higher expected returns.
- In particular, they may consider junk bonds, which are corporate bonds that are below investment grade and are perceived to have a high degree of default risk but that pay higher returns than better-quality corporate debt.

International Bonds

- International bonds are bonds issued by international governments or corporations.
- International bonds are commonly denominated in a foreign currency so that the coupon and principal payments must be converted into dollars which can lead to unanticipated gains or losses.
- International bonds are exposed to many of the same risks that are present in domestic bonds, but have an additional exchange rate risk component.

Bond Quotations

FIGURE 19.1

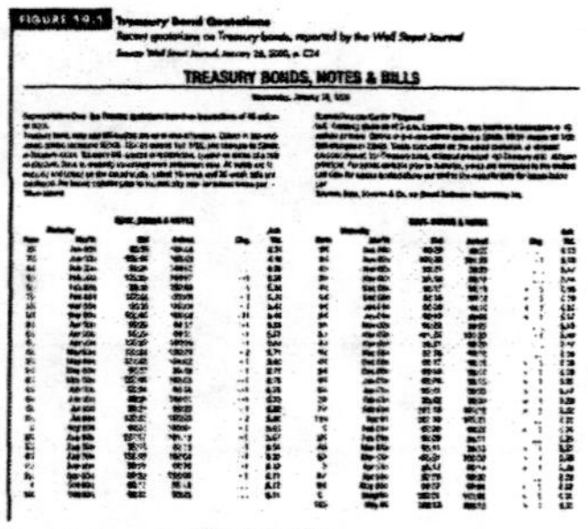

TREASURY BONDS, NOTES & BILLS

Figure 19.1

Bond Quotations

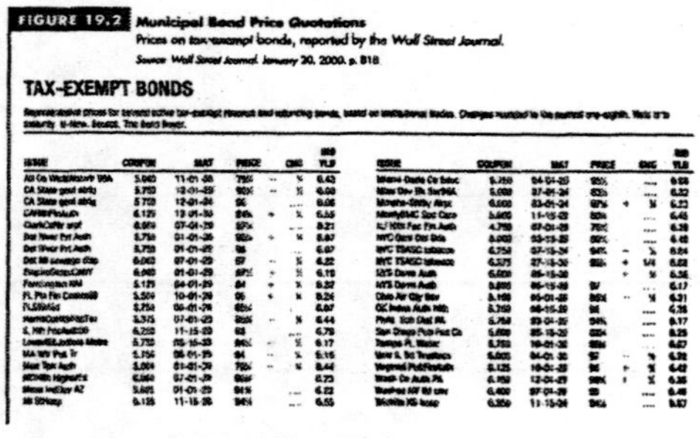

FIGURE 19.2 Municipal Bond Price Quotations
Prices on tax-exempt bonds, reported by the Wall Street Journal.
Source: Wall Street Journal, January 20, 2000, p. B18

TAX-EXEMPT BONDS

Figure 19.2

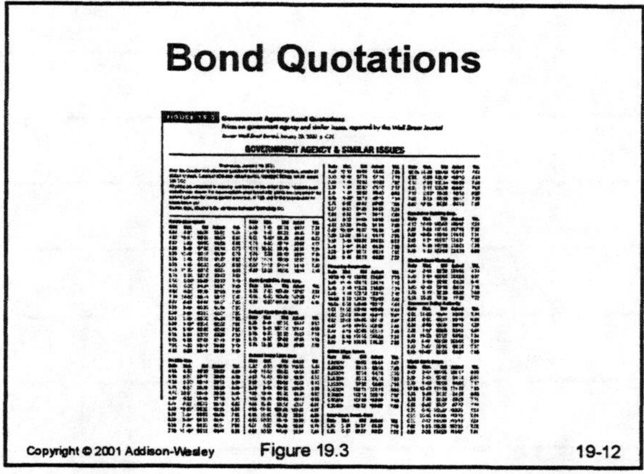
Bond Quotations
Copyright © 2001 Addison-Wesley
Figure 19.3
19-12

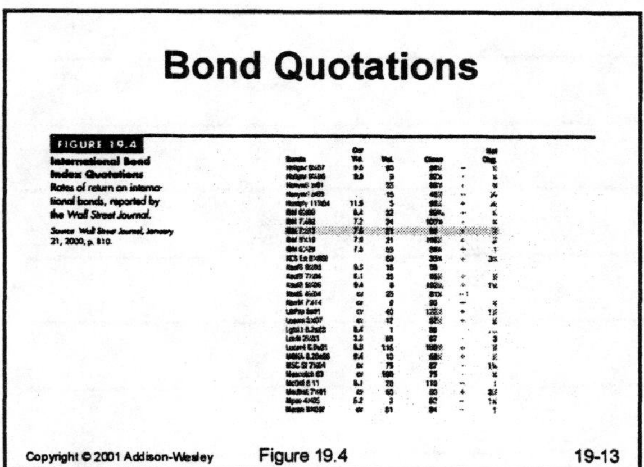
Bond Quotations
FIGURE 19.4
International Bond Index Quotations
Rates of return on international bonds, reported by the Wall Street Journal.
Source: Wall Street Journal, January 21, 2000, p. B10.
Copyright © 2001 Addison-Wesley
Figure 19.4
19-13

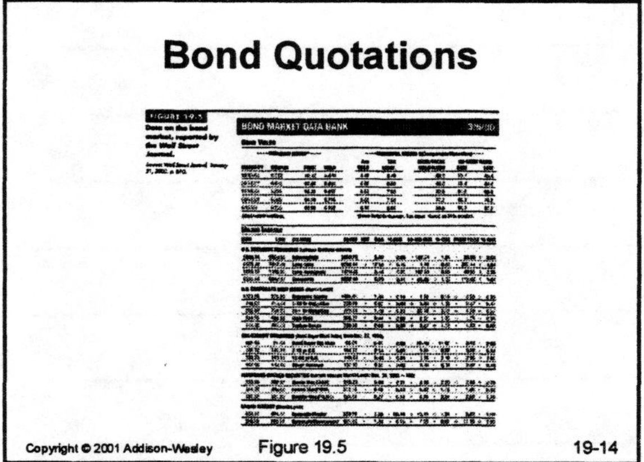
Bond Quotations
BOND MARKET DATA BANK
Copyright © 2001 Addison-Wesley
Figure 19.5
19-14

Bond Quotations

FIGURE 19.6

Corporate Bond Quotations

Selected bond quotations, reported by the *Wall Street Journal*.

Source: Wall Street Journal, January 21, 2000, p. C6

Total Rates of Return of International Bonds

In percent, based on J.P. Morgan Government Bond Index, Dec. 31, 1987 = 100

	LOCAL CURRENCY TERMS					U.S. DOLLAR TERMS				
	INDEX VALUE	1 DAY	1 MO	3 MOS	SINCE 12/31	INDEX VALUE	1 DAY	1 MO	3 MOS	SINCE 12/31
Japan	198.96	− 0.12	0.00	+ 0.50	− 0.41	229.55	+ 0.16	− 2.35	+ 0.69	− 2.38
Britain	332.34	− 0.29	− 2.44	− 1.03	− 1.69	280.48	+ 0.20	− 0.20	− 0.11	− 0.89
Germany	230.07	0.03	0.88	+ 0.73	0.73	178.21	0.06	0.77	3.89	0.01
France	281.64	− 0.04	− 1.15	+ 0.72	− 0.83	238.67	− 0.08	− 1.04	− 5.64	− 0.16
Canada	303.62	− 0.14	− 1.08	+ 0.75	− 1.08	277.87	+ 0.26	+ 1.28	+ 3.18	− 0.73
Netherlands	223.71	0.03	0.81	+ 0.84	− 0.79	188.56	0.06	0.40	5.58	0.07
Euro	288.12	+ 0.01	− 0.35	+ 1.84	+ 0.21	227.87	− 0.02	+ 0.46	− 5.35	+ 0.93
Global-a	280.58	− 0.08	− 0.70	− 0.89	− 0.60	235.80	+ 0.01	− 0.34	− 1.89	− 0.87
EMBI + -b	173.32	− 0.03	+ 0.70	+ 10.81	− 0.50	173.92	− 0.03	+ 0.70	+ 10.81	− 0.80

a-18 int'l gov. markets b-external-currency emerging mkt. debt, Dec. 31, 1993 = 100.

Figure 19.6

Bond Yields and Returns

- A bond's yield to maturity is the annual rate of interest that is paid by the issuer to the bondholder over the life of the bond.
- A bond's holding period return is the return from investment in a bond that is held for a period of time less than the life of the bond.
- Holding period returns for periods other than one year can be annualized for comparison.

Bond Yields and Returns

$$HPR_t = \frac{Coup + P_t - P_{t-1}}{P_{t-1}}$$

where

HPR_t = return on the bond during period t
$Coup$ = coupon payments received during the time period from the end of period $t - 1$ to the end of period t
P_t = price of the bond at the end of period t
P_{t-1} = price of the bond at the end of period $t - 1$

Bond Yields and Returns

- Six months ago Pat Bacavis purchased a bond with a par value of \$1,000,000 and a 7% coupon rate. She received \$35,000 in coupon payments over the last six months. She paid \$990,000 for the bonds and just sold them for \$970,000. The holding period can be calculated as follows:

$$HPR_t = \frac{Coup + P_t - P_{t-1}}{P_t - 1}$$

$$= \frac{\$35{,}000 + \$970{,}000 - \$990{,}000}{\$990{,}000}$$

$$= \underline{\underline{0.0152, \text{ or } 1.52\%}}$$

Bond Yields and Returns

- The expected holding period return [*E*(*HPR*)] is the projected value for the return on a bond over a particular holding period.

$$E(HPR) = \frac{Coup + E(P_t) - P_{t-1}}{P_{t-1}}$$

Bond Yields and Returns

- Lenz Insurance Company considers purchasing corporate bonds that have a par value of \$1,000,000 and a coupon interest rate of 8%. The prevailing price of the bonds is \$980,000. Lenz expects to sell the bonds in the secondary market one year from now for \$995,000. The *E*(*HPR*) can be calculated as follows:

$$E(HPR) = \frac{Coup + E(P_t) - P_{t-1}}{P_{t-1}}$$

$$= \frac{\$80{,}000 + \$995{,}000 - \$980{,}000}{\$980{,}000}$$

$$= 0.0969, \text{ or } 9.69\%$$

Bond Yields and Returns

- The holding period returns on international bonds must account for the exchange rate fluctuations over the holding period.
  - Stetson Bank of the United States considers investing in Canadian Treasury bonds because the yield to maturity offered on those bonds exceeds that of U.S. Treasury bonds. The prevailing price of the bonds is C\$100,000, the coupon rate is 9%, and the interest of \$9,000 (.09 × \$100,000) is to be paid at year end. Stetson plans to hold the bonds for 1 year and sell them for C\$100,000. The Canadian dollar is presently worth \$.60, but Stetson expects it to appreciate to \$.66 by year end. Based on this information, calculate the *E*(*HPR*).

Bond Yields and Returns

$$\text{Dollar value of coupon received at end of period Coup} = C\$9{,}000 \times \$.66 = \$5{,}940$$

$$\text{Dollar price paid at beginning of period } (P_t - 1) = C\$100{,}000 \times \$.60 = \$60{,}000$$

$$\text{Dollar price received at end of period } (P_t) = C\$100{,}000 \times \$.66 = \$66{,}000$$

$$E(HPR) = \frac{Coup = E(P_t) - P_{t-1}}{P_t - 1}$$

$$= \$5{,}940 + \$66{,}000 - \$60{,}000 \backslash \$60{,}000$$

$$= 0.1990, \text{ or } 19.9\%$$

Bond Yields and Returns

- Stetson is subject to the risk that the exchange rate of the Canadian dollar will weaken over the holding period. For example, assume that Stetson recognizes that under specific economic conditions, the Canadian dollar would depreciate over the year and would be valued at \$.56 by the end of the year. The *E*(*HPR*) is:

$$\text{Dollar value of coupon received at end of period Coup} = C\$9{,}000 \times \$.56 = \$5{,}040$$

$$\text{Dollar price paid at beginning of period } (P_{t-1} = 1) = C\$100{,}000 \times \$.60 = \$60{,}000$$

$$\text{Dollar price received at end of period } (P_t) = C\$100{,}000 \times \$.56 = \$56{,}000$$

$$= \frac{\$5{,}040 + \$56{,}000 - \$60{,}000}{\$60{,}000}$$

$$= 0.0173, \text{ or } 1.73\%$$

Bond Risk

TABLE 19.1 Exposure of Bonds to Various Types of Risk

Type of Risk	Description
Price risk	The risk that the bond's price will decline. The primary force behind a decline in bond prices is an increase in interest rates, bus this type of risk is also referred to as *interest rate risk*.
Default risk	The risk that investors will *not* recieve the remaining coupon interest and principal payments that they are due. The default risk is related to the issuer's financial condition.
Reinvestment rate risk	Reflects the uncertainty surrounding the return that investors can earn when reinvesting the coupon interest payments or principal they receive from investing in bonds.
Purchasing power risk	The risk that the purchasing power of the steady stream of income provided over time through fixed coupon interest payments will be eroded by inflation. In the late 1990s, purchasing power actually increased, because inflation remained very low. However, given the long-term maturities of bonds, investors should recognize that purchasing power can weaken over time.
Call risk (prepayment risk)	The risk that a bond with a call feature will be called before maturity. Issuers commonly call their bonds when interest rates have declined and new bonds can be reissued with a lower coupon interest rate. When bonds are called, investors do not benefit from the decline in interest rates as much as if they were able to retain the bonds or sell them in the secondary market.
Liquidity risk	The risk that a bond may not be easily sold at their current price in the secondary market. The bonds issued by well-known firms tend to have low liquidity risk. Bonds issued by firms that are not well known do not always have an active secondary market, and investors may have to sell these bonds at a lower price to attract investors.

 Table 19.1

Bond Risk

- How maturity affects bond price sensitivity
- How the coupon interest rate affects bond price sensitivity

Factors that Affect Bond Prices Over Time

- Factors that Affect the Risk-Free Rate
  - The Fed's monetary policy
  - Impact of inflation
  - Impact of economic growth
- Factors that Affect the Default Risk Premium:
  - Change in economic conditions
  - Change in a firm's financial conditions
- Bond Market Indicators
  - Indicators of inflation
  - Indicators of economic growth
  - Indicators of a firm's financial condition

Bond Investment Strategies

- A passive strategy is a strategy in which investors establish a diversified portfolio of bonds and maintain the portfolio for a long period of time.
- A matching strategy is a strategy in which investors estimate future cash outflows and choose bonds whose coupon or principal payments will cover the projected cash outflows.
- A laddered strategy is a strategy in which investors evenly allocate funds invested in bonds in each of several different maturity classes to minimize interest rate sensitivity.

Bond Investment Strategies

- A barbell strategy is a strategy in which investors allocate funds into bonds with short-term and long-term, but few or no intermediate-term maturities.
- An interest rate strategy is a strategy in which investors allocate funds to capitalize on interest rate forecasts and revise their portfolio in response to changes in interest rate expectations.

Chapter 19

Introduction to Finance

Lawrence J. Gitman
Jeff Madura

End of Chapter

Chapter 20

Introduction to Finance

Lawrence J. Gitman
Jeff Madura

Mutual Funds and Asset Allocation

Learning Goals

- Describe the operations of stock mutual funds, and explain how these funds are used by investors.
- Describe the operations of bond mutual funds, and explain how these funds are used by investors.
- Describe the operations of money market mutual funds, and explain how these funds are used by investors.
- Explain the meaning of asset allocation and the factors that influence a particular investor's asset allocation decision.

Stock Mutual Funds

- A stock mutual fund is an investment company that sells shares to individuals and pools the proceeds to invest in stocks.
- Mutual funds are popular because they enable individual investors to hold diversified portfolios of stocks with a small investment.
- In addition, they are managed by professional portfolio managers who specialize in making investment decisions.

Stock Mutual Funds

- How Stock Mutual Funds Operate
  - Each mutual fund is managed by professional managers who make decisions about which securities to select.
  - On some occasions, funds with large stakes in particular stocks will try to influence the management of poorly performing firm's rather than sell them.
  - The net asset value (NAV) is the current market value per share of the assets in a stock mutual fund.

Stock Mutual Funds

- How Stock Mutual Funds Operate
  - The NAV is calculated as the market value of all fund assets dividend by the number of shares outstanding.
  - When the prices of stocks within the mutual fund increase, so does the mutual fund's NAV.
  - Mutual fund investors can experience gains from three sources: increases in NAV, dividend distributions from companies within the fund, and capital gains generated by selling stocks within the fund for profit.

Stock Mutual Funds

- How Stock Mutual Funds Operate

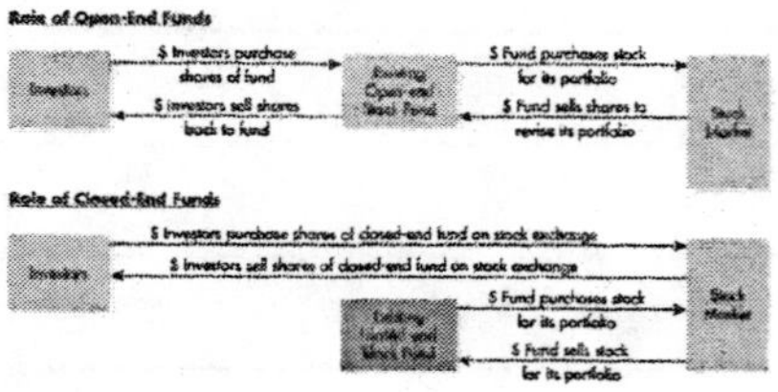

Figure 20.1

Stock Mutual Funds

- How Stock Mutual Funds Operate
  - Load funds charge fees or commissions to investors who invest in the fund while no-load funds do not.
  - More than half of all mutual funds charge 12b-1 fees which cover marketing and distributions costs.
  - These 12b-1 fees are limited to .25 percent for mutual funds designated as no-load funds.
  - There is currently no evidence that load funds outperform no-load funds.

Stock Mutual Funds

- How Stock Mutual Funds Operate
  - All mutual funds incur annual expenses, including administrative expenses, portfolio management fees, and trading commissions.
  - These expenses vary substantially among funds. And can be measured by the expense ratio which is equal to the annual expenses divided by the NAV.
  - Evidence suggests that mutual funds with lower expense ratios outperform those with higher ratios.

Stock Mutual Funds

- Fund Investment Objectives
  - Growth funds
  - Capital appreciation funds
  - Internet funds
  - Income funds
  - International and global funds
  - Index funds

Open-End Mutual Fund Quotations

FIGURE 20.2
Open-End Mutual Fund Quotations
Prices on open-end mutual funds, reported by the *Wall Street Journal.*
Source: *Wall Street Journal,* January 21, 2000, p. C20.

Copyright © 2001 Addison-Wesley | Figure 20.2 (Panel 1) | 20-9

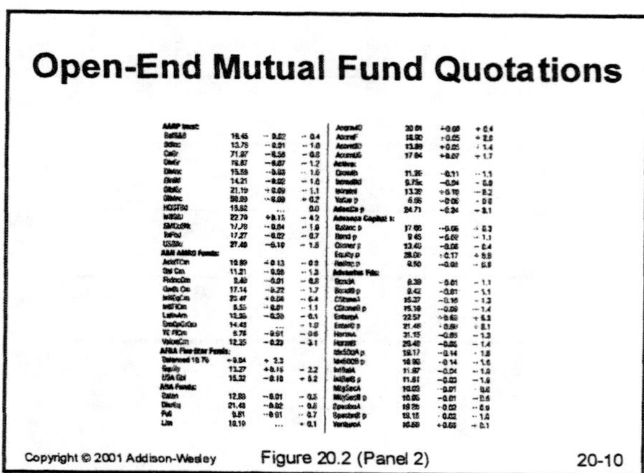

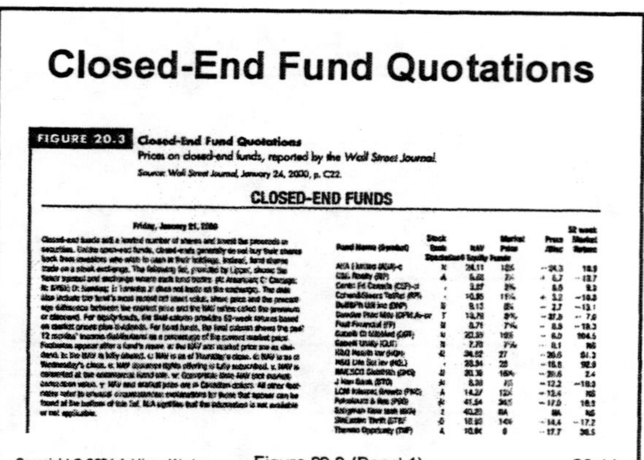

Closed-End Fund Quotations

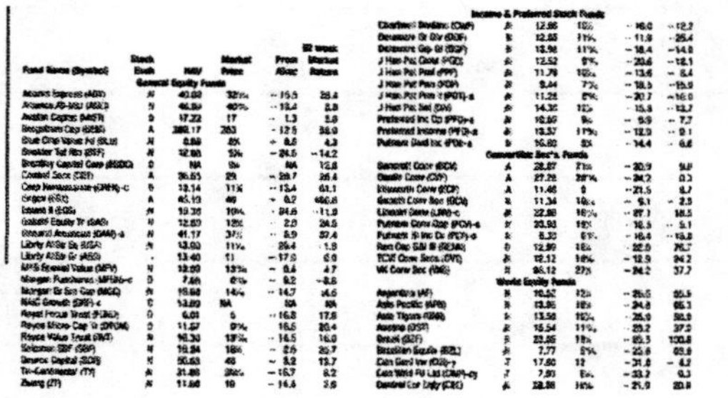

Fund Name (Symbol)	Stock Exch	NAV	Market Price	Prem/Disc	52 week Market Return
General Equity Funds					
Adams Express (ADX)	N	40.02	32[illegible]	-15.5	28.4
Alliance All-Mkt (AMO)	N	46.84	40[illegible]	-13.4	2.8
Avalon Capital (MST)	O	17.22	17	-1.3	2.8
Bergstrom Cap (BEM)	A	288.17	253	-12.5	38.0
Blue Chip Value Fd (BLU)	N	8.88	8[illegible]	[illegible] 8.6	4.3
Boulder Tot Rtn (BIF)	N	12.88	9[illegible]	-24.5	-14.2
Brantley Capital Corp (BBDC)	O	NA	9[illegible]	NA	12.8
Central Secs (CET)	A	36.65	29	-20.7	26.4
Corp Renaissance (CREN)-c	O	13.14	11[illegible]	-13.4	61.1
Engex (EGX)	A	45.13	49	+ 8.2	466.8
Equus II (EQS)	A	19.36	10[illegible]	-24.6	-11.9
Gabelli Equity Tr (GAB)	N	12.83	12[illegible]	2.0	24.5
General American (GAM)-a	N	41.17	37[illegible]	-8.9	27.4
Liberty AllStr Eq (USA)	N	13.03	11[illegible]	-26.4	1.8
Liberty AllStr Gr (ASG)	-	13.40	11	-17.9	6.9
MFS Special Value (MFV)	N	12.00	13[illegible]	- 0.4	4.7
Morgan FunShares (MFUN)-c	O	7.66	6[illegible]	- 9.2	-8.8
Morgan Gr Sm Cap (MGC)	N	16.68	14[illegible]	-14.7	14.6
NAIC Growth (GRF)-c	C	13.89	NA	NA	NA
Royal Focus Trust (FUND)	O	6.01	5	-16.8	17.8
Royce Micro-Cap Tr (OTCM)	O	11.57	9[illegible]	-16.5	20.4
Royce Value Trust (RVT)	N	16.30	13[illegible]	-16.5	16.0
Salomon SBF (SBF)	N	19.84	18[illegible]	- 2.6	25.7
Source Capital (SOR)	N	50.63	46	- 9.2	13.7
Tri-Continental (TY)	N	31.86	26[illegible]	-16.7	8.2
Zweig (ZF)	N	11.68	10	-14.4	3.6
Income & Preferred Stock Funds					
Chartwell Dividend (CWF)	A	12.86	10[illegible]	-16.0	-12.2
Delaware Gr Div (DDF)	N	12.65	11[illegible]	-11.9	-25.4
Delaware Grp Gl (DGF)	N	13.98	11[illegible]	-18.4	-14.8
J Han Pat Glob (PGD)	N	12.52	9[illegible]	-20.6	-12.1
J Han Pat Pref (PPF)	N	11.79	10[illegible]	-13.6	-8.4
J Han Pat Prem (PDF)	N	9.44	7[illegible]	-18.5	-15.9
J Han Pat Prem II (PDT)-a	N	11.26	8[illegible]	-20.7	-16.0
J Han Pat Sel (DIV)	N	14.30	12[illegible]	-15.8	-13.7
Preferred Inc Op (PFO)-a	N	10.87	9[illegible]	- 9.9	- 7.7
Preferred Income (PFD)-a	N	13.57	11[illegible]	-12.9	- 9.1
Putnam Divd Inc (PDI)-a	N	10.80	9[illegible]	-14.4	- 6.6
Convertible Sec's. Funds					
Bancroft Conv (BCV)	A	28.87	21[illegible]	-20.9	9.8
Castle Conv (CVF)	A	27.29	20[illegible]	-24.2	0.3
Ellsworth Conv (ECF)	A	11.46	9	-21.5	9.7
Gabelli Conv Sec (GCV)	N	11.34	10[illegible]	- 9.1	- 2.5
Lincoln Conv (LNV)-c	N	22.88	16[illegible]	-27.1	18.5
Putnam Conv Opp (PCV)-a	N	20.98	16[illegible]	-18.5	- 5.1
Putnam Hi Inc Cv (PCF)-a	N	8.32	6[illegible]	-16.4	-15.8
Rert Cap S&I II (RCS)	O	12.89	10[illegible]	-22.0	26.7
TCW Conv Secs (CVT)	N	12.12	10[illegible]	-12.9	24.2
VK Conv Sec (VXS)	N	35.12	27[illegible]	-24.2	37.7
World Equity Funds					
Argentina (AF)	N	16.52	12[illegible]	-25.5	55.5
Asia Pacific (APB)	N	13.95	10[illegible]	-24.8	65.3
Asia Tigers (GRR)	N	13.50	10[illegible]	-25.0	50.0
Austria (OST)	N	15.54	11[illegible]	-25.2	37.2
Brazil (BZF)	N	23.85	19[illegible]	-18.3	100.8
Brazilian Equity (BZL)	N	7.77	5[illegible]	-25.6	69.8
Can Genl Inv (CGI)-y	T	17.60	12	-31.8	- 4.2
Can Wrld Fd Ltd (CWF)-cy	T	7.93	5[illegible]	-33.2	0.3
Central Eur Eqty (CEE)	N	22.88	16[illegible]	-21.9	20.8

Figure 20.3 (Panel 2)

Bond Mutual Funds

- How Bond Mutual Funds Operate
  - Bond funds generate interest income and attempt to achieve appreciation in the fund's NAV.
  - In terms of expenses and sales charges, bond funds operate much like stock funds.
  - Like stock funds, bond funds can be load or no-load, and open or closed-end.

Bond Mutual Funds

- Bond Fund Investment Objectives
  - Maturity Classifications
    - Intermediate-term bond funds
    - Long-term bond funds
  - Type-of-Issuer Classifications
    - Treasury bond funds
    - GNMA funds
    - Corporate bond funds
    - Municipal bond funds
    - International and Global bond funds

Mutual Fund Performance

FIGURE 20.4

Mutual Fund Performance Review

Performance yardsticks on mutual funds, reported by the *Wall Street Journal*

Source: Wall Street Journal, January 21, 2000, p. C23

Performance Yardsticks

How Fund Categories Stack Up

INVESTMENT OBJECTIVE	YEAR-TO-DATE	ON A TOTAL RETURN BASIS: FOUR WEEKS	ONE YEAR	3 YRS (annualized)	5 YRS (annualized)
Large-Cap Growth	+ 5.57%	+ 2.31%	+ 54.13%	+ 31.5[illegible]	+ 30.88%
Large-Cap Core	− 0.84	+ 0.36	+ 18.80	+ 23.17	+ 25.08
Large-Cap Value	− 1.47	− 0.55	− 8.62	+ 17.08	+ 22.02
Mid-Cap Growth	+ 6.25	+ 10.15	+ 60.80	+ 24.98	+ 20.93
Mid-Cap Core	+ 4.55	+ 0.85	+ 43.73	+ 25.32	+ 21.95
Mid-Cap Value	− 0.08	+ 7.54	− 8.85	+ 16.73	+ 15.77
Multi-Cap Growth	+ 3.25	+ 6.47	+ 96.60	+ 31.33	+ 29.48
Multi-Cap Core	− 6.17	+ 1.86	+ 26.25	+ 20.84	+ 22.26
Multi-Cap Value	− 1.22	+ 0.36	+ 4.27	+ 11.55	+ 17.53
Small-Cap Growth	+ 5.76	+ 10.38	+ 68.71	+ 35.90	+ 24.76
Small-Cap Core	+ 5.71	+ 7.80	− 38.45	+ 12.77	+ 17.86
Small-Cap Value	+ 1.17	+ 4.79	+ 7.11	+ 7.38	+ 14.88
Equity Income	− 1.04	− 0.60	+ 2.20	+ 15.88	+ 18.83
International (ex U.S.)	− 2.82	+ 0.46	+ 34.17	+ 17.37	+ 15.48
Global (including U.S.)	− 6.01	+ 2.46	+ 38.57	+ 18.70	+ 18.80

Figure 20.4 (Panel 1)

Mutual Fund Performance

How Fund Categories Stack Up

INVESTMENT OBJECTIVE	YEAR-TO-DATE	ON A TOTAL RETURN BASIS: FOUR WEEKS	ONE YEAR	3 YRS (annualized)	5 YRS (annualized)
European Region	+ 0.26	+ 2.23	+ 24.08	+ 21.15	+ 20.52
Emerging Markets	+ 3.88	+ 6.36	+ 77.32	+ 3.74	+ 6.91
Science & Technology	+ 4.14	+ 7.18	+ 106.40	+ 51.83	+ 40.55
Utility	+ 2.42	+ 3.35	+ 16.25	+ 18.80	+ 19.11
Health & Biotech	+ 10.65	+ 13.09	+ 30.07	+ 19.32	+ 23.00
Balanced	− 0.90	+ 0.03	+ 6.05	+ 12.38	+ 15.93
Short Term Bond	− 0.18	− 0.10	+ 1.93	+ 5.20	+ 5.92
Intmdt US Govt	− 0.78	− 0.69	− 2.32	+ 4.80	+ 6.14
Intmdt Inv Grade	− 0.79	− 0.72	− 1.91	+ 4.88	+ 5.83
Mortgage	− 0.71	− 0.68	+ 0.25	+ 4.78	+ 6.65
Long Term Bond	− 0.90	− 0.78	− 2.83	+ 4.46	+ 7.11
Long Term US Funds	− 0.95	− 0.88	− 4.31	+ 4.57	+ 6.57
General US Taxable	− 0.58	− 0.40	+ 1.57	+ 4.17	+ 8.02
High Yield Taxable	− 0.57	− 0.38	+ 2.07	+ 4.79	+ 6.70
General Muni Debt	− 0.81	− 0.74	− 5.64	+ 3.58	+ 6.35
Single State Muni Debt	− 0.77	− 0.86	− 5.19	+ 3.14	+ 5.34
Intmdt Muni Debt	− 0.47	− 0.30	− 2.32	+ 3.96	+ 5.32

Figure 20.4 (Panel 2)

Money Market Mutual Funds

- Money Market Fund Objective
  - Money market mutual funds are investment companies that sell shares to individuals and pool the proceeds to invest in money market securities.
  - All money market funds are relatively low risk and highly liquid portfolios.
  - Money market funds can be distinguished according to their maturity (which affects interest rate risk) and issuer characteristics (which affects the default risk and tax status of the fund).

Money Market Fund Quotations

FIGURE 20.5 **Money Market Fund Quotations**

Yields on money market funds, reported by the *Wall Street Journal*

Source: *Wall Street Journal*, January 20, 2000, p. C2

MONEY MARKET MUTUAL FUNDS

Figure 20.5 (Panel 1)

Money Market Fund Quotations

Figure 20.5 (Panel 2)

Asset Allocation

- Asset allocation is the decision of how to divide investment funds across various classes of financial assets.
- Allocating funds across a diversified portfolio of securities within one type of financial asset class has limited benefits.
- By diversifying across classes, however, investors can reduce their exposure to any one force (such as stock market conditions or interest rates).

Asset Allocation

- Impact of Investor's Profile on Asset Allocation
  - Impact of investor's stage in life
  - Impact of investor's degree of risk tolerance
  - Impact of investor's expectations

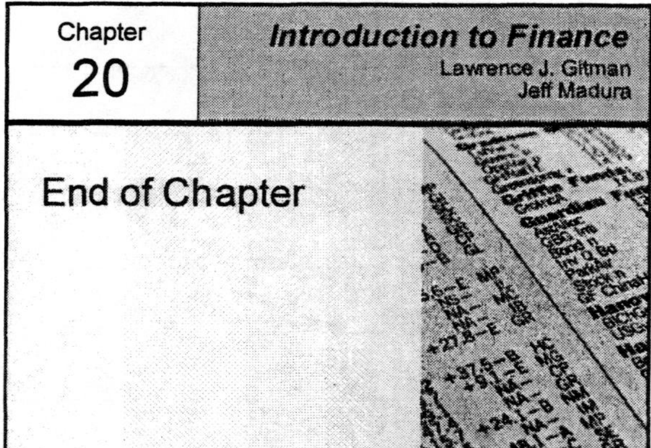

Chapter
21

Introduction to Finance

Lawrence J. Gitman
Jeff Madura

Derivative Securities

Learning Goals

- Explain how call options are used by investors.
- Explain how put options are used by investors.
- Explain how financial futures are used by investors.

Background

- Derivative securities are securities that are neither debt nor equity and whose values are derived from the values of other, related securities.
- Derivative securities are not used by corporations to raise funds.
- Rather, they serve as a useful tool for managing certain aspects of firm risk.
- Two of the most popular types of derivative securities are options and financial futures.

Options

- An option is an instrument that provides its holder with an opportunity to purchase or sell a specified asset at a stated price on or before a set expiration date.
- Options are probably the most popular type of derivative security.
- Three basic forms of options are rights, warrants, and calls and puts.
- This section will focus on call and put options.

Call Options

- A call option is an option to purchase a specified number of shares of stock (typically 100) on or before a specified future date at a stated price.
- They usually have initial lives of 1 to 9 months.
- The striking price is the price at which the holder of a call can buy the stock at any time prior to the option's expiration date.
- The striking price is usually set at or near the prevailing market price of the stock at the time it is issued.

Call Options

- Executing Call Option Transactions
  - Investors purchase call options in the same way they purchase stocks—by calling their broker.
  - The price of the call option is called an option premium.
  - American-style call options are call options that can be exercised at any time throughout the life of the option.
  - European-style call options are options that can be exercised only on the expiration date.

Call Options

Option/Strike		Exp.	Call Vol.	Call Last	Put Vol.	Put Last
[illegible]	[illegible]	Mar	657	[illegible]	10	[illegible]
[illegible]	[illegible]	Jan	947	3	[illegible]	6
[illegible]	[illegible]	Jan	1050	3	...	...
23	[illegible]	Apr	[illegible]	[illegible]	...	...
[illegible]	[illegible]	Feb	[illegible]	[illegible]	100	[illegible]
[illegible]	5	May	531	[illegible]	40	[illegible]
GTE	[illegible]	Jan	[illegible]	[illegible]	[illegible]	1
[illegible]	[illegible]	Jan	[illegible]	[illegible]	...	...
Gap	45	Feb	[illegible]	[illegible]	[illegible]	[illegible]
[illegible]	[illegible]	Feb	2149	[illegible]	[illegible]	[illegible]
[illegible]	[illegible]	Jan	[illegible]	[illegible]	[illegible]	[illegible]
[illegible]	[illegible]	Jan	[illegible]	[illegible]	1400	[illegible]
[illegible]	[illegible]	Jan	618	[illegible]	147	[illegible]
[illegible]	[illegible]	Feb	[illegible]	[illegible]	[illegible]	[illegible]
[illegible]	[illegible]	Jan	...	...	[illegible]	[illegible]
Gen El	[illegible]	Jan	[illegible]	12	[illegible]	[illegible]
146	[illegible]	Jan	1001	7	[illegible]	[illegible]
146	[illegible]	Mar	[illegible]	[illegible]	[illegible]	[illegible]
146	[illegible]	Jan	1047	[illegible]	1791	[illegible]
146	[illegible]	Feb	619	[illegible]	[illegible]	5
146	[illegible]	Jan	[illegible]	[illegible]	1034	[illegible]
146	[illegible]	Jan	[illegible]	[illegible]	42	[illegible]
146	[illegible]	Feb	[illegible]	[illegible]	60	[illegible]
146	[illegible]	Mar	[illegible]	[illegible]	...	...
[illegible]	5	Feb	[illegible]	[illegible]	[illegible]	[illegible]
[illegible]	[illegible]	Feb	546	1	[illegible]	[illegible]
[illegible]	[illegible]	Feb	[illegible]	[illegible]	[illegible]	[illegible]
[illegible]	45	Feb	[illegible]	[illegible]	...	...
[illegible]	[illegible]	Jul	[illegible]	[illegible]	[illegible]	[illegible]
[illegible]	35	Feb	67	[illegible]	1071	[illegible]
[illegible]	40	Jan	401	[illegible]	[illegible]	[illegible]
[illegible]	[illegible]	Feb	[illegible]	[illegible]	[illegible]	[illegible]
[illegible]	[illegible]	Mar	[illegible]	[illegible]	52	3

Source: Wall Street Journal, January 21, 2000, p. C13.

 Figure 21.1

Classifying Call Options

TABLE 21.1 Classifying a Call Option

Call OptioN	Exercise Price	As of September 1, When the Stock Price Is $85	As of November 13, When the Stock Price Is $88
1	$85	At-the-money	In-the-money
2	88	Out-of-the-money	At-the-money
3	90	Out-of-the-money	Out-of-the-money

 Table 21.1

Speculating with Call Options

- Bill Warden purchased a call option on Flight stock for $4 per share, with an exercise price of $60 per share. He plans to exercise his option at the expiration date of the stock price at the time it is above $60. He plans to sell immediately the stock he receives from exercising the option. Bill wants to determine what his profit per share would be under various possible outcomes for the price of Flight stock.

Speculating with Call Options

TABLE 21.2 Possible Outcomes of Investing in a Call Option

Possible Price of Flight Stock at Expiration Date	Premium Paid	Amount Received from Exercising Option	Profit from Investing in Call Option
$54	$4	Option not exercised	−$4
61	4	$ 1	−3
64	4	4	0
66	4	6	2
70	4	10	6

 Table 21.2

Speculating with Call Options

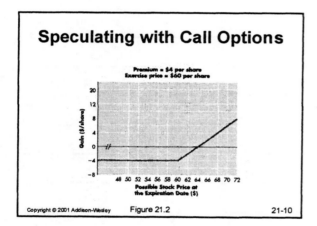

Premium = $4 per share
Exercise price = $60 per share

Gain ($/share)

20
12
8
4
0
−4
−8

48 50 52 54 56 58 60 62 64 66 68 70 72

Possible Stock Price at the Expiration Date ($)

 Figure 21.2

Speculating with Call Options

TABLE 21.3 Comparison of Returns from Investing in a Call Option with Returns from Investing in the Underlying Stock

Possible Price of Flight Stock at Expiration Date	Return from Investing in the Call Option	Return from Investing in the Stock Itself
$54	−100%	−10%
61	−75%	1.67%
64	0%	6.67%
66	50%	10%
70	250%	16.67%

$$\text{Return on option} = \frac{\text{Profit from option}}{\text{Premium Paid}}$$

$$= \frac{\$2}{\$4}$$

$$= 50\%$$

 Table 21.3

Speculating with Call Options

TABLE 21.4 Possible Outcomes for a Seller of a Call Option

Possible Price of Flight Stock at Expiration Date	Premium Received by Seller of Option	Difference Between Amount Received and Amount Paid for Stock When Call Option Is Exercised	Profit
$54	$4	Option not exercised	$ 4
61	4	−$1	3
64	4	4	0
66	4	6	−2
70	4	10	−6

Table 21.4

Speculating with Call Options

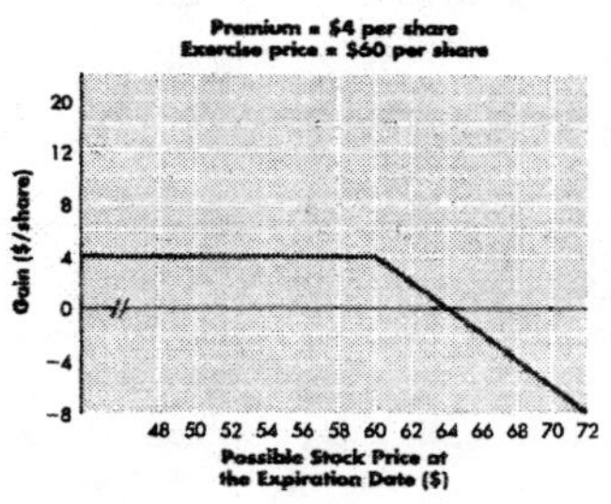

Figure 21.3

Speculating with Call Options

- Factors that Affect the Call Option Premium
  - Stock price relative to exercise price
  - Time to expiration
  - Stock price volatility

Put Options

- A put option is an option to sell a specified number of shares of stock (typically 100) on or before a specified future date at a stated price.
- They usually have initial lives of 1 to 9 months.
- The striking price is the price at which the holder of a put can sell the stock at any time prior to the option's expiration date.
- The striking price is usually set at or near the prevailing market price of the stock at the time the put option is issued.

Classifying Put Options

TABLE 21.5 Classifying Put Options

Put Option	Exercise Price	As of February 5, When the Stock Price is $49	As of April 22, When the Stock Price is $45
1	$45	Out-of-the-money	At-the-money
2	48	Out-of-the-money	In-the-money
3	50	In-the-money	In-the-money

Table 21.5

Speculating with Put Options

- Emma Rivers purchased a put option on Zector stock for $3 per share, with an exercise price of $40 per share. She plans to exercise her option at the expiration date if the stock price at that time is below $40. She plans to purchase the stock just before exercising her put option. Emma wants to determine what her profit per share would be under various possible outcomes for the price of Zector stock.

Speculating with Put Options

TABLE 21.6 Possible Outcomes of Investing in a Put Option

Possible Price of Zector Stock at Expiration Date	Premium Paid	Amount Received from Exercising Put Option	Profit from Investing in Put Option
$32	$3	$8	$5
34	3	6	3
36	3	4	1
39	3	1	−2
45	3	Option not exercised	−3

 Table 21.6

Speculating with Put Options

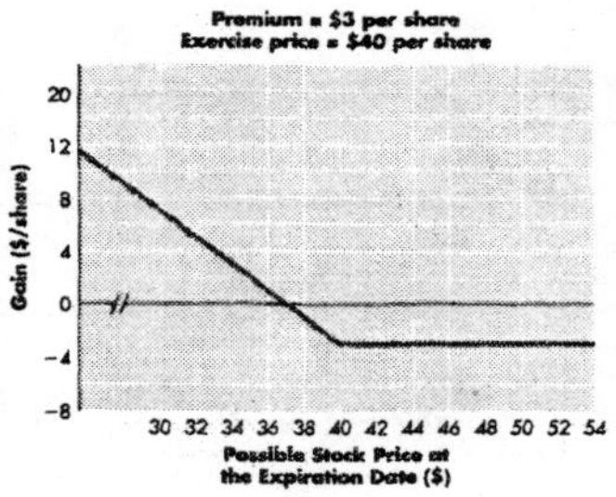

Premium = $3 per share
Exercise price = $40 per share

Gain ($/share)

Possible Stock Price at the Expiration Date ($)

 Figure 21.4

Speculating with Put Options

TABLE 21.7 Possible Outcomes of Selling a Put Option

Possible Price of Zector Stock at Expiration Date	Premium Received from Selling Put Option	Excess Amount Paid If Put Option Is Exercised	Profit from Selling a Put Option
$32	$3	$8	−$5
34	3	6	−3
36	3	4	−1
39	3	1	2
45	3	Option not exercised	3

 Table 21.7

Speculating with Put Options

$$\text{Return on option} = \frac{\text{Profit from option}}{\text{Premium Paid}}$$

$$= \frac{\$6}{\$3}$$

$$= 2.0, \text{ or } 200\%$$

$$\text{Return on option} = \frac{\text{Profit from option}}{\text{Premium Paid}}$$

$$= \frac{\$2}{\$3}$$

$$= 0.67, \text{ or } -67\%$$

Put Options

- Factors that Affect the Put Option Premium
  - Stock price relative to exercise price
  - Time to expiration
  - Stock price volatility

Financial Futures

- A financial futures contract is a contract in which one party agrees to deliver a specified about of a specified financial instrument to the other party at a specified price and date.
- The buyer of the financial futures contract receives the financial instrument on the settlement date.
- The seller delivers the financial instrument and receives payment on the settlement date.

Financial Futures Transactions

- Financial futures are traded on exchanges such as the Chicago Mercantile Exchange (CME) and the Chicago Board of Trade (CBOT).
- Brokerage firms require that investors maintain a deposit (margin) to cover any loss that might result from a futures position.
- Buyers (sellers) can "close out" a position by selling (buying) an identical contract before the settlement date.

Financial Futures Quotations

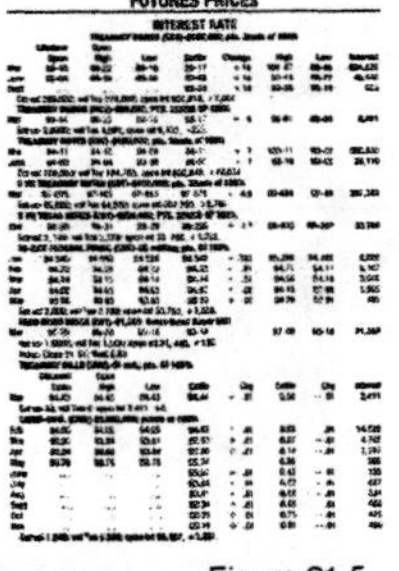

FUTURES PRICES

INTEREST RATE

Source: Wall Street Journal, January 20, 2000, p. C22.

Figure 21.5

Speculating with Treasury Bond Futures

- As of October 10th, Rita Richards expects that the price of Treasury bonds will rise over the next month. She can presently purchase a Treasury bond futures contract with a December settlement date for 101. The futures contract represents Treasury bonds with a par value of $100,000 that pay 8% and have 15 years to maturity. The price of 101 implies that $101 will be paid for every $100 of par value, so the total price to be paid by Rita on the settlement date is $101,000.

Speculating with Treasury Bond Futures

- Over the next month, Treasury bond prices rise and the price specified in a Treasury bond futures contract with a December settlement date at this time for 103. Rita will receive $103,000 as of the settlement date as a result of this contract. Rita now has one contract to buy Treasury bonds on the settlement date and another contract to sell Treasury bonds on the settlement date. The contracts offset each other. However, the amount she receives from selling the Treasury bonds exceeds the amount she paid by $2000.

Speculating with Treasury Bond Futures

Amount to be received from selling Treasury bonds, due to purchase of Treasury bond futures = $103,000

Amount to be paid for Treasury bonds, due to sale of Treasury bond futures = $101,000

Gain = $103,000 – $101,000
= $2,000

Speculating with Stock Index Futures

- On July 8th, Al Barnett notices that the DJIA futures contract with a September settlement date specifies an index level of 10,000, which is similar to the existing index today. Al expects stock prices to decline, so he anticipates that the price specified in the DJIA futures contract will decline in the future. Therefore, he sells a futures contract today. The sale of the futures contract creates a short position, in which the underlying instrument that will be sold is not presently owned by the seller.

Speculating with Stock Index Futures

- By August 24th, stock prices have declined, and the DJIA futures contract with a September settlement date specifies an index level of 9,400. Al does not expect further declines, so he purchases the DJIA index futures to offset his short position. The dollar value of the DJIA index specified in the futures contract is $10 times the index level.

Speculating with Stock Index Futures

- Thus, Al's gain is:

Dollar value of stock index futures when a futures contract was sold = $10{,}000 \times \$10 = \$100{,}000$

Dollar value of stock index futures when a futures contract was purchased = $9{,}400 \times \$10 = \$94{,}000$

Gain = $\$100{,}000 - \$94{,}000 = \underline{\underline{\$6{,}000}}$

Hedging with Financial Futures

- Stanford Mutual Fund manages a large portfolio of stocks. The portfolio managers anticipate that the prices of stocks will decline over the next month but will rebound afterward. They would like to hedge their portfolio against a loss over the next month. A stock index futures contract with one month to settlement is available on the DJIA at an index level of 10,000, so Stanford decides to sell a futures contract on the index because it is highly correlated with its mutual fund portfolio.

Hedging with Financial Futures

- In one month, just before the contract expires, Stanford will purchase the same contract. If stock prices decline over this period, the index will decline as well, and so will the futures contract on the index. Stanford will gain on its futures position because the price it paid for the index at settlement will be less than the future price at which it sold the index.
- After one month, the market declined as expected and the futures price of the DJIA is at an index level of 10,000.

Hedging with Financial Futures

- DJIA futures contracts are valued at $10 times the DJIA index, so Stanford's positions are as follows:

Sold DJIA futures for 10,000; receives 10,000 times $10 = $100,000

Purchased DJIA futures for 9,000; owes 9,000 times $10 = $90,000

Gain = $100,000 – $90,000 = $10,000
= $10,000

Chapter 21

Introduction to Finance
Lawrence J. Gitman
Jeff Madura

End of Chapter

Chapter 22

Introduction to Finance

Lawrence J. Gitman
Jeff Madura

Corporate Control and Governance

Learning Goals

- Describe the relationship between managers and investors, and explain the potential conflict in goals.
- Explain how a firm's board of directors can control the managers of the firm.
- Explain how investors in the firm's stock can control the managers of the firm.
- Explain how the market for corporate control can ensure that managers of firms serve their firm's respective shareholders.

Learning Goals

- Describe the relationship between managers and creditors.
- Describe the relationship between mutual fund management and investors.

Relationship Between a Firm's Managers and Its Investors

- Managers serve as agents for the firm's owners or shareholders and make decisions that are supposed to maximize the value of the firm's stock price.
- Managerial investment and financing decisions affect the performance of the firm, which affects the dividend payments.
- These decisions also affect stock price and therefore the size of capital gains realized.

Relationship Between a Firm's Managers and Its Investors

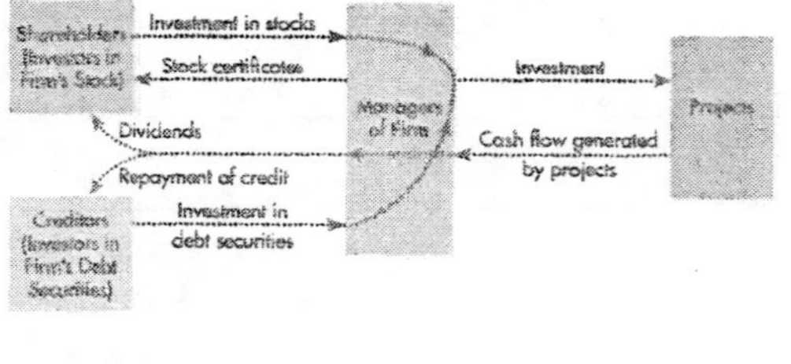

Figure 22.1

Relationship Between a Firm's Managers and Its Investors

- Ownership versus Control
  - The separation between ownership and control introduces conflicts, which lead to agency problems.
  - This encourages shareholders to monitor the firm's managers.
  - However, because the ownership of a typical corporation is spread across many shareholders, most are unwilling to monitor management because they would receive only a small proportion of any benefit.

Relationship Between a Firm's Managers and Its Investors

- Asymmetric Information
  - A problem called "asymmetric information" occurs because a firm's managers have information about the firm that is not available to shareholders.
  - This further complicates any attempt by shareholders to monitor the firm.
  - Although firms are required to inform investors by providing financial statements, some firms use accounting procedures that mislead investors.

 22-6

Relationship Between a Firm's Managers and Its Investors

- Asymmetric Information
  - Unfortunately, it is very difficult or impossible for shareholders to determine whether a particular management decision will enhance their wealth.
  - Thus, shareholders commonly use stock price performance as an initial indicator.

 22-7

Control by the Board of Directors

- Shareholders elect the board of directors, which oversees the key management decisions of a firm.
- Inside directors are those members of a board of directors who are also employed by the firm while outside directors are not.
- Outside directors may be employed or retired from high-level managerial positions at other firms.
- A typical term for a director is 3 years.

 22-8

Control by the Board of Directors

- Duties of the Board
  - Appoints high-level managers of the firm including Chief Executive Officer (CEO).
  - Monitors high-level managers.
  - Fires high-level managers.
  - Attend board meetings (usually between 5 and 10 per year).

Control by the Board of Directors

- Compensation for Board Members
  - Commonly receive between $15,000 and $25,000 annually for serving on boards of relatively small publicly-traded firms.
  - In 1998, the mean level of compensation for outside directors of the 200 largest firms was about $112,000.
  - The relatively high compensation levels was partially attributable to the strong stock price performance of many of the firms.

Control by the Board of Directors

- Impact of Outside Directors
  - In general, outside directors are expected to be more effective than inside directors at enacting changes that improve the firm's stock price.
  - Their independence gives them the flexibility to serve in the best interests of shareholders, even if their actions do not serve in the interests of the firm's managers.

Control by the Board of Directors

- Impact of Outside Directors
  - Impact of outside director as Board Chair
  - Impact of stock ownership by board members
  - Impact of the size of the board

Control by the Board of Directors

- How the Board Aligns Manger and Investor Interests
  - Three common methods are usually implemented by a firm's board of directors to align the interests of managers and investors:
    - Reducing free cash flow
    - Forcing stock ownership by high-level managers
    - Aligning compensation and stock price performance

Aligning Compensation and Stock-Price Performance

TABLE 22.1 Examples of Executive Compensation

Firm	Name of CEO	1998 Salary and Bonus	1998 Long-Term Compensation	1996–1998 Total Compensation	1996–1998 Dollar Return to Shareholders per $100 Invested
Boeing	P.M. Condit	$ 999,000	$ 2,027,000	$10,829,000	$ 86
Motorola	C.B. Galvin	1,513,600	0	7,382,000	110
Starbucks	H.D. Schultz	1,175,000	17,036,000	21,134,000	267
Kellogg	A.G. Langbo	1,028,000	1,836,000	10,424,000	95
Cisco Systems	J.T. Chambers	891,000	0	34,661,000	560
Cendant	H.R. Silverman	2,835,000	61,063,000	98,635,000	85
Maytag	L.A. Hadley	1,770,000	3,863,000	9,859,000	328
Disney	M.D. Eisner	5,764,000*	569,828,000	594,892,000	156

*Salary and bonus were waived.

 Table 22.1

Control by Investors

- Investors' Characteristics that Affect Their Degree of Control
  - Number of shareholders
  - Proportion of institutional ownership

Control by Investors

- Shareholder Activism
  - Communication with the firm
  - Proxy contest
  - Shareholder lawsuits or other actions

Market for Corporate Control

- To the extent that managers do not act in the best interest of shareholders, the stock price of the firm will be less than what it would have been if the managers focused on maximizing shareholder wealth.
- However, an underperforming firm is subject to the "market for corporate control," because it is subject to takeover by another firm.

Market for Corporate Control

- Barriers to Corporate Control
  - Anti-takeover amendments
  - Poison pills
  - Golden parachutes

Market for Corporate Control

- Barriers to Corporate Control

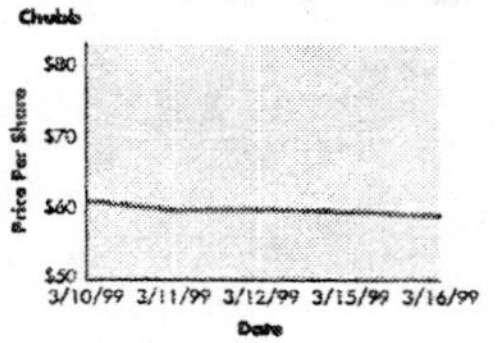

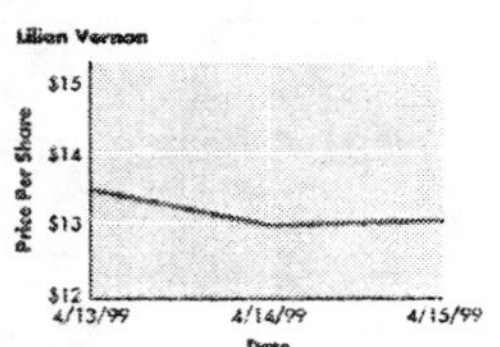

Figure 22.2

Monitoring and Control by Creditors

- Like shareholders, creditors must monitor a firm's management.
- However, creditors are more concerned with the firm's ability to repay its debt than with stock price.
- Creditors must monitor managers so that they do not make decisions that benefit themselves or shareholders at creditors' expense.
- Creditors commonly include restrictive protective covenants in loan or bond indentures to safeguard themselves against adverse managerial actions.

Conflict Between Managers and Mutual Fund Investors

- Just as a firm's managers may be tempted act in ways that benefit themselves at shareholders expense, mutual fund managers may be tempted as well.
- Two examples of situations where investors do not act in shareholders best interests include: (a) managing tax liabilities for shareholders, and (b) managerial expenses charged to shareholders.
- In addition, the boards of directors at mutual funds are relatively weak; thus, the agency problem in the mutual fund industry is typically more pronounced.

Chapter 22

Introduction to Finance

Lawrence J. Gitman
Jeff Madura

End of Chapter